As Old As Dallas Itself

AS OLD AS DALLAS ITSELF

⌘⌘⌘

*A History of the
Lawyers of Dallas,
the Dallas Bar Associations,
and the City They Helped Build*

⌘⌘⌘

DARWIN PAYNE

Three Forks Press
Dallas

THREE FORKS PRESS
P.O. BOX 823461
DALLAS, TEXAS 75382

LIBRARY OF CONGRESS CATALOG CARD NO. 99-90293

ISBN: 1-893451-01-1

PRINTED IN THE UNITED STATES OF AMERICA

FIRST EDITION

CONTENTS

⌘

ACKNOWLEDGMENTS

⌘

Such a genuine pleasure it has been for me to write this history. For one thing, it afforded me a new perspective for examining this city's always fascinating background, a subject which has given me much joy. Perhaps more of the pleasure, though, came from the subject itself—the lawyers of Dallas, their organizations, their profession, and the important and essential contributions they have made over the years to the remarkable progress of this entire North Texas metropolitan area. Beyond that, everyone associated with this project offered cooperation, assistance, and encouragement.

While the genesis of this work goes back a number of years ago to an earlier Dallas Bar Association historical committee, this present work was encouraged and made possible especially by the combined effort of the Dallas Bar Association and the Dallas Bar Foundation. Robert H. Thomas and John L. Estes, representing both organizations, initially discussed the project with me, and I was fortunate in winning their approval as author. Their friendship and support throughout the project has been very much appreciated.

Messrs. Thomas and Estes recruited an excellent editorial committee to help them oversee the work, and chapter by chapter we met over lunch in the Belo Mansion on an almost monthly basis for review sessions. The members' suggestions and guidance were invariably helpful, not just in reviewing the chapters as they were written but in suggesting new avenues to approach. L.A. Bedford Jr., who has been practicing law in Dallas since the 1940s, was a beacon in many areas, especially concerning African-American lawyers. Nina Cortell lent insights and observations concerning women lawyers, and her encouragement was much appreciated. William D. Elliott, whose involvement in this project dates to the original effort some years ago, was a conscientious reader whose comments were always insightful and helpful. His published work on law offices in the 1880s was indeed valued and is cited in this book as a source. Spencer C. Relyea's wide-ranging knowledge and friendly manner made him a pleasant luncheon companion. Actually, these words don't adequately convey the genuine enjoyment of our lunches together.

The support of two executive directors of the Dallas Bar Foundation was absolutely essential to the completion of this project. Ann Simmons, first, and then her successor in the office, Barbara Bratton, became friends as well as colleagues. The executive director of the Dallas Bar Association, Catherine M. Maher, always could be counted on for assistance, and I am indebted to her for all that she did. In October 1998 Ms. Maher was honored by the Bar Association for her twenty years of service to the organization. Sue Cady, editor of *Headnotes*, was kind enough to provide attention in her news columns for this project, and I also am thankful to Christina Melton for her interest and support. Ms. Melton and Brian Melton, who together oversaw a fine 125th anniversary video of the Bar Association, both were helpful.

Much of my research was done at the Underwood Law Library at Southern Methodist University and the Texas/Dallas History and Archives Division of the Dallas Public Library. At the latter facility, Carol Roark and her team of specialists made important contributions—as they have done before on other historical ventures of mine. Lois Hudgins of the Dallas Public Library's genealogy section provided exceptional assistance, and Jimm Foster was helpful in identifying and in making photographs available. The Dallas Historical Society provided another friendly environment for research. Thanks to Gaylon Polatti and to Executive Director Andy Wolber.

I have been blessed by the sharp-eyed assistance of a marvelous proofreader/editor, Denise Kuitunen. How fortunate I am indeed that she came along to save me from many embarrassing errors while at the same time offering inspiration.

My own family members have been cheerful companions, too—my wife Phyllis and daughters Sarah and Hannah. And while Mark and Scott are grown and out of the house now, their support—now augmented by daughter-in-law Kristin—continues.

DARWIN PAYNE
January 1999

FOREWORD

⌘

WHEN WE BECAME Chairs of the Fellows of the Dallas Bar Foundation and of the Trustees of Dallas Bar Foundation, respectively, in 1995, it was our view that the time was ripe for the Fellows to embark on a more expanded role in the Dallas legal community. We appointed a joint ad hoc committee to study possible projects for the Fellows, which concluded that nothing could be more appropriate for an initial grant than a history of the legal profession in Dallas.

We knew that the Dallas Bar Association had laid the ground work for the publication of such a history, but that its efforts had come to an unfortunate end as a result of the bankruptcy of the prospective publisher. The ad hoc committee determined that by jointly funding this project, the Fellows and the Trustees could avoid the problems that the Association had previously encountered.

One of the members of the ad hoc committee deserves special recognition for his dedication to this project. Robert H. Thomas—past president of the Association, founding member of the Fellows, and former trustee of the Foundation—had been involved in the early stages of the Association's efforts to publish such a history, and was well acquainted with the opportunities and risks which were attendant upon such an endeavor.

In addition, he not only observed a part of the history of the legal profession in Dallas while growing up as the son of Bascom Thomas, who also served as president of the Association, but also played a significant role in that history during the years that he served as president of the Association and trustee of the Foundation. Finally, his service as a member of the editorial committee for this book has enabled him to share his first-hand knowledge with the author and his fellow members of the editorial committee.

Darwin Payne has again distinguished himself by writing *As Old As Dallas Itself*, and we know that you will take great pleasure in reading it.

John L. Estes
Chair, Fellows of the
Dallas Bar Foundation
(1995)

Spencer C. Relyea
Chair, Trustees of the
Dallas Bar Foundation
(1995-96)

As Old As Dallas Itself

THE LAW IN A FRONTIER TOWN

⌘

Chapter One

THE HISTORY OF the legal profession in Dallas is as old as Dallas itself, for it was a lawyer who founded the town. John Neely Bryan (1810-1877) arrived on horseback in late 1841 along an ancient Indian trace leading from the Red River along the route now known as Preston Road. It was not Bryan's first visit to the area, and he evidently knew exactly the place he wanted. He picked a bluff overlooking the slow-moving Trinity River as the site for his town, less than a stone's toss from today's Old Red Courthouse.[1] Bryan, thirty years of age and a native of Tennessee, defied the usual frontier pattern which saw lawyers arriving only after some semblance of civilization and the promise of business had emerged. He intended to build the town first.

He had been educated as a lawyer in his native Tennessee in the usual frontier way, by "reading" law in an established attorney's office and being admitted to the bar only after his sponsor and other colleagues believed he was ready. Details about Bryan's life and his practice of law are sketchy, but the author of a short biography about him says he studied law "primarily in order to treat with the Indians on a legal basis."[2]

Certainly the practice of law never seems to have been a primary concern of his, for he loved the wandering, nomadic life of an Indian trader. He settled for a while in Van Buren, Arkansas, practicing law there while he traded and maintained his friendship with Indian tribes. Sometime around 1840 he began working as a wandering trader out of Holland Coffee's famous and rowdy establishment at the Washita Bend of the Red River.[3] Now, though, on the bluff of the Trinity, Bryan was ready to settle down and build a town. He had chosen this particular site—so very different from how it appears today—because it offered a natural and easy place for fording the river, because it was projected to be on the route of a military road planned by the Republic of Texas through the area, and because he believed it was the place that would become the head of navigation for the Trinity River. He envisioned steamboats coming upstream from the Gulf of Mexico to this northern-most point, unloading goods for the settlers, re-loading their own agricultural riches, then turning south to the Gulf and, eventually, the world. This, of course, never happened, but Dallas civic leaders in generations to come would also be concerned about transportation routes from Dallas to the rest of the nation. Although Bryan practiced very little law in his town, he would push hard for its development for much of the rest of his life, erratic though his life often appeared to be. And he would be followed rather quickly, as we shall see, by a second practicing lawyer and in the years to come by a long, ever-expanding line of lawyers who would perform the myriad tasks demanded of the profession in transforming a tiny, nondescript hamlet in an unsettled part of Texas into one of the nation's largest and most important cities.

This promising area was part of a new nation, the Republic of Texas. Independence had been won only five years earlier from Mexico. Now a steady stream of Americans emigrated to Texas, many of them crossing the Red River at the northern border or at the Sabine River to the east. While land was plentiful and much of it fertile, economic distress was endemic to Texas, in its government treasury as well as among its populace. The republic's generous land policy encouraged settlement. A married man could claim 640 free acres. Scores of American families and hearty individuals loaded up wagons with all of their belongings, posting a "gone to Texas" sign, to head west for this land of promise. Settlement in this new nation had concentrated first along the lower reaches of the rivers, in deep East Texas around Nacogdoches, and in towns like Galveston, Houston, San Antonio, and the new capital city of Austin, which was considered so far to the west that the Comanches were a menace.

Now it was time to populate other areas, such as that of the Three Forks of the Trinity.

This fledgling nation needed settlers—especially homesteaders who would clear the land and build fences and raise crops—but also merchants and bankers, teachers and doctors, and lawyers. By 1838 there was already a fair representation of the legal profession. However, as Texas statesman and physician Ashbel Smith wrote to a friend in the United States, while many lawyers had come to Texas, there remained a "very great demand" for "competent" lawyers.[4]

Bryan himself was too busy trying to lure new residents to his settlement to practice much law, and there was not enough population and certainly no commerce to sustain a practice in these earliest days. Bryan was thinking, though, about the importance of the law in an emerging society, and he made certain to reserve an entire block for a courthouse in his town. This he accomplished when surveyor J.P. Dumas arrived in 1844. Bryan had him lay out a half-mile square town centered around a potential courthouse, the same block occupied today by the Old Red Courthouse. Bryan deeded a single, worthless lot to Dumas as payment for his services. While there was no courthouse in sight, the Republic of Texas recognized Bryan's town by establishing a post office in his log cabin and making him postmaster.

The Republic of Texas shared Bryan's notion that this unpopulated section of Texas was ripe for settlement. It entered into a series of contracts with a group of land impresarios headed by W.S. Peters, headquartered in Louisville, Kentucky, to recruit newcomers to the North Texas area with the promise of a section of land for each household of settlers. Peters Colony, as the area came to be called, consisted of some 1,300 square miles in North Texas, including much of Dallas. To assist the newcomers in establishing clear titles to their land, the Peters Colony officials, organized as the Texas Emigration and Land Company, hired a lawyer from Indiana to move to the area in 1845 to be a sub-agent and surveyor.

This young lawyer, twenty-five years of age, was John Calvin McCoy (1819-1887). McCoy arrived in Dallas in 1845 by a circuitous route that must have severely taxed his patience and caused him to wonder what he was getting himself into in this distant land. He came down the Ohio and Mississippi rivers by steamboat to New Orleans, continued by sea to Galveston, then boarded another boat to go up Buffalo Bayou to Houston. There, he and the Peters Colony agent, Captain Charles Hensley, loaded their belongings on an ox-drawn wagon and proceeded north toward Dallas. For one portion of the trip they abandoned their wagon and rode for a while on a raft up the Trinity, but soon transferred once more to an ox-wagon. Finally, they purchased horses and rode to Dallas, the wagon trailing behind. Such were the travails of getting to the area of the Three Forks of the Trinity River.[5]

John Neely Bryan and his young bride, Margaret Beeman Bryan, the daughter of newly arrived settlers in the White Rock Creek area, hailed the newcomers from their log cabin. "We were cordially greeted by Colonel Bryan," McCoy later recalled, "who came out in buckskin leggings and moccasins and a red and black plaid blanket coat cut in high-water style. Through the solicitations of the colonel, aided by the sight of the inevitable gourd—the contents of which could be readily guessed—we were at home with him."[6]

McCoy, the youngest son of a frontier Baptist preacher, had studied the gospel himself for three years at seminaries, but his first job was as deputy circuit clerk of Clark County, Indiana. The position lent itself to the study of law, which McCoy did in his spare time. After working for a while as a surveyor, he was admitted to the bar in Indiana and Kentucky in 1842. Not long thereafter, officials of the Texas Emigration and Land Company offered McCoy a job in Texas as their land agent. Both a lawyer and a surveyor, he seemed ideally suited for the assignment.

WHEN MCCOY arrived in the area the seats of justice of the Republic of Texas were far away. The handful of people living in Bryan's settlement and the Peters Colony were under the jurisdiction of a district court in Nacogdoches County, 200 miles away. For those living just across the Trinity in Hord's Ridge (a forerunner of today's community of Oak Cliff), jurisdiction was in a district court located in Franklin, Robertson County, about 150 miles away. These circumstances were soon to change.

With the election of James K. Polk as president of the United States in 1844, annexation of Texas into the United States was virtually assured. In October 1845 an overwhelming majority of Texans approved the proposal to dissolve their independent nation and be annexed by their neighbors to the north. Thirty-two eligible voters in Dallas participated in the election. Only three opposed annexation. Among the three dissenters was John C. McCoy, who may have been lobbying against annexation because Peters Colony officials preferred dealing with a weak Republic of Texas over a powerful United States.[7] Even so, annexation into the United States, coupled with continuing problems within Peters Colony, probably were the two factors that prompted McCoy to resign his position with the Colony after one year's service and to begin the private practice of law in his adopted town of Dallas in June 1846.

Fortunate was Dallas to have such a man. McCoy's career as a lawyer and civic leader was long and active. By the time he died in 1887, he had performed an integral role in virtually every aspect of the town's development. He helped Bryan organize Dallas County in 1846; he served as the county's first district clerk; he helped organize the Tannehill Masonic Lodge (still in existence as the year 2000 approaches); he became the first district attorney of the 16th Judicial Circuit of the state;[8] and he served two terms in the Texas Legislature. He was an orator of note, compelling his listeners with flowing sentences and classical allusions. In 1849 McCoy built as his law office, the first frame building in Dallas. It was located on the east side of the courthouse square. In 1851 he married Cora McDermett in a log cabin ceremony in a grove of trees a mile east of the courthouse. Two years later Cora died in childbirth along with the infant. McCoy never remarried, but when his father-in-law died in 1854 McCoy assumed his family responsibilities, moving into his own house his father-in-law's unmarried sister, two daughters, and four small sons. Every Christmas throughout his life, McCoy held a party for all the children in Dallas and gave them all gifts. When he died in 1887 after forty-two years in Dallas, his body lay in state for four days at his home so that hundreds of friends could view him. The *Dallas Morning News* observed: "He left the impress of his energy, his wisdom, his enterprise and his conservatism. He was not only respected and honored by all who knew him, but he was loved by all, deeply loved by the very many."[9]

On March 30, 1846, after fierce lobbying efforts by John Neely Bryan, the new State of Texas Legislature authorized the creation of Dallas County, 900 square miles or some 576,000 acres. Less than three weeks later the legislature designated Dallas as the temporary county seat, the place where all court sessions would be held. At some unspecified time in the future, county voters would select the permanent county seat, but designation as the temporary site would give Bryan's community a decided advantage in that election. In May the legislature named Bryan as the authorized agent to organize an election for county offices, including a chief justice as the chief administrator, a probate judge, a district clerk, a county clerk, a sheriff, a coroner, and an assessor. He was also given authority to divide the county into precincts. To do this detailed work, Bryan promptly solicited McCoy to assist him. At the ensuing July 13, 1846, election, McCoy was chosen to be the county's first district clerk, a position he quickly resigned to resume his private practice after a visiting judge concluded his first session in Dallas in December. Among other officials chosen to govern the county's affairs were John Thomas as chief justice; William M. Cochran, county clerk; and John Huitt, sheriff.[10]

The designation of Dallas as the temporary county seat was a boon to the community and an acknowledgment of Bryan's skills in promoting his town. It boosted the community several notches above competitors in the county such as Farmers Branch, Scyene, Cedar Springs, Hord's Ridge, Lancaster, and a few others. By such designation Dallas became the place for recording such legal documents as wills, deeds, marriage licenses, brands, and land patents.

The new county, sparsely populated, was a part of the huge 6th Judicial District, consisting of Nacogdoches, Angelina, Houston, Cherokee, Rusk, Anderson, Henderson, Smith and Dallas counties.[11] Presiding over the district court was William Beck Ochiltree (1811-1867) of Nacogdoches.[12] To provide a semblance of justice and legal authority over such a far-flung area, Ochiltree followed the usual frontier pattern of traveling from county to county for court sessions. He held a session in Dallas for the first time on December 7, 1846, in the town saloon, which evidently had more space than the primitive courthouse that had been erected upon Dallas' designation as temporary county seat. Standing on a corner of Bryan's designated courthouse square, the log-cabin structure measured 16 by 16 feet. It had split logs for seats and a large fireplace and chimney. All government functions, save courtroom trials, were conducted here. The log-cabin courthouse was constructed on a corner of the designated square rather than in the middle so that it would not disturb Bryan's corn crop.[13]

Judge Ochiltree's work that 1846 session included the acceptance of sixty-one indictments returned by Dallas County's first grand jury, which had deliberated under a tree. The nature of the criminal offenses reflected the rather undisciplined ways of frontier life later reflected in countless Western stories and movies. Gambling, an illegal activity, appeared to be by far the predominant pastime for Dallas' early settlers. Fifty-one of the sixty-one indictments were for gaming. Other indictments included one for murder, one for challenging a duel, and four for assault and battery. Finding a jury whose members were not acquainted with those charged was impossible in such a small community. In fact, many of those charged with gaming were leading citizens. Nevertheless, those charged with gaming—including John Neely Bryan!—were found guilty and fined $10 each. Steep though these fines were for the times, they did not deter the residents' penchant for betting. Year after year gaming would be a common criminal indictment. One may speculate as to why charges for such a commonly accepted practice continued to be levied among men who, both prosecutors and defendants, were friends and neighbors. The gambling suggests the desperate need of men to inject some excitement into what otherwise was a rather dull existence in a land unmarked by the fast-paced life of later generations.[14]

At the court's second session, held June 7 to 12, 1847, Judge Amos Clark presided. After first selecting a grand jury, the judge admitted Smith Elkins to the bar "during good behavior" after Elkins presented "the requisite testimonials of good moral character and also license of two Circuit Judges of Indiana."[15]

Gaming indictments continued to monopolize, with fifty-three of them in 1847. The other indictments returned by the grand jury offer an interesting picture of life in this small frontier community. Next highest in number of indictments was trespassing with three; followed by "betting," a separate category from gaming, with two; and one indictment each for murder, "an affray," disturbing an election, assault and battery, and "challenging Elijah Carter to a duel."[16]

With plenty of visiting lawyers in town, days of court session were exciting. Considerable whiskey drinking, poker playing, and mock trials took place during the breaks. One day during a recess, (so a story goes), the grand jury decided to hold a mock trial. Charged was none other than the prosecuting attorney, Thomas Blake. The jury fined Blake a gallon of $5 whiskey, which he dutifully turned over. When Judge Ochiltree declined to join in the ensuing celebration, the jurors immediately fined His Honor two gallons of whiskey.[17]

ANY LAWYERS moving to the county almost surely would settle in Dallas to be near the courthouse, even though it was only a temporary county seat. In the late 1840s, several men chose to settle in Dallas who would play essential roles in developing both the town and county. One was John McClannahan Crockett (1816-1887), a native of Lancaster, North Carolina. Crockett arrived with his wife in the spring of 1848 and found lodging in a log cabin that doubled as office and bedroom. A year later he was chosen deputy county clerk, thus beginning a long career as a lawyer and public servant. Crockett was a delegate along with John Neely Bryan and the Rev. James Smith to a convention in Huntsville seeking to improve navigation on the Trinity. In 1851 he was elected to the state legislature, and in 1857 he became the second of Dallas' mayors. In 1859 he displayed yet another side of his accomplishments by serving the Smithsonian Institution as Dallas' meteorological observer. In 1861 he was elected to a two-year term as lieutenant governor during the Confederacy. Crockett eventually built a two-story farm house in the Hord's Ridge area on property now occupied by Methodist Hospital.[18]

Perhaps instrumental in Crockett's move to Dallas was the fact that his wife's brother, William H. Hord (1809-1901), was the leading citizen of the community named after him, Hord's Ridge. Hord, although not a lawyer, was a justice of the peace before being elected county judge in 1848.[19]

Yet another lawyer arrived in 1848 who was destined to be appreciated greatly by later generations for his many overall contributions to the Dallas area, to its nascent legal profession, and to the judiciary. He was Nathaniel Macon Burford (1824-1898). Burford, twenty-four years old, came in October 1848 with five dollars in his pocket and several letters of recommendation. This was the beginning of a long career of public service for Burford, a native of Tennessee. Admitted to the bar in his native state in 1845 after having studied at the law school at Lebanon, Tennessee, Burford moved first to Jefferson in East Texas in 1847, then on to Dallas the next year in hopes of finding brighter prospects in this promising area. He was right in his decision. Burford was elected as the first district attorney for Dallas County in 1850. He was re-elected in 1852, and was succeeded in that office by John E. Cravens. From 1856 to 1858 Burford was judge of the 16th Judicial District (newly organized that year from the 9th Judicial District which in turn had replaced the 6th Judicial District). This put Burford on the road for most of his time, away from his wife and children (although, presumably, not too much, for the couple eventually had eight children). Besides Dallas County, his district included Collin, Cook, Denton, Ellis, Grayson,

Johnson, Parker, and Tarrant counties. Later, Burford would become a colonel in the Confederacy, serve in the Texas Legislature, become Speaker of the House, and serve again as a district judge for two years beginning in 1876.[20]

An amusing anecdote concerning Burford's tenure as district judge was related years later in a speech to the Dallas Bar Association. Judge Burford, en route to a court session, was observed having a drink or two, after which he proceeded to the second floor of the primitive wooden courthouse to give his opening statement to a grand jury. "Gentlemen of the Grand Jury," he said grandiloquently, "they tell you that more men are killed in Texas than any other country in the world and I guess that's a fact, but Gentlemen of the Grand Jury, I tell you that more men need killing in Texas than any other country in the world."[21]

Years later Burford would have an entirely different recollection about the people who moved to Dallas before the railroads came: "They were plain honest people who were not roving about over the country, and the old pioneers knew each other, they shared with each other, they welcomed the honest, toiling stranger, and in social ties they became cemented with a bond of brotherhood. I could go to Dallas and lie down with $100,000.00 and it would be there the next morning."[22]

A lawyer who arrived even earlier than Burford but whose impact was less lasting was Smith Elkins, the lawyer who had been admitted to the Dallas bar by Judge Amos Clark in 1847. A native of New Hampshire, Elkins was senior to the many neophyte lawyers in town, being fifty-four years of age in 1847. He served as chief justice of Dallas County in 1850-51. Yet another lawyer in town prior to 1850 was James Wellington (Weck) Latimer (1825-1859), who, in a not uncommon practice, was also editor and publisher of the first newspaper in town, the *Dallas Herald* (published first under the title of the *Cedar Snag*). He had founded the newspaper in 1849 after bringing in his press and type by ox wagon from Paris, Texas. Latimer, from a family of lawyers, was admitted to the Texas bar in Red River County at the tender age of eighteen or nineteen after studying under his two brothers in the Clarksville area. He became justice of the peace of

Dallas County in 1851 and served as chief justice of the county from 1852 to 1854.[23]

To the handful of lawyers in town it soon became apparent that two one-week court sessions per year for Dallas were not long enough to handle all the business. The lawyers came together on November 25, 1849, to sign a petition to remedy the situation. This likely was the first organized effort by the Dallas bar to accomplish a mutual goal. Their petition began: "The undersigned members of the bar, District Attorney and Judge of the Ninth Judicial District of said state would respectfully represent to your Honl body. . ." In their one-page petition, Crockett, Burford, Elkins, John C. Easton, District Attorney A.J. Fowler, John H. Reagan (former legislator and future Congressman and U.S. Senator then living in Henderson County but a frequent visitor to Dallas), and District Judge Bennett H. Martin urged two-week sessions because of the excessive "accumulation of business." Moreover, they wanted the times changed because of their inconvenience. The fall session was scheduled *after* Christmas and the summer session during July. These times exposed the "officers of court, and the members of the bar to the severe inclemencies of winter, and to the burning suns of summer." A schedule starting a month earlier in both instances was requested. Their arguments proved persuasive. Both requests were granted in 1850.[24]

A brief analysis of the backgrounds of the eight lawyers who lived in Dallas in 1850 is intriguing. Of the five whose parentage could be determined, all were the sons of farmers. Only one of the eight was a college graduate. Five came from border states of the upper South, two were from the Midwest, and one was from South Carolina. Their average age was a very youthful thirty-two. Their talents as lawyers were in great demand, for three of them held local judicial posts, a fourth was a district judge, another was a district clerk, and a sixth sat in the state legislature from 1851 to 1857, after which he was elected mayor of Dallas. One lawyer combined his legal practice with newspaper editing, and another soon abandoned law to engage in land speculation and other promotional ventures.[25]

By 1851, with a total population of 160 residents (including 37 slaves), Dallas was home to nine attorneys, an unusually high proportion it would seem for any town. Undoubtedly, the presence of the courthouse made the town a promising environment. In addition to Bryan, McCoy, Crockett, Burford, Smith Elkins, and Latimer, there were Felix Eakins, John J. Elkins, and Samuel G. Newton. Felix Eakins, only twenty-one years of age as listed in the 1850 census, was born in Kentucky. John J. Elkins, twenty-seven years of age, also was a native of Kentucky. Samuel G. Newton was twenty-five years old and a native of Missouri.[26]

The strong presence of so many lawyers surely was an important factor in Dallas' favor when the time finally came in 1850 to select a permanent county seat. An election to choose that permanent seat was ordered by the Texas Legislature. Claimants for that honor included not only Dallas, but also Hord's Ridge on the west side of the Trinity and Cedar Springs. John Neely Bryan, now in California seeking his fortune in gold, recognized the importance of the election and came back to town to use his influence for Dallas. On July 19, a month before the election, he signed a bond which was entered in the district court minutes. The bond guaranteed that he would donate to the county the courthouse square, which he still owned, if the seat of government would be located permanently in Dallas.[27]

By this time there were some 2,700 residents scattered throughout the county. Those who were eligible and who took the trouble to vote cast 191 votes for Dallas as county seat, 178 for Hord's Ridge and 101 for Cedar Springs. No town gained the required plurality, and a runoff was held on the last day of August. Dallas defeated Hord's Ridge, 244 to 216. Dallas' role as the pre-eminent town in the county was assured.[28]

Now it was time to build a more proper courthouse, but more proper by the barest of margins. A contract was awarded to J.B. McPherson on December 9, 1850, to erect a structure that would be only slightly larger than the existing log-cabin building. It was to be sixteen feet wide by thirty-two feet long (as opposed to the original sixteen by sixteen foot courthouse), nine feet tall between the floor and joists, with "good plank flooring well jointed," a stone chimney in the center of the building, and individual fireplaces in each room. Each room was to have bookcases alongside the chimneys sufficient in size to contain the books and papers of District Clerk Edward C. Browder and County Clerk Alexander Harwood.[29]

In this wooden courthouse occurred the trial of Jane Elkins, a female slave accused of murdering a widower named Wisdom as he slept by splitting his head open with an ax. Wisdom had hired the slave from her owner to help him look after his children and to keep his house. In a trial presided over by John H. Reagan, the jury found her guilty on May 16, 1853, and sentenced her to death by hanging eleven days after the conviction. Sheriff Trezevant Calhoun Hawpe oversaw the hanging, which occurred on schedule. It was the first, but not the last, hanging to occur in Dallas County.[30]

That same year, a "roll of attorneys" appearing before the courts in Dallas County was inscribed in a small record book entitled "Motion Docket," covering the years 1849 to 1853. It listed thirteen lawyers: John C. McCoy, John M. Crockett, John E. Cravens, John J. Good, John W. Berry, John C. Easton, James Turney [or perhaps Gurney], E.H. Tarrant, E.P. Nicholson, Nat. M. Burford, Wm. J. Dyer, Barton W. Stone, and A.H. Martin. A fourteenth name on the list, that of John H. Reagan, was unnumbered, evidently because he was judge of the 9th Judicial District. Many of these men were planting deep roots in the Dallas community. Some of those listed, such as Tarrant, and perhaps a few others, came to Dallas only when court was in session.[31] That the names of some of those attorneys practicing in 1850 were not repeated in this 1853 list also suggests the tenuous nature of the profession in a frontier town.

The lawyer who made the biggest stir when he was in town surely was Edward H. Tarrant (1799-1858), a leading politician and former Indian fighter who by 1853 was living in Ellis County. Tarrant County had been named for him in 1849 because he led Texan volunteer troops in 1841 in decimating a large Indian settlement at Village Creek (in present-day Arlington), removing them as an obstacle to the early immigrants. Tarrant was a former chief justice (an early description for today's position of county judges) of Red River County during Republic of Texas days as well as a legislator in the House of Representatives from 1849 to 1853.[32]

THE EVER-PRESENT possibility of disputes over proper land titles, smoldering for almost a decade, flared into near-violence in a major civil disturbance in 1852 known as the "Hedgcoxe War." By now, some eight out of ten Dallas County residents had come to the area as Peters Colony settlers with grants of land to entice them. As these colonists arrived and sought to establish their land claims, Peters Colony agents often were unavailable to guide them in making their proper boundaries clear. As a result, many settlers established homes unwittingly on land originally intended to be part of the colony property.

One dispute after another arose as Peters Colony officials belatedly tried to move many settlers or adjust their boundaries. The litigation that arose over this volatile issue kept Dallas' lawyers and other people in the area busy, but tempers were rising. The Texas Legislature sought to calm the situation by enacting legislation intended ostensibly to satisfy all parties. Lawsuits between the Colony and the state were to be withdrawn, new guidelines were to be provided for the colonists and the time for filing their claims extended, and Peters Colony was to be given just over a million acres of land. This effort at compromise appeared to favor the Peters Colony officials, a fact which further provoked the settlers and caused them to protest and demand that the legislation be withdrawn. Henry Oliver Hedgcoxe, the principal agent for Peters Colony, announced in May 1852 that the settlers had until August 4, 1852, to submit their claims, an announcement viewed as unduly dictatorial, which exacerbated the situation. The angry colonists met in Dallas on July 15, 1852, to discuss the situation. They charged Hedgcoxe with fraud and corruption, and evidently laid plans for more direct action the next day.[33]

The colonists elected as their leader and "captain" John Jay Good (1827-1882), a lawyer who had settled in Dallas only the year before. On the morning after the protest, Good led a group of about a hundred armed colonists to Hedgecoxe's office in Collin County. They seized Hedgcoxe's files, brought them to the Dallas courthouse for safekeeping, and peremptorily ordered Hedgcoxe and Peters Colony clerks to leave the colony. Hedgcoxe fled to Austin the next day. This bit of heavy-handed vigilantism paid dividends to the colonists, for the legislature passed another compromise bill on February 4, 1853, which extended better terms to the colonists and effectively ended the difficulties.[34]

Good's war-like entry as a community leader gave him an early heroic status as well as the honorific title of "General." He would make many substantial contributions in future years to the Dallas bar (including service as the Dallas Bar Association's first president) and the general community. Born in Monroe County, Mississippi, he studied at Cumberland University in Tennessee, and then read law in Mississippi before being admitted to practice in that state in 1849. He was to serve with distinction in the Civil War after organizing an artillery company in Dallas. He became presiding judge of the Confederate military courts of three states, and after the war was elected judge of the 16th Judicial District, which included Dallas County, until General Philip Sheridan removed him as an "impediment to Reconstruction."[35]

As it turned out, those responsible for arranging for Dallas' new courthouse had not planned sufficiently for the growing needs of the county. Just five years after it had been built, yet another courthouse replaced it, this one brick, and authorized to be constructed at a cost of $7,400. John J. Good himself, assisted by James M. Patterson and W.W. Peak, drew up specifications that included a requirement for the "best brick that could be manufactured in the County, and to be covered by the best quality of lead roofing." This courthouse was fifty feet square and two stories high. Brick chimneys with fireplaces were placed in each corner of the building. It would serve as the Dallas County courthouse until 1871.[36]

In these ante-bellum days, Good and other lawyers in the area generally followed the typical frontier lawyer's lot: trailing the circuit court via horseback as it transferred operations from town to town over a wide area to mete out justice. Oran M. Roberts described the scene aptly, and it was a scene which surely applied to Dallas itself at times when court was in session there. "When the time for holding the courts arrived, it was not unusual to see a dozen or more lawyers and the judge mount their horses, with saddle-bags, blankets, and tie ropes; and thus equipped, start on their journey around the district, which then embraced many counties, comprising a large scope of country. As some of them would drop out of the company at different points, others would fill their places, so that about an equal number of traveling lawyers in addition to the local bar, would be found in attendance at nearly every court."[37]

On one occasion when court was in session in Dallas and numerous lawyers were making their headquarters at the Crutchfield Hotel, the alarm sounded to signal the approach of a band of Indians. The lawyers at the Crutchfield grabbed their arms and joined other citizens in racing off toward Turtle Creek to put the Indians to route. John H. Reagan, then of Palestine, was among the lawyers who joined the effort.[38]

On the road the lawyers would carry saddlebags in which they stored their clothing, some food, a blanket, lariat, tin cup, water gourd, and coffee pot. Often, if shelter was unavailable, a group of them would have to camp out at a place near water. They would unsaddle and stake their horses, build a fire, make coffee, and have their snack meals. After eating and drinking, they would sit around the campfire, tell jokes and stories, sing a song, and finally roll themselves in their blankets with their saddle for a pillow and sleep away the night.[39]

The hardships of this life were very aptly described by Good as he traveled the circuit on horseback in the 1850s, handling one criminal case after another. He wrote to his wife describing his associations with the "vulgar herd who generally hang round frontier court."[40] En route to Palestine on one occasion, Good wrote that he stayed at a crude hostelry where he "acted in the two-fold capacity of gentleman and servant, talked and acted like the former, but unsaddled, fed, and curried my own horse." His supper consisted of cornbread, "pale, muddy coffee, and tainted, fat bacon." His bed was dirty and infested with bedbugs and fleas which were "lying in ambush" for him. Their assault on his body forced him to leave the bed and settle down uneasily on the floor with his saddlebags for a pillow. He traveled long miles over areas where few houses could be found, fording swollen creeks and rivers, suffering from cold or heat, taking a grey mare or other items for a fee. Once, traveling from Weatherford to Mulkins Mills west of Fort Worth, he dismounted from his horse for the night "as near froze as any man ever was not actually to freeze, got out my box of matches and after much difficulty started a fire, thawed open my saddle bags, pulled on an extra pair of pants and vest, took a good drink of cold toddy, bid adieu to the fire and defiance to the norther." During his travels Good achieved an enviable reputation as a criminal lawyer, and in 1856 resisted the efforts of the leading men of Parker County to recruit him to become a candidate for the state senate.[41]

Berry B. Cobb, a Dallas attorney who in 1934 profiled Dallas lawyers of the nineteenth century, summarized the effects of traveling on the circuit. "These travels gave him [Good] and those who rode the circuit an opportunity to observe the territory, the character of the people, to hear their history from the older residents, and while this life was full of hardships and they had little money; while they lacked library facilities and were forced to practice under the two different systems, passed by crude and hasty legislation; while in their practice they were largely without precedent or controlling maxims; yet they were able to adjust the law to the facts with conscience, reason, and analogy as guides in an undeveloped field, and withal they endured their experience with the greatest satisfaction, and were thinkers rather than readers, as result of which wit, philosophy, and wisdom were evolved which enrich the history of our state today."[42]

AFTER DALLAS was incorporated in 1856, the residents elected a physician, Dr. Samuel B. Pryor, to be its first mayor, choosing him over another physician candidate, Dr. A.A. Rice. John M. Crockett, Dallas' second mayor, was only the first in a long list of Dallas attorneys to serve the city in that office.

Crockett held the position during the 1857-1858 term. A year later in August, 1859, he was again elected mayor, then re-elected for another term from August 1860 to August 1861.[43]

During this period of the 1850s John Neely Bryan left town after shooting and wounding a drunken man whom he believed had insulted his wife. By then he already had sold his landholdings to an entrepreneur named Alexander Cockrell, a shrewd if illiterate individual, who built a bridge over the Trinity, opened a sawmill, constructed an office building on the courthouse square, and had become the city's leading businessman. For some reason, Bryan believed that the attorneys of Dallas had unified in opposition to him. From California he wrote to Cockrell: "I am surprised at Colonel [B. Warren] Stone and the other attorneys in Dallas for turning against me and I shall meet them when they least expect it and will know the reason why they do so." Just why Bryan wrote in such a way is not known, but it is possible that he feared the attorneys would see to it that if he returned he would be brought to trial for attempted murder.[44]

Not until 1861 did Bryan, after an absence of six years, return to Dallas. When he arrived, his friend and confidante, Cockrell, was dead, victim of a shooting which resulted in the most sensational trial yet held in Dallas County. The courtroom battle involved the town's leading attorneys.

The shooting had occurred just off the courthouse square in 1858. The newly elected town marshal, Andrew M. Moore, confronted Cockrell after a long-simmering dispute over a debt that had been the subject of extended litigation.[45] According to a brief account in the weekly *Herald*, Moore was attempting to arrest Cockrell for "violating a corporation ordinance."[46]

Both men were armed with double-barreled shotguns and revolvers, and the result was that Cockrell was shot and killed. Moore was charged with murder, and his trial was held in July in the 14th District Court presided over by Nat Burford. McCoy, now the district attorney, prosecuted the case, and he was assisted by R.W. Lunday and G.W. Guess. Moore was defended by four attorneys: B. Warren Stone, E.P. Nicholson, Isaac Naylor, and John M. Crockett.

Sixty veniremen were summoned for the jury panel. Prosecutors made peremptory challenges of eight of them; the defense struck eleven prospective jurors; and twenty others were removed for cause. The trial lasted three days. Twenty witnesses testified for the prosecution, from twelve to fifteen for the defense. Spectators flocked to the courtroom, including an unusually large number of women. "A most searching investigation into all the facts was made," the *Dallas Herald* reported, adding that attorneys for both sides gave "elaborate and eloquent arguments, creditable to the talent of any bar." The jury deliberated only a moment before declaring Moore, a carpenter by trade before being elected town marshal, not guilty.

The verdict was followed by an irrepressible outburst of applause and demonstrations of satisfaction in the courtroom that carried forth to the streets. There is no ready explanation for such jubilation, but Cockrell evidently had numerous enemies in town despite—or perhaps because of—his success. Indexes to the 14th District Court show him to have been a defendant on thirty-eight occasions between 1850 and 1858, and a plaintiff on seventeen occasions.[47]

But anger between at least two of the opposing attorneys, Stone and Lunday, persisted because of harsh comments made during courtroom arguments that evidently crossed the borders of propriety. One of the two—it is unknown which—challenged the other to a duel. Each, according to the *code duello* custom, named a referee to handle the arrangements. Before the week ended, however, the referees had managed to resolve the differences on terms acceptable to both attorneys. The *Herald* reported, "We are gratified at this result, and we are pleased to know that there is now no cause to disturb the friendly relations of these gentlemen."[48]

Cockrell's widow, Sarah, became executrix of her husband's estate and went on to become one of the city's most dynamic entrepreneurs. When Andrew Moore died of pneumonia in 1870 at the age of 43 he was praised in the *Herald* as one of the city's "most esteemed citizens" whose "valuable works" would remain as his lasting monument to the city.[49]

After the trial of Andrew Moore and the hard feelings engendered, cordial relations returned to members of the Dallas bar. Ahead, however, lay the tragic events of the Civil War.

ORGANIZING A BAR ASSOCIATION

⌘

Chapter Two

REMOTE THOUGH Northeast Texas was from the parts of the nation where sectional rivalries threatened to tear it asunder, the citizens of Dallas on the eve of the Civil War strongly identified with the cause of the South. Slavery had not been particularly important to the area's agrarian economy, but its importance seemed to be increasing rapidly—the numbers of slaves in the county had grown from 207 in 1850 to 1,074 in 1860.[1] The *Dallas Herald* reported the growing controversy over slavery regularly and in alarming tones. Superimposed prominently on the newspaper's masthead appeared an unfurled American flag with the words "States Rights."

In the spring of 1860 fears abounded in the North Texas area that visiting abolitionists from the North were doing more than preaching the Gospel, that they were stirring up slaves and plotting insurrection against their owners. Stories in many area newspapers, including the *Herald*, warned of such matters. On June 20, 1860, the newspaper urged its readers to be suspicious of strangers and to demand that they give "a reasonable account of themselves."[2] On a hot Sunday afternoon on July 8, 1860, an event occurred that seemed to confirm the worst fears. A fire, "one of the most terrible conflagrations our State has ever known," destroyed practically the entire business district of Dallas and threatened many private residences. Since the *Herald* offices were in ruins it fell to other newspapers outside Dallas to describe the event. A *Houston Telegraph* "extra" edition summarized the story: "THE TOWN OF DALLAS IN ASHES! EVERY STORE AND HOTEL BURNED: LOSS $300,000."[3]

Saved from the ravages of the flames because of the "constant exertions of a few spirited individuals" was the five-year-old brick courthouse, located fortunately in the center of the town square, free from adjoining structures. Even so, the surrounding heat was so intense that curtains inside the courthouse windows were said to have burst into flames. The young trees surrounding the building perished.

Several of the town's lawyers suffered devastating setbacks through the loss of their offices and libraries. John C. McCoy's loss, valued at $3,000, was the greatest. E.P. Nicholson, B. Warren Stone, and John G. Good estimated the amount of their losses at $1,400, $500, and $1,200 respectively. Phillip Hay, whose law office was above Thomas Drug Store, was able to save part of his library. Judge Nat Burford, who had been holding court in Waxahachie, returned the day after the fire to find just one brick structure still standing around the courthouse square. He observed people gathering in small groups, talking in whispers.[4]

The fire had erupted suddenly and mysteriously in a box of wood shavings located in front of the W.W. Peak & Brothers Drug Store on the west side of the square directly opposite the courthouse. Few if any citizens believed the fire accidental, especially when word came that a series of fires in the area had broken out the same afternoon in towns such as Denton, Austin, Jefferson, Honey Grove, Milford, Pilot Point, Black Jack Grove and Millwood. And more fires would follow in the days and weeks to come.[5]

Throughout the parts of Texas affected, vigilante committees formed. Dallas was no exception. The town's impromptu vigilantes, fifty-two in number, consisted of "the most respectable and responsible gentlemen of this county." It probably is fair to assume that many if not most of the city's lawyers were involved. Judge Burford, however, was not. On the evening that the judge had arrived from Waxahachie, former Sheriff Trezevant C. Hawpe called upon him at his house to tell him that the vigilante committee was meeting at that moment at the courthouse.[6] Those present were angry, and the former sheriff expressed fears that the citizens were going to hang all the Negroes in the county in retribution, although he believed just three of them were guilty. Hawpe urged the judge to go to the meeting at once to see if he might offer a voice of moderation. Judge Burford agreed, but at the courthouse door he encountered guards who said that he would be admitted only if he abided by the action of the people's meeting. Upon agreeing to do so, he was admitted and permitted to speak. For nearly an hour he talked, urging the men not to violate the law and advising them against hasty decisions which they might later regret. It was their responsibility to conduct a legal investigation and to behave in a law-abiding manner, he told them. Having stated his convictions, Judge Burford decided that as a judiciary officer it would be improper for him to take any further part in the proceedings, and he left.[7]

The vigilantes' suspicions immediately centered around Dallas' own slave population, and in the days that followed nearly a hundred slaves were interrogated. Fifteen days after the fire had occurred the committee, meeting behind guarded doors at the courthouse, announced its findings. It was, they concluded, as suspected. Confessions by several slaves, said to have been independently obtained, indicated that slaves throughout the North Texas area, aided and abetted by visiting abolitionists, had plotted to rise up and overthrow their white rulers and the government after causing mass confusion with the series of fires. Three slaves were identified as ringleaders in Dallas. The vigilantes ordered that they be put to death by hanging and that all other slaves within the county be whipped. On the next day the three slaves—Sam Smith, "Old" Cato, and Pat Jennings—were taken from jail under a heavily armed escort and led through the town's charred ruins to the banks of the Trinity at Main Street. There, before a large crowd and without any show of emotion, they were hanged. Patrick Jennings, identified as the one who had put the torch to the town, died with a chew of tobacco in his mouth with what newspaper accounts described as "unparalleled arrogance." The three were buried at the place where they died, beneath the gallows. (Judge Burford declined to attend the hanging, but in a speech that he delivered in July 1892, he said he was convinced that "the town was fired by Negroes.") A committee of three, including the former chief justice of Dallas County, William H. Hord of Hord's Ridge, also detained two abolitionist preachers named Blunt and McKinney who were said, at least in Dallas County, to have inspired this "diabolical plot." Committee members confined the two men to the county jail, then publicly whipped them and ordered them out of the county. As an unidentified Dallas correspondent reported to the *Houston Telegraph* in summarizing these unusual events, "John Brown and his followers were fools compared with the men engaged in this affair."[8]

The full truth of the fire in Dallas and other fires at the time in so many Texas towns remains a subject of speculation. Even so, recent scholars have concluded that the fires indeed were a part of an insurrection plot.[9] Skeptics have speculated, though, that the extreme heat wave in the area caused spontaneous combustions of newly introduced "prairie matches" in the several towns and that documents such as the "Bailey letter" which seemed to confirm the existence of an insurrection plot were forged. (In this letter, written to a visiting Methodist minister who fled the state shortly after the fires, W.H. Bailey described in some detail the rationale for the insurrection plot. The minister, the Reverend Anthony Bewley, was said to have confessed to the authenticity of the letter before he was hanged in Fort Worth by a vigilante mob on September 13, 1860.) To Horace Greeley of the far-away *New York Tribune,* notions about conspiracies and slave uprisings throughout this broad area of Texas were absurd. Greeley dubbed the stories as "farcical."[10]

The entire event is, of course, an unfortunate commentary on the state of the system of justice in Dallas County in 1860, although such a statement is easy to make nearly 140 years after the event. If the authorized and legal system of justice had been followed rather than permitting vigilante action to reign, the truth behind Dallas' fire of 1860 and those occurring throughout the state might be found today in court records. Judge Burford made his stand against vigilante action, but if he received any degree of support from others members of the bar it was not recorded. And, given the emotions of the moment, it is likely that he knew he could go no further as a lone individual.

JUST A FEW MONTHS after these events, Abraham Lincoln of Illinois was elected president of the United States. The question of secession quickly arose, and Dallas residents voted 741 to 237 to join other states in seceding from the union. Having made this break, Dallas County residents' support for the war effort heightened. Voters, by a 516 to 3 majority, favored a plan offered by the county commissioners to allocate $5,000 in gold from the county treasury to buy arms and ammunition for the Confederacy.[11]

Members of the legal profession quickly assumed leading roles in the heightened activity that soon followed. John J. Good, especially devoted to the Southern cause, was the first of the town's attorneys to involve himself thoroughly in the Confederacy effort. Even before secession he had organized in 1859 his own "Dallas Light Artillery, Texas Volunteer Militia," with himself as captain. The unit, more social in its activities than anything, had a sterling list of Dallas' citizens, including John M. Crockett, John C. McCoy, John W. Lane, Samuel B. Pryor, Jefferson Peak Jr., Charles R. Pryor, and Nicholas H. Darnell. On February 22, 1861, the unit was "tendered to the State of Texas," and on June 10, 1861, to the Confederate States of America.[12] It became known as Good's Battery of Light Artillery. The unit of about one hundred soldiers, half from Dallas County and half from Smith County, trained on Good Street (presumably named for Good) between Swiss and Pacific. One of the privates in Good's battery was none other than the Honorable Nat Burford. Upon the unit's departure to join General Ben McCullough in Arkansas, the ladies of Dallas presented a Confederate flag to the men. At the battle of Elkhorn in Arkansas (Pea Ridge), Good distinguished himself and his company in saving the Confederate artillery from annihilation, but he injured himself and was forced to resign his commission in 1862. He thereupon received a commission as a judge in the military court with the rank of colonel, a duty which required him to hold sessions in Mississippi, Alabama, and Georgia.[13]

In this capacity Good evidently worked out of Dallas, for he also became the county's provost marshal. In July 1862 he issued General Order No. 1 to all county residents. The order required all males over the age of sixteen to register for military service. Good stated that all persons engaged in conduct that was injurious to the interests of the people and the Confederate states would "be arrested and imprisoned." Dallas men responded to the call, for they filled or helped fill at least nine cavalry companies in addition to Good's artillery unit.[14]

Judge Burford distinguished himself as a lowly private, resisting efforts by General McCullough to commission him as an officer and place him on his staff. Captain Good reported that "Judge Burford walks an average of ten to fifteen miles a day and resembles but little the dignified personage to whom I used to say, 'May it please your honor?' " Burford was, Good said further, "one of the finest specimens of a cornfield hand you ever saw."[15]

In 1862, with Good having departed from the active military service, Burford returned to Dallas, became a colonel, and established a regiment for the 19th Texas Cavalry. Still another Dallas attorney, B. Warren Stone, organized a regiment for the 6th Texas Cavalry and took part in the battle of Elkhorn along with Good's artillery unit. Yet other Dallas lawyers who were active in the war along with some 1,300 Dallas County men were George W. Guess and John T. Coit, both of whom became colonels, and Z.E. Coombes, who served as a captain under the former sheriff, Colonel Trezevant C. Hawpe, in the 31st Texas Cavalry.[16]

Although the town of Dallas was removed from the war fronts, besides sending soldiers, it was involved in other aspects of the hostilities. The Confederate government established a general quartermasters and commissary headquarters in Dallas for the collection of food and supplies for the Trans-Mississippi Department, a transportation and recruiting department, and a gun manufacturing and repair department at Lancaster in the southern part of Dallas County.[17]

John M. Crockett, serving as the city's mayor until secession, gave up his municipal office to become lieutenant governor for Texas under the Confederacy, then resigned that position in 1863 to become manager of the Confederate arms factory at Lancaster. During these war years municipal government in Dallas evidently took a sabbatical from elections, for there is no record of any elections held between 1861 and 1866. Crockett, though, found himself pressed into service as the city's mayor in presiding over municipal court just after the war ended, serving from November 15, 1865, until April 21, 1866. "I have no recollection as to how I came into office," he later told early Dallas historian John Henry Brown, but his own records showed that he had fined Sions Record the sum of $10 for shooting a firearm, fined George W. Baird $5 for assaulting Maxime Guillot, and fined John Edmondson $2.50 for riding his horse on the city sidewalks.[18]

WITH THE END of hostilities in the spring of 1865, the hustle and bustle associated with the war effort did not disappear. Dallas was thriving. A number of Southern planters who believed that the cultivation of cotton without slave labor was economically unfeasible moved to the Dallas area to grow wheat. Also, the general migration to Texas by individuals and families from other Southern states resumed, bringing to Dallas more lawyers, merchants and entrepreneurs. The editor of the *Herald*, John W. Swindells, having returned to business since the fire, urged residents to cooperate with the new guidelines imposed upon them, to register to vote, and to concentrate on building the community.[19] President Andrew Johnson's generous Reconstruction policies were accepted in Dallas without undue stress, and the county's lawyers readily took the amnesty oath so that their Constitutional rights and privileges would be restored. A new judge for the 16th District, R.W. Scott, appointed by Reconstruction Governor A.J. Hamilton, administered the oath to McCoy, Good, Burford, John T. Coit, John W. Payne, John M. Crockett, E.J. Brown, J.K.P. Record and James P. Bates. On November 11, 1865, the *Herald* reported with pride that 1,260 citizens in Dallas County had taken the amnesty oath from an authorized board that was visiting the various precincts in such towns as Lancaster, Cedar Hill, Scyene, and Farmers Branch in addition to Dallas. "What County can beat this?" the editor asked.[20]

Judge Scott, despite the basis of his authority, quickly made friends in town. A native of New York, he had lived in Texas since the 1850s. His jurisdiction included Dallas and six other counties. He presided over a session in Dallas in October and November, 1865, with no problems. A speech he made at the courthouse, recorded in its entirety in the *Herald*, was declared by the newspaper to be "sensible and timely." At the close of the court's session, members of the Dallas bar, under the chairmanship of John M. Crockett, praised his work in a unanimous resolution as meeting their "hearty approval." They thanked him for his "kind, courteous, and upright manner."[21]

Dallas County and other voters within the 16th District had an opportunity on June 25, 1866, to elect a permanent judge. Scott was a candidate, but one of the two candidates opposing him was Dallas favorite John J. Good. Good, a former Confederate officer, easily won the election, carrying not only Dallas County but also the overall district. (By the time Good held his first court session in Dallas in October 1866, the county had been placed in the 5th Judicial District.)[22]

Spirits were high these days. All Dallas seemed to be thriving. "Our town presents more business appearances within the past week or two than we remember to have seen for several years," Swindells wrote in mid-October 1865. The streets were "filled with wagons[,] some with goods, some with wool going to market, but the bulk of them with our principal producer, Flour, seeking a market in the Southern and Southwestern counties."[23]

A neighboring newspaper, the *McKinney Enquirer*, viewed Dallas County's actions this way: "The people of that county seem to have forgotten Congress, confiscation, territorial government, equal suffrage and the devil, remembering only their individual interests and looking forward to the future welfare of their children. Like sensible and enterprising citizens, the people of Dallas improve and beautify their city, thereby pleasing and catching immigrants who pass that way." Between 1860 and 1870 the city grew from a population of about 775 residents to nearly 3,000.[24]

Dallas' positive attitude—buoyed at least in part by the victory of Good as their favorite son—was reflected in a mass meeting held on July 18, 1866, a month after his election, to praise

President Johnson's conciliatory policies. Good and Burford both spoke in the president's favor. In this era of good feeling, the circumstances for Good's tenure on the bench had changed since last he had served before the war; now he had to rule upon a myriad of complex legal matters brought about by neglect during the war and the adoption of a new legal system. The cases he heard included such charges as theft, assault, horse stealing, unlawfully cutting timber, altering marks illegally, unlawfully carrying away timber, malicious mischief, failing to discharge duties as overseer of a road, failing to put mile posts as overseer, disturbing public worship, aiding escape of prisoners, and using estray unlawfully.[25]

But Good had not long to dwell on such matters. The positive post-war mood quickly darkened when Radicals in Congress seized the initiative from President Johnson and began to pass a series of punitive measures impacting the South. Judge Good did not hesitate to express his concerns over the new "Jury Order" issued by the military commander of the Department of Texas. The regulation prohibited citizens from serving on juries unless they swore that they had never voluntarily supported the Confederacy. The order also printed Section 2 of the Civil Rights Act of 1866 requiring equal rights for all citizens. Under these rules most white men would be excluded from jury duty, and it was not legal to deny black citizens from serving on juries even though a state law forbade it.[26]

Unionists in Dallas had been alarmed at the ease by which ex-Confederates such as Good had resumed their previous roles in government. Eighty of the Unionists sent a petition to the nation's capital asking for a purge of all district and county officers who displayed too keen an allegiance to the South's lost cause. Good and other judges, they contended, were treating Unionists in their midst harshly, favoring former Confederates, and allowing men who had murdered pro-Unionists to run free. Their ire was directed, of course, not just to Judge Good but to a large number of Dallas County officials. These officials, including Good, were removed from office in 1868 by General Joseph Jones Reynolds, commander of the Department of Texas during Reconstruction, from his Austin headquarters.[27]

D.O. Horton of Weatherford was appointed by the military authority to succeed Good. During court session in December 1867 Horton—as had been the case for Scott—apparently faced no special obstacles from Dallas lawyers. He won praise from the *Herald* for his "courteous and gentlemanly bearing."[28] After this favorable beginning, though, Horton died three months later. Great support arose in Dallas to have James K. Polk Record succeed him. Even two of the county's leading Republicans urged Governor E.M. Pease to appoint Record to the office. Record, however, had been a Confederate officer himself, and the governor appointed instead a man destined to become a leading and popular figure in Dallas, Anthony Banning Norton (1821-1893).[29]

Norton, one of the most intriguing and colorful attorneys ever to practice law or preside over a court in the county, would become one of Dallas' leading and most fascinating citizens over the next twenty-five years. As a young lawyer/editor in his native Ohio, he had vowed in 1844 never to shave or cut his hair until Henry Clay was elected president. Clay, of course, was never elected, and Norton never cut his hair or shaved for the rest of his life. After leaving Ohio for Texas in the mid-1850s, he was elected to the Texas legislature from Henderson and Kaufman counties in 1857 and 1859 as a Unionist and supporter of Sam Houston. Besides his legal career, he published newspapers in Fort Worth, Austin, and eventually Dallas. After the series of fires in 1860 which destroyed so much of Dallas and which were blamed on abolitionists and slaves, Norton himself was suspected as an instigator. A grand jury in Weatherford recommended that he be hanged, and within a month Norton gave up his Fort Worth newspaper and left that town.[30] During the Civil War, which he opposed, he returned to the friendlier climes of his native Ohio. He ventured back to Texas after the war and became a stalwart of the newly empowered Republican Party. Norton would remain judge of the 5th Judicial District until 1875, when President U.S. Grant appointed him postmaster of Dallas.

Norton, like the other pro-North sympathizers who had been appointed to judgeships in Dallas County, quickly made a positive impression in most circles. Shortly after his first court session in Dallas County beginning on November 30, 1868, the *Herald* editorialized about the "fine impression Judge Norton is making by his urbanity as a man and genuine dignity and ability as a judge." In December 1868 with the launching on the Trinity River of the Dallas-built steamboat, *Sallie Haynes*, Norton, upon being introduced to the crowd of enthusiastic businessmen there, made an optimistic speech about the prospects for river transportation and for Dallas in general which was "received with most hearty applause by the audience." The next month Norton moved his residence from Van Zandt County to Dallas. Norton would remain as judge of the 5th District until 1870 when a new Constitution was adopted which provided for district judges to be appointed by the governor.[31]

The governor's first appointee, C.T. Garland, seemed to be of no conciliatory mind. Garland had been a Republican Radical in Jefferson, attended the Radical Republican state convention in 1869, published a paper called the *Jefferson Radical*, and already had served as a military-appointed judge in the 8th District in 1869-1870 before arriving in Dallas in October to preside over the 5th District. When only two of the twenty men summoned for grand jury reported, he ordered those absent to be fined and for Sheriff J.M. Brown to summon more grand jurors. Among the sixteen he impaneled was Melvin Wade, a young black man from Tennessee who had arrived after the war in time to serve on the Dallas County Board of Registrars in 1867. Wade became the first African-American ever to serve on a jury in Dallas County.[32]

Even so, two weeks after Garland's arrival the *Herald* reported that "Judge Garland, we are informed, in his rulings upon all questions of law, has given universal satisfaction to members of the bar." When he attended a dinner given by the businessmen of Dallas to honor a Missouri, Kansas, and Texas Railway Company surveyor recently arrived in town, Judge Garland responded to a toast that was offered to "The Judiciary" with a speech in which he praised the town's lawyers for their support of railroads.[33]

Garland presided over only this single term in Dallas because his appointment for some reason was not confirmed, and when the next court session opened in Dallas in June 1871 the presiding judge was Hardin Hart of Greenville, whose career would be marked by controversy. Hart had come to Texas with his father in the 1830s. Without formal education he was admitted to the bar in the 1840s, starting his practice in Greenville with his brother Martin D. Hart.

During the war both brothers supported the Union. Martin Hart joined a group of Texas "irregulars" who fought with Union forces in Arkansas. He was captured by the Confederates and executed for treason. Hardin Hart stayed in Texas and survived, although he was "severely abused and roughly handled" during the war. Afterwards, he took Republican assignments for a number of positions, including military appointment as judge of the 7th District in northeast Texas. He became very unpopular because of his outspokenness, and was so alarmed by threats that at one point he requested Governor Pease to give him a military escort. Pease denied the request, but in September 1869 Hart and seven soldiers were ambushed outside Bonham. Hart's wounds caused his arm to be be amputated. In 1871 he became judge of the Civil Court in Dallas. Unlike his Reconstruction predecessors, Hart won few friends in Dallas. The *Herald* carefully avoided mention of him as Hart continued Garland's practice of permitting African-Americans to serve both on grand and petit juries.[34]

Judge Hart was to play a role in the most controversial episode of Reconstruction in Dallas. Governor Davis, empowered by the much-debated Enabling Act which gave him authority to appoint public officials at all levels, attempted in 1872 to remove Mayor Henry S. Ervay and City Attorney John M. McCoy from office and replace them with his own appointees.[35] Ervay refused to give up his office or to surrender the city's records, and Judge Hart ordered Ervay placed in jail. In the midst of this brouhaha Dallas lawyers protested the governor's high-handed actions, holding a public meeting to denounce Davis's action as a "usurpation" of his authority. McCoy, Dallas' recently elected city attorney—the first to hold that office—and nephew of the venerable John C. McCoy, traveled to Austin to obtain a writ of habeas corpus to free the mayor from jail. Vindication soon came when the state attorney general ruled that Governor Davis no longer had the power to remove city officials from office.[36] And the next year the state's voters—by a far greater margin in Dallas County than in the rest of the state—elected Democratic candidate Richard Coke over Davis as governor. The carpetbagger regime in the state thus ended. Dallas County voters cast 2,032 for Coke and just 336 for Davis, whereas the rest of the state favored Coke by only a 2-1 margin.[37] Judge Hart resigned from office in February 1874.

He was replaced by man far more favored in Dallas, Hickerson Barksdale, a nephew of Nathaniel M. Burford. Barksdale was a native of Tennessee who had studied law at Lebanon College. He had served three years as an officer in the Confederate Army before coming to Dallas in 1870. Barksdale presided over the 14th District until 1876 when the new Texas constitution removed the last vestiges of the Reconstruction regime in the state. When Barksdale left office, members of the bar presented him with a gold-headed ebony cane in appreciation of his "spotless integrity as a Judge, his courtesy and impartiality as a presiding officer, and his learning and ability as a lawyer."[38]

The new Texas constitution created twenty-six judicial districts for the state. Judges were to be elected by popular vote. Dallas and Ellis counties constituted the 11th District, and three familiar candidates with impeccable Southern and Dallas credentials campaigned for the judgeship in the first election. They were the Confederate veteran and former district attorney and district judge Nat Burford; Zachariah Ellis Coombes, also a Confederate veteran and former county judge who had been removed from that position in 1867 as an "impediment" to Reconstruction; and attorney John M. Crockett, second mayor of Dallas. The easy winner was Nat Burford, who presided over his first court session in June 1876.

JUDGE GOOD, upon his removal from office in 1868, had joined with Judge Burford and another attorney, T.C. Jordan, to form one of the city's first law partnerships. The union lasted only until 1869 when Jordan left the firm to become president of the

City Bank of Dallas. Then Good joined into a partnership with E.G. Bower in the firm of Good and Bower. In the early 1870s another former jurist, Judge Zachariah Ellis Coombes, joined the partnership, the firm's name becoming Good, Bower, and Coombes. This partnership was to last until 1878 when Good's son, John G. Good Jr., completed his legal education at Cumberland University and joined his father in a firm known as Good and Good. Their partnership, located at 107 Main St., was to last until Judge Good retired in 1881 because of ill health.[39] After the dissolution of the partnership with Good in 1869 Burford evidently resumed a solo practice until 1873 when he united with Richard Morgan Jr., in the firm of Burford and Morgan. Their office was on the north side of Main between Austin and Lamar streets.[40]

While their partnership was only a brief one, Good and Burford had been great friends, dating from the earliest pioneer days when they frequently played poker together. Another early-day lawyer, Alfred H. Benners, recalled a humorous story about the poker-playing pair in those days when formality in court was often a rarity. In this instance, Judge Burford was presiding and Good appeared in his court opposite a young lawyer fresh from law school named Ed Bower. Benners recalled the incident this way: "The case was called. Good announced ready! Bower said, 'Hold on, Judge, I have a demurrer!' Good said, 'I do not know anything 'bout these newfangled tricks, Nat, you will have to show me.' The Judge said, 'Hand up your demurrer and let me see it.' When the Court had looked at the papers, Good said, 'Well, Nat, what about this young shorthorn's demurrer?' The Judge said, 'John, you have antied your petition, but this young man has raised you, with his demurrer. I have looked over it and his raise is good.' Good said, 'Well, Nat, what must I do?' The Judge said, 'You must see his raise and come in with some more facts.' Good said, 'I have not got any more facts.' The Judge said, 'The young man takes the pot.' And he dismissed Good's petition."[41]

ONE OF THE SEVERAL attorneys who arrived in the period after the Civil War and just prior to the coming of the first railroad was the man Governor Davis had attempted to remove from office in 1872, John Milton McCoy (1835-1922). Although a newcomer, McCoy wrote the city's 1871 charter and was elected by the city council in 1872 to be the first designated attorney for the City of Dallas. He represented a new wave of younger attorneys. A native of Indiana, he held three degrees from Indiana University, the B.A., M.A., and LL.D. He settled in Dallas in his mid-30s to be with his "Uncle Johnny" in "the wilds of Texas" and to try to overcome grief from the loss of his wife from tuberculosis. As he later recalled, McCoy "came to Dallas in November 1870 before any of the railroads. . . . I staged it across the Indian territory in a seat beside the driver, on top of the stage-coach, for there was no room on the inside beside the nine passengers that were already there." He was let out along with the other passengers, "tired, wornout, cold, and hungry," at the Crutchfield House on the northwest corner of the courthouse square. "I seized a rawhide bottomed chair and seating myself, braced my feet up against the jamb of the fireplace in which was a blazing fire, surveyed the premises about, and meditated: 'Well, I have come a long distance and under many difficulties for just this and these surroundings, and a tempestuous disgust overshadowed my entire being.' " Primitive though these surroundings seemed to McCoy, at least the city now had replaced its log cabins with clapboard houses.[42]

Young McCoy was surprised to learn what a formidable presence his uncle was in Dallas. He found him to be "not merely the peer but the prince of everybody." McCoy wrote home that the court, members of the bar, and citizens alike held the pioneer attorney in reverence. "I heard him make several speeches and had no idea there was either so much of the orator about him or learning. He is simply a power in this country. He can speak the most gracefully sarcastic and the most eloquently digging [sic] of any man I think I ever heard. [He] can say murder with such intonation as to make the hair rise on your head. Withal, everybody is his friend and nobody his enemy."[43]

McCoy moved in with his uncle. Residence and office were one and the same. The house had two rooms, one for a bedroom shared by the two men and the other an office and law library. "We make our own beds and do our own sweeping," the younger McCoy wrote home. However esteemed McCoy's uncle was in the area, McCoy viewed his uncle's situation as a dismal one, for it seemed to him that many had taken advantage of his kind nature. "It never will be known the amount of money Uncle has given away, spent, lost, burnt up, and [had] stolen [from him]. Oh, it makes my heart weep to think one so noble, so kind and affectionate, so princely a man has not had a home for these 17 years. Of course he has friends. . . but he has needed a sacred home."[44]

Also arriving in Dallas at about the same time was the man who soon would serve as judge of the 14th Independent District Court from 1874 to 1876, Hickerson Barksdale, who was Nat Burford's nephew. Young McCoy and Barksdale promptly joined the other lawyers in following the circuit court, trying whatever cases came along. They had hardly arrived when the two found themselves appointed along with their uncles on opposite sides of a Fort Worth case in which a man was charged with killing a Choctaw Indian. The McCoys, along with two other lawyers, prosecuted, and Barksdale, Burford, and three other lawyers defended the man, contending that the man was within his rights in killing the Indian wherever he found him because of recent Indian depredations. The trial lasted ten days; closing arguments took another day and two nights. Young McCoy won lavish praise for his own summation, which had lasted for an hour and forty minutes. After all this effort, though, the jury could not reach a verdict and the result was a mistrial. The defense attorneys' fee for representing the accused murderer was 320 acres of land, worth about $5 per acre, to be divided among themselves.[45]

Still another ambitious lawyer who was attracted to the promise of Dallas even before it had a railroad was Robert Blake Seay, only twenty-two years of age when he moved to the city far from his family and friends in Tennessee. Seay kept a diary which provides a colorful portrait of life in Dallas for a beginning lawyer. Seay, after studying law at Cumberland University in Lebanon, Tennessee, had declined to begin a practice with his brother

George's established firm in his native town of Hartsville. Instead, he chose to move to Dallas for a fresh if uncertain beginning. He explained to his father that if he had stayed and had become a successful lawyer in Tennessee he never could have known "whether I did it myself or just had it handed to me." Thus emboldened to try it on his own, he traveled by boat from New Orleans to Galveston, took the Houston and Texas Central Railroad to its northernmost terminus, Corsicana, then came to Dallas by stagecoach. The allure of Dallas as a good place to begin a practice seemed to be confirmed by the fact that traveling with Seay for at least part of the journey to the city were two other lawyers who were planning to settle and practice in Dallas.[46]

"Life in Texas will be a stern thing to me for a while," he recorded. "I must earn my bread." A frightful stagecoach ride from Waxahachie, on which Seay was the only passenger, was made in early December during a sleet and rain storm. When he arrived in Dallas he readily enough found a room for himself in one of the numerous rooming houses, but commercial space was available only at a premium. He also realized right away that there would be a great deal of competition in his chosen profession. "The prospects here are not very flattering for a young lawyer to get a start. There are I think about 30 of the profession in this little town and a fair prospect for more," he wrote just three days after his arrival. Seay shared his first office with a dentist, then, over the months to come, dutifully aligned himself with a church and various civic groups. Desperately he looked for a client, but nearly three weeks after arriving he still had not found one. When court was in session in nearby towns such as Lancaster, Scyene, Breckenridge (now Richardson), and Kaufman he traveled there in hopes of obtaining a case. "I have nothing to do but read. . . . If I can't get any cases I can at least improve my mind," he wrote. "The town is filling up with lawyers," he recorded. "They are coming in almost every day," he wrote on December 19, 1871.

By spring of 1872 Seay continued to struggle. "I am going through the starvation process in a manner not at all suitable to myself. I am still in good spirits and feel that I will come out right in Texas," he wrote. In June that year, although he had found a few clients, he was forced to write home for money, something he had never expected to do. "If my clients would only pay me what they owe me I would not be forced to do this," he said. His brother asked him to return to Tennessee to join him in his law firm, but Seay declined. Things picked up in September, and he wrote at the end of the month that he had "taken in more business this month than I ever did in my life." He had collected $57 in fees. "If my business will only continue to increase as it has done, I will make a great deal of money next year," he wrote. Setbacks were inevitable, though, such as the time in January 1873 when he traveled to Breckenridge, thinking it was the day for the justice of peace court to be in session there, only to find that the court was in Scyene instead. Next day he went to Scyene, but he got no cases. "So I had two good rides for nothing," he recorded. But on New Year's Day, 1874, Seay exclaimed in his diary: "Bless the day I ever came to Dallas!"

Seay would go on to become one of the city's most distinguished lawyers. After losing his first bid to be city attorney in 1874, he was twice elected county attorney beginning in 1878, served as a member of the Dallas City Council, formed a firm with Colonel W.L. Williams that would last more than a hundred years,[47] and in 1908 was elected criminal district judge, serving through 1922. At the time he was elected judge in 1908 it was said that he had the "longest continuous legal practice of any member of his profession in the city."[48]

STILL ANOTHER YOUNG lawyer arriving in Dallas at the same time was also a graduate of Cumberland University in Lebanon. He was Richard Morgan Jr. (1850-1908), who came from Georgia in 1871 and explained in a lengthy letter to his father just how he had chosen this place on the Three Forks of the Trinity. He had not stayed in his native Savannah, he told his father, because it would have taken too long to work into a practice in competition with other more established lawyers. Morgan had weighed the merits of Galveston, Houston, Jefferson, Marshall, San Antonio, Austin, Waco, and Dallas, and he had concluded that the latter location was the best even though it lacked the size of many of the other towns. Galveston and Houston were liable to yellow fever epidemics. San Antonio or Waco were more established in the legal profession and lacking in the same opportunities for beginners as Dallas. Finally, the choice was between Austin and Dallas. While Austin was twice as big as Dallas, Morgan said that "its people rely too much upon the fact that it is the capital and there does not seem to be that public spirit and enterprise and determination among them to build the city up by their own private efforts which prevails here [Dallas]. If there is anything to be done, they want the State to do it." Dallas was situated in the heart of the "richest and most thickly populated portion of the state," and while it did not have a single railroad it was destined to be a railroad center. Moreover, Morgan foresaw a forthcoming division of Texas into five states, as permitted by terms of its admission into the union. In that event, he believed that Dallas would be the inevitable capital of the wealthiest and most populous of those states. As was true for Seay, Morgan would become one of Dallas' leading attorneys, a partner with Nat Burford and others, and elected judge of the 44th District Court in 1898, serving until his death in 1907.[49]

Another pioneer lawyer, John D. Kerfoot, arrived in Dallas in 1867 from his native Virginia and served two terms as justice of peace of Precinct No. 1. He became mayor of Dallas on April 5, 1876, the second attorney to hold that office since the city was incorporated in 1856, following John M. Crockett.[50]

Seay, Morgan, Kerfoot and the other young attorneys attracted to Dallas seemed to be blessed with visions of the future, for they arrived even before the great boom that followed the arrival of railroads in 1872 and 1873. While they may have anticipated it, it was by no means certain that the city would win either of the two railroads headed in its direction. But if Dallas were to prosper, it had to be successful in the effort if it were to end its isolation.

THE TOWN WAS ASTIR, surely as never before, as it followed the progress of the Houston and Texas Central Railroad moving slowly northward from the settlements around Houston toward the Red River. No group was more vocal in seeking to entice it to pass through Dallas than the members of the bar. Burford, Good, the elder McCoy, Z.E. Coombs, and others organized meetings, formed committees, and wrote resolutions assuring the railroad favorable treatment if it would come through Dallas. When it appeared that, despite all these efforts, the railroad would bypass the city, cash and real estate enticements were offered that succeeded in winning the favor of the H&TC officials. On July 16, 1872, the Houston and Texas Central Railroad arrived in Dallas from the south, ushering in a boom period that dramatically changed the city and increased its population from 3,000 citizens in early 1872 to more than 7,000 by September of the same year. The following year the Texas & Pacific, crossing the continent from east to west, similarly was entreated through some bold maneuvering in the Texas Legislature by Dallas' John W. Lane to come through Dallas, thus making the town the railroad crossroads of North Texas. The economic boom prompted by the H&TC was intensified even further, and by 1890 Dallas would be the state's most populous city. [51]

Even before the railroads arrived, lawyers in Dallas, a sizable number now, had begun gathering as a group to discuss and to take actions on matters of mutual concern. One of the first references to one of their meetings was a resolution passed in February 1872 upon the death of fellow attorney James K.P. Record, a native of Tennessee who had arrived in Dallas in 1859 and who had been instrumental in the important civic project of having an iron bridge constructed over the Trinity. It appears that the meeting had been called spontaneously with John J. Good being elected chairman of the meeting (he also would be elected as the first regular president of the Dallas Bar Association the next year). Colonel McCoy was delegated to appear before the 14th District Court and present the resolution to Judge Hardin Hart on February 5. "May it please the court," he said, "I have been elected as a Medium through whom to present to this Court the Resolutions adopted by the Members of Dallas Bar upon the death of Capt. J.K.P. Record. The resolution, carefully recorded in ink in the court's huge record book, stated that the bar had lost "one of its most courteous, able, and eloquent advocates." (Record's memory was to be remembered in Dallas probably through Record Street and until recent times through Record Crossing on the Trinity River west of town.)[52]

Soon after, McCoy's nephew wrote home on March 3 with another reference to the bar, this time concerning the death of another attorney, John T. Coit, a native of South Carolina who had moved to Dallas in 1870 and established a partnership with J.D. Kerfoot. "We had a bar meeting this morning and you will likely see the resolutions of the bar in the next Herald," he wrote. The bar was arranging Coit's funeral and paying "every attention and respect" to his widow and their four small children.[53]

In September 1872 the "bar" came together to form a "Legal Association," and on November 9, 1872, they agreed on a schedule of fees for services. Their numbers had increased from the nineteen in the entire county, as listed by the census of 1870, to thirty-two.[54] Eighteen of them listed their services, either individually or as partners, in discreet front-page advertisements in the *Dallas Weekly Herald*.[55] In 1875 the first directory published for Dallas listed fifty-seven lawyers in a town with a population of 12,000. This new directory profiled a number of the leading citizens, and the esteem in which attorneys were held is indicated by the fact that four of the first five men featured represented the legal profession. The directory listed a number of partnerships, including McClure & Goldthwaite, Hughes & Tucker, Bookout & Edwards, Morgan & Gibbs, and Shannon & Oldham.[56]

These partnerships generally amounted to a casual agreement between two barristers to share an office and set of lawbooks. Philip Lindsley (1843-1911), an attorney who arrived in town amidst this boom in 1875 and who later wrote a history of Dallas, described how A.T. Watts and Bob Cowart formed one such partnership. Watts was on his way to the courthouse one day when Judge George N. Aldredge (1846-1908), who went on the bench in 1879, encountered him on the corner of Main and Austin streets. "Watts," Aldredge said, "how'd you like to have Bob Cowart as a partner?" "All right," said Watts. Cowart, conveniently, was nearby. "Bob," called the judge, "Watts says yes." The deal was done, and they remained partners until Watts was appointed to an appellate court.[57]

Sometimes, Lindsley added, the partnerships dissolved just as suddenly. "S. and H. had their office over a store on Main Street, opposite Sanger Brothers. One morning a wild commotion was heard in their room—it sounded like tables and chairs being knocked over, while occasionally a heavy book or poker would crash through one of the windows, to the street below. A passer-by on the street anxiously inquired of another lawyer coming leisurely down the stairs, what was the matter? Oh, was the reply, it's S. and H. dissolving partnership."[58]

The Dallas bar was growing bigger and being infused constantly with new and more sophisticated ideas. Yet, frontier ways lingered. "I have seen a prominent attorney, lying behind the chair of District Judge Aldredge, his coat off, enjoying his afternoon nap, while the case was on trial," Lindsley wrote. He characterized Aldredge's predecessor, Hardin Hart, in this courtroom exchange as Judge Hart brashly responded to one attorney's motion: "Steele, you know that aint law!" "I know it aint," Steel replied, "but I thought your Honor might accept it as such." "That may not be contempt of court," Judge Hart said, "but it's an awfully close shave."[59]

Aldredge, a native of Georgia, arrived in Dallas sometime before the 1870 census that listed him as twenty-three years of age. He entered into a partnership with John T. Ault, also a Georgia native, and Olin Wellborn, and it lasted until Aldredge was elected county attorney in 1875. From 1879 until 1888 he served as judge of the 11th District Court. Berry Cobb recalled an incident when the judge and Sawnee Robertson were fishing together on an area lake. The boat tilted and Aldredge fell into the mud. Furious, the judge blamed Robertson for doing it on purpose. "Yes, I did," Robertson admitted, "but I just got even with you for ruling against me the other day."[60]

One day in March 1873, A.B. Norton stopped by the office of one of the city's leading lawyers and found it empty except for a "rough-looking" customer who was obviously unhappy at the delay. The man said that he had been waiting far too long, and before striding away in disgust placed on the office table a hand-scrawled note. Norton read it and noted its very direct comments. The top of the page, entitled "Take Notice," was followed by this message: "[Norton deleted the attorney's name] will please stay at office during business hours, and he will succeed a damm, site better. [signed] A CLIANT."[61]

WHILE THE SEVERAL references to the Dallas bar in 1872 suggest a casual affiliation of lawyers who came together as needed (although the agreement upon a schedule of fees in November 1872 suggests something rather official), in 1873 the "Bar Association of Dallas" appears to have organized on a more formal basis. Its first president was John J. Good; the date of his election is unknown. In the spring of 1873 Good requested District Judge Hardin Hart to excuse "jurors, parties and witnesses" from June 2 until June 16 because the county's wheat crop was ready to be gathered. This request, granted by the judge, was recorded in the minutes of the court. On October 7, 1873, the bar association's secretary, Richard Morgan, Jr., presented a resolution in behalf of the organization requesting Judge Hart to adjourn court for two weeks because of the great fear of an epidemic of yellow fever which had occurred in Shreveport and Calvert. The bar's resolution quickly pointed out that there was no evidence of such an epidemic in Dallas County and that the physicians of Dallas would sound an immediate alarm at the first sign of it. Judge Hart granted the request, adjourning until October 20, 1873. [62]

In late November 1873 the bar met on a Friday evening for a convivial time which included a mock trial with a jury of lawyers. The jury assessed the guilty party a basket of champagne. "Things were going gloriously and everybody getting drunk fast when I left at midnight," Robert B. Seay recorded in his diary.[63]

The actual date for the founding of the Bar Association of Dallas has been accepted on the basis of the above activities as 1873, but as we have seen, local lawyers began gathering and passing resolutions as early as 1872. (In November 1849 they evidently had come together to sign the petition requesting a change in court sessions.) This post-war era was a time in the nation's history when many professionals were forming associations and developing common standards, nationally as well as locally.

Insofar as the legal profession is concerned, Texas was a pioneer in this regard. In fact, the first local bar association in the nation may have been founded in Galveston when thirty-five members of the Galveston bar came together on April 11, 1868, to create the Galveston Bar Association. They prepared a constitution and bylaws and soon began drafting bills on such matters as judicial reform. They also lobbied at the state legislature for their adoption.[64] Lawrence Friedman, in his authoritative work, *A History of American Law*, seems not to have noticed the founding of the Galveston Bar, for he states that the first record of a local bar association founded anywhere in the nation was that of New York City on February 5, 1870, when eighty-five lawyers formed the Association of the Bar of the City of New York. Not until seven years later was the American Bar Association formed at a meeting in Saratoga, New York, with purposes to "advance the science of jurisprudence, promote the administration of justice and uniformity of legislation. . . uphold the honor of the profession. . . and encourage cordial intercourse among the members of the American Bar." [65]

DALLAS WAS TAKING on airs; its rapid growth showed no signs of abating. It was big enough and brash enough in 1873 to create a poster, 13.5 inches high by 9 inches wide, inviting "all who wear the badges of industry, honesty, and morality" to settle in Dallas. The poster bragged of the city's many benefits, and it listed by name the bankers, druggists, grocers, attorneys, and other merchants. Under the category of attorney were listed at least five partnerships, surely a sign of growing sophistication in the profession. Partnerships listed were Ault & Wellborne, Burford & Morgan, Barksdale & Eblen, Good & Bower, and McCoy & McCoy. Individual lawyers named were R.D. Coughanour, J.T. Downs, W.M. Edwards, O.E. Finlay, W.C. Holland, J.W. Payne, C.G. Payne, John M. Stemmons, H.H. Sneed, and J.M. Thurman.[66] These were not all the lawyers in town, for not even listed were the city attorney, James H. Field, who had succeeded John M. McCoy in that office in 1872, nor Field's successor, Olin Wellborn, who held the office from 1873 to 1874, nor A.B. Norton, the publisher of *Norton's Union Intelligencer*.

Lawyers advertised their services in tiny newspaper advertisements. Nat. M. Burford was "Attorney & Counselor at Law" with his office "upstairs in the Harsh building." H.L. Ray, similarly an "Attorney & Counselor at Law," would "regularly attend all the courts of the 14th judicial district." He promised "prompt attention to all legal matters."[67]

On February 3, 1875, the Dallas Bar Association met during a court recess to pass a resolution of condolence for the death of Colonel H.H. Sneed, a fellow bar member, beginning a tradition of memorials that continues to the present day. The lawyers resolved that each member of the bar would wear "the usual badge of memory" (presumably a black armband) for thirty days. Colonel McCoy presided at this meeting.[68]

With news of the early-morning death in 1876 of the county's deputy clerk, Pierce Mitchel Brown (son of prominent pioneer John Henry Brown), members of the bar again came together to plan a proper showing of respect. At this noon meeting they elected Good as chairman and Seay as secretary, then named a five-person committee to assist the two in preparing an appropriate resolution.[69]

Good's term as first president of the Dallas Bar Association ended in 1875. He was succeeded by the elder McCoy, who presided at a meeting held in the courtroom on March 10,1876, in which a resolution was adopted praising the learning and integrity of Judge Hickerson Barksdale, retiring from the 14th Independent District Court after two years' service. For his contributions the bar presented him with a gold-headed cane. McCoy held the presidency through 1877, being succeeded by A. H. Field, whose presidency lasted until 1880.[70]

Surely a unifying topic for all lawyers in Texas was the dreaded state occupation tax, imposed on members of the profession by the state legislature in 1873, 1876, 1879, and 1881. Lawyers widely believed the $10 tax (reduced to $5 in 1881) to be discriminatory and a reflection of the legislature's animus toward the profession. Most members of the bar refused on a matter of principle to pay it, and almost every lawyer in town was listed as being unpaid in 1879 and 1881.[71]

THE BOOM PERIOD introduced by the railroads and the increasing amount of legal work in the city and county rendered the old 1855 courthouse too small to serve its purposes, and it was unsafe as well. The structure was dismantled and its materials sold for $465. Work began on a new two-floor courthouse, 66 by 120 feet. Progress, though, was slow, and by early 1873 construction had stopped for lack of funds. The *Dallas Herald* complained: "Our Court House has stood still too long, and its unfinished walls admonish us that they should go on until the last stone is in place, and until justice is enthroned within them." Already $50,000 had been spent on the building, and the Herald wasn't certain how to raise the necessary additional funds, but it did stress the need to "bring back the ring and hum of skilled artisans." A serious question was whether to scale down the plans or to find the funds to go ahead as originally envisioned. Finally, in April 1873, voters approved $40,000 additional in bonds to complete the building as originally planned.[72] This new courthouse, a handsome, well-proportioned structure as opposed to its ungainly predecessor, was constructed of limestone rock quarried from around White Rock Creek. It was ready for occupancy in 1874. Two stories high with a splendid dome and graceful architectural detail, it was saluted by the 1875 city directory as the finest and most substantial public building in the state. A large courtroom occupied the entire second floor.[73]

The pride felt by all citizens in the new courthouse and the entire city was summarized by John M. McCoy in an 1872 letter to his parents. "Look out here with me now out of my window at the beautiful stone courthouse going up surrounded by the beautiful grove of trees that Uncle John [McCoy] put out with his own hands years ago. Then look with me across southward to the river and see the beautiful river bridge spanning the Trinity and long causeway leading through the forest on the other side. Then look with me to the east far up Commerce and Main Street and they stretch out through the little cottage groves, cedar forests etc. to the prairie. Away yonder, then see the flowers everywhere–the beautiful sandy roads. See the pleasant faces, the social people. Hear the church bells ringing and see the orderly companies going here and there as I did this morning. . . each going to his little church around the corner."[74]

Every week the *Dallas Herald* was praising the county's attributes and urging more and more settlers to come to Dallas, as indeed they did, a fact which continued to burden the legal system. The county's growth was recognized by the state legislature in what became a constant realignment of judicial district boundaries to accommodate the ever-increasing amount of litigation. In July 1870 Dallas became one of just three counties served by the 14th Judicial District, the others being Tarrant and Ellis counties. (Rockwall County was added to the district in 1874.) Five-week sessions were held beginning on the first Mondays in February, June, and October. On June 4, 1873, the legislature created a Criminal District Court for Dallas County alone. Its terms, four weeks each unless more time was needed, began on the first Mondays of January, May, and September.[75] As a part of the continuing reorganization of the state court system, this court, presided over by Silas Hare, ceased to exist in 1876.

Progress and growth, even in these early days, brought expressions of remorse for the loss of older, simpler times. One of the casualties of growth was Judge Burford's old home at Main Street and Akard. It had been purchased and torn down by the Rock Island Railroad, which put its local office there. Under Burford's roof had slept over the years such honored guests as Sam Houston, Thomas J. Rusk, Louis Wigfall, John H. Reagan, and General Jubal A. Early. [76]

The earliest, pioneer days of practicing law were ending. A bar association had been founded and was meeting regularly. Dallas' lawyers could take pride in the fact that their association was an early one, preceding by a decade the 1882 founding of the Texas Bar Association and also antedating the 1878 founding of the American Bar Association. The coming of the railroads, the telegraph, new businesses, and new problems were emerging as Dallas' growth—slowed only slightly by the nation-wide depression of the 1870s—continued on a pace that would make the city the biggest in the state in 1890. The number of lawyers of Dallas was increasing rapidly, but the growth of the city and its bustling commerce required it.

ATTORNEYS OF AMBITION

⌘

Chapter Three

THE SUDDEN EXPLOSION in population after the railroads arrived made Dallas, as described by its own 1878-79 city directory, pre-eminently the "grand central point of a vast territory." By 1880 its population had mushroomed to 10,385. Only a few decades earlier, buffalo had grazed on its heights. Now, a sprawling and rapidly growing city extended eastward from the cluster of buildings around the courthouse along Main, Commerce, Elm, Jackson, and Pacific streets toward the H&TC Railroad terminal almost a mile away. This "great railroad centre," the city directory predicted, would become a "great manufacturing city." A brief list of some of the town's major institutions suggested its increasing complexity and a growing workload for the attorneys. There were four daily and six weekly newspapers (among them a weekly German-language publication, the *Texas Volksblatt*), six flouring mills, three street railroads, two cotton compresses, a woolen factory, two large foundries, a waterworks, a gas works, several broom factories, a hoop factory, three planing mills, two theatres, a cement factory, fifteen to twenty common schools, a dozen or more brick kilns, three railroads with three depots, four stagecoach lines, and a fine fair grounds.[1]

Although this new town was just more than three decades old, in June 1875 residents formed a historical group called the Pioneers of Dallas. The organization planned a reunion that summer of the city's surviving pioneers. John C. McCoy was elected first president, and at least two other lawyers, John M. Crockett and Nat Burford, had prominent roles in the work. It was perhaps hard at this early date to generate widespread interest in a historical society. The record of its activities fades, although a committee met again in January 1877 to discuss the historical society.[2]

The founder of this thriving town, John Neely Bryan, was among its surviving pioneers, and he still could be seen on occasion. But he was not doing well. The *Herald* reported briefly and rather harshly in February 1877 that "the venerable John Neely Bryan, the founder of Dallas, has lost his mind." The newspaper urged the people of Dallas to "see that the old pioneer may be carefully looked to and cared for."[3] Bryan soon entered the state institution for the insane in Austin, and before the year was over he was dead. His grave site remains unknown to this day.

Later in 1877 *Herald* editor J.L. Bartow wrote that the "great tide of immigration that is constantly flowing into Texas is almost beyond conception." Dallas' progress and its growing reputation continued to be a magnet to attorneys of ambition looking for a promising location. They moved to Dallas in ever-increasing numbers, typically from friendly Southern states such as Tennessee and Kentucky or from Texas towns such as Jefferson or Kaufman or McKinney. In many cases those coming from other states first made brief stopovers in the smaller towns, learning Texas' ways in these environments, and then, after a while, moving on to the bigger and more rewarding playing field offered in Dallas. Some lawyers wandered so much from town to town that they seemed almost like itinerant peddlers. Many of these men—and they were all men—had been admitted to the bar prior to reaching to Dallas. Almost without exception this took place after a private course of study in a law office. Their authorization to practice law came through their local courts after cursory examinations. Usually, their acceptance in Dallas or Texas was routinely approved upon the motion of a local attorney who knew them. Minutes of the courts prior to 1890 reveal only two instances in which applicants were rejected.[4] Many men who had studied in the older Southern states were admitted to practice in their home states with the understanding that they were moving west to start their legal careers. Many were veterans of the Civil War, fleeing the disruptions of the Old South and seeking new beginnings in Texas. Of those few who had formal legal training, many of them came from Cumberland University in Lebanon, Tennessee, which by 1859-1860 had an enrollment of 180 students, fourteen more at the time than Harvard's law school.[5]

BY 1877 THERE were some six dozen lawyers in Dallas. Typical of those newly arrived was Samuel N. Braswell, born in Georgia in 1827 and admitted to the bar there after having read law in an office. From Barnesville, Georgia, he moved in 1858 to Mount Pleasant, Texas, where he was elected a state senator. Then he moved to a larger town, Corsicana, in 1871, and finally made his way to Dallas in 1874, where he became the county's second elected justice of the peace, serving for three consecutive terms beginning in 1886.[6]

Following the same general pattern as Braswell was a Kentucky native, Colonel John Martin Stemmons (1830-1890), who would become an important member of the bar and who also would have descendants whose names would become well-known in Dallas for their leadership in legal, civic, and business activities. Stemmons, a Confederate veteran, was licensed to practice law in Tennessee and Mississippi. After the war he moved to Texas and was admitted to the bar in Dallas in 1868. Colonel Stemmons was one of those lawyers who got together in 1872 and agreed upon a schedule of fees for the city's lawyers.[7]

A younger lawyer, William Beriah Gano (1830-1912), was unique in two special ways—he grew up in Dallas and, rare for the area in that time, he was a Harvard graduate. Gano was the son of a dashing Confederate general, Richard Montgomery Gano, who had five horses shot from beneath him during the war. With the war over, General Gano moved his family, including his young son William Beriah, from Kentucky to Dallas. Upon graduation from Harvard Law School in 1877, young Gano returned home to Dallas to begin a law practice. "Prompt attention given to all legal business entrusted to his care," he stated in an 1878 newspaper advertisement, listing his office as 607 Main Street.[8] Gano became a leading member of the local bar, serving three times as president of the bar association and becoming in 1890 a special judge for the 44th District Court. Besides his legal prowess, Gano would leave another interesting legacy to the American nation, for his daughter would give birth in Houston to a son who became one of the nation's richest and most intriguing individuals, the reclusive movie-maker and industrialist, Howard Hughes, Jr.[9]

One who became an early legend was Colonel William L. Crawford (1839-1920), who before establishing a practice in Dallas already had achieved state-wide distinction as a lawyer in Jefferson. He had been reared in that East Texas town after being born in Kentucky and brought to Texas by his parents at the age of five in a covered wagon. He moved to Dallas just after chairing the committee that drafted the Bill of Rights to the Texas Constitution of 1876. In the preceding year he had been a delegate to the Texas Constitutional Convention. In Jefferson, Crawford was the protégé of a powerful East Texas politician, Congressman Dave Culberson. At Culberson's suggestion the young Crawford took and passed the state bar examination after an intensive six-week period of study. In a sensational murder trial in Jefferson, the "Diamond Bessie" case, Colonel Crawford won an acquittal for the accused woman murderer and instantly became recognized as one of the greatest trial lawyers in the state. Colonel Crawford's move to Dallas represented a powerful statement as to the city's growing prestige, for Jefferson at the time was a bigger and more prominent town. Crawford, whose flowing locks and beard gave him the appearance of an eternal Confederate—and, in fact, he had risen in the ranks in the Confederate army from private to colonel at the age of 22—became the first Dallas man to be elected president of the Texas Bar Association, serving in 1887-88. Despite his special skills as a criminal lawyer, until he died in 1920 he also represented the powerful new institution that arrived in town in 1885, *The Dallas Morning News*. In his obituary Crawford was described as "the foremost criminal lawyer of Texas, if not the entire South."[10]

When Harry P. Lawther, who would become one of the city's outstanding attorneys and president of the Bar Association in

1929, arrived in Dallas in the fall of 1883 to begin his practice, Judge John L. Henry gave him this warning: "Young man, I wouldn't advise you to locate in Dallas. Dallas is too big a town. There are too many lawyers here. You pick you some county seat with about 2,500 people. You can become acquainted quicker and get some business sooner." This advice was given when Dallas had a population of some 25,000 and about forty lawyers.[11]

THERE WAS YET another breed of lawyer in Dallas during these post-Civil War days—those who hailed from the North rather than from the South and who were Republicans in an area that was overwhelmingly Democratic. They were far fewer in number, of course. Some of these attorneys fared well under the Republican administration's Reconstruction period, gaining important federal appointments and becoming prominent individuals. One of the foremost of these was the highly principled Anthony Banning Norton, who generally had made a positive impression on Dallas lawyers despite his Unionist views upon his appointment in 1868 as a Reconstruction judge. In 1878 and in 1884 Norton was an unsuccessful Republican candidate for governor, and in 1866 and 1871 he lost Congressional races.

While it appears that Norton was well-liked in Dallas, during the tense Reconstruction period and for a brief while afterwards he was viewed with suspicion in some quarters. The *Herald* printed a letter in late 1876 from a man in Warren, Illinois, describing a "political speech" Norton had delivered while visiting that town. He was said to have related in his speech many instances of cruelty practiced on the Union men of Texas, and especially on Republicans, by unregenerate Southerners now exacting retribution. "From his statements there would be no safety for Northern men, were they Republicans, to settle in your state," stated the letter-writer, John D. Platt. "He [Norton] related many instances in his court where rebel juries acquitted men for flagrant crimes committed on black and white Republicans, and where the most trifling charges against black men and women terminated in cruel punishment in jail and penitentiary." Norton, he said, had given lurid details about an occasion in which fourteen black men in Texas had been murdered for being Republicans and a white Republican who tried to bury them also murdered. "I write to you to learn whether his statements are true or not," Platt asked of the *Herald*.[12]

The *Herald* responded with a bitter attack upon the man who was the town's postmaster, and, it should be said, editor of an opposition newspaper. "The utterances of A.B. Norton are as untrue as they are slanderous; they are deformed by falsehoods at which perjury would hesitate; they are founded in an inspired malignity at which hell itself rejoices; they are the insidious declarations of a reptile calumny ever upon the watch to strike down a gallant though luckless people. They are the utterances of a Southern spy, from the restlessness of whose malice there is no interval save when he disgorges his venomous slanders to the bidding of Chandler, his master." The newspaper said that during his Dallas residency Norton was receiving "naught but the most courteous and considerate treatment," but that now it was evident that he was "like a viper warmed in the bosom of friendship." As to the murder of fourteen black men, the *Herald* said that six cattle thieves had been killed in West Texas and that later a white man had been killed when called to his door. No actual connection between the incidents had been made.[13] Despite these vituperative comments, in time any harsh feelings that existed in the community toward Norton faded away.

The *Herald* denied that it held ill-will toward Unionists in general. It constantly solicited for more settlers for Dallas, no matter their political viewpoints or backgrounds. "Union men, Republicans, Old Line Whigs, Democrats, all men, of whatever political persuasion, are welcomed to Texas, and *shall* and *will* be protected here."[14]

A DALLAS LAWYER who was even more prominent in his uniqueness than Norton and the other Union men was Sam H. Scott. Scott was the first African-American to practice law in Dallas. He moved to the city in March 1881 from Memphis, Tennessee. Despite the racial prejudices of the times, he established a law practice evidently without any major problems.

Scott set up his office at 301 Main Street in the immediate vicinity of the courthouse and in the heart of the area where the city's white attorneys were located. Unlike most of the other lawyers, however, Scott lived in his office. A white attorney, C.G. Payne, also listed 301 Main Street as his office. Just a few doors down at 313 Main Street was Dallas' venerable Nat M. Burford. Whether or not Scott attended the occasional meetings of the Dallas bar is not recorded. If Scott's practice was confined to the area's black residents, as surely it was, certainly his clientele and opportunities were limited in a city whose black population was 18.6 percent of just more than 10,000 residents.[15]

Scott stayed in Dallas only seven months. He moved in October 1881 to Pine Bluff, Arkansas, to begin a practice there. Upon his departure, the *Dallas Herald*, in a news story under the rather proprietary headline, "Our Colored Lawyer," commented favorably. "He came to this city highly endorsed by the bar of Memphis, and leaves here recommended by a number of the most prominent members of this bar, the judges of the courts, and some of our best citizens. He was the first and only colored lawyer who ever practiced his profession in this city, and at first there was perhaps a slight prejudice against him on account of his race, yet it must be said that he conducted himself with [such] propriety and discretion that he soon won the good will of all with whom he came in contact, and he leaves carrying with him the good wishes of those who knew him, both white and black."[16]

Information on his later career is sketchy, although in 1885-86 a man named S.H. Scott served in the Arkansas State Legislature from Jefferson County, Arkansas, which is where Pine Bluff is located. It appears that the two men were the same, for the African-American population in Pine Bluff outnumbered whites at the time by an approximate two-to-one margin. In Pine Bluff, Scott was not the only black lawyer in town, for African-Americans had been practicing there since the 1870s.[17]

Scott remains a curious and enigmatic figure. The 1880 census for Memphis, Tennessee, shows him to be a divorced man, forty years of age, a lawyer, born in Massachusetts, with the birthplace of his parents listed as unknown. In the designated space for race, the census enumerator recorded "mu" for mulatto, indicating that Scott was the offspring of black and white parents. As one who was born in Massachusetts, Scott certainly was not a former slave. A reference to him in the *Dallas Daily Herald* suggested that he had lived for a while in Oberlin, Ohio. Beyond these scattered facts, nothing is known of this path-breaking pioneer lawyer.[18]

A year after Scott had departed another African-American, J.H. Williams from Mineola, Texas, applied to the district court for admission to the bar. Judge George N. Aldredge appointed a four-man committee to examine him and review his qualifications, and their decision was split, two to two. Aldredge appointed a second committee to settle the issue, and the three attorneys on this committee agreed unanimously that Williams was not qualified. His admission to the bar thus was denied. Williams said he would continue his studies until he was able to pass the examination, but there is no record that he did.[19]

The second African-American attorney to successfully practice law Dallas was Joseph E. Wiley, who arrived in 1885 from Chicago. Wiley's first office was in A.B. Norton's own building, Elm and Sycamore (now Akard), which raises the possibility that he was encouraged to come to Dallas and assisted by the Republican Norton. Later in the decade, Wiley's law office was in the immediate vicinity of the courthouse at 755 Elm Street, where so many of the town's lawyers had located. The first reference to Wiley's work evidently came on October 6, 1885, when *The Dallas Morning News* published a routine article about a divorce petition he filed in district court for a black client, Semantha Wilson, who accused her husband of "abusive, cruel and outrageous treatment."[20]

Wiley moved his office several times early in his career, usually finding a place on Elm Street near the courthouse. The 1898 Dallas city directory lists him as being a law partner with John L. Turner. Their offices were at 155 Main Street across the street from the courthouse. Wiley was a remarkable individual who ultimately branched out from the practice of law into real estate and business to become the city's most prominent early black entrepreneur as owner of the New Century Cotton Mill and as organizer of the Colored Fair and Tri-Centennial Exposition in 1901. The attention he gained as an entrepreneur ultimately overshadowed his work as a lawyer.[21]

The 1898 city directory notation for Wiley & Turner was the first time John L. Turner (1869-1951) appears on its pages as an attorney. Turner, who attended Kent Law School and was the son of a farmer, would go on to practice law in the city for fifty-five years. In 1952, when the city's African-American attorneys—still excluded from membership in the Dallas Bar Association—came together to form their own association, they named it in his honor, the J.L. Turner Legal Association.[22]

Another pioneer African-American whose lengthy career as a lawyer in Dallas began at the same time as that of Turner's was Ammon Scott Wells (1876-1936). Wells also appears for the first time as a lawyer in the 1898 city directory, being listed as the partner of Isaac L. Henson in the firm of Henson & Wells at 790 Elm Street. In Wells' first listing in the 1894-95 city directory he is identified as an employee of the George W. Brooks' carriage and wagon manufacturing shop, located on Main Street at its juncture with the H&TC Railroad. In 1935 Wells became one of the first if not the first black citizen in Dallas to run for public office. He sought to succeed Sarah T. Hughes as state representative after her appointment as judge of the 14th District Court. Despite powerful pressure from the city's established leaders that he withdraw from the race, he held on to his candidacy but was not elected.[23]

There seemed to be plenty of business for all Dallas lawyers. The *Herald* observed that there was enough "to make all the attorneys rich." And indeed, the *Herald* continued, they *would* be rich "if they got their fees." The expanding legal activities kept courthouse officials busy, although few people seemed to have any idea of just how much legal business was being conducted. Two justices of the peace, a county judge, a district judge, a sheriff, constables and deputies, and county and district clerks were dealing with the processes of the law. And the city's seventy-odd lawyers, the *Herald* wrote, "are busy examining papers, making speeches, and trying cases." One small indication of how busy the courthouse personnel were came through a statement by the Dallas County Clerk, who said he issued sixty-four marriage licenses in the month of December 1876 with no let-up in sight. "Golly, how fast they are marrying up there," observed the *Caldwell Eagle*. So many legal notices were being posted on the courthouse walls, it was observed, that the situation had become chaotic and many matters of vital interest were being missed.[24]

Some of the cases being tried in the courts required considerable sophistication and knowledge. For instance, attorneys in a suit against the Houston & Texas Central Railroad had to prepare themselves to examine and cross-examine medical experts to determine whether a man's death had been caused naturally by rheumatism of the heart or whether the rheumatism had been "superinduced" by injuries sustained in a railroad accident.[25]

IN THE EARLY morning hours of February 4, 1880, the courthouse that had been completed after so much expense and trouble suffered a disastrous fire. Only the walls were left standing. Two employees happened to be sleeping in the courthouse when the fire broke out at about 2 a.m. One of them, C.B. Gillespie of the tax collector's office, managed to save the county's records by raising a window and passing the documents through it undamaged.[26] Taking advantage of the walls that were still intact, the courthouse was rebuilt. A third floor, a mansard roof, and a large, square clock tower were new features. This building was destined to stand another ten years before another fire would consume it, too. Meanwhile, the 1880 fire prompted officials to erect on the southeast corner of the courthouse square a small, fireproof building for records that would remain standing until it was demolished in the early 1960s.

In 1876 the Dallas bar drew up and presented to the U.S. Congress an "ably drawn and exhaustive petition" asking that an additional federal district be created for the state with headquarters at Dallas. A year later, with no progress toward that goal being evident, a new petition was circulated among members of the bar with the same purpose. "Its importance to this city can scarcely be overestimated," wrote the *Herald*. The advantages seen were many: attendance of persons from all adjacent counties would bring large sums of money to Dallas; the federal offices of marshal, clerks, registrars and assignees in bankruptcy would "increase the business of the city"; the building of a new federal courthouse estimated to cost from $100,000 to $150,000 would generate considerable work. Beyond that, the savings to the federal government brought about by creating a court in Dallas also would result in savings in transportation costs for all concerned. The *Herald* urged the Dallas bar to dispatch to Washington, D.C., at once a representative to press the issue.[27]

In March 1878, with Alexander White presiding, the bar met at the courthouse and passed yet another resolution urging "speedy passage" of a bill creating a new federal district. Three of the places holding court sessions in Texas were fixed at locations in the southern half of the state and the remaining location, Tyler, was remote from a large portion of the people of Northwest Texas. A certified copy of the petition was sent to each Texas member of Congress.[28]

Finally, in early 1879 Congress responded, creating the new Northern District of Texas. Dallas' wishes to be named the headquarters, however, failed to materialize, for the tiny and remote town of Graham in Young County was awarded that honor, with Dallas and Waco being new divisions within the Northern District. A.P. McCormick was named district judge; A.B. Norton yielded his postmaster's position to become the U.S. marshal; and Fred Miner was named United States attorney.[29]

Since there was no proper federal courthouse, the court's first session in Dallas, May 23, 1879, was held on the second floor of a store at Main and Murphy. At that session Judge McCormick swore in Norton and Miner, and also Andrew Jackson Houston (Sam Houston's son) as court clerk. This done, court recessed until July when the first trial, dealing with a tobacconist's failure to display a dealer's license, was heard.[30]

A belief arose that Dallas was the center of so much legal activity that it was also the best place to locate the state's higher appeals courts. In January 1881 the county commissioners asked the state legislature to place the supreme and appellate courts in Dallas instead of Tyler. "The Supreme Court at Dallas—Justice Demands It," read a headline in the *Herald*. Population figures were cited showing the "vastly greater number of people" who would be served in Dallas. "Dallas county tenders the state indefinitely a splendid suite of rooms in our elegant courthouse for the use of these courts, free of charge," the commissioners offered.[31] The *Herald* argued that the railroads made Dallas particularly accessible for litigants and that hotel accommodations were superior, too. "And we have the court house building, all ready and prepared, one of the handsomest temples of justice in all the state, and the most commodious, with spacious court rooms, library rooms, private rooms for the judges, and vaults for their books and records. Dallas is ready to receive the courts and tenders all these facilities and accommodations."[32] But these wishes were not to be granted until 1893 when the 5th Judicial District of Texas at Dallas was created by the Legislature.

MORE AND MORE there seemed to be a need for the growing Dallas bar to be better organized. Sometime in 1878—the exact date is uncertain—the city's lawyers went a step further in formalizing their organization by adopting a charter. The event, in retrospect, was not without its humor. There was some thought at the time that this occasion constituted the actual birth of the association, for it was declared that all those who attended the first meeting and paid within three months an initial membership fee of $2.50 would be considered "charter members of the Association." As the meeting adjourned only the president, Colonel W.W. Leake, paid the $2.50 fee to treasurer Philip Lindsley, remarking that he felt obliged to do so since he was president of the association. That very day Lindsley used 50 cents of this amount to purchase a blank receipt book so he could issue receipts to other members as they paid their dues. But at the next meeting the attorneys, concerned about the high dues, unanimously voted to reduce the membership fees from $2.50 to 50 cents. Colonel Leake immediately called upon Lindsley to refund him the $2 owed, explaining lamely that he had a special investment he wished to make with the money. As Lindsley reported seven years later when he resigned his office and submitted his treasurer's report, not another lawyer since that day had ever paid his 50-cent dues.

"By the very terms of your charter," Lindsley told the members in the courtroom meeting on that October 1885 occasion, "the association ceased to have a legal existence within three months after it was born, because only one member paid his initial fee, and no attorney was to be considered a member unless said fee was paid by the date named in the charter." The audience seemed non-plussed as Lindsley continued. "And yet, sirs, no man can successfully say this fact ever disturbed the moral, intellectual or professional equanimity of any member, or of the association as a body."

All the association's acts since that day, Lindsley reminded the attorneys, had been "illegal," but that fact, he said, had never for one moment kept the bar from coming together and advising the courts on how their business should be run, "nor, when one brother has passed over the river, of meeting in subdued feeling, passing touching and eloquent tributes to his memory." As Lindsley continued with this disquieting although ineffective summation, the *Herald* reporter observed "several legal lights. . . fumbling with their pockets, but the only development was a plug of tobacco, which was freely passed around as a symbol of harmony."[33]

Florid indeed were the bar's inevitable resolutions when one of their members died. The death of Judge John H. Carleton, who had moved to Dallas five years earlier from Arkansas, prompted such a resolution: "Resolved, That while we bow in humble submission to the fiat of the great judge, who ordereth all things well, we will so order our own lives that when the dread summons shall come we may one and all, like our departed brother, lay us down to die, with the happy reflection of a well spent life and the blessed assurance that death is but the gate to our eternal rest."[34]

Such as this undoubtedly prompted the *Herald*'s humorous editorial note, "When Lawyers Die." The editor wrote that "the newspaper man hates to have a lawyer die. Not that he thinks any more of lawyers than he does of other classes of people, but he knows there has got to be a meeting of the bar, and resolutions are going to be drawn up. . . and speeches made eulogizing the deceased, principally by rival attorneys who hated him like sin when he was alive." Then, of course, these resolutions would be printed in the newspaper and distributed to the courts. Only at this point did the community discover, too late, "what a jewel they have had among them."[35]

Half a century later Harry P. Lawther would recall—too harshly—that the Bar Association of the 1880s was "nothing more than a mere gesture." It, he said, had no committees and performed no functions. Memorials to the deceased were prepared, he acknowledged, and "once in a while we had a banquet and elected a president."[36]

LIFE IN DALLAS was a far cry from those earlier pioneer days which now seemed distant but actually had not been that long ago. Nowadays, passengers arriving at the city's train depots had to put up with a mob of ne'er-do-wells intent on stealing whatever luggage might be left unattended for a moment. Men described as "tramps" were seen lolling about town. Con artists with stories of hardship preyed on the innocent. Robberies and shootings were constant fare. Sam Bass and his gang of masked train robbers created a reign of terror on all sides of the town in the spring of 1878. A young man named Doc Holliday who had practiced dentistry in Dallas ("well known in this city") was erroneously reported shot and killed in Fort Worth.[37]

Growth brought more than ne'er-do-wells to town. It brought trash. "I lost my breakfast while crossing the ford of the Trinity this morning," one letter-writer to the *Herald* said in 1881. "The approach to the ford is lined with dead cats, hogs and dogs, and piles of matter taken from the privies by scavengers have been emptied here on the bank of the river and in the stream." Those arriving at the city by way of this ford either came to the city vomiting or else were incapable of nausea," said the writer, who urged police to arrest those who were dumping refuge there.[38]

The county jail, located apart from the courthouse, was in dire need of repair. Prisoners charged with capital offenses were kept in an iron cage in the late 1870s that was so heavy it was threatening to fall through the floor onto the twenty-odd prisoners kept below. If so, they "would inevitably be killed." Temporary supports were being used.[39]

Capital punishment was not routinely administered, despite popular contemporary notions of how the justice system harshly treated felons in those earlier times. Descriptions of the execution of a 27-year-old black man and former slave named Adam Thompson in July 1881, the fourth legal execution ever to be held in Dallas County, provide a glimpse of how authorities carried out the ultimate punishment. Thompson's case is a reminder that justice was not as swift in those days as we often think it was. Thompson, convicted for the murder and robbery of a storekeeper named Schumaker about seven and a half miles west of town, had seen his first conviction overturned on a technicality by the court of appeals because a court clerk had failed to sign the charge. County Attorney Robert B. Seay, after much difficulty and delay, had rounded up witnesses once more and obtained a second conviction and death sentence. Not until five years after the crime had been committed was the penalty carried out. Before being led to the gallows, Thompson praised his attorney, "Mr. C. Clint," who he said "had done everything in his power" to save him and who when it became evident that his client could not be saved had "cheered and comforted" him in every possible way. Once the appeals process had been completed and execution certain, Special Judge Sawnie Robertson had allowed Thompson the full sixty days permitted by the law to prepare for his death.

The execution, by hanging, was carried out "privately" on an outdoors gallows behind a tall plank fence around the jail. Despite the fact that the execution was not intended to be public, large numbers of witnesses gathered around the jail, finding elevated viewpoints on surrounding housetops or peering through every available crack in the fence so they could see the event.

Prisoners within the jail were able to witness the hanging through windows, and members of the press, the police force, visiting sheriffs, several physicians, and a few citizens were allowed to be present. Prior to his execution, Thompson, wearing a black suit and white cotton gloves, was visited by two black ministers who sang and prayed with him in his cell before he was led outside and the noose placed around his neck at two minutes before 2 p.m. When the trap door was sprung, Thompson fell a distance of seven and a half feet. His death was not immediate nor easy; it was caused by strangulation rather than by a broken neck.[40]

BY 1882 MANY lawyers in Texas believed that it was time to begin a state bar association. A number of them—including at least four from Dallas (A.T. Watts, A.H. Field, E.G. Bower, and Richard Morgan Jr.)—circulated a petition calling for an organizational meeting. Dallas and two other cities, Galveston and Austin, accounted for more than 50 percent of the sponsors of the movement.[41] The Dallas Bar Association eagerly supported the idea, passed a favorable resolution at a meeting in Leake & Henry's law office, and elected eighteen delegates to the July 15 organizational meeting in Galveston. Some sixty-nine lawyers from throughout the state attended, although only three of Dallas' delegates (Richard Morgan, Jr., W.L. Crawford, and James P. Simpson) were able to attend.[42] In the years ahead Dallas lawyers would continue to be active participants in the state bar association.

A NEW RED COURTHOUSE

⌘

Chapter Four

THE VISION OF SO many lawyers who had chosen to locate in Dallas in anticipation of its growth was confirmed by 1890. That year's federal census revealed that the "Queen City of the Southwest" was now the biggest city in the state, its population of 38,067 outdistancing such older cities as Galveston and San Antonio. Dallas County's 67,003 residents made it the state's most populous county, as well. Evidence of the city's prowess was everywhere. A powerful new newspaper, *The Dallas Morning News,* had begun publishing from a handsome three-story building on Commerce Street on October 1, 1885, as a branch of the venerable *Galveston News* to take advantage of the obvious promise of the Northeast Texas area. Within days the new journal had purchased and absorbed the *Dallas Herald.* Already the *News'* special train, the "Comet," was extending Dallas' sphere of influence by rushing daily editions to towns to the north and displacing the St. Louis newspapers. The older annual Dallas County fairs had been transformed into an actual "state fair" that attracted huge crowds. A handsome new planned community, Oak Cliff, had been established in 1887 as a separate city just across the Trinity River. Way up town at Akard and Commerce, many blocks from the courthouse square, a new city hall had been built.

By the end of the 1880s the roster of Dallas lawyers had climbed to about 150. Most of them worked independently; some had partnerships with one or sometimes two other attorneys. Most lawyers in Dallas and elsewhere were general practitioners whose typical services included preparing and probating wills, handling real property conveyances, and appearing before the courts on various litigation manners. Practically all of them devoted a fair portion of their time to criminal matters, too.[1] Some of them, admittedly, were not well prepared for the profession, although too rarely was this recognized. In 1890, however, a committee of eight lawyers, headed by J.K.P. Record, expressed their doubts on an applicant who wanted to be admitted to the bar by recommending that he be licensed to represent himself only. For all other cases "he [must] have 12 months longer to prepare himself."[2]

For most lawyers an office within walking distance to the courthouse was mandatory, a preponderance of the offices being located on Main Street no more than half a dozen blocks away. A customary arrangement was to have space on the second or third floor of a building that was occupied on the first floor by a retail establishment. Many of the offices now offered such amenities as reception rooms for clients, conference rooms, and private offices. Roll-top desks, wooden chairs, and wood stoves were common features. Secretarial help inevitably was provided by men, for women still stayed at home in these Victorian days. Telephones were rare, not being introduced in Dallas until 1881, and still scarce also were the new-fangled typewriters. Preparation or copying of documents was done laboriously with the steel pen.[3]

There was camaraderie among the profession, for the lawyers of Dallas were not so numerous as to prevent practitioners from being acquainted with all their peers. This was reinforced by the fact that so much of their work still involved litigation, and the courthouse served as a common meeting ground for all. The romantic and spirited fellowship of frontier circuit riding, though, by now was just a memory. Despite the growing sense of professionalization and sophistication, the casual informality of earlier days still lingered. A large majority of the lawyers had come to Dallas from areas even less formal and more rural, places where decorum was the exception. "We indulged in the freedom born of such environments," observed one of the leading lawyers, Philip Lindsley. "A little nonsense, now and then, was not tabooed."[4]

Sawnie Robertson (1850-1892) and Jim Eblen kept open house for their fellow attorneys at their office in the rear of the Exchange

Bank at Main and Lamar streets. "Here, oft-times came together much that was brilliant of the North Texas Bar," Lindsley wrote. What amazed Lindsley was the fact that Robertson and Eblen, despite their perennial open house, were always well prepared when their cases came on for trial. "One wondered when and where they were able to accomplish so much—for when the visitor or visitors entered—and he came often and stayed a long while— pen and book was laid promptly and cheerfully aside, the glad handshake was heartily given, welcome beamed in their friendly smile, while the moments, or the hours, flew away on sunny wings of wit, and humor, and wholesome mirth."[5]

Robertson, who began practicing law in Dallas in 1870, was appointed associate justice of the State Supreme Court in 1885— the youngest man ever to serve up to that time—but after just one year on the bench he resigned to resume his law practice in Dallas. Roberton's influence across the state was great, and in 1890 he used that influence to persuade James S. Hogg to run for governor.[6]

For their occasional official bar association meetings, the lawyers gathered in a courtroom. At their October 1885 meeting, their numbers "about filled" the room, and one on-looker observed that "it ought not be a difficult thing to pick a good governor out of the crowd." The observation perhaps was prompted not only by the good looks of those present but also by the fact that within the past several years the Dallas bar already had provided some distinguished state-wide leaders, including Barnett Gibbs, lieutenant governor of Texas; J.M. Hurt, associate justice of the Court of Appeals; Sawnie Robertson, associate justice of the Supreme Court; Olin Welborn, member of Congress; and A.T. Watts, commissioner of appeals.[7]

The organization by now had become far more than a group of men who met to pass flowery resolutions honoring the memory of those who had crossed the bar; its involvement in the administration of the courts was quite thorough. A committee, for example, responding to its assignment to come up with a better method of arranging court dockets to facilitate the trying of cases, presented an elaborate plan.[8]

A number of lawyers got together in 1891 to establish the kind of library that was expensive and difficult for an individual to have. The Dallas Law Library Association incorporated that year with a capital stock of $50,000. They put their fledgling library in the courthouse. The 1894-95 Dallas City Directory listed John M. Avery as president; A.T. Watts, vice president; W.L. McDonald, secretary; D.A. Eldridge, treasurer; and James R. Cole Jr., librarian. Ten years later the association's librarian was G.W. Blair, and three trustees were listed: J.J. Eckford, J.M. Dickson, and DeEdward Greer. The desire to create a fine library open to all lawyers has continued to the present.

THERE WAS no let-up in the arrival in the city, year after year, of lawyers whose eventual deeds would make them long-remembered. The contributions to the bar and community by many of this new generation would last far into the twentieth century, making their names still familiar by mid-century and even later.

Coming in 1885 and opening an office at 739 Main Street was William H. Clark (1861-1931), who like several others arrived after graduating from the Cumberland Law School in Tennessee. Clark was the son of a prominent Georgia lawyer and legislator who moved to East Texas in 1835 and gained further distinction in Texas politics. At the age of thirty-five William H. Clark would become in 1897 the youngest man to that date to be elected president of the State Bar of Texas and the second lawyer from Dallas to hold that position. Beyond his daily practice of law, Clark became noted for his scholarly writing on legal topics, including textbooks dealing with the law of land titles, wills and inheritances, and railroad law. His paper on deeds of trust in 1896 was said to demonstrate "exhaustive study and legal talent of the highest order." In 1902, a New York newspaper declared him as "rapidly becoming one of the most favorably known lawyers of Texas." In 1888, Clark was joined in his law practice by William M. Alexander, and then in 1894 by William H. Hall. The firm, undergoing numerous name changes over the years, was still in existence in the 1990s as Clark, West, Keller, Butler & Ellis. One of Clark's three sons, Thomas Campbell Clark (1899-1977) would become a national figure. After beginning his law practice in Dallas, Clark became attorney general under President Harry S. Truman. Truman then appointed him to the Supreme Court, making him the first Texan ever to serve on the high court. Thomas C. Clark's son and William H. Clark's grandson, Ramsey Clark, would be appointed the nation's attorney general by President Lyndon B. Johnson.[9]

Arriving soon after Clark was a University of Texas law school graduate, William Thompson (1862-1949), destined to be a founding partner of one of Dallas' longest-lived and most prominent law firms. Thompson, who had become a school principal in his home town of Brenham just two years after finishing high school, moved to Dallas to take a more lucrative position selling furniture, books, and supplies in order to save money for law school. The law school at the University of Texas, newly formed, had a two-year course which Thompson, a native of the state, completed in just half that time—not because of genius, he quickly pointed out, but because he had saved only enough money for one year.[10]

Upon opening a law office in Dallas in 1887, Thompson waited patiently for a client to appear. None came, until finally a letter arrived from a law-school classmate who had begun a practice in New York City. Thompson's friend had a rather strange request concerning a private matter for a wealthy client. Thompson, having no other business, agreed to undertake the assignment. The man's uncle had died with the wish that he be cremated and his ashes buried in the family plot in Dallas. An urn of the man's ashes soon arrived, and Thompson placed them atop his roll-top desk awaiting further instructions. Finally, they came, along with a check written for a substantial sum. None of the deceased man's relatives could attend, but they wanted the man's ashes to be interred with the finest services available, no expense spared, to include a carriage, mourners, a rector, and a funeral oration. Thompson duly arranged for the services, renting a carriage, locating and paying individuals to take on the role of mourners, engaging a rector, personally carrying the urn of ashes to the cemetery, and delivering himself the eulogy for the man he had never met. Thus began Thompson's practice of law.[11]

It would not be long before he gained more regular work, work bolstered by the new Oak Cliff development just across the river. Home builders in this new town began calling upon Thompson to examine their titles. Not long afterwards in 1890 he became counsel for a fire insurance company, and as he learned more and more about insurance law, he became recognized as one of the first lawyer specialists in the state.[12]

A man who would join Thompson a few years later as a partner was Robert E. Lee Knight (1865-1936), who started his practice in Dallas in 1889. Knight, named for Confederate General Robert E. Lee, was born about two weeks before Appomattox on the family plantation encompassing part of the property ultimately taken in by Love Field Airport. He was the youngest child of well-to-do Dallas pioneer Obediah W. Knight, who had come to Texas and the Dallas area in 1846 and bought a plantation of 1,000 acres. Young Knight, after being educated in Dallas private schools and academies, earned bachelor's and master's degrees from Southwestern University at Georgetown, Texas, and a bachelor of law degree in 1888 from the University of Texas. Still, he was not finished with his studies. He attended the University of Virginia for post-graduate work before returning to Dallas to set up a practice in his native city.

Knight, a splendid orator even as a college student, soon became a pillar of the legal society and community. Stories abounded about his colorful life and prominent law practice. Once during a trial he displayed to a jury a pocket knife and related a story. About ten years ago, he said, a cutlery salesman had given him that knife with the explanation that it was a trophy for being the ugliest man the salesman had ever seen. "I was enjoined, however," Knight said, "to pass this trophy on if I ever see an uglier man. In satisfaction of that injunction I now present this knife to opposing counsel."[13]

Knight, who like so many had gained the honorific title of "Colonel" without benefit of military service, told the following story on himself. One evening he was entertaining a handful of old friends, and when midnight came they were enjoying themselves so much that he implored them to stay longer. Several guests said they feared they would be upsetting the rest of the household at this late hour. "Oh, that is all right," Knight said. "I am Caesar in my house." At that moment Mrs. Knight stepped into the room and spoke with a smile. "Gentlemen, I shall be most happy indeed to have you continue. There are more refreshments being prepared and it will be my pleasure to have them served to you. But as for Caesar, he is going to bed."[14]

Knight was a large landowner and a long-time bank director of the National Bank of Commerce. He served also as president of the State Fair of Texas. It was in 1908 that he joined with the formidable William Thompson to form the law partnership that continues to this day, Thompson & Knight.

Another distinguished lawyer emerging in this period whose name, reputation and legacy would be sustained throughout the twentieth century was Maurice E. Locke (1861-1918), a scholarly but imposing 6-foot-5 man who came to Dallas in 1888 not as an attorney but as the manager of Jarvis-Conklin Mortgage Trust Co.'s Texas operations. Locke earlier had taught languages at a small college in Valparaiso, Indiana. His passion for reading and for books was a life-long affair with him. A year after arriving in Dallas the principal owner of the mortgage trust company decided to establish a bank with Locke as president. This was not a timely decision, for the economic troubles of the early 1890s caused the bank to fail. Just one year later, though, the 1893 Dallas City Directory carried this listing: "Maurice E. Locke, attorney, office Room 514 North Texas Bank Building." Just how Locke had become a lawyer in one year after the demise of the bank later remained somewhat of a mystery even to family members, but Locke's grandson, Maurice E. Purnell, said that some recalled that Locke's wife, Mary Dixon Locke, had gambled her small family inheritance to support the family while Locke immersed himself in law books. (However, in his profile of Locke, Philip Lindsley declared unequivocally that Locke was admitted to the bar in Indiana in 1879.)[15]

Locke, like William Thompson, became a noted specialist in insurance law. It was Locke's goal to create a library containing "every statute of every English-speaking jurisdiction from the beginning and every reported decision of every English-speaking country from the beginning." The immense law library in many languages which he developed was said to be the most nearly complete private law library in the country. By 1929, the firm's library was said to exceed 20,000 volumes, embracing the statutes and reports of all the states and of England, Ireland, and Canada.[16]

Locke's love of literature was reflected in his successful leadership of the drive to establish a public library for Dallas, followed by his long service as a trustee. In 1904 he and his son, Eugene Perry Locke (1883-1946), joined in a partnership, Locke & Locke, and so faithful and regular in their habits were they that it was said that residents of Bryan Street could set their clocks by the time the pair emerged each day to board the streetcar for town. Locke died prematurely at the age of fifty-seven, but his firm would continue through the years as one of the city's most prominent. His sons, grandsons, and great-grandsons—Lockes and Purnells—would participate in the firm which under different configurations would have those two names listed first.[17]

DALLAS LAWYERS, having been instrumental in founding the Bar Association of Texas, brought the organization's fifth annual meeting to their own city in 1886 on July 13-15. Some 200 lawyers attended sessions in which a key consideration was "how to improve the machinery of the state judiciary,"[18] a matter which focused on a constitutional amendment to create an additional appellate court.

Another concern was the issue of how best to educate and qualify a lawyer for admission to the bar. The Committee on Legal Education and Admission to the Bar expressed concern about the lack of uniform standards applied throughout the state by the many district judges and their ad hoc committees formed to examine the candidates. Rigid examinations were an exception rather than the rule, the committee reported. The committee recommended a "collegiate or classical" education followed by a fixed period of study, and then the creation of permanent committees for their examination. The best way to study the law, the committee concluded, was through a properly organized law school. Even so, a minority report stated a belief that individual study in a law office was superior to a course of study in any law school. "The average lawyer turned out of the 'law schools' is running down the bar, I think, pretty fast," the report quoted Senator George F. Edmunds as saying.[19]

A magnificent banquet at the Windsor Hotel concluded the two days. The very colorful banquet menu began with "green turtle consommé de volatile" and ended with after-dinner cigars for all. Despite such nice touches, preparation for this state-wide meeting seemed casual at best. On the very morning of the arrival of the visiting lawyers Dallas Bar Association President A.T. Watts summoned his members to the offices of Crawford & Crawford "to perfect such arrangements as have not been completed."[20]

What the Dallas lawyers seemed unable to do, though, was to ensure the election of one of their own as the next state-wide president. It had been expected to be the venerable Colonel W.L. Crawford, who as vice president of the state bar was expected as a matter of course to succeed to the presidency. However, Colonel Crawford recently had made a sympathetic speech at a Farmers' Alliance picnic which alarmed some members, and the result was an upset win by Fort Worth's T.J. Beall as president of the state bar.[21] The slight to Colonel Crawford was remedied the following year, though, when he was elected seventh president of the state bar, becoming the first man from Dallas to hold that position.[22]

In 1891 the state's attorneys chose a second Dallas lawyer to fill the presidency of the state bar. He was Seth Shepard.

REALIGNMENT of the state's judicial system in a manner capable of handling an increasingly heavy load of cases, both jury trials and appeals, was (and continues to be) a constant concern. The number of counties included in judicial districts had been steadily diminishing as new ones had been added over the years, and in 1883 the 14th Judicial District was designated to include only Dallas and Ellis counties. In 1885 Dallas County alone was placed in the 14th District. Four years later the dockets were so crowded that the state legislature divided Dallas County into two districts, adding a new 44th District to the existing 14th.

Judge George N. Aldredge, one of the town's veteran public officials, continued as judge of the 14th District, serving until 1888 after becoming a district judge in 1878. A native of Georgia, he earlier had been elected county attorney in 1876.[23] Charles Frederick Tucker (1847-1908) was appointed judge of the 44th by Governor Lawrence Sullivan Ross. Tucker, from a family of lawyers in Louisiana, had moved to Dallas in 1873 in search of a newer and more open environment to begin a law practice. He would serve until 1893 when he resigned to re-enter private practice.[24]

Finally, it was perceived that congestion in both the 14th and 44th District Courts could be alleviated in another way—by creating a district court that handled criminal cases only. This was accomplished in 1893 by the 23rd State Legislature with its creation on May 4 of the Criminal District Court of Dallas County. Charles F. Clint was appointed to the judgeship, a position he held through 1902. With the addition of this new court, the 14th and 44th District Courts would handle only civil cases.

Relief in the appellate courts also was critical. A history of the new appellate court created in 1893 for the area, the Court of Appeals for the 5th District, stated plainly that Texas' "business development was in serious danger of being thwarted by the lack of an adequate appellate court system that allowed businessmen to resolve their commercial disputes in an efficient and speedy manner."[25]

The 5th District had jurisdiction over appeals of all civil cases from trial courts in the thirty-two northeast Texas counties in its district. Governor James Hogg appointed Henry W. Lightfoot of Paris as first chief justice and W.W. Finley of Tyler and Anson Rainey of Waxahachie as the two associate justices.

THE COURT assumed commodious new offices on the third floor of yet another new courthouse for Dallas County, the stately Romanesque Revival building now affectionately referred to as "Old Red." The structure, crowned on top with a center tower and clock, made it the second tallest building in Texas, surpassed only by the state capitol in Austin. Judge Lightfoot expressed his profound gratitude to the county commissioners for providing "the most comfortable and convenient courtroom, library room, consultation rooms, clerk's office and judge's rooms in the state."[26]

The previous courthouse, built in 1880 as the pride and joy of Dallas' citizens, was destroyed by a fire in 1890, just as its predecessor, constructed only in 1874, also had been consumed by flames. Ironically, on February 7, 1890, just after a jury in the 44th District Court had given an 18-year-old man a five-year sentence for horse theft, a deputy sheriff yelled, "Fire! Fire! Fire!" Simultaneously, a red hot piece of debris fell through the ceiling between the two courtrooms. In the next few seconds jurors, judges, lawyers, deputy sheriffs, and the newly convicted defendant were fleeing in "grand confusion." In only a few minutes the fire was raging and roaring like a furnace, and despite the best efforts of the fire department the courthouse was rendered a "total ruin" as high winds kept the fire going. "The County Courthouse Reduced to Ashes Yesterday," read a sub-headline in *The Dallas Morning News*. The fire evidently had started from the boxing of a hot air pipe at its junction with the ceiling. All records were saved except those of the new 44th District Court, thanks to the fire-proof building that had been constructed for the district clerk's records after the previous fire.[27]

A remarkable coincidence had occurred. At the time of the 1880 fire it happened that the Grand Lodge of Odd Fellows was holding its meeting in Dallas. In 1890 the organization once again had come to Dallas for its meeting, and in the welcoming address on Friday, February 7, the speaker noted that the last time the group had been in town the courthouse had been burned for their entertainment. This would not occur again, he promised the audience. But at three o'clock that very afternoon the Dallas

County courthouse once again caught fire and was reduced to ashes.[28]

This new courthouse, County Judge E.G. Bower and other members of the Commissioners Court determined, would not suffer the same fate as its predecessors, and their first specification was that it must be fire-proof. Maximillian Orlopp Jr., one of the state's foremost architects, won an advertised competition to design the new courthouse. He was a Brooklyn native, child of German-born parents, and a graduate of the U.S. Naval Academy. County commissioners awarded a contract to construct the building at a winning bid of $276,967.50. The building's basic material, red sandstone, was to come from Pecos City, Texas; its marble columns from Burnet, Texas; and its Little Rock blue granite from Arkansas.[29]

At the laying of the cornerstone in November 1890 an honored guest was Mrs. S.H. Cockrell, a pioneer resident who had witnessed the building of every one of Dallas' courthouses. Recollection of past events occurring at the site caused tears to flow from her eyes. A large number of relics were placed in the cornerstone for future generations to enjoy. These included numerous paper documents of all sorts, including the last issue of *Norton's Union Intelligencer*, numerous business cards, and a large sampling of coins. Silver-haired Norton himself was present, and when his paper was presented for deposit, moderator John Henry Brown looked to the audience and said, "Here is the old man himself. We had better put him in, too."[30] Two years later Norton was dead.

By December 8, 1892, work was nearly finished, and the county clerk on that date was first to move into the building. Atop the building the handsome central tower had a huge clock with four faces and a three-ton bell that rang out the hours so distinctly that it could be heard ten miles away. An observation tower attracted scores of visitors and provided a wonderful view of the surrounding area. The building was said to be "unsurpassed in the grandeur of its architecture, the magnificence of its proportions and the elegance of its finish and appointments" by any other courthouse south of the Mason and Dixon Line. Unfortunately, the peal of the three-ton bell was so loud that eventually fears arose that vibrations were endangering the structural integrity of the building. In 1919 the tower, clock and bell were dismantled.[31] In 1966, after sixty-three years of service, the building was "retired" by Dallas County from active service. Some time afterward the need for additional space caused it to be re-opened, and then it was closed again. In 1998, after years of being shut down, the first floor was being restored for use as a Dallas visitors' center with a historical exhibit.

By now Dallas had another courthouse, too, a federal courthouse and post office constructed in 1889 at Ervay, Main and Commerce, far "uptown" from the courthouse square. It was a three-story structure with graceful towers on both ends, and held other federal offices as well. The streets were filled with traffic, all the way from the county courthouse to the federal courthouse.

T H E O N L O O K E R who in 1885 had said it should not be difficult to pick a governor out of the crowd of lawyers at the Dallas Bar meeting was not far off the mark, for in 1887 a man who would twice be elected governor and four times U.S. senator became one of the Dallas legal fraternity. He was Charles Allen Culberson (1855-1925), who left his prominent father's law firm in Jefferson to move to Dallas just as others, including two of the city's most distinguished lawyers, Nat M. Burford and Col. William L. Crawford, had done before. Culberson's father, David, was an important political figure, serving as a U.S. Congressman from East Texas from 1875 to 1897. Before moving to Dallas, the younger Culberson, a graduate of Virginia Military Institute and the University of Virginia Law School, already had served as county attorney of Marion County, of which Jefferson was county seat. In Dallas he formed a partnership with John Bookhout, and in 1890 he was called upon in his office by Democratic gubernatorial candidate James Hogg and Dallas powerbroker lawyer Sawnie Robertson. They persuaded him to run for attorney general. Culberson agreed, and he became the Dallas Bar

Association's anointed candidate for the position. When Robertson announced Culberson's candidacy, as Culberson later wrote, he did so "on behalf of the bar of Dallas."[32] Elected as a Democrat by a large majority, Culberson helped Hogg in his reform program and was returned to office a second time in 1892. In 1894, after earning high praise for his successful defense of the Railroad Commission, he was elected governor of Texas.[33]

During his two terms in the governor's office surely one of the most vexing legal issues Culberson confronted was a unique dilemma in Dallas involving a sporting event of national significance. It was billed as "the fight of the century," a heavyweight championship boxing match between two famous pugilists, Gentleman James L. Corbett, the reigning champion, and the challenger, Fighting Bob Fitzsimmons, a fight that would bring crowds from throughout the nation to Dallas. A leading sports-man, Dan Stuart, had won the right to stage the fight in Dallas by raising enough money to offer a $41,000 purse. The fight was set for October 31, 1895. To accommodate the expected huge crowds, construction began on a gigantic wooden amphitheater with a seating capacity of 52,815. This new facility would seat about 7,000 more people than lived in the entire city of Dallas, and it would be the second biggest building—so far as seating capacity was concerned—in the known history of the world. Railroads announced special excursion cars that would bring fans from as far away as New England and California, and by midsummer eleven miles of track had been laid next to the amphitheater site.[34] A Santa Fe Railroad official said the event would bring "more men and money into the state than any other event that ever occurred here."[35] Dallas' merchants and hotel owners waited expectantly for the financial bonanza that seemed certain. The city was on the verge of gaining national headlines as never before.

A dilemma, however, arose over a law which seemed to declare prizefighting illegal in the state of Texas. Prominent members of the bar and the state's attorney general debated both sides. County Attorney John P. Gillespie obtained an opinion from the state's attorney general who said that the prize fight would violate the law. Other members of the bar, including Col. W.L. Crawford, disagreed. Finally, James M. Hurt, presiding judge of the state's Court of Criminal Appeals, rendered an opinion that the law against prizefighting was invalid. Now came a rash of new arguments couched in moral terms. If the law was invalid, then a new and valid law should be written. One minister declared boxing to be "an abomination not to be tolerated by any civilized community." Mayor Frank P. Holland countered that the match would be "the premier event in the domain of sport."[36]

Despite its touted economic benefits for Dallas, Culberson publicly opposed the fight as a "public display of barbarism." He said he would prevent the fight "if it takes the entire police force of the State to stop it."[37] Public interests required that the exhibition should be suppressed, he said, and to back his words Culberson called a special session of the Twenty-fourth Legislature, the so-called "Prize-Fight" session, to pass a new law prohibiting prizefighting. The legislature met on October 1, suspended its rules to expedite the matter, and on the third day of the session passed a new prize-fight law which prohibited the Corbett-Fitzsimmons fight and all others as well. The huge amphitheater, still incomplete, was dismantled.[38]

The "fight of the century" finally occurred in 1897 in Carson City, Nevada, with Fitzimmons the victor in a bout that was the first in the history of boxing to be recorded by motion picture cameras. Fitzsimmons won with a blow to Corbett's "solar plexus," thus originating and making popular this widely used boxing term.

Governor Culberson, the first Dallas man to hold that high office, went on to the U.S. Senate. In 1899 the state Senate and House, meeting in joint session, elected him to that office before the 17th Amendment of 1912 permitted the popular election of U.S. senators. Culberson would hold the office until 1922, being recognized as a power not only in state politics but nationally as well. He became minority leader for the Democratic Party in the Senate, and before the 1908 election he was mentioned as a possible presidential candidate. *The Independent* described him in December 1907 in these words: "His smooth, shaven skin has something of a Greek cast about it and his slow-coming words and quick-coming motions are carefully constrained by unobtrusive dignity." He was, the magazine said, "colossal on infinitesimal details" and a man who "loves to use the microscope," statements which suggested the other side of the coin—he was "woefully lacking in personal magnetism."[39]

Poor health and opposition from the Ku Klux Klan led to Culberson's defeat in 1922. It was the only political defeat he ever suffered. Culberson, the Dallas Bar Association's best-known member up to that time, had held high political offices from 1890 to 1922.

New Times, New Century

⌘

Chapter Five

PHILIP LINDSLEY, who came to Dallas in 1873 to practice law, recalled fondly in 1909 the happier times that had worn away with the coming of the twentieth century. He urged his fellow practitioners to remember always the early lawyers who had preceded them and who had brought honor to the profession. "There will never be bigger hearts, nor redder, warmer, richer blood," he wrote. The work of these men and their Dallas Bar Association had been a powerful influence for good in the community, Lindsley avowed. "The memory of the good it [the bar association] has done, the wrongs it has righted, the evils it has turned aside, as well as the picturesque characters of its membership, will find an enduring resting place in the chronicles of the city. It will live, in local history, long after all its members have crossed over the river."[1]

Pioneer attorneys still alive at the time of his writing that he deemed worth listing included: Jeff Word, J.W. Thompson, William G. Sterett, John Bookhout, Charles F. Flint, R.E. Cowart, W.L. Crawford, M.L. Crawford, W.M. Edwards, John P. Gillespie, John M. McCoy, T.S. Miller, George H. Plowman, R.B. Seay, Gen. W.L. Cabell, and himself. And he named and characterized in capsule form with rhetorical questions those who were dead: "But what of the 'grand old man,' Judge John L. Henry," he asked, "of the polished and learned W.W. Leake, of the patriarch of the Dallas Bar, John C. McCoy, of the brainy Jerome Kearny, of the whole-souled Jim Eblen, of the able judge, George N. Aldredge, the impartial judge, Thomas F. Nash, of the imperious W.H. Barksdale, of the well named John J. Good, of the lawyer, judge and Mason, Ed. G. Bower, of the partner of the last two, J.E. Coombes, of the courteous judge, R.E. Burke, of the brilliant, lamented, Sawnee Robertson, of the genial judge, Charles Fred Tucker, where are these?"[2]

Lindsley's comments bespoke of an age in which the bar and the community were tied closely together. Their interests were recognized to be mutual. Progress for Dallas was progress for the bar. And so was the opposite just as true. The arrival of a new railroad, the opening of a bank, a situation at the courthouse, a municipal or county or state election—all these mattered to members of the bar. Even now and certainly in the future these mutual interests, while still in existence to no less degree, would seem far less immediate, the ties far less binding.

Certainly the town itself was evolving rapidly into the modern age. Automobiles had arrived. One could read in the newspaper each week the names of those who obtained automobile licenses. Thirteen were obtained during one week in 1904. Speeding was condemned in harsh terms. A woman who drove through downtown at 20 miles per hour was arrested, tried by jury in the city court, and fined $5.[3] The ability for man to fly not only was understood to be a fact, it could be observed in Dallas. Daily dirigible flights were made over the city during the October 1909 State Fair, and daring pilots put on daily exhibitions at Fair Park for a week in January 1911. Beginning that same year, one could dial a telephone number automatically—no more going through the operator. Streetcar lines now wound their way through the city streets, and interurban rail links existed with rapid and regular transportation to surrounding cities.

The passing of the old and the arrival of the new was especially evident for the legal profession in two new developments. One was the manner in which lawyers received their legal training and were admitted to the bar. Historically, after the American Revolution and during the rise of Jeffersonian and Jacksonian democracy, admission to the bar had been purposely intended to be open to the common man rather than the exclusive province of the privileged few. Now the old practice of "reading law" gave way to university training as the norm and a more formalized procedure for admission to the bar. A state legislative act in 1903 tried to bring some order to the process. It required each of the several courts of civil appeals to appoint three-member boards of legal examiners who would conduct written examinations for all applicants at least four times a year. The examinations would use standards established by the State Supreme Court. More refinements would occur in the years ahead, bringing an end to the casual oral examinations that sometimes permitted favored candidates to be admitted to the bar over a drink and without having to answer even a single question.[4]

A second new development could be seen in the emergence of lawyers who reflected the new age in America—the age of corporations, of big business, of railroads, and of insurance. These new lawyers with corporate specialties did not spend hours and hours at the courthouse. They worked more and more out of high-rise office buildings instead of easily accessible second-floor offices up the stairs above retail shops. They became directors of banks and other corporations.

By 1900 a favorite location for lawyers' offices was the city's first "high-rise" office building, the North Texas Building, constructed in 1895 on Main Street between Lamar and Poydras. By 1902 twenty-eight lawyers maintained their offices there, and as late as the 1920s it continued to be a highly popular site. The National Exchange Building in 1902 was the second favored location, with sixteen lawyers listed at that location in the city directory. The Linz and Gaston buildings in the same year also each held a half dozen lawyers' offices.[5]

A SAMPLING of lawyers working in the first decade after the turn of the century reveals the marked change away from general law practices towards business law practices. The railroads—the dominant industrial force in the nation—represented especially prized clients for the city's corporate-minded attorneys, and when such a relationship was announced it was news. "Alexander S. Coke Is Katy Attorney," read a newspaper headline. William L. Hall, who had come to Dallas in 1876, became the local attorney for Texas & Pacific Railroad in 1892, and in 1906 he advanced to the position of general attorney for the railroad. W.J.J. Smith, former 14th District Court judge, resigned his judgeship after three years to resume practice on civil and corporate law, and by 1909 he was representing three railroads and several large corporations. Elijah B. Perkins, who seconded the nomination of William Jennings Bryan at the Democratic National Convention in 1900, became in the next year the general attorney for the Cotton Belt Railroad. Thomas Scott Miller, a Harvard law school graduate, in 1895 became general attorney for the MK&T Railroad.[6]

Other lawyers reflecting the shift away from general practice to business law represented a multitude of corporate clients. General Alfred P. Wozencraft, whose son Frank would become a prominent mayor of Dallas, was attorney general for Southwestern Telegraph and Telephone Co. Cecil Lane Simpson, who had practiced law in Mississippi before coming to Dallas in about 1900, was the attorney for the Dallas Independent Telephone Co. Lawrence Lindsley, Philip Lindsley's uncle, represented Western Union Telegraph Co. and other corporations. Still other corporate clientele included especially insurance companies, banks, and other financial institutions. One lawyer, John M. Spellman, despite the warnings of friends about the field being too specialized, established a practice in patent law and developed a reputation throughout Texas and the Southwest for his expertise.[7]

The insurance industry was becoming more and more important in Dallas as a profitable part of corporate practice. The Robertson Act of 1907, passed by the state legislature, required insurance companies doing business in the state to invest 75 percent of their reserves on Texas policies within Texas. This prompted an initial flurry of protests and withdrawal of firms from the state, but it also served to stimulate a large number of new fire, life and casualty companies, many of them forming in Dallas. The Modern Order of the Praetorians, a fraternal order chartered in 1899 to do insurance business; Southwestern Life Insurance Company, organized in 1903; and Southland Life Insurance Company, organized in 1909 and merging in 1915 with the Sam Houston Life Insurance Company, were some of the larger companies. These firms and a large number of smaller ones all required legal counsel.

One attorney who specialized in insurance, banking, and taxes and who became a state-wide political leader as a Democrat was Thomas Bell Love (1870-1948). Bell was a Missouri native who came to Dallas in 1899 and quickly entered political life. Just three years after his arrival he was elected to the Texas House of Representatives and re-elected in 1904 and 1906. During his last term he served as Speaker of the House. The experience he gained in reform legislation related to his legal specialties prompted Governor Thomas Mitchell Campbell to appoint him in 1907 to be commissioner of the new Department of Insurance and Banking. In 1910 he returned to Dallas to practice law, where he remained active in public affairs and was an outspoken foe in the early 1920s of the Ku Klux Klan. In 1927 he was elected to a four-year trm as state senator.[8]

WILLLIAM H. CLARK, who in 1897 became the third lawyer from Dallas to be elected president of the State Bar of Texas, contrasted himself with those lawyers who sought railroad or corporate clients. Clark made it known that he did "not desire railroad employment or that of any other large corporation which would take him out of the general practice."[9]

A number of other attorneys, of course, also preferred to retain general practices. Many of them identified with liberal causes or criminal law. Recognized as one of the most outstanding liberal lawyers in the state was Jerome Claiborne Kearby (1847-1905). Kearby, a Populist, sprang to prominence because of his defense of several Knights of Labor leaders following the Great Southwest Strike in 1886 against Jay Gould's Texas and Pacific Railroad. Afterwards, Kearby was labeled "Populism's most urbane speaker." Kearby's support of Greenback economic principles endeared him to workers, farmers, and small-business owners. He proudly retained many of his small-town ways such as squatting on the sidewalk in front of his office while whittling a stick. [10]

Having grown up in Denton, the son of a physician, Kearby at the age of 15 enlisted in Colonel Charles DeMorse's 29th Texas Cavalry, reputedly the youngest enlisted man in the Confederate Army. After the war he studied law in McKinney, then practiced in Kaufman and Canton before becoming district attorney in Palestine in 1872. Two years later he moved to Dallas, where he practiced law until 1903. Active at first as a Democrat, in the 1880s Kearby affiliated himself with various minority parties, finally campaigning unsuccessfully for Congress in 1892 and 1894 as a Populist. His second loss was so close that he obtained a recount, and while it did not change the outcome of the election, recent research indicates that except for ballot stuffing he would have won.[11] In 1896 he was the Populist nominee for governor, and ran an unsuccessful but spirited race against a fellow member of the Dallas bar, the incumbent Democrat, Charles A. Culberson, losing by 60,000 votes.[12]

Succeeding Kearby as the Dallas lawyer who was closely identified with liberal causes was a native of the city, George Clifton Edwards (1877-1961), a dedicated Socialist and son of pioneer Dallas attorney and justice of the peace William M. Edwards. As the Populist movement waned in Texas following Kearby's defeat in 1896 and William Jennings Bryan's loss that same year in the presidential campaign, Edwards and other like-minded Dallas professionals pulled various liberal elements, including alienated Populists, into a grassroots movement under the Socialist banner. In addition to his practice of law, Edwards published a radical newspaper, the *Laborer*, in which he championed the working classes. Throughout the first decade of the 20th century and even beyond, Edwards and fellow Socialists campaigned vigorously but largely unsuccessfully for municipal office, often winning several precincts.[13]

Edwards' admission to the bar had come late. With degrees from Sewanee and Harvard, he began his career as a Dallas schoolteacher, but his activist politics brought his dismissal from the school district. He read law in his father's office, attended some classes in a night school operated by A.A. Cocke and Shearon Bonner, and was admitted to the bar in 1909. As a lawyer, he represented and gained wide attention for his work toward labor causes, the poor, minorities, and the disadvantaged. His son, who became a federal appeals judge in Michigan and who wrote a biography of his father, remembered that for Dallas his dad was *"the* labor lawyer, *the* ACLU lawyer, *the* NAACP lawyer."[14]

FROM THE VERY beginning, as has been true for virtually all communities, Dallas lawyers had been making important contributions to civic life. Gilbert Haven Irish (1872-1946) was especially active in municipal civic affairs. He gained credit as the alderman who pushed the local government into purchasing as rapidly as possible property for public parks and for levying sufficient taxes to maintain them. After one of his ambitious campaigns toward this goal the City acquired the property on which Fair Park was located and the annual State Fairs were held. Irish also wrote the municipal ordinance requiring the city's streetcars to be heated in cold weather.[15]

Rhodes S. Baker (1874-1940) first gained special attention through his energetic leadership of the 150,000 Club, so named because it was dedicated to bringing to reality Jay Gould's prediction in 1887 that Dallas would become a city of 150,000 people. Along with other noted city leaders, Baker worked on a committee that examined a very important question for the future of the city—a means of taming the Trinity River so that its frequent floods could be controlled. His work on this committee brought about the first city plan department and also the employment of George S. Kessler as Dallas' first city planner. Baker also helped materially in securing in 1914 a grand coup for Dallas, designation as the regional headquarters for the new Federal Reserve Bank, a move which guaranteed the city's prominence as a banking center of the entire Southwest. A few years later Baker helped secure the removal of the T&P railroad tracks from Pacific Avenue, a project deemed essential for the growth of the downtown area to the north.[16]

Baker was no less distinguished for his legal work. In 1930 he argued a case before the U.S. Supreme Court, *Poe v. Seaborn*, which established that in most community property states, income belonged one-half to the husband and one-half to the wife. In 1914 Baker joined three other Dallas lawyers, William Thompson,

R.E.L. Knight, and William R. Harris in the firm that survives today as Thompson & Knight.[17]

THE BAR ASSOCIATION itself was "meeting subject to call" at the district courtroom, and the old practice of passing resolutions on the deaths of attorneys still provided the main reason for these called meetings. Other than that, what especially concerned the legal community and the Bar Association were the constantly overcrowded court dockets. As Dallas and the Dallas County area grew, so did the courts' business. It was difficult to be timely in creating enough courts to accommodate this litigation.

To a called meeting of the bar in late 1906, County Court Judge Hiram F. Lively explained his dilemma in handling his docket. For the twelve-month period, December 1, 1905, through November 30, 1906, a total of 464 civil cases were filed and disposed of, yet 220 cases remained on his docket. In the same period 1,500 criminal cases were filed and approximately 500 were disposed of, leaving approximately 1,000 still on the docket. Approximately 1,000 probate cases were pending. It was "impossible" for a single county judge to get this work done, he said, and there existed an "urgent necessity for some remedial legislation." The bar responded by naming a committee to draw up a bill to present to the legislature for the creation of another court, and in 1907 the County Court of Dallas County, At Law, was created with William M. Holland appointed as judge. Ten years later, with more assistance still needed, County Court at Law #2 was created.[18]

Congested dockets also confronted the 14th and 44th District Courts, and in 1907 and 1908 this matter was the topic of bar meetings. The usual pattern was followed—the hearing of reports, the appointment of committees, and the presentation of resolutions to the legislature. Routine though such matters seemed to be—few if any could deny the crowded conditions of the courts—feelings became so ruffled at a meeting in January 1907 that a motion to appoint a committee to study the crowded conditions of the 14th and 44th District Courts created "great excitement." Such a flurry arose that one member was obliged to call for the appointment of a sergeant-at-arms to maintain order and establish calm. The only issue that seemed to be at stake for the 150 members present was whether or not the bar's organization was "sufficiently complete" to move on the matter, and Judge M.L. Crawford believed that it was not.[19] By the end of 1908 the bar association was ready, though, and a committee was appointed to appear before the 1909 session of the State Legislature to seek a new district court.[20] This was done promptly, and on February 1, 1909, Judge J.C. Roberts was appointed to preside over the newly authorized 68th District Court.

While these new courts helped alleviate the growing burden of civil litigation, the county's Criminal District Court, created in 1893 with Charles F. Clint presiding from that date to 1902, was saturated with cases as well. The court congestion had familiar dimensions. In the year 1910 the court had disposed of 121 cases, which Dallas lawyers believed to be "the largest number of felony cases ever disposed of by one court in the same length of time in this state." The grand jury that same year returned 420 felony indictments. These numbers prompted a bar meeting on January 7, 1911, to review the situation. "We cannot conceive of any rational change in our present code of criminal procedure that would enable the present criminal district court to transact three times the volume of business which it transacted in 1910," reported a five-member committee. The Bar Association, meeting in the 14th District Courtroom, urged the State Legislature to create an additional criminal district court for Dallas County. Before the year was over, the 32nd Legislature had created Criminal District Court #2, and the chairman of the five-man committee which had urged that action, Barry Miller, was appointed its judge.[21]

ONE DALLAS LAWYER whose rise to fame resembled a Horatio Alger story was Hatton William Sumners (1875-1962), who began in 1900 a distinguished career of public service that spanned the first half of the twentieth century. Sumners grew up on a Tennessee farm, and at the age of eighteen moved to Garland with his parents. Ambitious but without resources, he persuaded City Attorney Wozencraft to let him read law in his office.

Wozencraft and his partner, Lauch McLaurin, not only permitted Sumners study in their office, they also allowed him to sleep there. In 1897 Sumners was admitted to the bar, and only two years later launched a successful campaign to become the county attorney. Taking office in 1900 at the age of 25, he launched a vigorous crusade against saloons and gambling interests, prosecuting them with skill. So successful was he that representatives of these elements of Dallas life organized to defeat him in his bid for re-election in 1902. Afterwards, though, Sumners again turned the tide against them, accusing them of sponsoring illegal voting. The next year the Texas Legislature passed the Terrell Election Law, incorporating many of his recommendations. Under the provisions of this law, he was re-elected county attorney in 1904. A high point in Sumners' crusade against vice undoubtedly occurred on November 29, 1904, when the famous Carry Nation arrived in Dallas and headed straight for the courthouse, where she lectured bystanders on the evils of drinking. Following her talk came the requisite visits to the city's saloons, where she bantered with bartenders and pinned her small hatchet emblems on customers. A few months later a city charter amendment was passed which required the city's saloons to close their doors between midnight and 6 a.m.[22] After serving this second term, Sumners returned to private practice to continue his reform efforts.

In 1912 he was elected to an at-large Congressional seat as a Democrat, and in 1914 he was elected to represent the 5th Congressional District, of which Dallas County was a part. As a freshman Representative, Sumners sponsored a successful bill that made Dallas a port of entry for customs. Hatton Sumners' lengthy career in the House, which lasted until his retirement in 1947, saw him acclaimed along with Sam Rayburn as one of the two most powerful people in the House.[23]

Sumners was the fourth member of the Dallas bar to be sent to Congress. First was Olin Wellborn (1843-1921), who began practicing law in the city in 1871 and served four terms as a Congressman, representing the Dallas area and surrounding environs from 1879 through 1887. In the House of Representatives he served as chairman of the Committee on Indian Affairs. After failing to get the Democratic nomination for a fifth term, he moved to San Diego, California, and in 1895 was appointed a U.S. district judge by President Grover Cleveland.[24]

Next was Robert E. Burke (1847-1901), yet another attorney who moved to Dallas from Jefferson in 1870. In Dallas he served as a member of the city council, as county judge, as judge of the 14th Judicial District, and finally as a Democratic Congressman from 1897 to 1901.[25]

Burke was succeeded in office by Dudley Goodall Wooten (1860-1929), who came to Dallas in 1889 after a prominent legal career in Austin, during which time he helped secure for that city the location of the University of Texas at Austin. He spoke at the university's opening in 1883. In Dallas, Wooten was elected county judge, serving from 1890 to 1892, then as state representative, in 1899-1900, and finally as Congressman from 1901 to 1903. Wooten also was an accomplished historian, author of a two-volume history of Texas, contributor of articles to national magazines about the South and Mexico, and president of the Texas State Historical Association. Wooten left Dallas after his term in Congress, to settle in Seattle, Washington, and then became a professor of law at Notre Dame University in 1924.[26]

A DALLAS ATTORNEY whose career as a public servant roughly paralleled that of Sumners but who belonged to the Republican Party was William Hawley Atwell (1869-1961). A native of Wisconsin, as a child Atwell moved with his parents in the 1870s to Dallas County, first to Mesquite and then to Hutchins. He graduated from Southwestern University in Georgetown, Texas, in 1889, then read law in the Dallas offices of Williams and Turney. In 1890 he was admitted to the bar, and in a reversal of normal procedure, then attended the University of Texas Law School, received a degree after a year's study, and began practicing law in Dallas. As a Wisconsin resident, Atwell's father had served with the Union in the Civil War, and Atwell— despite his new geographical setting—followed this parental precedent and became active in Republican politics. A reward came in 1898 when President William McKinley appointed him U.S. attorney for the Northern District, a position he held until 1913. In 1922 Atwell ran unsuccessfully as the Republican candidate for governor, and in 1923 President William G. Harding appointed him U.S. district judge, where he served until retirement in 1958 after becoming a pronounced fixture in Dallas affairs. During his long tenure on the federal bench Atwell became noted for the rapidity with which he tried cases, for his insistence on decorum and proper attire in the courtroom, and for his refusal to permit frivolity of any sort during court sessions.[27]

Especially during his younger years, Atwell traveled over the state and debated widely against such Democratic politicians as James S. Hogg, Joseph Weldon Bailey, and Charles A. Culberson. As a boy he had been inspired upon hearing the polished oratory of Congressman Olin Wellborn, and he determined that he would take every opportunity to emulate him. An especially memorable debate occurred when Governor Hogg enticed him to debate him without preparation over the question, "Resolved, that we shall turn loose the Philippines." In his opening comments Hogg belittled the Republicans who hoped to retain the 1,300 Philippine islands but did not even know their names. If his opponent Atwell could name thirteen of the islands, Hogg said, he would concede the debate. Atwell did not know the names of thirteen of the islands, but he remembered one, Luzon. In a moment of inspiration he quickly made up the names of twelve others, and when it was his turn to debate—knowing instinctively that Hogg didn't know their names either—he readily reeled off the fake names, to the governor's great chagrin. [28]

MUNICIPAL POLITICS also attracted the attention of many of Dallas' lawyers. One who seemed incapable of resisting the lure of elective municipal office was Bryan T. Barry, who was elected mayor three times, none consecutively. His most noteworthy race was his first one in 1893 against incumbent Winship C. (Bud) Connor, who was seeking his fourth term in office and boasted of some significant accomplishments. Barry had worked his way up to Dallas from Houston, where he had been admitted to the bar in 1873. He followed the H&TC Railroad on its northward route to Corsicana to begin his practice there. From his Corsicana base he achieved considerable success in state-wide Democratic politics, and finally in 1888 he moved to Dallas. In the 1893 contest with Connor, Barry lost by just two votes. His appeal to a Dallas district court failed to reverse the results. However, in February 1894 the State Supreme Court ruled in his favor and Barry found himself mayor of Dallas. In his first term Barry is credited with building the first surface water reservoirs for the city and ending reliance on dwindling underground sources by constructing dams at the Elm Fork of the Trinity at Record Crossing and also at California Crossing. In the 1895 election Barry, challenged by magazine publisher Frank P. Holland and fellow bar member A.P. Wozencraft, lost to Holland. In the next election in 1897 Barry and another fellow bar member, E.G. Bower, former county judge, vied for the mayor's office, and Barry once more was returned to office for a single term. His final election as mayor came in 1904, after having served in the interim a term as an alderman.[29]

The aldermanic form of city government was proving, in the opinion of many, to be too cumbersome a vehicle to solve the increasingly vexing urban problems. Perhaps it erred on the side of being too democratic, for there was an amazing array of elective offices. Voters picked ten aldermen from as many wards; they also elected five others to serve on an at-large basis to represent the overall interests of the city; and beyond that, they directly elected a dozen key administrators—including the city attorney. Certain influential leaders began to feel that the long-term solution to solving the growing municipal problems lay in adopting a more streamlined form of government, specifically, the commission form of government implemented so successfully by Galveston after its devastating 1900 hurricane. In this plan only a mayor and four commissioners were elected. They divided the city's departments among themselves, then supervised them as full-time administrators.

To achieve this drastic change the State Legislature approved a new charter for Dallas, and attorney Philip Lindsley's rising young son Henry organized a high-powered group of Dallas' leaders into a civic group called the Citizens Association which selected a slate of candidates and then launched a massive campaign to elect them. Thus was conceived the first civic/political organization which in decades to come would give Dallas the reputation of being a city led by inside groups of powerful businessmen.

Realization that Dallas' once close-knit group of lawyers now had become a diverse group with widely varying ideas could hardly have been more apparent than in the effort by the Citizens Association to gain control of municipal politics and to unseat the incumbent mayor, Curtis Pendleton Smith, a lawyer who had come to Dallas twenty years earlier to start his practice. His election in 1905 had been preceded by his two terms on the city council, four terms as city judge, and occasional other stints as city judge, but now he faced a formidable organized force in being elected. Supporting him as a vigorous spokesman in the harsh campaign was one of the city's most prominent lawyers, Judge William H. Clark, who argued that the Citizens Association was proposing a startling proposition—that the people of Dallas were incapable of self-government.

Many of the city's most powerful businessmen, though, affiliated themselves with the Citizens Association, as did a number of leading attorneys. This included one candidate for election as a commissioner, Harry L. Seay, brother of Criminal District Judge Robert B. Seay. And when final results came in, the entire Citizens Association slate was elected, thus beginning a legacy of leadership in the city that would endure for years to come.[30]

JUST ACROSS the river another town with its own municipal government and its own school system had sprung suddenly into prominent existence—Oak Cliff. A Dallas entrepreneur, Thomas L. Marsalis, created Oak Cliff as a planned community for upper middle-class citizens after buying Judge William L. Hord's 640 acres and adding to it another 1,360 acres. Judge Hord was still alive, but the old Hord's Ridge that had challenged Dallas to be the county seat in the election of 1850 had basically ceased to exist as a municipal entity. On this beautifully situated property, Marsalis, beginning in 1887, developed a planned community with fine houses, beautiful parks, and a separate school system. The new town, incorporated in 1890, attracted many prominent residents, including the artist Frank Reaugh and a number of prominent lawyers, including Judge Charles Frederick Tucker, Judge William Charlton, Robert Cowart, George Aldredge, Hugh Ewing, James Dickinson Thomas, and Martin L. Morris.

Thomas and Morris became closely intertwined with the affairs of Oak Cliff. Thomas arrived in Oak Cliff in 1889 and became a key ally to Marsalis in promoting the new town. As a major in the Confederacy during the Civil War, Thomas had been captured by the Yankees but released upon signing an oath never to take up arms against the Union again. After gaining his freedom he declined to honor his oath, rejoining a cavalry unit and then enduring the lengthy siege at Vicksburg before it fell finally to Union forces on July 4, 1863. By the time he moved to Oak Cliff, Thomas already had served as president of the board of trustees at Texas A&M, and in that capacity had selected the university's site at College Station. The property he purchased in Oak Cliff along Cedar Creek became known as Thomas Hill, a name it retains to this day.[31]

Even more closely tied to Oak Cliff's fortunes was Judge Martin L. Morris (1855-1927), who served as the town's fifth and last mayor from 1899 until its incorporation by Dallas in 1903. Morris, a native of Georgia, had been county judge and county attorney in Pittsburg, Texas, before moving to Oak Cliff in 1890 and practicing law out of his office in the North Texas Building in Dallas. He took an active role in Dallas County politics, and in 1894 in his capacity as chairman of the county's Democratic Convention he was active in nominating Dallas attorney Charles A. Culberson to be governor. In addition to his law practice, he was president of the Oak Cliff State Bank & Trust Co.[32]

Morris was a key figure in the controversy surrounding the annexation of Oak Cliff by Dallas, an event which he heartily opposed and which brought about a deep split in the community's residents. The financial crisis that struck the nation in the 1890s and brought depressed real estate values to the nation had stymied the continued development of Oak Cliff, sent Marsalis into bankruptcy, and prompted him to move to New York City. Despite the lack of commercial development in Oak Cliff, many of the residents felt deep pride in their town's amenities and lifestyle. An early issue concerning annexation centered around the differences in municipal ordinances governing livestock in the two towns. Dallas' municipal ordinance required cattle, horses, and hogs to be fenced or restrained twenty-four hours a day. Oak Cliff, with 3,624 residents in 1900, required only that animals be restrained at night, permitting them to wander freely during daylight hours. This emerged as one of the heated issues in the debate over annexation. In the debate that raged for several years, Morris and the previous mayor, Rufus Porter (who gained the nickname "Greater Dallas" Porter), took leading and contrasting roles. Besides the differences in livestock ordinances, another key distinction between the two communities was their policies toward alcohol. Oak Cliff was "dry" and Dallas was "wet."

Finally, on March 17, 1903, an election was held on the matter of disincorporation as a city as a prerequisite to annexation to Dallas. Morris, seeking a way to discourage annexation, sent queries to the state's attorney general and to local judges asking if annexation would cause Oak Cliff to lose its status as a dry community. With this issue unresolved, by a slim margin of 201 to 183, voters chose to disincorporate the town of Oak Cliff.[33] Those favoring annexation by Dallas successfully lobbied the Texas Legislature to pass an emergency bill accomplishing this act, and on April 3, 1903, Governor S.W.T. Lanham signed the bill into law. Annexation would be effective on July 1, 1903.

Even after that date Morris and other city and school officials still refused to accept the legality of the annexation, persisted in performing their perceived municipal duties, and filed a series of lawsuits to challenge it. The unusual reality was that two sets of city officials—those from Oak Cliff and those in Dallas—sought to exercise their authorities. Dallas City Attorney Will Henry obtained from Judge Richard Morgan of the 44th District Court an order to oust the Oak Cliff authorities, but this too was challenged with an appeal. Finally, in March 1904, the Texas Supreme Court upheld the annexation.[34] Celebratory cannons were heard in parts of Oak Cliff, but Morris and the other unhappy city officials yielded the city's municipal records and went on a hunting trip.[35]

THE RULE OF LAW UNDER CHALLENGE

⌘

Chapter Six

IT WAS TRUE IN DALLAS AS well as in other places in the still-developing American nation that the rule of law, so carefully nurtured from pioneer days as a civilizing influence, still remained vulnerable to impatient and emotional forces. Such clearly had been the unfortunate case in 1860 when Dallas vigilantes disdained legal processes and peremptorily hanged without benefit of trial three slaves whom they believed had torched the town. Because of advancements such as improved educational requirements for lawyers, more responsive courts, and greater sophistication among the public concerning its functions, the legal system that had developed in the state and in Dallas since then was far removed from those pioneer times. Yet, sadly, episodes and situations occurred or existed in the first quarter of the twentieth century which suggested that Dallas residents— although by no means unique in this respect—sometimes were unwilling to rely on the slow but orderly processes of the law as a means for achieving societal goals.

The first sad episode, occurring in 1910, saw an angry mob kidnap a man accused of sexually assaulting a small child. The mob exacted its own immediate and cruel punishment on the suspect. Painful as it is to recount, the incident does provide a startling snapshot of the manner in which the criminal justice system was rendered impotent.

The series of events began on a Thursday morning in late February 1910 when an African-American man, Allen Brooks (his age was reported at different times as 50 and 58) was seen emerging with a two-and-a-half-year-old white girl from a barn loft behind her parents' house at Ross Avenue and Pearl Street (across the street from the Belo Mansion that today is headquarters for the Dallas Bar Association). The girl's underclothing, according to an afternoon newspaper account that same day, outrageous in overstatement, not only was torn but it was covered with "blood and black marks where it came in contact with the hands of the negro." Brooks was arrested almost immediately, placed in city jail, and then transferred to county jail. The newspaper that afternoon described the incident as "one of the most terrible crimes that has been committed in the city of Dallas, or Dallas county." Fears arose immediately that angry citizens would assault the jail and lynch the suspect. As a precaution, the sheriff transferred the prisoner that night to an undesignated out-of-town location.[1]

That evening, a mob estimated at a thousand and unaware that Brooks already had been whisked away to safety, surrounded the county jail and demanded that he be turned over to them. They refused to believe deputies' explanations that he was no longer there. County Judge John L. Young, speaking from the jail steps, was jeered when he implored the group to let the law take its proper course. Some twenty men then made a futile attempt to batter down the jail's front door, then paused to ponder their next step. To forestall violence, Sheriff Arthur Lee Ledbetter permitted the father of the victimized child to tour the jail to see for himself that the suspect was not there. Upon hearing the father's report that he indeed was gone, mob members still expressed disbelief. Sheriff Ledbetter now agreed to permit a committee of six men, including one who recently had served eighteen months in the jail and who knew "every bit of the building from dark cell to tower," to be admitted for a more thorough search. After this futile search, finally convinced that the suspect was gone, the mob dispersed at 2:30 a.m.[2]

Next day the Dallas County grand jury indicted Brooks for rape. His trial was set for the following week. In explaining such a prompt trial date, County Attorney Dwight L. Llewelling pointed out that the State Code of Procedure adopted in 1897 provided that prosecution for the crime of rape "shall take precedence of all cases in all courts."

A *Times Herald* editorial enflamed the community's still-angry mood with a fiery message: "To the judges and prosecutors of Dallas county: Get busy. To the jurors: Break the necks of brutes. This is the message and it is a message from the people. The law should be uppermost, but there should be no delay. This is not a time for inaction or technicalities. The clock of Justice should strike twelve and then oblivion for a brute who will attack a child. Crimes against women and children must cease or there come a terrible day of reckoning."[3]

Assistant County Attorney B.M. Clark stressed that "in this case there is absolutely no need for mob violence." If the people would wait a "few days" and permit the law to take its course, he said, "prompt justice will be administered."[4]

J.C. Muse, a member of what probably was the city's most outstanding law firm (Crawford, Muse, and Allen) and a neighbor to the family whose daughter had been attacked, had visited the girl's home on the afternoon of the incident. He announced that he would volunteer to be a special prosecutor in the case. His rationale, he told the district attorney's office, was to obtain "a speedy prosecution and punishment of the negro guilty of the crime."[5]

The case was set for trial in Judge Robert B. Seay's Criminal District Court. Seay, a member of the Dallas bar since those early days in 1871 when he had struggled so hard to find clients, had been a member of the legal profession in Dallas longer than anyone living. To represent Brooks in his trial, Seay appointed two attorneys, Wilson T. Pace and J.E. Thomas. Pace, former court reporter for the 14th District Court who had been admitted to practice in 1905, balked immediately. He absolutely would not represent the accused man. He would rather go to jail himself, he said, and he accordingly made arrangements to serve as many as three days in jail if necessary.[6] Thomas said he could not serve because he had a previous engagement that would call him out of town on the day of the trial. Judge Seay excused both men. On March 1, he named three other attorneys to defend the hapless suspect: F.D. Cosby, R.H. Capers, and T.F. Lewis. A day later Cosby said he was ill, and did not know if he could be in court for the trial. Capers said that he would obey the mandate of the court, just as any other officer of the court would do.[7]

When a rumor arose that Brooks would be executed publicly—his guilt seemed accepted as a foregone conclusion—County Judge Young told the newspapers that he knew nothing of the rumor. Assistant County Attorney C.G. Evans said that a public execution could not occur, for state law prohibited public executions in counties such as Dallas with jails that could accommodate an inside gallows.[8]

Before dawn on the morning of the trial, Thursday, March 3, Brooks was brought by interurban rail to Dallas from Sherman (the secret location where he had been transferred as a precaution), met by former Sheriff Ben E. Cabell and Sheriff Arthur Lee Ledbetter, hurried to the courthouse in a touring car, and hidden in the jury room of the second-floor Criminal District Court to await trial. Three attorneys were present to represent the defendant: Capers, Lewis, and a new appointee, the liberal-minded George Clifton Edwards, who had replaced Cosby. None of the three had had an opportunity to visit with their client before the trial that was to begin minutes later.

By 9 a.m. a large, unruly crowd was surging around the courthouse. To protect Brooks, Sheriff Ledbetter had placed on duty his entire staff of deputy sheriffs as well as a large contingent of city police officers under Police Chief John W. Ryan. The glass doors leading into the courtroom were papered over for privacy. The only persons admitted into the courtroom were thirty prospective jurors out of a special venire of 150 men from whom the jury would be chosen, officers of the court, newspapermen, sheriffs deputies, and attorneys for the prosecution and defense. Outside the courtroom a struggle ensued as deputy sheriffs and police officers held back the increasingly rambunctious crowd, now estimated at a thousand. As this struggle ensued outside, inside the courtroom the three defense attorneys consulted for half an hour with their client. Then Judge Seay gave them an hour to prepare a motion in writing. Evidently, they intended to make a request for a change of venue.[9]

Meanwhile, Judge E.B. Muse of the 44th District Court went outside to address the crowd, pleading that the law be allowed to take its course and promising that if the defendant were found guilty the jury's sentence would be quickly carried out. Judge Seay also stepped out of his courtroom and urged the crowd, now on the second floor of the courthouse itself, to be calm. Officers managed to cajole crowd members into retreating to the first floor of the courthouse, but shortly before 11 a.m. word circulated that a change of venue was to be requested and the crowd's mood dramatically changed. There was a sudden surge of angry men pushing toward the courtroom, overcoming the resistance of officers who struggled to hold them back but still were forced to retreat to the second floor. The mob smashed open the courtroom door, surged inside, then fought steadily against the officers to reach the jury room where Brooks stood trembling. Mob leaders grabbed him, carried him to the window, caught a rope thrown up from below, then placed it around his neck despite efforts by officers to prevent it. This done, crowd members from below pulled Brooks head-first through the second-floor window. Mob members fell upon him immediately, stabbing him with knives and kicking him.

Forty or fifty men grabbed the rope and with cries of "to the Elk's arch" began at a trot to drag the apparently dead victim over brick-surfaced streets up Main Street to Akard where the arch had been erected two years earlier for an Elks' convention. An excited and noisy crowd of thousands followed. At Main and Akard, Brooks' body, now covered by only a few scraps of clothing, was strung up on a utility pole. Scuffling broke out among some crowd members as they fought to claim strips of the victim's remaining clothing as souvenirs, and soon even the pole on which the body was hung was whittled away by souvenir hunters so that it almost collapsed.

Mayor Stephen Hay and three city commissioners, conferring outside nearby city hall, ordered the town's saloons to shut down, a fire engine company to go to the county jail, and every Dallas member of the Texas National Guard to report for duty. The mayor and commissioners realized that the mob did not consider its work finished, for, pleased at their success, many now were shouting the names of three more African-Americans in jail as their next victims. Unbeknownst to the mob, though, the sheriff already had rushed these prisoners away by automobiles with armed escorts.

Now there gathered at the county jail—located on Houston Street near the future site of Union Terminal—a crowd estimated at 5,000, intent on taking the three men by force. To appease the mob, authorities selected a committee of six to enter the jail and see for themselves that the trio was not there. While awaiting word on this inspection a man identified in the newspapers as a young lawyer from Rockwall urged the crowd on. "What are we here for, men? Burrell Oates [one of the three] has been eating at the state's expense for five years; let's save Texas some money." After some interchange with a deputy, the Rockwall lawyer again spoke: "Let's get twenty men of our own to go through the jail. If the sheriff won't agree to that, then down with the doors." Without waiting, the mob used an iron rail in an effort to push down the walls, then switched its efforts to the locked door. Just as the door was about to give way, Sheriff Ledbetter appeared and agreed to let twenty men of the group's choosing search the jail. After that search was concluded and it was realized that the prisoners had been taken away, the disgruntled moved to the Katy railroad depot where they encountered the newly gathered militia. At this point the mob's energy was dissipated, and the horrendous day was over.

What was the reaction of those representing law and order to this horrendous crime? What would happen to those nameless individuals responsible for this day?

County Attorney Llewelling sought to explain the mob's anger. He blamed the lynching on frustrations felt by the public over technicalities in the legal system. "In my judgment the flimsy technicalities resorted to by criminal lawyers and sustained by the courts, and especially the higher courts, are responsible for such a condition of the public mind. If the public believe that under the law swift and prompt justice would be meted out to the criminal, affairs of this kind would not happen. . . . If the higher judges would pay less attention to technicalities and more to substantial justice, law in Texas would be more respected by all good citizens."[10]

The governor of Texas, Thomas M. Campbell, had no comment, but it was reported in the newspaper that he was "likely to order a special grand jury to investigate the affair" and that it also was very probable that "the district judges of Dallas may be directed to order a special grand jury of investigation."[11]

Two days afterwards, Judge Seay said he would ask the grand jury to investigate the situation. Former sheriff Cabell, who had assisted Sheriff Ledbetter through so much of the affair, said he had not recognized a single man in the crowds.[12] Ledbetter, criticized for reportedly having struck a Confederate veteran with his pistol during the melee, unequivocally denied it and said he never drew his pistol at any time. The Confederate veteran issued a statement confirming Ledbetter's denial.

On the Monday following the Thursday affair, Judge Seay appealed to the grand jury to examine the affair and to indict lawbreakers. In remarks quoted in the newspaper, he told the grand jury that the mob was guilty of riot, burglary, and murder, and that such violence threatened the existence of society. He urged a thorough inquiry, not sparing any details in his comments of the gruesome character of the incident. "Gentlemen," he said, "I want to ask you this question: What are you going to do about it?"[13]

The grand jury, appearing to take the judge's comments to heart, began calling in witnesses, but the *Daily Times Herald* reported that no one believed the investigation would result in "anything of a definite nature." As the news story pointed out, officers who had lived in Dallas County all their lives stated that they were "unacquainted with the ring leaders."[14]

No indictments were ever returned.

Several days after the lynching an unusual legal question was addressed to U.S. Attorney William Hawley Atwell. Thousands of postcards had been printed bearing photographs of the lynching scene at Akard and Main. Would it violate any federal laws to send them through the U.S. mails? Atwell acknowledged that indeed they could be mailed. "Unfortunately, there is no law against it except the law of common decency and love of the city in which one lives," he added.[15]

And what of the general reaction of the city's lawyers to this frightening event? Within a week the affair inspired a number of them to form a new club: the Dallas Law and Debating Club. Its purpose would be to debate and discuss issues and the law, with meetings to be held every Tuesday evening in the 44th District Court. Wilson T. Pace, the lawyer who had refused to accept Judge Seay's appointment to represent Brooks, was elected president of the organization. J.J. Fryer was chosen as secretary The first topic chosen for debate was "Is mob action justified?" Taking the affirmative were Fryer (the club's secretary) and Craddock. Opposing it were R.S. Loving and an unnamed associate.[16]

The debate occurred as promised, and afterwards the resultswere announced: "The decision of the club affirmed such action to be justifiable." Twenty-five members were present.[17]

AS THE LYNCHING of Allen Brooks under the very nose of the Criminal District Court so dramatically demonstrated, when the laws of the State of Texas contradicted the notions of a particular community about how best to handle its affairs, those laws sometimes were disregarded. Another far less sordid example of this came in the same year in which the lynching occurred, 1910, when the elected City of Dallas commissioners adopted an ordinance designating an official district in which prostitutes could operate with impunity despite a state law prohibiting prostitution. Earlier, the city's prostitutes had centered their activities in the South End of the city, but in 1907 an expansion of the railroads in that area forced them to begin to move to different parts of the city. This had prompted Criminal District Judge W.W. Nelms, in making a charge to the grand jury, to observe that for many years "either by the tacit consent of our officers or the common consent and toleration of our people," prostitutes had been segregated in that area. Now, as prostitutes moved from that area, he said, they were inflicting a "condition" on reputable families which should not be tolerated. His message clearly implied, if not specifically stated, the need for a designated district.[18]

This district turned out to be an area known as "Frogtown," a neighborhood along Griffin Street just north of McKinney Avenue and within a mile of the courthouse. City commissioners confirmed that fact by adopting an ordinance decreeing that neighborhood to be a safe haven for prostitutes. It was intended not so much to protect the prostitutes as to isolate them and thus protect decent and respectable neighborhoods from their encroachment. Some 240 to 400 prostitutes ultimately worked in this district, which came to be known as "the Reservation."[19]

The fact that this ordinance conflicted with state laws outlawing prostitution was not a problem to County Attorney Currie McCutcheon, nor to Police Commissioner Louis Blaylock, nor to Police Chief Ryan. But in 1913 the city's ministers, working through the Council of Churches, decided to mount public pressure to put an end to this official sanctioning of prostitution. A series of meetings was held, with Dallas' leading ministers speaking from pulpits. Under growing pressure the county attorney, police commissioner, and police chief were persuaded that they had been wrong to sanction the Reservation. They now agreed to enforce the laws against prostitution. Thus, County Attorney McCutcheon advised the women in the Reservation to move out by 6 p.m., November 3, 1913, or face arrest and prosecution. The break-up of this huge area was hailed as the biggest clean-up of vice ever made in the United States outside of Chicago and the Barbary Coast area of San Francisco.[20]

SURELY ONE of the most bizarre series of criminal trials and appeals processes ever to occur in Dallas County revolved around the convicted murderer Burrell Oates, one of the three African-American inmates sought by the 1910 lynch mob as candidates for summary justice. Between 1904 and 1911 Oates underwent seven trials for the murder of a grocer, Sol Aronoff, before he was hanged in 1912. He was represented in every trial by the same attorney, Albert Sidney Baskett, a native of Smith County who had been practicing law in Dallas since 1902. Because of the unusual number of trials, convictions, and reversals, Oates became a minor celebratory as his execution was delayed time after time.

The crime had occurred on November 30, 1904, when Oates and an accomplice, Holly Vann, entered Aronoff's small grocery store at the corner of Houston Street and the Missouri, Kansas and Texas Railroad, not far from the courthouse. At pistol-point they ordered Aronoff to turn over the money from his cash box. When Aronoff's wife rushed to his aid with a pistol, shots were fired. Aronoff was killed and his wife slightly grazed by a bullet. The robbers fled, only to be arrested the following day and identified by Mrs. Aronoff.[21]

Within a month Oates and Vann were convicted in separate trials and sentenced to death. Vann was hanged at an outdoors gallows adjacent to the jail on May 12, 1905, before a crowd of more than 2,000 spectators, many of whom had admission tickets. Oates' 33-year-old attorney, Baskett, appealed his client's conviction and won a reversal because of improper selection of jurors. Shortly afterwards, a new jury was called and Oates again was found guilty and sentenced to death. Once more Baskett won a reversal, this time on the grounds that the court had not allowed him an opportunity to present to the jurors the possibility that Mrs. Aronoff might have accidentally shot her own husband in trying to protect him. In 1906 Oates again was convicted, and the verdict again was reversed due to an error "in the court's charge on accomplice testimony and with reference to implied malice on the robbery plea." Later in 1906, in a trial before a special judge another jury found Oates guilty and sentenced him to death. This verdict, too, was reversed because the appeals court believed the selection of a special judge to have been wrong.[22]

Early in 1907 Oates, with Baskett continuing to be his lawyer, again was tried and found guilty. A mistrial was declared when Oates became ill with pneumonia and three of the jurors suffered from grippe.

The 1910 lynching of Allen Brooks and the mob's effort to find Oates and lynch him as well caused a change in venue to Waxahachie for the next trial. A jury there again found Oates guilty and sentenced him to death. Baskett's appeal to a higher court was successful, and another new trial was granted. In November 1911 Oates' seventh trial also took place in Waxahachie. Again a jury convicted him and sentenced him to death. This time the higher courts affirmed the verdict.

Oates' execution was set for November 29, 1912, at a gallows outside the Dallas County jail. Oates, all this while, had maintained his innocence. On the evening before he was hanged he repeated his claim of innocence to former Sheriff Arthur Lee Ledbetter. And to a minister on his way to the gallows, he said, "I can't confess to a lie. I am innocent." According to legend, Oates had threatened that if he were hanged the clock on the tower of the courthouse would stop working and never would run again. Finally, the death sentence was carried out. The clock did later stop. Experts from St. Louis who came to fix it informed the county commissioners that it was beyond repair. In 1919 the clock and tower were removed from the top of the courthouse because of structural instability.[23]

IN 1921 THERE arose in Dallas an organization which sought on numerous occasions to supersede the legal system with its own values and practices—the Ku Klux Klan. This version of the Klan originated in Georgia as a post-World War I revival of the notorious Ku Klux Klan of Reconstruction Days. Its proclaimed values—a return to morality and traditional values, especially as reflected by fundamentalist Christianity—attracted many followers during these post-war years in the South and Midwest as they proclaimed the importance of native white Americans. Dallas Klan No. 66, headed by dentist Hiram Wesley Evans, developed almost overnight into what was described as the largest Klan chapter in the nation. It reportedly had 13,000 Dallas members in a city of 160,000 population. Its presence in the city was announced in a dramatic Saturday night parade with sign-bearing members wearing masks and Klan regalia. It included many of the city's most prominent citizens, who seemed to be well-intended if naive.

Concerned that the nation's criminal justice system was failing to do its job, Klansmen took it upon themselves to discipline individuals they deemed guilty of immoralities. By the spring of 1922 masked Klansmen in Dallas had abducted and whipped some sixty-four individuals. Support for these extra-legal activities, always couched in moralistic terms, was widespread in prominent circles, including the ministry as well as law-enforcement. Klansmen and Klan-supported candidates successfully campaigned for local political offices, and they took control of the courthouse in 1922 and of city hall in 1923. Klansmen included the county sheriff, the police commissioner, two consecutive district attorneys (the first of whom angrily resigned from the organization, only to be defeated by a Klansman in the next election), the police chief, judges, doctors, bankers, public utility executives, ministers, businessmen, journalists, and lawyers.[24]

One of the supporters of the Klan in its earliest days in Dallas was none other than the district attorney, Maury Hughes (1894-1955), who afterwards would become one of the city's most noted criminal attorneys. Hughes was the son of a widowed mother who had brought Hughes and his brother to Gainesville, Texas, after her husband, a California Supreme Court justice, died in 1900. Hughes attended Austin College in Sherman and the old Dallas University, earned a law degree from the University of Virginia in 1916, and returned to Dallas in time to enlist as a private in the Army to serve in World War I. He left the service as a captain, earning the Croix de Guerre for having led a successful charge against a German machine-gun emplacement. He had hardly returned to Dallas when he decided to campaign for Dallas County district attorney. In November 1920 he was elected to that office at the age of twenty-five, the youngest man ever to hold that position in Dallas County.[25]

Although he was soon to break from the Klan and oppose it, Hughes was among those Dallasites who at first were captivated by the Klan's strong moralistic message. Indeed, few if any Dallas residents who harbored doubts about the organization were willing to oppose it publicly, especially given its strong support by law enforcement officials, ministers, and businessmen. An exception was *The Dallas Morning News,* although it suffered significant circulation and advertising losses when the Klan organized a boycott against the newspaper.

Hughes was by no means the only Dallas attorney who affiliated with the Klan. Their numbers included some of the best-known members of the legal profession, including officers of the Bar Association of Dallas and others who were active or soon would become active in the Association. According to a document in the Dallas Historical Society's archives, in 1922 three of the ten members of the local Klan's "Executive Committee of Ten" and eleven of the "Steering Committee of One Hundred" were lawyers.[26]

The incident which dramatically illustrated the nature of the Klan menace to the orderly processes of law and order occurred in Dallas in the spring of 1922. A Jewish picture-framer, accused without specificity of violating moral codes, was kidnapped by masked men from his home on McKinney Avenue in the presence of his wife, taken to a remote area, beaten severely, and ordered to leave town within twenty-four hours. This appears to have been the moment when District Attorney Hughes, suddenly alarmed at the Klan's blatant disregard for legal processes, quit the organization in disgust. The terrified beating victim, Phillip J. Rothblum, fled town as ordered. But Hughes located him in St. Louis and persuaded him to return to Dallas under protective custody so that he could testify in the trial against one of his assailants, a police officer known by Rothblum and recognized by him when the officer's mask had slipped as he administered the beating. When the jury quickly found the policeman—a Klansman—innocent despite Rothblum's positive identification, a number of prominent Dallasites who had been quietly viewing the situation with alarm decided that the time had come to organize themselves and to begin a movement to point out the perils of the Klan's lawlessness.[27]

Some prominent members of the legal community took leading roles in organizing this opposition, and it is not difficult to imagine that intense debates arose among members of the bar over this issue since a number of them were Klan committee members. Those willing to take public stands against the extra-legal organization included Judge C.M. Smithdeal, who became temporary chairman of the committee of twenty-five citizens who were assigned to gather signatures of more than 400 anti-Klan residents. Among the attorneys signing the petition, in addition to Smithdeal, were Martin M. Crane, M.M. Crane Jr., D.L. Llewelling, W.L. Crawford, W.H. Clark, E.B. Muse, J.C. Muse, John B. Muse, Ben E. Cabell, William Clark, James P. Simpson, C. Tom Knight, M.A. Holland, and A.J. Reinhart. Their names were published in the newspapers—a daring move at the time considering popular public sentiment—as a sign of their resolve. The petition called for a mass meeting of concerned citizens, and it forcefully outlined the dangers of the Klan's extra-legal activities: citizens had been driven from their communities by violence and threats of violence; men had been seized by masked mobs in the presence of their wives and daughters and dragged away for beatings in secluded locations; at least sixty-three individuals had been punished by masked mobs. The petition stated:

> Not one of these marauders has been indicted. The officers seem to be powerless. . . . These crimes are being committed by an organization thoroughly trained and disciplined. They must know that if they can commit sixty-three crimes and escape punishment, they can commit others as well and likewise escape, and thus inaugurate an absolute reign of terror in this county. . . . No man should be a Klansman and a public officer at the same time. . . . We must provide adequate protection to our people against mob violence. We must give to the people, who live here, and whom we are constantly inviting to come into our midst assurance that their homes will again be their castles, and that they shall not be convicted and punished for a crime without a public trial before a lawful tribunal. . . . We must determine whether we are to have a government of law or government by the mob, which means anarchy and ruin.[28]

Of particular concern was the widespread belief—later to

be confirmed—that a large number of police officers were Klansmen. Smithdeal suggested that a citizens committee be appointed to visit the courthouse and "inquire of every placeholder, from District Judges, County Court Judges, County Commissioners and on through the Sheriff's office and Justices of the Peace down through Constables and their deputies and make searching inquiry concerning their affiliation or sympathies with the cohorts of outlawry."[29]

A huge crowd of citizens, 5,000 strong, responded to the call, filling the City Hall auditorium, overflowing onto Harwood Street, and cheering loudly as speaker after speaker—including Sam P. Cochran and former Governor O.B. Colquitt—denounced the Klan and pledged the supremacy of the Constitution. A number of resounding resolutions were adopted, all emphasizing the importance of due process of law and including such statements as: "The jury box destroyed, the whole fabric of a free government fails. The jury box destroyed, man's struggles for liberty and security have been in vain."[30] Another resolution "cheerfully" conceded that "many good men" had joined the Klan for what they conceived to be "lofty purposes," but the end result of the Klan would be "subversive of our democratic institutions and the enthronement among us of chaos and anarchy."[31]

Those present created a new organization, the Dallas County Citizens League, with the express purpose of opposing the Klan, and named a group of nine members to work as an executive committee. Martin M. Crane, former attorney general, was the consensus choice to head the committee and the League. The executive committee included two other members of the Dallas bar, Judge Smithdeal and former Governor Colquitt.[32]

Martin McNulty Crane (1855-1943) had risen to prominence in a way reminiscent of Horatio Alger. He came to Dallas in 1899, where he was to practice law for forty-four years. By the time he arrived, he already had gained state-wide acclaim for his high-level involvement in Texas politics and public service. A native of West Virginia and son of a husband and wife who were natives of Ireland, Crane lost both his mother and father to death before he was five years of age. At the age of seventeen, Crane decided to seek his fortune in Texas, and after a journey by ox wagon landed in Johnson County, where he worked on farms, attended school, taught school, studied law, and at the age of twenty-two was admitted to the bar. Six years later, voters in Johnson County elected their adopted son to be their prosecuting attorney, re-electing him in 1880 and advancing him in 1884 to the state legislature for a single term. There, he developed a reputation for supporting progressive causes, sympathizing with farmers and the Farmers' Alliance program, expressing alarm at the growing power of railroads, and helping Governors Hogg and Culberson in their efforts at political reform. In 1890 Crane broadened his constituency by being elected state senator for the 21st District (Ellis, Hill, and Johnson counties), then lieutenant governor in 1892, and attorney general in 1894.[33]

Crane gained distinction in a series of cases as attorney general, notably in enforcing Texas' anti-trust laws and driving from the state the Waters-Pierce Oil Co. This celebrated case brought political repercussions for years, symbolizing for progressives the need for stronger regulation of corporations, and serving as a beacon for reforms occurring in the state from 1906 to 1920. After his initial work in this case, Crane, still in his forties, chose in 1899 to move to Dallas, where he would practice law for forty-four more years and continue to be active in public affairs. He again gained headlines in 1906 when he debated with Senator Joe Weldon Bailey against the practice of politicians' accepting fees from businessmen. In 1917 he was the chief counsel in the impeachment trial of Governor Jim Ferguson. With such a reputation for fearlessness, probity, and a willingness to take controversial stands, Crane was a logical choice to become the leader of the Dallas County Citizens League and to lead its drive to combat the Klan.

One of the important goals enunciated at that first meeting and in the days that followed was to remove from office all city and county officials who were members of the Klan. Another was to educate Dallas as to the dangers of the "Invisible Empire." In its effort to identify officials who belonged to the Klan, the Citizens League prepared a questionnaire which went to city and county officials asking if they now belonged to the Klan, whether they intended to affiliate with it, and whether they were in sympathy with its purposes and practices. The questionnaire produced little if any results, for officials generally disregarded it.

The League also prepared a thirty-page miniature pamphlet, "The Case Against the Ku Klux Klan," which was widely distributed, and organized a group of speakers who visited neighborhoods and nearby towns to discuss the menace of the Klan. These efforts were greeted with hostility and some derision. Speakers at public meetings found themselves harassed.

A key test as to the effectiveness of the League's efforts came in the 1922 Democratic primary, and it was not favorable to the anti-Klan forces. Klan-supported candidates swept the courthouse, winning every race. The winners included three admitted Klansmen, two of them attorneys—Felix D. Robertson and Shelby S. Cox. Robertson, a municipal court judge, won the nomination for Criminal District Court, and Cox defeated Maury Hughes to become the Democratic nominee for district attorney. The third Klansman, Dan Harston, gained the nomination as sheriff. Democratic Party primary victories were tantamount to victory in the general election, which indeed proved to be the case in all these instances. The results, a bitter pill for anti-Klan forces, spelled the end of the Dallas County Citizens League's efforts. In the next test, the spring 1923 municipal elections, pro-Klan candidates once more won every commission seat. It was apparent that public sentiment in Dallas County overwhelmingly supported the Ku Klux Klan.[34] The widespread acceptance of Klan activities could be seen in the 1923 State Fair of Texas when an official Ku Klux Klan Day drew a huge number of Klansmen from across the nation.

Despite its sudden and powerful emergence as a force, the Klan's dominance in Dallas and its national support declined just as precipitously as it emerged. Internal dissension in both the local and national organizations, a growing public awareness about the dangers of the Klan as an extra-legal organization, and the defeat of Klansman and District Judge Felix Robertson in his bid to become governor of Texas all signaled the demise of the organization. By 1926 the Klan in Dallas had lost its power as suddenly as it had attained it. Perhaps the educational efforts of the Dallas County Citizens League had paid off after all.[35]

WHEN THE NOTED attorney William L. Crawford died in 1920 he left his entire estate of some $250,000 to his second wife, Katherine Lester Crawford, much to the dismay of the three children from his first marriage. Colonel Crawford's first wife had died in 1873. In 1880 he moved from Jefferson with his children to Dallas to set up a noted law partnership with his brother, M.L. Crawford. In 1896 he married Katherine two weeks after her divorce from Lucius Q.C. Lamar.[36] With Colonel Crawford's support, Katherine Crawford, herself an artist, created the city's most outstanding art gallery at the side of their home on Ross Avenue. In 1898 a son, William Lester Crawford was born to the couple. He became an attorney, too, and by the 1920s he was practicing law out of second floor offices in the Crawford Building on Main Street. Somewhat of a loner, it was said that much of his time was spent reading law, literature, poetry, novels, and current magazines.[37]

Colonel Crawford's first three children employed one of the city's leading firms, Locke & Locke, to represent them in challenging the will which left them nothing. Representing Mrs. Crawford as her lead counsel was another attorney with impeccable credentials, Francis M. Etheridge, who had been the first president of the re-organized Bar Association of Dallas in 1914. In various pleadings it was contended that the colonel had been induced to leave his entire estate to his second wife because of her undue influence on him. The challenge had been unsuccessful in probate court, unsuccessful in Judge Kenneth Foree's 14th District Court, and in September 1924 an appeal to the 5th Court of Appeals was pending.

Paul O'Day, a bright young attorney in Locke & Locke who was designated to be in charge when Eugene P. Locke was away, was given primary charge of the case. O'Day was no stranger to controversy. That previous spring, in representing an out-of-state insurance firm, he had gained headlines by charging that the state courts were dominated by the Ku Klux Klan and that his client could not get a fair trial in the state courts.

In seeking to prove undue influence by Mrs. Crawford, O'Day had introduced testimony from Colonel Crawford's coachman in which he said that prior to the couple's marriage he often drove the colonel to Mrs. Lamar's home and had to wait outside for him until he was ready to go home. There was evidence that Colonel Crawford would often emerge from her house after having had too much to drink and being accompanied to the door by Mrs. Lamar in scanty attire. These and other charges unfairly impugned his mother's integrity, William Lester Crawford believed, and he determined to have revenge in his own manner.[38]

On a Thursday morning, September 11, 1924, Crawford appeared in the lobby of the American Exchange Bank Building (later the First National Bank Building) on Main Street bearing a loaded shotgun. The shotgun attracted some notice, but he calmly told one inquisitor that he was going dove hunting. The firm of Locke & Locke was on the seventeenth floor of the building. At 8:45 a.m. O'Day's wife dropped him off for work, and inside the lobby near the elevator Crawford leveled the shotgun at O'Day, was heard to say, "Paul, fall dead," and then fired two rounds of buckshot into him. O'Day fell without a word, a pool of blood widening about his body, and he soon was pronounced dead. "He insulted my mother and I killed him," Crawford said to a friend who walked up to him and took him by the arm.[39]

Crawford was jailed, freed on $15,000 bond, then jailed again without bond upon the grand jury's indictment. Ultimately, he was convicted for the murder of O'Day and sentenced to prison. As a result of the case, Eugene P. Locke never permitted the firm or anyone connected with it to accept representation in any matter that might involve a domestic dispute.[40]

BREAKING THE GENDER BARRIER

⌘

CHAPTER SEVEN

FOR SOME TIME THE Dallas Bar Association believed a need existed to reorganize, and as early as the presidency of Judge John L. Henry in 1907-08 a committee had been appointed to propose such a plan. Under T.T. Holloway's presidency, 1909 to 1915, the preparatory work was done, and the reorganization finally took place at a meeting on May 16, 1916, at the Oriental Hotel. The Dallas lawyer widely acknowledged as the prime mover was Alexander Pope, whose father and grandfather also had been attorneys and whose son Jack would be chief justice of the State Supreme Court from 1982 to 1985.

In fact, the new arrangement seemed by common consent to be far more than a reorganization; it was, literally, a "new" organization. *The Dallas Morning News* headline on May 17, 1916, quite conclusively announced: "BAR ASSOCIATION OF DALLAS IS FORMED," with a subheading, "New Organization, With 100 Charter Members, Has Wide Scope." A picture of the new president, Francis M. Etheridge, was accompanied by the caption, "First President of Bar Association of Dallas."[1] The new organization received a charter as a "literary society" from the Secretary of State of Texas—"literary society" because the statutes of Texas did not authorize the granting of a corporate charter to a local bar association.[2] The new association was understood to replace not only the old Dallas Bar Association, but, according to newspaper accounts, a group known as Lawyers' Lunch Club. A key distinction was this: the old organization was known as the Dallas Bar Association; the new one, the Bar Association of Dallas.

Etheridge (1859-1925), the new president, 57 years of age, was one of those many lawyers who had moved to Dallas from a smaller Texas town, but politically he was in a minority. He had been among those followers of Theodore Roosevelt who in 1912 had formed the Progressive Party in the split with the Republicans. Etheridge had been practicing law in Dallas since 1891 when he had come from Groesbeck, Texas, after being admitted to the bar in Pittsburg, Texas, in 1881, having studied law in the evenings while teaching school.[3]

Shortly after the turn of the century he and J.M. McCormick, son of the first federal judge in Dallas, Andrew P. McCormick, created a partnership. They were joined in 1900 by Henri L. Bromberg, a University of Texas graduate, and the firm became Etheridge, McCormick, and Bromberg. It developed a reputation as expert trial counsel and astute business advisors.[4]

The Bar Association of Dallas would have four regular meetings a year on the second Tuesday in March, June, September, and November, an annual meeting each January, and luncheon meetings strictly for pleasure once a month. At these luncheons no business would be transacted. Officers would be elected on the second Tuesday in January each year. In addition to Etheridge as president, new officers included three vice presidents: William Thompson, Wendel Spence and Maurice Locke. L.M. Mays was secretary and G. Drummond Hunt, treasurer.

It was unclear just how the one-hundred charter members were selected, but it was emphasized that no discrimination had been intended. As to future members, any member of the profession in good standing could be admitted upon recommendation of the committee on admission and upon vote of the association. There evidently was great interest among those attorneys not included as charter members to join the organization, for the admissions committee (W.S. Bramlett, Rosser J. Coke, L.M. Dabney, William Flippen, John C. Harris, Hiram F. Lively, Eugene Locke, Albert Walker, and Joseph A. Worsham) met the very next afternoon to consider membership applications.

An executive committee (Edward Crane, J.J. Eckford, A.B. Flanary, William M. Holland, Charles C. Huff, J.C. Muse, C.M. Smithdeal, Cullen F. Thomas, and T.B. Williams) would take charge of the association's affairs and make all appropriations of its funds. The board of trustees was named as Henry C. Coke, M.B. Templeton, W.J.J. Smith, Robert B. Allen, T.T. Holloway, M.M. Crane, Joseph E. Cockrell, and Col. W.L. Crawford.

The association's new standing committees were expected, according to *The Dallas Morning News*, "to have an important bearing not only on the practice of law in Dallas, but on future legislation and on law reform."[5] Standing committees were planned for these areas: amendment of the law, law reform, grievances, constitutional amendments, legal education, and ethics. The committee on amendment of the law, to consist of five members, would watch and report on all pending legislation in the state, especially as it pertained to the general rules of practice, and either support or oppose that legislation on behalf of the association. The law reform committee, consisting of seven members, would entertain and examine projects for change or reform in substantive law or procedure not pending before the legislature. The five members of the grievance committee would hear all complaints against members of the association or anyone else practicing law in Dallas and also concerning matters affecting the interests of the legal profession, the practice of law and the administration of justice.

The committee on constitutional amendments would watch all resolutions in the state legislature proposing changes to the state constitution. The committee on legal education would inquire into the methods of legal education and requirements for admission to the bar. It would recommend changes or improvements that it felt necessary. A library committee and a house committee were charged with finding quarters for the association and a library. The development of a code of ethics was a duty charged to the executive committee. Its recommendations in this matter were to be presented to a meeting of the association at an early date.

An editorial in the *Daily Times Herald* congratulated the new association, calling its organizers "among the most brightly shining lights of the local bar" and congratulating them for establishing important standing committees to improve the "poor workings" of the legal machine. "That the law and the constitution are not perfect they [the association's members] tacitly admit. And they recognize that if perfection is ever to be approached it will be through the efforts of the lawyers."[6]

Four days after the new Bar Association was formed, it held a gala banquet in the Palm Garden of the Adolphus Hotel, the city's finest hotel in town and its tallest building. Besides members' wives, special guests included Chief Justice Nelson Phillips of the Supreme Court of Texas; the mayor and city commissioners of Dallas; Louis Lipsitz, president of the Dallas Chamber of Commerce; and Dr. R.E. Vinson, president-elect of the University of Texas. It was a grand evening of eloquent speeches and toasts.

The association's new president, Etheridge, spoke of the group's mission of maintaining the honor and dignity of the profession, of its need to be useful in promoting the administration of justice, and of its goal to cultivate social intercourse among members. "The true lawyer must be actuated by conviction," he said. "He must possess courage and candor."

In his comments, the venerable Colonel W.L. Crawford divided law into four systems—moral, divine, municipal and international. "The greatest of all these systems is the moral law, a law not enacted by any legislature. It is the conception of right and wrong, of personal duty in respect to private transactions, of personal obligation, of our relations to our fellow-man and our duties to our country."

Chief Justice Phillips commended the new organization for its high ideals. He predicted that the Bar Association of Dallas would have an important bearing not only on the legal profession in Dallas but for future legislation in the state.[7]

The new Bar Association of Dallas was off to a fine start. In the ensuing meetings, for the first time, formal minutes were kept of meetings and maintained as a permanent record. Presidents began to serve limited terms of one or two years rather than the indefinite terms that had marked such tenures as W.B. Gano, who had served from 1891 to 1900; John L. Henry, 1901-1909; and T.T. Holloway, 1909-1915. Regular meetings would be held at the Oriental Hotel until 1919 when they began alternating between the 14th and 44th District Courtrooms. Then, from 1923 until mid-June 1924 meetings returned again to the Oriental Hotel at

Commerce and Akard streets, ceasing when the Oriental was torn down to be replaced by the Baker Hotel. (This site is now occupied by Southwestern Bell Telephone Co.)[8]

When the new Bar Association of Dallas met on June 13, 1916, at the Oriental for its first regular meeting after its formation, the association's president, Etheridge, had just returned from the final Progressive Party convention in Chicago, where signs of disintegration appeared. As a prominent Bull Moose leader, Etheridge had been a member of the convention's platform committee. Alex Pope formally welcomed him back to Dallas in behalf of the association, and suggested that with the demise of the Progressive Party he might come into the Democratic Party. Etheridge's response drew loud cheers—he, indeed, had decided to join the Democratic Party. "I cannot subscribe to the 'standpatism' of the Republicans," he said.[9]

At this same meeting the names of fifty-two prospective members, submitted by the membership committee, were presented and elected to membership. Their numbers included several appeals court judges as well as local judges.[10]

More significantly, the new code of ethics, devised by the executive committee under the leadership of Alex Pope and committee chairman William M. Holland, was adopted by a unanimous vote. The code was patterned closely after that of the American Bar Association. Titles of its major sections reflected the subject matter: "The Duty of the Lawyer to the Courts," "The Selection of Judges," "The Defense or Prosecution of Those Accused of Crime," "Fixing the Amount of the Fee," "How Far a Lawyer May Go in Supporting a Client's Cause," "Candor and Fairness," "Attitude Toward Jury," "Advertising, Direct or Indirect," "Stirring Up Litigation," "Upholding the Honor of the Profession," and "The Lawyer's Duty in Its Last Analysis." A committee on grievances would handle all complaints—coming from lawyers or their clients—concerning violation of the code.[11]

Besides a code of ethics, there was another pressing interest to the membership: the manner of admission to the bar. By this time there were two means of admission: graduating from the University of Texas Law School or passing the state bar examination. In January 1917 the legal education committee, headed by Alex F. Weisberg, reported to the annual membership meeting that it had no problems with University of Texas graduates being automatically admitted to the bar, but it was highly critical of the state bar examination and recommended drastic changes in procedures.

The passing of the bar exam, being administered by each Court of Civil Appeals district since 1903, was said to be so simple that it was "little more than a travesty upon a so-called learned profession." A large number of men were being admitted to practice with "only a superficial and desultory reading of some of the prescribed books or after only a few months of cramming." Committee members had the figures to back up their comments. In the Sixth District (Texarkana) 634 applicants had taken the examination since 1903 and only fourteen had failed. In the Eighth District (El Paso) forty-nine applicants had taken the examination and only one had failed.

"No general education or previous mental discipline is required," the report read. "There is no uniformity in the character of examinations or strictness of grading among the various boards. Many of the examiners are inexperienced, either in the preparation or conduct of examinations. Many of them regard their duties as more or less perfunctory."

As a result of its study, the committee recommended abolishing the nine examining boards throughout the state and replacing them with a centralized examination prepared and conducted by a single state board consisting of five members to be appointed by the Supreme Court. Moreover, no one would be permitted to take the examination until he had satisfied the state board that he had passed the "necessary requirements for entrance to the collegiate department of the University of Texas." Candidates would be required to study law for a time equivalent to the twenty-seven months required at the University.[12]

The prescience and effectiveness of the committee's report was seen two years later when the Texas Legislature passed a statute based on its recommendations. The nine separate examining boards were replaced by a single State Board of Legal Examiners consisting of five members appointed by the Texas Supreme Court.

Another committee reporting at the same meeting was less successful. It recommended that the state's Court of Criminal Appeals be abolished and its work be assumed by a single Supreme Court consisting of nine judges.

THE STRUGGLE by women to become lawyers had been a difficult but persistent one in the latter part of the nineteeth century, and it was a struggle that continued into the early decades of the twentieth century. The nature of the cultural obstacles they faced was reflected in a concurring opinion by three justices of the U.S. Supreme Court in 1873 in *Bradwell v. The State,* in which the court upheld an Illinois statute barring women from the practice of law. "The civil law, as well as nature herself, has always recognized a wide difference in the respective spheres and destinies of man and woman," the high court reasoned. "Man is, or should be, woman's protector and defender. The natural and proper timidity and delicacy which belongs to the female sex evidently unfits it for many of the occupations of civil life."[13] The urge to achieve equality in all areas, not just in the profession of law could not be denied, however, and by 1900—two decades before suffrage—some three percent of the nation's lawyers were female. [14]

In Texas the first female to be admitted to the bar and the first to practice law was Hortense Sparks Ward (1875-1944) of Houston, whose introduction to the profession was typical for many of the early women lawyers. Mrs. Ward's husband was a lawyer, and she worked in the firm by day, served also as a court stenographer, and studied law at night. She was admitted to the Texas bar in 1910.[15]

Dallas' first woman lawyer came four years later when Lilian D. Aveilhe represented a plaintiff in a divorce case before Judge E.B. Muse in the 44th District Court, appearing on a Saturday afternoon, December 26, 1914. The *Daily Times Herald* reported the event under the headline, "Dallas Woman in Court as Lawyer; Starts New Era." Not only was Mrs. Aveilhe the first woman to appear in a Dallas district court, the *Daily Times Herald* believed that she possibly was the first to do so in Texas. (The newspaper was unaware of Mrs. Ward in Houston.) Previously, the newspaper recorded, Mrs. Aveilhe "recently" had won a verdict in a "small civil suit" in the Oak Cliff justice of the peace court. Her admission to the bar after examination in Dallas County also had occurred "recently." Mrs. Aveilhe's appearance in Judge Muse's court evidently caused quite a stir, for courthouse officials and spectators seemed to make a special point of being in the courtroom to witness the event. They noted with some sense of astonishment her "familiarity" with the statutes. While the opposing attorney made several objections to Mrs. Aveilhe's arguments, not once did Judge Muse sustain one. Mrs. Aveilhe "for the present" was sharing an office with William Hawley Atwell in the North Texas Building. [16]

Before her admission to the bar Mrs. Aveilhe had been a clerk in the law firm of Spellman & Murray in the Sumpter Building. She appears to have been the wife of Jules B. Aveilhe, a contract agent with Southwestern Telephone and Telegraph Co. This pioneer female attorney evidently did not remain in Dallas for long, for after her appearance in the 1915 City Directory, which still listed her office as being with Atwell at 506 North Texas Building, she disappears from view. [17]

The second female to be admitted to practice law in Dallas County became a familiar and prominent figure for many years. She was Hattie Leah Henenberg (1893-1974), a native of Ennis in Ellis County, who had gone to public schools in Dallas before being admitted to practice on October 20, 1916, in Texarkana upon certification by the State Board of Legal Examiners. [18] Much of her legal training likely came from her work as a stenographer for Albert Walker, an attorney working out of the Busch Building, but she also was a graduate of a program being operated by the downtown Young Men's Christian Association, the Dallas School of Law. [19] Miss Henenberg's early practice involved civil work, and during the first World War she was an associate member of the legal advisory board, assisting registrants to the draft in filling out their questionnaires. In 1924 she became director of the Dallas Bar

Association's new free legal aid bureau, and in the next year went on to be appointed by Texas Governor Pat M. Neff as one of three women to serve as special associate justices of the Texas Supreme Court. The three sitting male justices had to disqualify themselves because of a conflict of interest in a case involving the fraternal organization, Woodmen of the World, of which they all were associated.[20]

In 1932 she was a delegate to the Democratic National Convention in Chicago, where Franklin Delano Roosevelt was nominated for the first time. In the following years she served as an assistant secretary to the state Democratic Convention. Miss Henenberg held a number of public offices, including assistant attorney general of Texas, 1929-1930, and assistant district attorney of Dallas County, 1941-1947.[21]

Third of the female attorneys in Dallas was Frances Hexamer, who, like Mrs. Aveilhe and Miss Henenberg, had worked in a Dallas law firm and had read law there before being admitted to practice in 1918. Miss Hexamer practiced alone with an office at 811 Great Southern Life Building. She was active in the Professional Women's Club in Dallas, lobbied the legislature for equal treatment of women in hiring and promoting, and participated in the Young Lawyers Club.[22] Miss Hexamer, like Mrs. Aveilhe, also disappears from view.

These pioneer women and a few others had been admitted to the bar even before women became eligible to vote, but passage of the 19th Amendment in 1920 seemed to spur a number of other women to enter the profession. In 1925 the *Daily Times Herald* identified and portrayed eight "prominent women attorneys" practicing in the city: They were Hattie L. Henenberg, Sarah C. Menezes, Grace Fitzgerald, Hollie B. Martin, Isabell Abright, Helen Viglini, Edith Wilmans, and Sarah T. Hughes.

Sarah Cory Menezes (1886-1977) was the first woman to be appointed as an assistant U.S. attorney for the Northern District of Texas. She was named to the position in 1925 under U.S. Attorney Henry Zweifel, and she would continue in the position under two subsequent U.S. attorneys through June 1933. She would not be followed by another female in the position until

1961 when Martha Joe Stroud began a twenty-three year career in the office.[23] Miss Menezes was a Kansas native who been secretary to her lawyer-father there, had studied law at the University of Kansas, and moved to Texas with her husband, Major Harry Menezes. She was elected unanimously to membership in the Bar Association of Dallas on April 5, 1924.[24]

Grace Fitzgerald was admitted to practice on October 10, 1918, after having studied law in the offices of the U.S. Referee in Bankruptcy in Dallas. She went on to have a legal career that touched at least four decades in the city, being listed as late as 1951 in the Dallas Bar Association directory. Many of her clients were women. She told the *Times Herald* in 1925 that, contrary to common assumptions that many women preferred men to represent them, she had found that numerous women came to her *because* she was a woman. She also said she longed for the day when a woman would not be conspicuous when she argued a case in court. In 1926 she was the only female member of the Bar Association to have a committee assignment, hers being on the Membership Extension Committee.[25]

Hollie B. Martin had graduated from Dallas High School, attended Denton State Normal School, and then studied and graduated from the Jefferson Law School in Dallas. She was admitted to practice law in 1923. In 1925, the year she was elected to membership in the Bar Association, she was working in the credit department of a "large mercantile firm" in Dallas.[26]

Another native Dallasite and graduate of Jefferson Law School was Miss Isabell Abright, who was admitted to the bar in 1924. In 1925, the year she was elected to membership in the Bar Association on the same day as Mrs. Martin, she worked in the legal department of the Cotton Belt Railroad. Miss Abright, as was true for so many of the early women attorneys, joined the Business and Professional Women's Club and was also active in the Democratic Women of Dallas. For a while Miss Abright worked in a partnership with Hallie Harper, but in the years following World War II she was in a solo practice.[27]

Two of the women listed in the *Times Herald* article were sisters, Helen Marion Viglini (1880-1965) and Edith Therrell

Wilmans (1882-1966). The sisters had been reared in Louisiana but brought to Dallas as children in 1885 by their parents. Each of them achieved notable "firsts" in the state. Mrs. Viglini, who in 1917 was left with several small children when her husband died, was admitted to the bar on June 16, 1919. She early had a strong interest in criminal law, a field she had been introduced to when she became Dallas County's first woman assistant district attorney under Maury Hughes. Later, Mrs. Viglini would become the first woman in the state to argue a case before the Texas Supreme Court. She was elected by unanimous vote to membership in the Bar Association of Dallas on December 8, 1920, the first woman to appear in the official minutes as a member. (Attorneys were not eligible for membership in the Bar Association until two years after being admitted to the bar.) On the day she was elected, a toast entitled "Women and the Law" was offered at the meeting. Mrs. Viglini continued to practice law in Dallas until her retirement in 1963.[28]

Her sister, Edith Eunice Therrell Wilmans, achieved even greater prominence as the first female ever elected to the State Legislature, a deed accomplished in 1922. She was a virtual whirlwind of activity, and her rapid rise to prominence as a state-wide figure and crusader for women's rights makes it surprising that her name seems to have been forgotten in recent times. In her one term in the legislature Mrs. Wilmans campaigned for legislation for child support and child care and for the establishment of a district court of domestic relations for Dallas County. (Not until 1957 was the Domestic Relations Court established. Its name was changed in 1977 to the 301st Family District Court.) In 1924, instead of running for re-election, Mrs. Wilmans decided to campaign for governor, but did not win, and she lost again in 1926 in a second bid for the governor's mansion.[29]

Mrs. Wilmans was admitted to the bar in March 1918 after deciding to study at the YMCA's law classes because of her interest in Texas laws that restricted the rights of women. She was a founding member of the Dallas Equal Suffrage Association, a founder of the Dallas Housewives League, and a founder of the Democratic Women of Dallas County. She was elected president of the Democratic Women's Association of Texas. In June 1919 Mrs. Wilmans, still shy of the two-year minimum required for membership, urged Bar Association members to support the creation of a Dallas County District Court of Domestic Relations, but after a favorable motion to do so by F.M. Etheridge, a flurry of substitute motions effectively killed the request.[30] There is no record of when Mrs. Wilmans was elected to membership in the Bar Association, but she first appears in the minutes of November 25, 1922, as favoring a motion supporting the creation of two new civil district courts. Governor Pat Neff appointed Mrs. Wilmans to the all-woman State Supreme Court in 1925, but she was disqualified when it was discovered that she lacked by a few months the required seven years' legal experience. In 1935 Mrs. Wilmans retired to a farm in Jack County, conducted two unsuccessful campaigns for the 13th District congressional seat in 1948 and in 1951, returned to Dallas to live with her daughter in 1958 after a hip fracture, and died on March 21, 1966, at the age of 84.[31]

At the time of the *Times Herald* article in 1925, Mrs. Wilmans was clearly the most prominent of the eight women featured. However, the woman who ultimately made the most lasting mark and achieved an enduring national reputation was Sarah Tilghman Hughes (1896-1985). Born in Baltimore, Maryland, and educated at Goucher College with a degree in biology, Sarah Tilghman taught science in North Carolina for two years before deciding to enroll in the George Washington University Law School in Washington, D.C. While studying there she became a member of the Washington, D.C., police force and also married a Texan classmate, George Ernest Hughes. Upon graduation with LL.B. degrees in 1922, the couple decided to begin their legal careers in Dallas, and before doing so Sarah Hughes wrote letters to a number of firms in the city asking for a position. She received no answers, but George Hughes found a job with the Veterans Administration and the couple came to Dallas anyway. In Dallas Mrs. Hughes persisted in her search for employment with a law firm, but she met with resistance from every major firm in town. "It just seems like there are too many handicaps in the law profession for me," she wrote to her brother. "I'm too young, a woman and unknown in Dallas. Whether I will ever overcome those handicaps or not I do not know."[32]

Finally, the firm of Priest, Herndon, and Ledbetter agreed to provide free space for her in an unoccupied anteroom. It also agreed to refer some cases to her. Soon she became a member of the firm, and on April 5, 1924, was elected to the Bar Association of Dallas. Through Andrew Priest she became an instructor and secretary of the Jefferson Law School. Quickly becoming known in the city, she also joined numerous organizations, including the Business and Professional Women's Club, the Zonta Club, the League of Women Voters, and the American Association of University Women. In 1927 she was a member of the Bar Association's Membership Extension Committee.[33] During her public career Sarah T. Hughes would become widely known as a liberal Democrat who served not only as Texas' first female district judge but as a state repre-sentative, a federal judge, a nominee for vice president of the nation, and as the federal judge who in 1963 would swear in President Lyndon B. Johnson aboard Air Force One on a fateful day in Dallas.[34]

Indeed, as the *Times Herald* article in 1925 stated, "the legion of 'lady lawyers' " in Dallas was steadily advancing. Still, they were a novelty and their ability to practice law seemed surprising to many. "What makes it so uncomfortable for the skeptics who predicted dire things when they admitted women to the bar is that many of the women have made better attorneys than many men," said the newspaper, adding that they seemed to excel especially in closing arguments.[35]

When in 1926 the Bar Association on a rare occasion recognized its women members by turning over to them a luncheon program at the Adolphus Palm Gardens Room, it was Sarah C. Menezes who was placed in charge. Mrs. Menezes and the "several" ladies at the speakers' table presented a male speaker, E.M. Baker, a referee in bankruptcy, who spoke on "Similarity Between Bankruptcy and Probate Practice."[36]

Far more visible than Dallas' female lawyers, although auxiliary in nature, was the Lawyers Wives Club, an organization founded in 1926. This organization, now known as the Dallas Lawyers Auxiliary, became a prominent factor not only in the Bar Association but in the life of the city because of its many events. The idea to form a club especially for the wives of Dallas lawyers came from the president of the Bar Association, M.N. Chrestman, during a reception being held for members of the State Supreme Court, other appellate courts, and the Dallas judiciary. Chrestman asked Mrs. Kenneth Foree Sr. if she would not extend an invitation to the wives of Bar Association members to form an organization to "co-ordinate with and aid the Bar association." Mrs. Foree readily agreed and called for the first meeting at the Chrestman home on Country Club Circle on the afternoon of March 17, 1926. A large number of wives gathered there and heard Chrestman explain that it was just as essential for the lawyers' wives to form an association as it was for the men. Ninety-three charter members were announced at the first meeting. Mrs. Foree became the organization's first president, and meetings began to be held monthly, the early ones at various members' homes. One of the club's first major acts was to establish a scholarship fund for students. The Lawyers Wives Club frequently took over the chore of hosting special events such as banquets, providing musical entertainment, and sometimes they attended regular bar meetings. At the November 22, 1930, Bar Association meeting Tom Clark urged his fellow male bar members to "learn a lesson" from this "very active" association which was "accomplishing much good work."[37]

IT WAS, OF COURSE, growth and the promise of growth that had brought more and more lawyers to Dallas and made it a fine place to practice law. What local boosters once had called the "City of Splendid Possibilities" by now had become the "City of the Hour." Growth not only had brought commercial activity— and its accompaniment, litigation—it also had become a problem as old boundaries expanded and the city's character transformed willy-nilly. Between 1900 and 1913 Dallas' population almost tripled to more than 130,000 residents. Just as the legal system sought to bring order into the affairs of society, so did the need arise for planning to bring order into the city proper. In 1902 the president of Dallas' Civic Improvement League declared that there was "scarcely a more slovenly community in the United States than this city."[38] An effort to bring order into civic affairs already had been made in 1907 with the adoption of the commission form of municipal government, and, as he presented Dallas' first master plan in 1910, city planner George Kessler commented that "no apparent thought" had ever been given to the requirements for accommodating a growing city.[39]

While it was not incumbent upon the city's legal community to provide this particular form of guidance, the means to achieve stable and orderly neighborhoods did lie through the law—zoning laws in particular that could divide the city into designated commercial or business and residential neighborhoods. A first requirement here came in 1915 when the City of Dallas amended its charter to take advantage of a new state Home Rule law that granted municipalities self-government powers that were unique in the nation.[40] Laws passed by Home Rule municipalities took on the force of any statute passed by the state legislature, the only exception being that municipal law could not supersede state law.

Three months after a progressive new mayor, Henry Lindsley, who had been the motiving force behind the formation of the Civic Association, took office, the city passed in July 1915 its first zoning ordinances. Residential and business districts were established with the clear intent of protecting residential areas from commercial encroachment. No business could locate nearer than 300 feet to a residential area without consent of three-fourths of the property owners within a 300-foot radius. The legality of this ordinance came into question when John R. Spann purchased a corner lot at the intersection of Ross and Fitzhugh with the intention of building a warehouse. When building inspector H.J. Emmins, at the direction of street commissioner Otto Lang, denied Spann a permit to do so, Spann filed suit, contending that his private property rights were being denied. District Judge Kenneth Foree upheld the legality of the ordinance, and the Court of Civil Appeals upheld his ruling. Spann, represented by the firm of Lowrance and Bates, appealed to the Texas Supreme Court, and that court held in 1921 that zoning conducted under police powers violated the "natural right of property owners." The city's early efforts at zoning thus were invalidated, not to be realized until the mid-1920s when Dallas and Fort Worth lawmakers coordinated efforts to provide for state-sanctioned zoning.[41]

Another aspect of the city's zoning, an ordinance that segregated individual residential blocks by race, also was challenged in court. This ordinance forbade black citizens from living in a block designated as white and neither could whites live in black-designated blocks. One of the few Republican attorneys in Dallas, William Hawley Atwell, who had served fifteen years as U.S. Attorney for the Northern District of Texas before returning to private practice, challenged the ordinance in 1921 when he took on the case of Roby Williams, a black man who had moved to an all-white residential block in Oak Cliff and was brought to trial for his transgression. Atwell argued before City of Dallas Municipal Judge Felix D. Robertson—not yet but soon to be a self-proclaimed Klansman—that the segregation ordinance was unconstitutional because of a 1917 U.S. Supreme Court decision, *Buchanan v. Warely*. Nevertheless, Robertson upheld the validity of the ordinance. Williams was found guilty and fined $150. County Judge T.A. Work confirmed the decision on appeal. In January 1923 Atwell and Williams were denied a new trial, and in the next month President Warren G. Harding appointed Atwell to be a federal district judge, a position he would hold until he retired at the age of 87 while presiding over a case involving the desegregation of the Dallas Independent School District.[42]

A . B . N O R T O N, the Reconstructionist lawyer/editor, was not the only Dallas lawyer who became associated with the practice of journalism. One who followed him and became a leader in both professions was Tom Finty, Jr., (1867-1929) of *The Dallas Morning News*. Finty played a key role in 1914 winning for the city one of its most important economic coups of all time—designation as one of twelve regional headquarters for the Federal Reserve Bank. Finty also developed a state-wide system of gathering election results which formed the basis for the Texas Election Bureau. He published a number of brochures on the law, including *Anti-Trust Legislation in Texas* (1915), *Texas Homestead Exemption Law* (1918), and *Penitentiary System of Texas* (1909). He also served as legal counsel and an editorial executive of the A.H. Belo Corporation.

Finty had not been drawn to the study of law until he was nearly 30 years of age, by which time he had had experience as a general store clerk, telegraph operator, railroad station agent, bookkeeper, journalist, and, from 1892 to 1894, court reporter. In this latter occupation he became attracted to law, began studying it part-time, and was admitted to the bar in 1894. In the same year he began working in Galveston as a newspaper reporter, and from 1901 to 1914 was political editor in Dallas for both the *Galveston News* and its northern branch, the *Dallas Morning News*.[43]

It was Finty's wide political acquaintances that permitted him to play an important part in winning for Dallas the coveted designation as a regional headquarters for the Federal Reserve Bank. The city's bankers, the Chamber of Commerce, the *Dallas Morning News,* and various civic leaders had been working hard and meeting often in strategy sessions to achieve this goal, but perhaps the most important breakthrough came when it was learned that a member of the site selection committee, U.S. Postmaster General A.S. Burleson, was coming to Texas. Finty was a long-time friend of Burleson's, and on the basis of this friendship he and banker J. Howard Audrey were dispatched to St. Louis to intercept Burleson, board his train for the ride into Texas, and present to him Dallas' case in a comfortable setting. They obtained a spacious drawing room, invited him to to leave his modest Pullman car and join them in their superior quarters for relaxation and conversation. As the train headed south towards Texas they regaled him with the merits of Dallas as the best site for the new regional bank.

The exercise, carried out in deep secrecy with an elaborate secret code devised for communications, was successful. When the selection of Dallas was announced on April 2, 1914, its significance was summed up by Dallas Trust and Savings in a huge newspaper advertisement: "It means a great increase in population. It also means a great expansion of our commercial and industrial interests. It means that many new and important enterprises will seek a home in Dallas. In short, Dallas is on the eve of an era of prosperity seldom if ever experienced by another city."[44]

A Surge of Maturity

⌘

Chapter Eight

JUST AS THE COURTHOUSE itself no longer was the focal point for so many of the town's lawyers in these early decades of the twentieth century, no longer was the courthouse square the center of town. As we have seen, attorneys were moving away from the courthouse and its surrounding walk-up offices in favor of fancy new uptown buildings. This transition coincided with the development of the business corporation, particularly banks, railroads, and insurance and petroleum companies, all of which had major presences in Dallas, as a commanding influence in the nation's economy. Courtroom work no longer dominated the lawyer's daily routine; the Bar Association of Dallas had taken to meeting regularly in big hotels instead of the courthouse.

The commercial life of downtown Dallas had been experiencing this gravitational pull away from the town square since 1872 when the H&TC Railroad stubbornly placed its tracks and terminal not adjacent to the courthouse square but almost a mile away (on a route that many decades later would be used for Central Expressway). And when the city fathers decided a few years later to construct a new city hall, they put it on Akard Street, midway between the courthouse and the H&TC tracks. Adding to the concentration of activities in this newly emerged primary section of downtown was the ornate Oriental Hotel, opening in 1893 at the southeast corner of Akard and Commerce, followed in 1912 by the new Adolphus Hotel at the northwest corner of the same intersection. Even further uptown at Harwood Street was the new City Hall, also finished in 1912, and the

Dallas Public Library, built in 1901 at Harwood and Commerce. The erection of the magnificent Magnolia Petroleum Building just across from the Adolphus and Oriental hotels in 1921 settled the matter for certain. The intersection of Elm and Akard streets seemed to be the center of town. Dallas indeed was no longer a town whose activities centered around a square dominated by a courthouse.

One of those lawyers whose practice no longer revolved around the courthouse was Maurice Locke. Even before the turn of the century Locke had started specializing in insurance law, and in 1902 he twice argued cases before the U.S. Supreme Court in behalf of insurance companies. After his son Eugene P. Locke joined his practice in 1904 the two continued to represent some of the nation's largest insurance companies.[1]

When the Robertson Act of 1907 was enacted into state law, many companies with headquarters outside Texas protested and withdrew from the state rather than to comply with what they considered to be a punitive measure. The firm of Locke & Locke unsuccessfully sought on behalf of their clients to forestall the enactment of the law. Although unsuccessful, the Lockes gained great visibility throughout the state for their efforts. As new insurance companies were formed to fill the void left by the departing firms and as other firms returned to the state, Locke & Locke took on even more insurance clients.[2]

So did other law firms in Dallas respond to the need of new insurance companies for corporate counsel. Listings of corporate clients by Dallas law firms in the *Martindale-Hubbell Legal Directory* during these early decades of the 1900s showed more insurance clients than those of any other industry. In addition to Locke & Locke, the firm later known as Thompson & Knight developed a large practice in insurance law during its many years as the city's largest law firm.

The Praetorian Building, a fourteen-story structure at Main and Stone streets completed in 1909 as the home office of the Praetorian National Insurance Order, gave vivid evidence of the emergence of the industry in Dallas. Construction of the even taller Southwestern Life Insurance Co. building at Main and Akard streets in 1913 confirmed insurance as one of the dominant economic forces in town. By the 1930s Dallas would be fourth among all American cities in the volume of life insurance handled by its companies.[3]

The Magnolia Building, soaring home of the Magnolia Petroleum Co. (at twenty-nine floors the tallest building in the South), signified another powerful new force in Dallas and in the state that would spawn volumes of business and new legal specialties to represent the oil and gas industry. The company's origin lay in the accidental discovery of oil in Corsicana in 1894. It was the first major discovery of oil west of the Mississippi River, and it was the harbinger of an industry that would become so important to the state and to Dallas. By 1920, a decade before the discovery in 1930 of the vast East Texas oil field, Dallas already had become a center of activity for the industry because of its proximity to a number of oil fields being developed in North and Central Texas. A Chamber of Commerce publication in 1922 declared the city to be headquarters for thousands of oil men, "lease-hounds," and organizations that were prospecting for oil or gas.[4] In fact, it was a wildcatter operating out of Dallas, C.M. "Dad" Joiner, who discovered in 1930 in East Texas the world's richest oil field. As a result of this discovery and because of its proximity to Dallas, oil rather than cotton became the driving force for the city's economy. It was a complex industry requiring far greater reliance on legal skills than did growing and selling cotton.

Banking, an important force in the city, continued to prosper, especially in light of the petroleum industry's lending requirements for exploration and development. City National Bank and American Exchange National Bank were formidable presences along Main Street, and in 1920 the Federal Reserve Bank moved into a commanding new structure at Akard and Wood streets.

EVEN THE appearance and character of the courthouse square was changing. Across the street from the courthouse itself at the northeast corner of Main and Houston streets, a new red-brick, eight-story structure that was combination courthouse and jail opened in May 1915. It was said to be the finest jail and court building in the entire nation, "as clean and sanitary as any private home."[5] Marble walls, marble stairways, and modern furniture and fixtures gave the building a sumptuous quality that bedazzled curious spectators, some 25,000 of whom toured the building on the weekend before it opened. The interest in the new courthouse surprised officials, who had expected a far smaller crowd. To accommodate the curious they extended tour hours. Built at a cost of $675,000 and designed by H.A. Overbeck, the Dallas County Criminal Courts Building provided quarters on the first floor for the sheriff's office, the county attorney's office, and the justice court rooms. On its second floor were the two criminal district courts, jury quarters, and private offices for the judges. On the upper six floors were the jail cells. It was a "skyscraper jail" from which escape was deemed all but impossible.[6]

Escape-proof though the skyscraper jail was believed to be, this soon proved not to be the case. Only a month after the building opened, two 16-year-old youths, having been confined there for two weeks pending petty theft charges, made a daring escape. In the dark of night they tied together sheets and blankets into a make-shift rope, removed a grate from a jail window on the sixth floor, slid seventy-two feet down the side of the wall to the ground, and raced to freedom into the Trinity River bottoms. "A break of the improvised rope would have meant certain death," *The Dallas Morning News* recorded in astonishment at the deed. Escape from the building, the *News* article continued, had been considered "practically impossible."[7] In years to come other escapes would be made from the building, and the early hopes that it would be escape-proof were forgotten.

A few years later the main courthouse itself was transformed in appearance. The distinctive tower, holding a clock with four faces and a three-ton bell which sounded the hour of the day for miles around, was dismantled in 1919—seven years after the condemned killer Burrell Oates had predicted its demise. Removal was ordered by county commissioners because the pealing of the bell was so loud that the building's structural integrity seemed jeopardized by the vibrations. The new look was a jolt to the eyes—it left a courthouse that was much lower and squattier than the familiar version. It had become the building that would become so familiar to residents as "the Old Red Courthouse."

Reaffirming the continued importance to Dallas of the courthouse area was the opening in 1916 of a new Union Terminal just a block away down Houston Street. The gleaming, glazed white-brick railroad station served as a single train depot for passengers. It consolidated into a single facility the five separate stations that previously had represented a great obstacle for those transferring from one line to another. In an age when travel by rail was dominant, the Union Terminal and its passenger service brought a constant flow of activity to the entire courthouse area.

In the World War I era, many of the city's lawyers were in the military. Bar Association minutes for June 28, 1919, reported that "due to the absence of so many of our younger members in the war and due to war conditions, no meeting of the association was held last January."[8]

By the 1920s the firm of Locke & Locke had a handful of attorneys, but there was no doubt as to who was in charge. Eugene P. Locke had taken over from his late father with an iron hand. In a memo addressed "To Each Member of the Office," he advised them that he was going on vacation. "I cannot enjoy the time in which I am away unless I know that the office is running as usual," he said. Then he directed the staff as follows: "The office must not have a lazy, slouchy, do-nothing appearance during my absence. No one who enters the office should find at any hour of the day anyone lounging at the entrance or at any of the other desks in the office, chewing gum, eating candy, or reading newspapers. Regular hours should be observed by everybody in the office during my absence, just the same as when I am here. Though there may not be as much work to do, there nevertheless is plenty of work of various kinds to be done if one only tries to find it."[9]

AS THE PRACTICE of law matured in the city, more and more examples could be seen of sons following their fathers into the legal profession. Their fathers, in effect, had gambled their professional careers that Dallas would become a large and important city and a good place to practice law and to raise a family, and their gambles had paid off. If these second-generation lawyers, inspired by their fathers' successes, did not exactly start their practices with silver spoons in their mouths, they at least enjoyed certain advantages that were a far cry from what almost all their fathers had experienced in earlier days. Fathers tended to be generalists; their sons, more and more, were specialists. And, of course, there were brothers and nephews and other relatives, too, who entered the profession and sometimes the same firm. Among these father-son teams were Colonel William L. Crawford and his sons William L. Jr. and M.L.; J.C. Muse and sons J.C. Jr. and John B.; E.B. Muse and Cavin; Judge John L. Henry and William T.; William H. Clark and his three sons, William H. Jr., Tom C., and Robert L.; and still others. An African-American attorney, Daniels Mason (1872-1915) had two sons who followed him into practice. Roger Mason and D.B. Mason both graduated from Howard University in 1922 and began practicing law in Dallas. Many more father-son examples would arise in the years to come as the profession continued to grow.

An early father-son example could be seen in William C. Holland, who had emigrated to Dallas from Tennessee in the 1870s, and his son, William Meredith Holland. In his new Texas home the senior Holland achieved prominence as a lawyer and in municipal politics, serving three terms as alderman in 1878, 1889, and 1890. Holland especially had been active in the organized and seemingly endless effort to bring navigation to the Trinity River.

In 1907 his son, William Meredith Holland, was appointed judge of the newly created County Court of Dallas County, At Law, a position he held until late 1910 when he resigned to campaign for the office of mayor. He was elected mayor in 1911 and re-elected in 1913. Holland held the distinction of being Dallas' first native-born mayor, and at the age of 38 he also was the youngest up to that date to hold the office. During his first term Holland oversaw the construction of a new city hall at Main, Harwood and Commerce (where the Dallas Police Department now has been headquartered for many years), the start-up of municipal garbage collection, the initiation of work toward the new Union Terminal Building, and the installation of a sewage disposal plant.

Another noted example of Dallas father-son attorneys was General Alfred Prior Wozencraft (1859-1917) and Francis Wilson Wozencraft (1892-1966). Their experiences were not dissimilar from those of the Hollands. General Wozencraft had been admitted to the bar in Arkadelphia, Arkansas, in 1882, but the possibility of a more lucrative practice in a growing city brought him to Dallas that same year. Eight years later he had become Dallas' city attorney, an office he would hold for another eight years. (It was during this period that he took a young and penniless but promising Garland man, Hatton Sumners, under his wing and permitted him to study law in his office, thus launching Sumners on a prominent political career.) Wozencraft served as city attorney until 1898 when Governor Charles A. Culberson appointed him adjutant general of the state, a job which earned him his title of "General." After further service as brigadier general of the Second Brigade of the Texas Volunteer Guard, he resigned in 1909 to become attorney general for the emerging and prosperous public utility firm, Southwestern Telegraph and Telephone Co.[10]

During his service as city attorney, his son Francis was born to Wozencraft and his wife in 1892. Francis, or Frank as he would be called, graduated from Dallas High School in 1909, and earned a bachelor of arts and a law degree from the University of Texas in 1913 and 1914. As a fledgling attorney, Frank Wozencraft joined his father's legal department at Southwestern Telephone. With the U.S. entry into World War I, young Wozencraft became commanding officer of a Dallas infantry unit, the "Grays," and saw service on the front in Europe. After the war and fresh out of the Army, having just returned to the city of his birth, Wozencraft found himself nominated for mayor of Dallas.

Wozencraft, only 26 years of age in 1919, was the candidate of a "fusion" ticket of the Citizens Association and the Democratic Party in a campaign that saw a dramatic split in the ranks of the dominant Citizens Association. Wozencraft had served as an aide to Dallas' prominent businessman and civic leader Henry Lindsley during the war in Paris, and when Lindsley himself declined the Citizens Association entreaty for another term as mayor, he evidently recommended Wozencraft instead.

In the campaign, in which he faced the incumbent mayor, Joe E. Lawther, Wozencraft was criticized as the candidate of privilege, a man "born with a silver spoon." Wozencraft won in a race described by the *Daily Times Herald* as "one of the hottest political campaigns in the history of Dallas." The "boy mayor" thus became only the second native-born Dallasite to hold that office, and at the age of twenty-six he was said to be the youngest mayor of any major American city.[11]

No matter how divisive the young Wozencraft's election had been, he became one of the city's most successful mayors. Continuing the progressive platform that Henry Lindsley had initiated during his 1915-17 term, Wozencraft nominated women for several appointive offices, arranged to remove the now menacing T&P railroad tracks from Pacific Avenue, prevented a proposed rate hike by the power and light company, appointed a committee of women to examine local milk prices, and joined police officers and firemen as they performed their duties. In 1919, knowing that the Army's use of Love Field for training military pilots was nearing its end and recognizing the importance of aviation for the city's future, he visited Washington, D.C., to investigate the possibility of securing that facility for the city.[12]

Near the end of his term, sixty-four of the state's mayors, meeting in Dallas, urged that "on the basis of his record" Wozencraft be nominated the next governor of the state of Texas. Wozencraft pointed out that this was impossible—he was two years away from the constitutionally mandated minimum age of 30. After his one rather spectacular term as mayor, Wozencraft declined to stand for re-election. Instead, he returned to private practice with the firm of Leake, Henry, Wozencraft, and Frank and began handling the Texas affairs of Radio Corporation of America, a new company organized on the eve of the broadcasting communications explosion of the 1920s. In 1931 he left Dallas to join RCA's corporate headquarters on the 53rd floor of the new RCA Building in New York City, officing on the same floor with David Sarnoff, and eventually being named general counsel and vice president.[13]

William H. Clark, who had been the youngest attorney ever elected president of the Texas Bar Association, was joined in his law firm in 1922 by his son Thomas C. Clark (1899-1977). But the younger Clark did not stay long. He gained appointment from the county commissioners as the civil district attorney for Dallas County, and in 1932 entered private practice with his colleague, William S. McCraw, who had just completed five years as district attorney. McCraw soon itched for public office again, and in 1934 with Clark's help he campaigned across the state and won election as the Texas attorney general. Clark also had an undeniable urge for public service. In 1937 he left Dallas for Washington, D.C., to work in the U.S. Attorney General's office. Less than a decade later he would hold that office himself, and soon thereafter he would become the first U.S. Supreme Court justice from Texas.[14] (For more on Tom C. Clark see Chapter 12.)

DAILY LIFE MOVED at an increasingly faster pace in the nation and also in Dallas during the 1920s. Modern times had begun. Radio for the first time provided an instant, nation-wide communications system. The omnipresent automobile, most evident in Henry Ford's black Model T, was chasing the horse and buggy from city streets. Movies with characters who actually could be heard talking were replacing silent films in the theaters that dotted Elm Street.

The city, forty-second in population in the nation after the 1920 census, ranked consistently higher than that in the value of buildings under construction. Faith in business, in the economic prosperity it was bringing, and in the efficient, business-like approach to all activities was at an all-time high. Similarly, a move toward business-like efficiency and expansion into new areas of endeavor also marked the activities of the Bar Association of Dallas as its membership expanded from 127 members in 1920 to 428 in 1926, with dozens of new members being added annually.[15]

No longer was the organization a rather loose confederation of attorneys whose primary business seemed to be a concern over perpetually crowded courts and the preparation of finely honed memorials for departed members (although those concerns certainly continued). Regular luncheons with prepared programs and speakers—sometimes of national renown—with defined topics were held in banquet rooms of the finest downtown hotels; auxiliary groups were formed for young lawyers and the wives of lawyers; women not only had begun practicing law in the courts but now were being elected to Bar Association membership; a successful drive was mounted to get a new courthouse records building; a full-time secretary was hired for the organization at $25 a month; a grievance committee was hearing complaints and in some occasions recommending disbarment proceedings; and a myriad of other activities important to the well-being of the entire city took place in an association which by 1926 was spending about $2,500 a year on its activities. Communications with its members was and would continue to be a priority. In 1929 the association authorized publication of a short-lived, monthly, magazine-style publication, *The Dallas Law Journal*, which carried news of the association. W.H. Reid was chairman of the publications committee which oversaw the magazine.[16]

For some reason, the 1920s was a decade in which death came to an unusually high number of pioneer lawyers who had provided leadership in the legal community for many years. Colonel W.L. Crawford, Maurice E. Locke, Alfred P. Wozencraft, John M. McCoy, Francis M. Etheridge, Joseph E. Cockrell, and Kenneth Foree were among them. Truly a new generation of leaders was emerging.

One of the most prominent attorneys in the city was Robert E. Lee Saner (1871-1938), who in 1924 was elected the first Texas lawyer ever to be president of the American Bar Association. Saner, born on a farm in Arkansas, worked as a newsboy, janitor, railroad agent, and teacher, studied at Searcy College and Vanderbilt University, and in 1896 earned his LL.B. degree from the University of Texas School of Law. He devoted much of his legal practice to business and corporate affairs, and although he was an outstanding orator his appearances in the courtroom were rare. From the beginning of his practice he devoted much attention to bar association work. From 1920 through 1937 Saner served as chairman of the board of editors of the American Bar Association Journal. As chairman of the ABA Citizenship Committee he initiated public speaking contests in 1923 and 1924 on subjects pertaining to the Constitution that were conducted in about 13,000 high schools in the nation. President Calvin Coolidge asked him to preside over the finals in Washington, D.C., for which members of the U.S.. Supreme Court were judges. In 1925 he presided over the first national intercollegiate oratorical contest in Los Angeles, and later he established an endowment for an annual oratorical contest at Southern Methodist University.[17]

For thirty years, from 1900 to 1930, Saner served as Land Agent for the University of Texas, an assignment that required him to be familiar with the details of the hundreds of thousands of acres of land owned by the permanent fund of the university in West Texas. This vast amount of property returned millions of dollars to the university, making it one of the nation's wealthiest institutions of higher education. In 1926 Saner filed a suit in behalf of the university to recover disputed oil royalties on the property, and he won a judgment of $1 million, said to be the largest judgment recovered up to that time in Texas with the exception of the Waters-Pierce Oil Company case.[18]

THE MOVE IN RECENT decades to provide and also to require better legal training for lawyers continued. Three schools of law, with varying degrees of success, attempted to establish a credible presence in the city. First was the Jefferson School of Law, founded as a proprietary school by Andrew J. Priest, a Dallas attorney and resident of the city since childhood. His first class in 1919 consisted of just three students, but enrollment steadily increased during the decade, and until the Depression darkened in the 1930s the school's future seemed bright. By 1930 Jefferson had its own three-story building in downtown Dallas and a Fort

Worth branch. Its curriculum had expanded to include not only law but also a School of Commerce and Accounts and a School of Secretarial Training. Its progress was recognized on March 4, 1930, when the Supreme Court of Texas placed Jefferson on its list of approved law schools, only the fourth such institution in the state to be so recognized. This meant that a student who graduated from Jefferson was automatically granted a license to practice law without having to take a bar examination. In the fall of 1931 Jefferson's enrollment included forty-nine senior students, twenty-one of them in the School of Law, including two women. Completion of their studies would lead to the LL.B. degree.

By then Jefferson's law faculty had grown to ten attorneys, all of whom presumably continued their law practices while they taught on a part-time basis: N.R. Crozier Jr. (whose father was superintendent of the Dallas public schools), Hawkins Golden, J. Henry King, Russell Allen, Owen George, Robert Lee Guthrie, Richard J. Dixon, M.B. Solomon, T.C. Burroughs, and Lt. Col. A.C. Burnett. Priest himself continued to practice law at the same time he oversaw his college, for he was chief prosecutor for District Attorney William S. McGraw, whose term of office was 1927 to 1932. Beginning in 1931 Jefferson University, as it now was called, occupied a new building at Harwood and Jackson streets with the words, "Jefferson University," engraved boldly over the front door. Besides the Sigma Delta Kappa legal fraternity, Jefferson even had a football team and a baseball team which played such institutions as North Texas Teachers College, Paris Junior College, and Hillsboro Junior College. Its fight song, played to the tune of "Washington and Lee," went like this:

Oh! We are jolly students of the law;
We have the best old crowd you ever saw.
We have high ideals of law and right.
and for these things we will always fight;
The spirit of Jefferson guides us all along;
We will uphold the right and denounce the wrong,
For Law and Justice in this land,
We jolly students always stand.

Jefferson University's tenure as a Dallas institution of higher learning was bright but brief. An unsuccessful struggle for students during the Depression of the 1930s brought about its demise. Priest resumed his work as a prosecutor, working under District Attorney Andrew Patton, 1937 to 1940, and he later unsuccessfully campaigned for Dallas County District Attorney.[19]

The other two institutions offering programs in law in this period both opened their doors in 1925. The Dallas School of Law, established as an evening program by the Young Men's Christian Association, operated out of the YMCA building on Ervay Street in downtown Dallas. Its evening classes were popular since they allowed those with full-time jobs to study law after work. But maintaining high standards was difficult, and while there continued to be sufficient numbers of students, in 1938 the Dallas School of Law united with the other institution that had started offering classes in 1925, the one that emerged as the dominant one in the city and the one that gained national stature—Southern Methodist University's School of Law.[20]

In this successful venture the Bar Association of Dallas played an integral role without which it seems unlikely that the law school could have been established until years later after the Depression and World War II. Former Bar Association President Joseph E. Cockrell was most influential in founding the SMU Law School. Besides his keen participation in the Bar Association, Cockrell was also active as a trustee of Southern Methodist University. In 1925, while serving as chairman of SMU's board of trustees, Cockrell argued that no university could achieve first-rank status without the presence of a law school. SMU, as an institution founded and supported by the Methodist church, already had a strong academic presence and a well-planned, handsome campus in University Park even though classes had begun there only in 1915. As early as 1919 mention had been made of establishing a law school at SMU.[21] Finally, at Cockrell's urging, SMU President C.C. Selecman agreed, and on February 10, 1925, he asked the board of trustees for permission to authorize one. The board agreed unanimously with the understanding that money for it would be raised outside SMU's regular budget.[22]

Only three days after SMU's decision, Bar Association President Charles D. Turner and a committee of his choosing met with SMU's executive committee to discuss the matter. A second meeting followed on February 18. It was agreed that the Bar Association of Dallas would give full support to the law school, and at the May 9 meeting Judge Cockrell pledged that the school would be a "model school, based on standards laid down by the American Bar Association for associated law schools." Cockrell asked Bar Association members to underwrite the salaries of two full-time faculty members for the first two years.[23]

Turner appointed a committee composed of C.W. Starling as chairman and Rhodes S. Baker and Judge S.P. Sadler as members to advise the university and work with Cockrell on the project. Cockrell, acting dean of the law school until a permanent one could be hired, led the fund-raising drive for the school. He leaned heavily on his friends in the Bar Association for both monetary donations and law books for the library.

Surely no law school of such stature was ever started with such a short time for planning. Classes began in the fall of 1925 with a total of twenty first-year students, all men. Two faculty members hastily recruited were William Alexander Rhea and Robert B. Holland. Rhea, who had practiced law in Dallas between 1895 and 1917, had been teaching law for the past six years at the University of Texas School of Law. While in practice in Dallas he had served as counsel in drawing up the incorporation papers for the town of Highland Park. Holland, a practicing attorney with the firm of Touchstone, Wight, Gormley & Price, taught on a part-time basis until 1928. A second member from Holland's firm, Hobert Price, joined the faculty in 1926. Additional beginning classes were admitted in 1926 and 1927, giving the school a three-year program. In 1927 it was placed on the approved list of the American Bar Association. Two years later it was admitted to membership in the Association of American Law Schools.[24]

n N. Bryan, a
yer, founded
las when he
led on a bluff
the Trinity
er at what is
ay Dealey
za. (1)

This courthouse was built in 1857 at the site of today's Old Red Courthouse at a place designated by John Neely Bryan. (2)

handsome new courthouse, made of limestone, was completed in 1874. The Dallas y directory of 1875 saluted the courthouse as the finest and most substantial public ilding in the state. A large courtroom occupied the entire second floor. (3)

John C. McCoy, the first full-time practicing lawyer in Dallas, was a powerful force in the young community. (4)

By about 1880 McCoy's success as an attorney was suggested by his fine frame house on Commerce Street. (5)

The Old Red Courthouse, shown here as it appeared in the late 1930s, was opened i 1892. In front of it is the tiny log cabin that for years was believed to be John Neely Bryan's first home in Dallas. Just visible at the right is the corner of the small fireproof building constructed in the 1870s to hold county records. It later was torn down. (6)

John J. Good, left, first president of the Dallas Bar Association, 1873-1875. (7)

A.H. Field, right, president, 1878-1880. (8)

W.B. Gano, left, president, 1891-1900. (9)

John L. Henry, right, president, 1907-1908. (10)

F.M. Etheridge, left, president, 1916-1917. (11)

Nelson Phillips, right, president, 1933. (12)

Deputies of the Dallas County Sheriff's Department, posing outside the Old Red Courthouse in about 1910, were in a stage of transition—the old days of horses and horse-drawn carriages were about to yield to the new "horseless carriages." (13)

William Hawley Atwell, left, moved to the Dallas area as a child in the 1870s. He was a life-long Republican who was appointed a federal district judge by President Warren G. Harding in 1923. (14)

Harry P. Lawther, right, was president of the Dallas Bar Association in 1929. He was a leader in both local and state bar activities. (15)

sea of padded chairs awaited spectators in an Old Red Courthouse courtroom. (16)

1926 the center of town was far removed from the courthouse area. Most lawyers had ved uptown, too, as their need for frequent visits to the courthouse diminished. (17)

In 1935 Sarah T. Hughes became the state's first woman district judge. In 1961 President Kennedy appointed her to be the state's first woman federal district judge. (18)

Woodall Rodgers, four-time Dallas mayor and Bar Association president in 1937. (19)

D.A. Frank, Bar Association president in 1936, started the weekly clinics. (2

Glenn Turner served as president of the Bar Association in 1939. (21)

Paul Carrington was president of the Bar Association in 1940. (22)

Henry W. Strasburger was president of the Bar Association in 1955. (23)

Judge Joe B. Brown swears in a shirt-sleeved jury in the summer of 1951 in his County Criminal Court No. 1. The occasion was noteworthy as the first time summer jury trials were held in the mid-July to mid-September period. (24)

Two Dallas attorneys played key roles in the Nuremberg war criminal trials. Robert G. Storey, standing at the podium at right, was deputy prosecutor under U.S. Supreme Court Justice Robert H. Jackson. George E. Seay, seated at left in the Army uniform, was in charge of Section VI in compiling evidence against Nazi organizations. (25)

In the 1950s Louise Raggio was the only female prosecutor in the district attorney's office. She and her husband later established their own firm. Mrs. Raggio became a specialist in family law. She was inducted into the Texas Women's Hall of Fame for her accomplishments in this area. Here she is seen in 1952 with her children. (26)

allace H. Savage was one of the many young attorneys who returned to Dallas after
erving in World War II and assumed important civic and political roles. Savage was
ayor of the city from 1949 to 1951, and afterwards he served as chairman of the
emocratic Party's state executive committee. (27)

t. Atty. Henry M. Wade, seated, second from left, confers with staff members. Wade
d office from 1951 to 1986, longer than anyone in the county's history. He became
ely known as one of the nation's most successful district attorneys. (28)

Former Congressman Hatton Sumners (seated, dark suit) retired to an apartmen
at SMU's School of Law. Here, outside the dean's office in about 1955, he is sur
rounded by law students and Professor Moss Wimbish, seated beside him. (29)

SMU's Law School quadrangle, marked by this handsome monument to the
study of law, was brought to a completion in 1970 with construction of the
Underwood Law Library, from where this photograph was taken. (30)

Barefoot Sanders was appointed by President John F. Kennedy in 1961 to be U.S. Attorney for the Northern District. President Jimmy Carter appointed him a U.S. District judge in 1979. (31)

ounty Judge W.L. (Lew) Sterrett, left, gives the oath of office to Dean Gauldin, appointed st judge of County Criminal Court No. 2 in 1951. Judge Sterrett was the county's chief dministrative officer from 1949 through 1974. Judge Gauldin served until 1969. (32)

The George L. Allen Sr. Courts Building, opened in 1966 and named after the former Dallas city councilman and justice of the peace, provided a gleaming contrast to the Old Red Courthouse, its neighbor at the right. (33)

Just over a block from where President Kennedy was assassinated in 1963, citizens of Dallas erected a memorial (right) in his honor. The memorial, designed by Philip Johnson presented a pleasing contrast to its historic neighbor, the Old Red Courthouse. (34)

H. Louis Nichols, Bar Association president in 1963, visited Lee Harvey Oswald at the city jail to inquire about is need for an attorney. Nichols also as instrumental in bringing about the integration of he Dallas Bar Association. (35)

W.J. Durham was lead attorney in some of the most noted civil rights cases in the city and state. (36)

ouis A. Bedford Jr., one of the first African-merican members of the Bar Association, as named the organization's "Trial Lawyer the Year" for 1998. (37)

Royce West, attorney and state senator representing District 23. (38)

John L. Hauer, Bar Association president in 1981 and author of a history of Dallas lawyers and the legal profession entitled *Finest Kind!* (39)

In 1976 Jerry Jordan alerted fellow Bar Association board members to the possibility of acquiring the Belo mansion a its new headquarters. (40)

William E. Collins was chairman of the Dallas Bar Foundation from 1978 to 1982. (41)

For his work in helping acquire and renovate the Belo mansion as headquarters for the Bar Association, Robert Thomas earned a nickname: "Father of the Belo mansion." (42)

At left, a detail of the columns of the Belo mansion. (43)

Belo mansion on Ross Avenue, home of the Dallas Bar Association since 1979. (44)

To commemorate the Dallas Bar Association's 100th anniversary, members commissioned this statue of Lady Justice, blindfolded with sword and scales, and placed it at the entrance to the George L. Allen Sr. Courts Building. Separate markers acknowledged each of the six sovereign nations of which Texas had been a part. (45)

Henry D. Schlinger, right, president of the Bar Association in 1972, passes the gavel to his successor in office, John L. Estes. (46)

The impressive entrance to the Crowley Courts Building, a part of the new Justice Center at Commerce Street and Industrial Boulevard. In this building, opened in 1989, are located all the criminal courts in Dallas County as well as office space for the district attoney, sheriff, and other county agencies. (47)

Spencer Relyea was president of the Dallas Bar Association in 1989, and chairman of the Dallas Bar Foundation in 1976-1977 and 1995-1996. His wife Nancy served as a president of the Dallas Lawyers Wives Club. (48)

Vincent W. Perini, president of the Bar Association in 1986, in the late 1970s led the drive for improved courthouse facilities at the Justice Center. (49)

Harriet E. Miers became in 1985 the fi woman president of the Bar Associatic In 1992 she was elected the first wom president of the State Bar of Texas. (5

Elizabeth A. Lang-Miers, third woman president of the Bar Association, held office in 1998. (51)

Pablo Alvarado, president of the Mex can-American Bar Association, reflecte the growing number of minority attorney since the 1970s. (52)

. Alex Bickley, city attorney for the City of
allas from 1965 to 1976, became especially
:tive in civic affairs afterwards through his
ork for the Citizens Council. (53)

Jerry Buchmeyer did not give
up his folksy style after President Carter appointed him to be
a federal judge in 1979. In 1983
American Lawyer named him
the best federal judge in the 5th
Circuit. (54)

Morris Harrell has been president
of the Bar Association, the State
Bar of Texas, the American Bar
Association, and the American
College of Trial Lawyers. His
contributions to law earned him the
American Bar Association's 1998
ABA Medal for rendering "conspicu-
ous service in the cause of Ameri-
can jurisprudence." (55)

When the lawyer/frontiersman John Neely Bryan settled on a high bluff of the Trinity River in 1841 with the idea of founding a town, he surely never would have envisioned a setting such as this. Bryan designated the block now occupied by the Old Red Courthouse (the building with turrets immediately right of center) as the site for a courthouse, and that area remains today the center for county, state and federal courtrooms in Dallas County. In this view is visible, left to right, the Crowley Courts Building in the immediate foreground, then the Records Building Annex, the Dallas County Criminal Courts Building, the Old Red Courthouse, the Earle Cabell Federal Building (which houses federal courts), and at top right the George L. Allen Sr. Courts Building. (56)

Photo Credits

The library, housed in the basement of Dallas Hall beneath two classrooms allotted to the law school, reached nearly 7,000 volumes by 1926, largely under Rhea's guidance. Just a year later it had almost 10,000 volumes. Members of the Dallas Bar were cordially invited to use the library as needed. Among the several generous donations were a 1,000-volume collection from former State Senator J.J. Faulk, 400 volumes from former U.S. Senator Charles Culberson, and 250 volumes from the law firm of Saner, Saner, Turner and Rodgers.[25]

In 1926 a "permanent" dean, Judge Peter J. Hamilton, was hired, but poor health forced him to retire after only one month (not before he addressed the Bar Association at an October meeting). He died soon thereafter. His duties were then divided among the handful of faculty members and a member of the Dallas Bar, Lawrence Rhea, until the spring of 1927 when a new dean, Charles Shirley Potts, was hired. Potts was a former law school professor at the University of Texas who came to SMU from a teaching post at Washington University in St. Louis. In 1928 SMU graduated its first class, and that fall Dean Potts brought thirty-four of the law students to a meeting of the Bar Association. Among the graduates was a woman, Erin Bain Jones, who had entered the program late but graduated early.[26] Dean Potts would continue as dean for twenty years, providing strong leadership during a period which included the challenging years of the Depression and World War II.

IN ADDITION TO ITS important work in helping found SMU's law school, the Bar Association's energy was evident in another important endeavor—the creation of a clinic to enable Dallas citizens with little or no financial resources to obtain free legal assistance. The idea began to be explored in May 1924 when President W.R. Harris appointed a three-person committee to examine the advisability of such a clinic. D.A. Frank, who made the motion for such a study, was appointed chairman, and he was joined on the committee by the liberal activist George Clifton Edwards and C.K. Bullard.[27] A month later the committee recommended that the clinic be established for the City of Dallas but under the supervision of the bar, and before year's end one of the Bar Association's few women members, Hattie Henenberg, had been appointed to serve as attorney for the clinic. Funds totaling $300 were raised to finance the activity. The clinic opened on July 1, 1924, and continued at least into 1926 when the Bar Association allotted $50 to it.[28]

Another affiliate to the Bar Association was the Young Lawyers Club, which had organized in about 1913 even before the reorganization of the Bar Association. This was about a dozen years before the national Junior Bar Association movement began. Evidently disgruntled because the Bar Association in these pre-War World I days seemed mostly preoccupied with passing resolutions to honor recently deceased members, a group of two dozen or so young lawyers formed and began meeting once a week in the Oriental Hotel.[29]

But the organization evidently was not long-lived, for any evidence of their continued meetings is missing. The idea, though, had proved worthwhile. In the summer of 1928 J.W. Randall, a recent SMU Law School graduate, brought notice to a number of young lawyers the existence of junior bar organizations in Cleveland and Los Angeles. A committee of members of the Bar Association of Dallas was appointed by its president, Carl B. Callaway, to determine if such an organization might be formed in Dallas. This committee called the first meeting of the city's young lawyers in the probate courtroom. About seventy attended, and they elected their first officers as C.A. Matthaei, president; R.J. Dickson, first vice-president; Jimmie McNicholl, second vice-president; William Harry Jack, secretary-treasurer; and Pat O'Keefe, sergeant-at-arms. For the first several weeks this group continued to meet in the probate courtroom, but soon they began gathering at 12:15 p.m. every Friday in the seventh-floor cafe of Sanger Bros. Department Store.[30]

In September 1929 they organized as the Dallas Junior Bar Association, the first Junior Bar Association in Texas. It was agreed that members of the Junior Bar could join the Dallas Bar Association with a reduced membership fee of $3 per annum until they had been engaged in the practice of law for five years, at which time regular dues would be required.[31] That same year the Dallas Bar Association designated members of the Junior Bar to give a speech to every civic organization in town during Constitution Week. (The Bar Association also tried to gain the support of the Pastors' Association to encourage the city's various ministers to give sermons on the subject.)[32]

The Dallas Junior Bar was the first in the state, but it was followed by others. In 1930 some 200 young lawyers organized the Texas Junior Bar Association at a meeting in Fort Worth. Six years later the Texas Junior Bar became a section of the State Bar of Texas.[33]

A year after the formation of the Dallas Junior Bar, its weekly luncheon meetings were drawing as many as a hundred. More than half of the membership also belonged to the Bar Association of Dallas, and at all meetings members of the regular Bar Association were welcomed as guests. By December 1932 the Junior Bar Association of Dallas listed some 190 members on its roster.[34] Over the years ahead the organization of young lawyers would continue to be active, and its members would also take leadership roles in the Texas Junior Bar Association.

WHEN THE NEW Records Building, adjacent to the Criminal Courts Building, was completed in 1928, it became the new home for the Court of Civil Appeals, 5th Supreme Judicial District of Texas. To commemorate the occasion, the Bar Association presented photographic portraits of all former and present members of the court, as well as of its chief clerk, George Blair. C.W. Starling, in making the presentation, expressed hope that the portraits would be placed on the walls of the sixth-floor courtroom. "I believe their presence will prove an inspiration to both bench and bar for generations to come," he said. Indeed, the practice of placing portraits of judges in all the county's courtrooms became a routine practice for the Bar Association.[35]

Reaching out to the city's civic groups—Rotary, Lions, Kiwanis, Chamber of Commerce, and others—became a particular goal during the last half of the decade. Inviting speakers from those groups to appear before the Bar Association, volunteering attorneys to speak to those groups, and holding joint meetings were some of the techniques used. In March 1926 members heard a speech from Albert Reed of the Dallas Chamber of Commerce concerning the relationship of the Bar Association with the Dallas Chamber. To commemorate San Jacinto Day a month later, a joint meeting was held with the Rotary Club in the Junior Adolphus Ballroom that was attended by 500 to 600 persons. The key speaker, introduced by Bar President M.N. Chrestman, was the president of the American Bar Association, Chester I. Long.[36] In November 1928 members heard a presentation by the banker and civic leader who years later would become known as "Mr. Dallas," Robert L. Thornton. Thornton, president of a Chamber-sponsored group dedicated to developing industry in Dallas, gave a "splendid" address on "The Business and Industrial Opportunities of Dallas and How the Lawyers May Assist in Expanding the Same."[37] (Thornton's brother, W.L. (Jack) Thornton, served as judge of the 44th District Court from 1937 to 1961.)

One of the most ambitious projects in bringing these groups together occurred on Texas Independence Day, March 2, 1929, when U.S. Senator Joe Weldon Bailey gave a talk on Texas independence. Members of every civic group in the city were invited to the special luncheon meeting in the Baker Hotel's Crystal Ballroom. Attendance was estimated to be about 350.[38]

Speeches concerning city-wide projects were frequently heard at Bar Association meetings. The Ulrickson Plan, an improvement plan that proposed long-range improvements for Dallas, especially realization of the Trinity River levee project, was carefully explained at a meeting in 1927.

Two years later speakers extolled the merits of changing the city's municipal government from the commission plan to the council-manager plan. Problems had emerged, it was now widely believed, because the commission plan divided responsibilities among four commissioners and the mayor, a system which led to separate political fiefdoms in which cooperation between municipal departments was difficult or non-existent. Alarming deficits also had become apparent in some city departments. The council-manager plan, touted especially by Tom Finty Jr., *The Dallas Morning News'* lawyer-editor, and reporter Louis Head, specified a professional city manager who would be in charge of all municipal affairs under the direction of city council members who would confine themselves to setting policy. Thus, politics and administration were separated. In late 1928 Mayor R.E. Burt selected a prominent member of the Bar Association, Hugh Grady (as of January 1929 the organization's first vice president), to head a commission to devise and recommend a new charter for the city. Grady presided over a March 1929 meeting of the Bar Association at which Head spoke of the virtues of the plan.[39] Grady and his commission's recommendations that a council-manager plan be adopted for the city ran into political problems, and to overcome them a new organization, the Citizens Charter Association (CCA), was created to go directly to Dallas voters to obtain enough signatures to force an election for a charter change. Grady became the organization's first president and Louis Head of the *News* the vice president.

The ensuing drive to gain signatures on the petition succeeded, and on October 10, 1930, after a comprehensive campaign that gained widespread support among the businesses of Dallas and civic groups, voters approved the charter plan. The Citizens Charter Association, still under Grady's presidency, now selected a slate of business-minded candidates to run for the nine City Council positions. The candidates all won in a landslide, and the CCA became an organization that would guide the municipal political destiny of Dallas with almost no interruptions until the early 1970s. Grady, who had played such an important role in creating this organization, became the city attorney for Dallas. And the council-manager plan of government for which he had been so responsible in convincing Dallas' citizens to adopt would continue to provide a very stable and efficient municipal framework for the city into the twenty-first century.

ACCLAIMED FOR GOOD WORKS

⌘

Chapter Nine

WALL STREET'S CRASH of October 1929 and the Great Depression that followed did not bring the same degree of despair to Dallas as it did for so much of the nation. Indeed, while the city did not altogether escape economic distress, significant events and developments indelibly marked the 1930s for Dallas. These included replacing the old commission style of municipal government with the new council-manager form, a change which brought enhanced efficiency to city hall by separating politics from city management; completing the long-term goal of diverting the Trinity River from its menacing position near the courthouse and placing it in the middle of its flood plain between protecting levees; and celebrating on the State Fair grounds the Texas Centennial of 1936, an international exposition which brought so many visitors from faraway places to the city that it suddenly had a national reputation. In all these events, the skills and involvement of the legal profession were essential.

Even more important, though, was the discovery in East Texas of the world's richest oil field by the former Tennessee lawyer and legislator, C.M. "Dad" Joiner. As the vastness of the reserves over a five-county area began to be realized, a mad rush developed. Dallas, the nearest major city to the fields, became a major headquarters for corporations, independent producers, wildcatters, promoters, investors, pipeline operators, oil-scouts, lease hounds, and drilling contractors. What had been an activity in Dallas secondary in importance to cotton became by the end of the decade the dominant economic force. During the first two months of 1931 alone, twenty-eight oil-related companies either began operations in Dallas or moved there. By August of 1932 the Chamber of Commerce listed 787 companies in the city that were dedicated to the oil business. Dallas banks quickly recognized the needs of this industry. Accustomed to lending money for prospective cotton crops that were dependent upon the vagaries of weather, they found no problem in financing deals based on oil reserves that were protected beneath the earth's surface. In 1934 the American Petroleum Institute recognized Dallas' growing importance in the industry by holding its annual convention there, an occasion which prompted the Magnolia Petroleum Company to place a double-sided flying red horse atop its 29-floor building. By the beginning of the 1940s it was estimated that as much as 20 percent of Dallas' population relied on the oil industry for income.

All of these developments brought not only volumes of business to the city's attorneys and expansions in sizes of law firms but also a growing demand for specialized legal knowledge in oil and gas matters. In the earliest days of this boom most of a lawyer's work lay in examining title to properties desired for oil exploration (natural gas frequently was an accompaniment to oil). Soon thereafter leasing arrangements had to be completed and contracts prepared so that drilling could begin. As the industry matured the legal work became more complex, involving such matters as unitization, pooling, waste disposal, gathering systems, and gasoline plants. Complying with the various regulatory matters outlined by the Railroad Commission in Texas was a major concern, too.[1]

The manner in which Dallas law firms grew and profited from such work may be seen through what was then the city's largest firm, Thompson, Knight, Baker & Harris (later just Thompson & Knight), and its involvement in oil and gas affairs. A 1929 legal directory lists just four oil companies among the firm's clients; by 1939 that number had grown to twenty-eight.[2] The firm's reputation for offering special expertise in the field of oil and gas was derived especially through its relationship with one of the nation's foremost oil operators, Everette Lee DeGolyer. When DeGolyer financed J.C. Karcher and Eugene McDermott in 1930 to organize Geophysical Services, Inc., for the purpose of using Karcher's development of seismic methods to search for promising geological formations, Thompson, Knight, Baker & Harris was hired to provide legal counsel. In the next few years GSI (which ultimately evolved into Texas Instruments) and those associated with it formed many other companies, many of which also turned to the firm for its expertise. When DeGolyer and Lewis MacNaughton formed their own consulting firm in 1936—immediately recognized as the premier petroleum engineering firm in the world—Thompson, Knight, Baker & Harris became their legal counsel. Many spin-offs from DeGolyer & MacNaughton also turned to the firm, and still other oil and gas companies retained their services. The inevitable result was the hiring of additional attorneys to take care of this growing volume of business. By 1935 the firm had nineteen attorneys.[3]

FOR THE BAR Association of Dallas the decade of the 1930s also was the period of its greatest accomplishments to date, bringing the organization national recognition. The Association's many new activities ranged afar—from conducting a regular Saturday morning legal clinic, to sponsoring radio broadcasts on legal subjects, to forming a relief committee to assist lawyers needing financial help, to campaigning against loan sharks in the city. With this expansion of activities came growth—to more than 1,000 members by 1939.

The overall mood of these uncertain Depression times and the quandaries of how to cope with its exigencies was reflected clearly in the 1932 inaugural address of the Bar Association's new president, Charles W. Starling, a member of the Dallas bar for thirty-five years. As Starling spoke, Herbert Hoover in the White House was timidly experimenting with government programs. The more radical New Deal presidency of Franklin Delano Roosevelt was a year away. Yet, already the specter of Big Government and the upsetting of traditional boundaries of state authority loomed. Starling expressed his alarm to members of the association as they gathered on January 8, 1932, in the Palm Garden of the Adolphus Hotel for their first meeting of the new year.

Constitutional rights were being threatened, he believed, by the selfish rapacity of special interests. Demands for government controls and regulation of business affairs, appeals by commercial interests for special governmental aid and privileges, and a growing disposition to use the power of taxation to accomplish that which could not be accomplished otherwise all demonstrated a dangerous movement toward broadened police powers of the state. "We are still in the twilight zone of constitutional power and construction," he said. In this troublesome new age the "business of the Bar is to see that the great questions arising . . . are properly submitted to and correctly decided by our courts." He summed up with considerable acumen his belief that "this age is destined to mark and define constitutional grants, powers and limitations as important as those of the era of John Marshall."[4]

The same concern about the growing powers of government was repeated the following year by Starling's successor, Nelson Phillips (1873-1939), former chief justice of the Texas Supreme Court. Phillips, with oratorical flourish, said: "A determined effort must be made to protect this people from the insatiate greed of power on the part of their own government, which is destroying the integrity of these States and despoiling the citizen of his inherent rights; and from that lavish and profligate expenditure of public money which has largely contributed to encompass the nation with the dangers of economic ruin."[5] These comments Phillips made two months before Franklin D. Roosevelt's inauguration and the beginning of the New Deal. Phillips, a Democrat, as were so many of the city's attorneys and others in this age of the one-party system in Texas, had served on the Texas Supreme Court from 1912 until 1921, when he resigned to begin private practice in Dallas.[6]

Just how far the "police power" of the state should be extended was a difficult question in these twilight years of laissez-faire government, for it appeared that some extensions were necessary for the good of the people. This very issue had been at the heart of the 1921 decision by the Texas Supreme Court when it struck down Dallas' municipal zoning ordinance as an excessive use of power because it violated the "natural right of property owners."[7] Since then Dallas' municipal authorities had struggled to find a balance between the natural rights of its citizens and an ordinance that would create an enforceable standard for achieving orderly growth, protection of residential neighborhoods from undesirable intrusions, and designation of appropriate areas for commercial and industrial purposes. This was a special problem for all growing cities, but Alex Weisberg, an attorney who chaired Dallas' City Plan Commission during the 1920s and who urged the adoption of a comprehensive zoning ordinance with enforcement authority, pointed out that 57 percent of America's urban population already lived under zoning laws. Dallas, he and others believed, should join that majority. Members of the Bar Association were thoroughly briefed on such issues, having heard many visiting civic leaders talk on the need for master planning.

To assist in this matter, Thomas B. Love, the Dallas attorney who was a former speaker of the Texas House of Representatives and now in 1927 a newly elected state senator, joined a Fort Worth senator in introducing and winning passage of an enabling act to permit cities to enact comprehensive zoning regulations. Thus encouraged, Weisberg and his fellow City Plan Commission members launched a large-scale campaign to favor a zoning ordinance for Dallas. On September 9, 1929, city commissioners approved a comprehensive zoning plan.[8] The new plan designated unusually generous portions of land to commercial, retail, and industrial use, but it also sought to protect and provide for single-family homes in traditional neighborhoods as well as apartments and duplexes.

Of course, the important question now was whether the zoning ordinance could withstand the scrutiny of the courts, especially regarding the matter of whether such an ordinance was an undue exercise of government authority over individual freedom. The test was assured on June 6, 1930, when a challenge was filed in Judge T.A. Work's 68th District Court by attorneys W.S. Bramlett, J.T. Kelly, and Angelo Piranio in behalf of V.A. Lombardo, whose request to build a gasoline filling station on a corner just inside an exclusive residential neighborhood had been denied by the city. Lombardo's challenge was rejected by Judge Work, and then by the Court of Civil Appeals in February 1932 with an opinion written by Justice Ben F. Looney. It was then appealed to the Texas Supreme Court, where on June 30, 1934, that body upheld

Dallas' comprehensive zoning ordinance. "No man who is able to do otherwise lives in a factory or commercial district, because experience has shown that a home where the noise and confusion of business do not obtain is of direct benefit to his family's health and peace of mind," the court stated. The power to regulate such matters was held to be "within the police power of the state."[9]

The travails of establishing zoning ordinances that could withstand the scrutiny of the courts had been a special challenge for one long-time Dallas lawyer whose name was the first of the five listed in the decision as representing the City of Dallas.[10] He was James J. Collins (1873-1933), who unfortunately died six months before the Supreme Court decision was rendered. The favorable decision would have represented a fitting finale to his life. Collins' legal career had been an inextricable part of city government since 1899 when he became assistant city attorney. Promoted to city attorney in 1904, he held that position except for a few years until 1931, then was advisory counselor to the city until his death on December 21, 1933, just a few months before the ultimate victory in mid-1934 in the Lombardo case. The drafting of the necessary legislation for city zoning and involvement in the trials that challenged the ordinances had constituted a large part of his life's work. Born in Dallas, he had studied law in the office of Barry Miller before being admitted to the bar. In a resolution passed by the Bar Association upon Collins' death, it was pointed out that in Collins' long career as city attorney he had attracted nation-wide attention for his knowledge of municipal law.[11]

Collins' death had been preceded only six months by that of his early mentor, Barry Miller (1864-1933), whose passing also served as a milestone. Born in Virginia, Miller moved to Dallas as a young man and studied law under the venerable Sawnie Aldredge in the office so noted for its conviviality and wisdom. He became assistant district attorney of Dallas County, served a term in the State Senate, was appointed by the governor to be the first judge of the new Criminal District Court No. 2, was elected to the State House of Representatives, and then three times was chosen to be lieutenant governor of the state.

Besides his political prowess, Miller would be remembered in Dallas for another reason. In 1885 he married the daughter of William B. Miller, a noted Dallas County pioneer. Eventually he and his wife moved into her family's handsome plantation-type estate in Oak Cliff known as Millermore.[12] That Dallas County landmark, constructed between 1855 and 1862 as perhaps the most lavish house in North Texas, many years later would be saved from demolition through a drive led by another Dallas lawyer, John Plath Green, and moved to Old City Park, where it became a well-known and photogenic centerpiece for that park's collection of historical buildings.

WHEN IN THE 1920s the Ku Klux Klan gained approving nods from so many of the city's leaders and officials as an ex-officio enforcer of morals, the Bar Association of Dallas had not as a group taken official notice of those dramatic and frightening events. In 1931 another situation arose in which unnamed individuals again sought to administer justice in extra-legal fashion, and this time the Association loudly and clearly condemned the action.

The incident centered around an abduction of the Dallas lawyer who for so many years had been identified with liberal causes—George Clifton Edwards—and two of his clients. In late February two young men who were identified as Communist Party organizers from Kansas City began passing out pamphlets and speaking on Dallas streets about economic and racial justice. ("Black and White Workers Unite" was the title of one pamphlet.) Their actions, which included provocative addresses before groups of unemployed men in front of city hall, attracted police attention. In early March officers arrested the two men for vagrancy and placed them in jail, where they were beaten by an inmate with implied approval of police. Edwards, concerned as always with the rights of minorities, free speech, and Socialist causes, visited the two men in jail and agreed to defend them in Judge Cavin Muse's municipal court against vagrancy charges. Edwards evidently was so vigorous in his defense that Judge Muse fined him $105 for contempt of court and assessed him a one-day jail sentence. After Judge Robert B. Allen Sr. of the 116th District Court ordered Edwards' release from jail on a writ of habeas corpus, Edwards visited Police Chief Claude Trammell to advise him that the two agitators had assured him that they would leave town immediately if turned loose. After a few hours' contemplation, Trammell informed Edwards by telephone that he would drop the charges and free the men. Edwards returned to the jail to see to their release. As Edwards and his clients were leaving the building, a group of men, some of them bearing arms, abducted all three of them. Their hands were tied and they were driven in separate cars out of town. Edwards was released with the warning that he "must not defend Communists in Dallas or he would be called upon again." The two alleged Communists were driven farther away to a more remote area near Hutchins, whipped severely with a doubled rope, and abandoned there with their hands still tied.[13]

All these alarming events received extensive newspaper coverage, attracting the immediate interest of the Bar Association's executive committee, chaired by C.K. Bullard. A special meeting was called to discuss the situation in the law office of Paul Carrington. The committee heard Edwards' full account of the incident. Edwards believed that the Ku Klux Klan, still active in the city, had been involved and that persons inside the police department had tipped off the Klan about the impending release of the two men. He said he had not bothered to report the kidnapping to the police department or to the sheriff's office because he believed it would be "wasting my time and breath."[14] (Ironically, the executive committee included at least one ex-Klansman, Maury Hughes, the former district attorney who had angrily resigned from the Klan at the height of its power in the early 1920s.) Committee members then passed a fiery resolution which fully supported Edwards and condemned the kidnapping:

> It is not only Mr. Edwards' right to defend an individual charged with the violation of the criminal law, but it is duty to do so. . . .While this Committee views with alarm and condemns without reservation the activities of

communists in our community or elsewhere, it also views with alarm and condemns without reservation the conduct upon the part of those individuals responsible for the abduction of Mr. George Clifton Edwards. . . . And it severely condemns the breakdown in respect for the law evidenced by the abduction, and calls upon all good citizens and all law enforcement agencies, to condemn severely such action, and to aid in the discovery and punishment of such criminals.[15]

To this latter end, Dallas attorneys H. Bascom Thomas Sr., Alex Spence, O.T. Compton, W.J. Moroney and others followed up on the executive committee's resolution by sending a telegram to Governor Ross Sterling. "We appeal to you as governor of this state to order Rangers to investigate this infamous outrage and further ask that a reward be offered."[16] The governor promptly complied. Two Rangers from Kilgore quickly arrived and began their investigation although Mayor J. Waddy Tate implored them to leave.

Edwards, meanwhile, gave full statements of the affair to U.S. District Judge William Hawley Atwell and to Sarah Menezes of the U.S. Attorney's office. Miss Menezes, one of Dallas' earliest women attorneys and now an assistant U.S. district attorney for the Northern District, said that if it were found that federal statutes had been violated the case would be referred to the federal grand jury in May. Dallas Police Commissioner W.C. Graves said he would ask the Dallas County grand jury to investigate the affair, which it soon did to the accompaniment of further newspaper headlines. When the two victims, missing for days with their whereabouts unknown, showed up in Kansas City, Dallas County District Attorney William S. McCraw and *Daily Times Herald* reporter E.K. Mead went there to interview the two men at Trade Unity League headquarters and attempt to persuade them to return to Dallas to testify before the grand jury.[17]

An interesting sideline to these events was the issue—which years later would become a far more celebrated one—of whether or not a journalist could be compelled to reveal confidential sources. *Dallas Dispatch* reporter Eddie Barr, called before the Dallas County grand jury, declined to identify a source for his detailed news story about the beatings of the two victims. Judge Grover Adams of Criminal District Court promptly jailed him for contempt. After one night in a cell, Barr had a change of heart and identified his source as an employee of the district attorney's office who, according to newspaper reports, was a former Klan cyclops now leasing his building in Oak Cliff to the Klan for its regular meetings.[18]

No indictments ever were returned for the kidnapping and beatings. However, the aggressive and prompt response of the Bar Association in lamenting the event and the summoning of Texas Rangers by prominent lawyers in behalf of a controversial cause suggested the growing influence, maturity and self-confidence of the organization.

A few years after this episode, Edwards again found himself involved in controversy. This concerned the effort in Dallas by unions to organize workers in the Ford Motor plant on East Grand Avenue, an effort often accompanied by violence. A young Dallas attorney who acted as a spokesman for the United Auto Workers, W.J. Houston, required hospital treatment after he was attacked on Main Street in downtown Dallas by a gang of a dozen men who knocked him to the ground, kicked him repeatedly, and broke three of his ribs. As violence continued with union organizers being assaulted—one of them was tarred and feathered—Houston concluded that he should leave town, which he did in October 1937. Charges against his assailants were dropped.[19]

Edwards, who had always been an active member of the Bar Association and occasionally served on its committees, this time believed that the organization was remiss in not speaking out. He criticized his fellow lawyers in *The Dallas Morning News*. "The lawyers and the Bar Association of Dallas are strangely silent just now at a time when it would seem that courage, conscience, and principle ought to make them speak vigorously. . . . There is need for a resounding protest by all lawyers who are sincere in their concern over the Constitution and its basis, the Bill of Rights.

Dallas lawyers ought to speak out and to rouse the public to the dangers threatening our constitutional rights."[20]

THE NUMBER of women in the Bar Association of Dallas had not substantially increased since the 1920s. Of 470 members in 1934, just eleven were women. Female members that year included a number of the earliest pioneers: Grace N. Fitzgerald, Hattie L. Henenberg, Sarah T. Hughes, Sarah C. Menezes, and Helen Viglini. Others who now had been admitted to membership were Mrs. Sam P. Cochran; Sarah Daniels, who had an office in the Santa Fe Building; Mildred M. Douglass, a legal aid attorney with the City of Dallas Welfare Department; Florence Dunigan, assistant courthouse reporter for the 95th District Court; Alice Winsor, whose office was in the Fidelity Building; and Regina Urbish, who had the distinction of being the first woman to receive a degree from the Dallas Y.M.C.A. School of Law.[21]

The energy of these early female lawyers had been exemplified especially in the 1920s by the two sisters, Edith Eunice Therrell Wilmans and Helen Viglini. Following her sister's achievements in state-wide politics, Viglini became Dallas County's first female assistant district attorney. In 1928 she unsuccessfully campaigned as a Democrat for Dallas County's Place 3, 50th District, in the Texas Legislature. Two years later, with the incumbent deciding to be a candidate for state treasurer, she once again announced for that legislative office.

But another female member of the bar, Sarah T. Hughes, also filed for that position as a Democrat. Hughes' interest in politics had been whetted by her success on the state campaign trail in 1928 by speaking for presidential hopeful Al Smith. During this campaign she became friends with Texas Congressman Sam Rayburn, who described her as an "explosive, never-say-die campaigner." Now, as past president of the Dallas Zonta Club and second vice president of the Texas League of Women Voters, she was ready herself to campaign for office. In her announcement she expressed her opposition to higher taxes, a belief in a need to reorganize and consolidate state departments on a business-like basis, and a need to establish a civil service system.[22]

Neither Viglini nor Hughes was expected to be successful in the race. There were three other candidates, all male. Alton E. Stewart, also an attorney, was · active in the Junior Bar Association. Another candidate was Henry F. Juergens, a photographer. The favorite was D.C. Bell, a boxing promoter and lobbyist who, like Hughes, had campaigned for Al Smith in 1928. As expected, Bell gained the most votes in the July primary, but he was followed closely by Hughes and Viglini. The August run-off for the Democratic nomination was between Hughes and Bell. Hughes, supported strongly by the women's organizations in which she had been so active and surely picking up some of Viglini's voters, defeated Bell for the Democratic nomination, 15,333 to 12,953. This was tantamount to victory in the general election, which indeed was the case for the woman described by a newspaper as "small and fiery."[23]

Sarah T. Hughes would be re-elected twice more to the office, gaining a reputation in Austin as a feisty activist favoring progressive causes such as women's rights and a state income tax despite the conservative tone of her initial announcement for office. Hughes' legislative record prompted one fellow representative to charge in 1933 that she had sponsored "more idealistic measures under vote-catching names that would wreck Texas business than any other member of this body."[24] But the capitol press corps in 1934 voted her the "most valuable member" of the House.

Shortly after her third election to the legislature, a Dallas lawyer asked Hughes in early 1935 to recommend him to Governor James Allred for appointment to the bench of the 14th District Court. It had become vacant when Judge William M. Taylor Sr. resigned to accept an appointment to the Supreme Court Commission of Appeals. Hughes did as requested, but the governor was not enthusiastic about her recommendation. Instead, another person came to his attention—Hughes herself. Women's groups had begun urging that she be appointed to the judgeship. As a progressive Democrat with a political kinship to Hughes' record in the Legislature, Allred saw much merit in appointing her, and to Hughes' surprise, he did so. However, State Senator Claud

C. Westerfeld of Dallas, an associate of Hughes in the Bar Association of Dallas, announced that he would exercise the traditional prerogative of a home district senator and oppose her nomination. The secretary of state informed Hughes of her colleague's opposition. Since confirmation seemed hopeless with Westerfeld's position, he asked if under the circumstances she still wanted him to send her name to the Senate. Aside from the temporary all-woman Supreme Court of 1925 which made a single decision, the state had never had a woman judge. Nor could women sit on juries in Texas. Only recently, Hughes had co-sponsored a constitutional amendment to permit women to serve on juries (not to pass until 1953), and now she was determined to go a step further. Yes, she replied, she wanted her name sent forward.

So informed, Senator Westerfeld exclaimed that Sarah T. Hughes "should be home washing dishes" instead of aspiring for the bench.[25] It was a statement he surely regretted, although it did not deter him from leading a spirited campaign to the last minute to stymie her appointment. Hughes, infuriated at the comment, launched a determined campaign to win support and defy his opposition. She contacted all other senators from Dallas County, requested support from prominent attorneys and women's organizations, and in the process gained national attention over the prolonged brouhaha. Dallas female attorneys Grace Fitzgerald, Sarah Menezes, and Hattie Henenberg were prominent in their support of her. When Westerfeld suggested that the Bar Association should vote on whether or not Hughes should be confirmed, Fitzgerald said she already was polling the members and gathering their support.[26]

On February 12, 1935, the State Senate confirmed Hughes' appointment by a vote of 23 to 7. She promptly resigned her seat in the House and returned to Dallas, assuming the bench the next day before a welcoming crowd of about one hundred supporters. Even so, opposition lingered. Dallas attorney C.K. Bullard, a Westerfeld ally in opposing Hughes' appointment, held out a threat that he would challenge the legality of her appointment. But the opposition soon died away, and at the age of thirty-eight

Sarah T. Hughes became the state's first female district judge. She served with distinction, and was re-elected time and time again until 1961 when President John F. Kennedy appointed her to the federal bench despite some protests that she was too old. Judge Hughes would retire in 1975.

THE GROWING COMPLEXITY of the Bar Association of Dallas was indicated in 1934 when new president Robert G. Storey appointed seventy-six members to fourteen standing committees. Their responsibilities were as diverse as law reform, history, grievance, "sunshine," admissions, and constitutional amendments. The annual meeting and banquet, held jointly each January in a fine hotel, gave way by the mid-1930s to a separate annual meeting and a banquet held a few days apart. Presidents continued to serve one-year terms. An executive committee met monthly, frequently at the Adolphus or Baker Hotel, to handle the organization's primary affairs, and monthly membership meetings usually were held in a courtroom. At these meetings members frequently discussed and adopted resolutions from the various committees.

The organization's record-keeping had not kept pace with its growing complexity. In January 1932, in a three-hour meeting in the Adolphus Hotel, Secretary Harry D. Page informed the executive committee of the desperate need for better maintenance of records. The files needed systematizing and indexing, and membership rosters for past years had not been maintained. Page said that improved record-keeping was critical if a historical record of the organization were to be maintained. Hearing this, the executive committee authorized Page to purchase a filing cabinet with a lock and visible index system, to spend no more than $25 to hire stenographic and clerical assistance for installing a filing system, to list the association's telephone number in the city telephone directory, to establish a petty cash account from which the secretary and president could purchase any necessary supplies not to exceed $10, and to arrange for the printing of Bar Association stationery.[27] Still, the organization had no permanent office or headquarters.

Other efforts at house-cleaning continued. At its April 1932 meeting the executive committee voted to drop from membership rolls seventy members unless they became current within a month. Some of them had not paid their dues since 1930. Those targeted included some of the organization's most prominent attorneys.[28] Evidently, the announcement was sufficient, for later minutes reflect no large-scale dismissal of members.

The realization that much of the history of the association had been lost through a lack of attention to record-keeping perhaps is what prompted Berry B. Cobb, chairman of the historical committee, to prepare a history of lawyers in Dallas. Cobb's exemplary research was well-documented, and it gave invaluable account of the subject from Dallas' earliest days. By 1934 the manuscript was ready. The association printed 400 copies of *History of Dallas Lawyers*, presenting a copy to each member upon payment of dues.[29]

ONE OF THE MORE important issues studied by the Association and its Committee on Legal Education was the long-standing, complicated issue of what standards to have for admission to the state bar—the right to practice law. Committee members and many lawyers shared a sense that the legal profession was overcrowded. They believed that standards for admission should be higher. In a speech before the Bar Association, Robert G. Storey pointed out that in England there was approximately one lawyer to every 2,100 citizens; in Italy, Belgium, and Denmark, one to 2,500; and in France and Germany, one to 4,500. The ratio in the United States was approximately one lawyer to every 800 people.[30]

M.N. Chrestman's hard-working Committee on Legal Education perceived the so-called "diploma privilege" to be a special problem. As the old practice of reading law in an office had yielded to more formal studies in law school classrooms, the state legislature had exempted graduates of certain law schools from admissions exams. They were certified to practice automatically through graduation. More than half a dozen schools in Texas, including such schools as Jefferson in Dallas, had been given this privilege. Compounding the situation was an influx of lawyers arriving from other states who were admitted to practice in Texas upon presentation of a diploma from more than twenty state universities even though those states did not similarly recognize graduates of Texas law schools.[31]

A lengthy report by the legal education committee dissected the issue, made recommendations to upgrade minimal requirements, gained the support of the full Association, and was sent to the State Supreme Court, the body in charge of setting standards. Among its many recommendations, the committee urged that the Supreme Court repeal the diploma privilege entirely, treat all candidates alike, and require all aspiring lawyers to take a qualifying exam. The committee and Bar Association argued that Texas should adopt the basic standards promulgated by the American Bar Association.[32]

Several members of the Supreme Court responded quickly and favorably, announcing that they already had modified their rules in a way that covered "practically all of the propositions submitted in your communication."[33] Eventually, the Supreme Court honored the growing stature of local bars by requiring candidates for the examination to obtain first a certificate from the local bar association. The Bar Association of Dallas capitalized on this opportunity by issuing its own requirements for obtaining the certificate—no candidate would be certified to take the examination unless he or she had graduated from a school approved by the American Bar Association. After June 7, 1937, the diploma privilege was entirely abolished in Texas. Privately operated law schools such as Jefferson vanished, and the Dallas YMCA Law School merged with Southern Methodist University's Law School, which continued to offer evening classes in downtown Dallas. As late as 1941 the evening division continued to be identified as the YMCA school.[34]

THE COMPLICATED new age of the 1930s—economic distress at home, new federal legislation which seemed to overturn years of tradition, and turmoil in Europe—seemed to demand higher standards for those entering the legal profession. Robert G.

Storey, president of the Bar Association in 1934 and later dean of the SMU Law School, summed up succinctly the demands upon the lawyers of this age and the justification for stricter admission standards:

"Not only has the practice of law become complicated, but the development of the law has become difficult. New conditions of life surround us; capital and labor, machinery and transportation, social and economic questions of the greatest, most vital interest and importance, the effects of taxation, the social structure, justice to the poor and injustice to the rich—a vast array of difficult and complicated questions that somebody has got to solve."[35]

Recognition of this growing complexity of law and its role in bringing order into a chaotic world inspired the Bar Association in the 1930s to launch an ambitious program of education. On one level the association sought to educate the general public. This was through a series of weekly fifteen-minute broadcasts in 1935 over Radio Station WRR. Storey, Nelson Phillips, and F.M. Ryburn formed a committee to arrange for speakers to appear on the station.[36]

The 1936 president of the Bar Association, D.A. Frank (1875-1955), brought great enthusiasm to the office. Born in a log cabin in Montgomery County and graduating from high school at the age of fourteen, Frank taught school for nine years before earning his law degree from the University of Texas in 1905. For many years he was an attorney for Southwestern Bell and American Telephone and Telegraph Company, but since 1921 he had been in private practice.[37]

To instruct their own members and to raise the levels of their competencies, the association at Frank's urging initiated regular Saturday morning meetings at the courthouse for speeches on a wide variety of topics. These meetings were held before the regular Saturday morning docket calls. Well-attended and highly popular with weekly attendance reaching some 200 lawyers, they became known as the Saturday Morning Legal Clinic (later they would be held at noon on Fridays). The idea was to schedule speakers on topics that were of "immediate relevancy" and "compelling importance" to Dallas lawyers.[38] The topics in the first year of the Legal Clinic included such subjects as cross-examination of witnesses, solicitation of business, legal aid clinics, lawyers and politics, the trial of Aaron Burr, a biographical portrait of Colonel W.L. Crawford, and a history of the courts of criminal appeals.

At the end of the year the association decided to publish these addresses as well as some speeches made at regular meetings. They appeared in the form of what became an annual yearbook entitled *The Dallas Bar Speaks*, published from 1936 through 1956. The books, properly bound in a standard trade-book format, included annual membership rosters, committee memberships, and officers. The first issue, 493 pages long, listed 727 members.

Dedication to special members of the bar began with the 1937 edition of *The Dallas Bar Speaks*. The first dedication was to Harry Preston Lawther (1859-1942), who had practiced law in Dallas for more than fifty years and who had served as Bar Association president in 1929 and president of the Texas Bar Association in 1931-32. Lawther frequently regaled those around him with stories of the difficult times he experienced during his early years of practice in Dallas. He said he often slept in the courthouse and considered returning to Galveston, where he had been reared. In 1890 he was elected a Dallas alderman, and a fellow alderman was his own father, who also had moved to Dallas. Lawther married Mary Ross, the young lady for whom Ross Avenue in Dallas had been named. In 1937 he was one of the few attorneys in town to vigorously defend Roosevelt's "court-packing plan."[39]

In 1938 *The Dallas Bar Speaks* was dedicated to Nelson Phillips, described as "preeminent among the great men who have served upon the Supreme Court of Texas." In 1939 the dedication went to William Hawley Atwell, federal judge and former U.S. attorney.

During his term as president, Frank also appointed a committee, with William H. Duls as chairman, to investigate the possibility of acquiring portraits of all former district judges in Dallas County and hanging them in the courtrooms. Upon the committee's eventual recommendation, the Bar Association provided funds to do so, beginning a practice that was expanded by the end of the decade to include U.S. District Judge William H. Atwell and justices of the state Court of Civil Appeals at Dallas.

Frank's enthusiasm seemed boundless. During his one-year presidency, membership jumped from about 400 to more than 700 at the end of 1936. Upon the conclusion of his term, Bar Association members by resolution declared him to be one of the greatest presidents in the association's history.[40] In the following year, the Bar Association unanimously voted to nominate him as president of the Texas Bar Association and to pledge "all honorable means to secure his election."[41] As it happened, Frank was elected vice president of the Texas Bar Association in 1938 and nominated for president in 1939. The other candidate for president that year was Angus G. Wynne of Longview, who formerly had maintained his law practice in both Dallas and Wills Point. Both lawyers were immensely popular. When it was evident that the vote would be badly split, Frank withdrew his candidacy so that Wynne could be elected by acclamation.[42]

In keeping with the move to upgrade standards for the practice of law was the effort for the state to have an "integrated bar"; that is, a bar that would give it and the courts full control over the admission to the practice of law and the discipline and disbarment of members. W.M. Holland, chairman of the Bar Association's committee on law reform, made a report on the proposal for a self-governing bar in April 1926, and later that year, on behalf of the Bar Association of Dallas, M.N. Chrestman presented at the Texas Bar Association's meeting in Texarkana a petition requesting that a bill for such a "self-governing" bar be presented to the Texas Legislature. Besides Chrestman, Harry P. Lawther, T. Whitfield Davidson, A.H. McKnight, and W.E. Spell signed the petition. The idea soon was adopted as a crusade by the Texas Bar Association. It would be Harry P. Lawther, who for ten years—much of that time as chairman of the Self-Governing Bar Committee and then the State Bar Act committee—led the fight for passage of the bill. J. Cleo Thompson of the Dallas Bar also served as chairman of the State Bar Act committee in the late 1930s. In 1939 the bill passed, and on April 12 Governor W. Lee O'Daniel signed it into law. The bill took effect on July 6, 1940, at which time the old voluntary Texas Bar Association was replaced by the new compulsory State Bar of Texas. The State Bar had become an integrated department of the state government, and it had been Dallas lawyers who had played key roles in making it happen.[43]

THE RED COURTHOUSE, barely older than four decades now, already was viewed as being outdated. It was a building that, as Harry P. Lawther said, would be declared unsafe for occupancy and a fire hazard if it were being used by private enterprise. Most everyone agreed to the need for a new courthouse, but when the possibility of using federal funds to help pay for it was recommended in March 1936 by Paul Carrington, chairman of the "New Courthouse Committee," a vigorous debate ensued at a bar meeting. The former state Supreme Court justice, Nelson Phillips, believed that accepting federal funds would be unwise as well as unconstitutional, and other attorneys such as Carl Callaway, Ernest McCormick, and John White agreed. But Lawther contended that the appropriations bill providing federal funds must be presumed to be constitutional, and that the money would be spent elsewhere if not in Dallas. Thomas B. Love joined Carrington and Lawther in favoring a motion to ask the county commission to set a bond election for additional funds. The motion carried by a 31 to 23 vote.[44] As it finally turned out, the Old Red Courthouse was retained, but the debate over the growing impact and the role of the federal government continued, especially in President Franklin Roosevelt's "court-packing" plan of 1937.

Having seen some of his key social legislation programs declared unconstitutional by the Supreme Court in 1936, the President on February 5, 1937, sent to Congress a plan to enlarge the number of justices by as many as six. This seemed clearly to be a way to "pack" the High Court with new appointees who would favor the President's legislation. The day after Congress received Roosevelt's proposal, Bar Association President J. Cleo Thompson called a special meeting prior to the regular Saturday Morning Legal Clinic to discuss the unusual plan. D.A. Frank introduced a resolution disapproving it; Thomas B. Love argued against Frank's resolution; but the vote was postponed until the following Saturday when full notification of members could be effected. Almost 200 members of the Bar Association attended this meeting, an unusually large number, and many of them debated Frank's motion against the President's plan. Frank, Lawther, Phillips, John W. Pope, Allen Wight, W.R. Harris, and Robert G. Storey were among those favoring the motion, with Love, M.M. Crane, Eugene DeBogory, W. Gregory Hatcher, and John Davis arguing against it. The vote overwhelmingly opposed the President's plan, 152 to 25, and the results were sent to both U.S. senators from Texas and also to the representative in Congress from Dallas, fellow Bar Association member Hatton Sumners.[45]

Sumners, since his election to the 5th Congressional District in 1912 as a Democrat, had become one of the most powerful men in the House. As chairman of the House Committee on the Judiciary he would be a key figure in winning support for the President's plan. But when Roosevelt surprised Sumners and other key Congressional leaders with his plan in a White House meeting on February 5, 1937, Sumners sat with a growing sense of unease at what appeared to be an indirect assault at unfavorable Supreme Court rulings. Upon leaving the White House and joining several of them in a taxi ride, he said, "Boys, here's where I cash in my chips," a phrase that would be quoted frequently in the years ahead. It was a major break from the President. Sumners permitted the court-packing plan to languish without action while opposition to it mounted, and the scheme was defeated. Sumners had been widely believed to be in line for the next vacant Supreme Court position. His opposition to the President's plans doomed those chances and he became recognized nationally as a man who had put principle before expediency.[46] Later in 1937 Sumners spoke to the Bar Association on "Our Constitution," and, as the minutes reflected, "discussed some very interesting side lights on recent happenings in Congress."[47]

On April 7, 1938, the House of Representatives spent most of its day celebrating the beginning of Sumners' twenty-sixth year in Congress. One after another of the Congressmen paid tribute to him. Three years later *The Saturday Evening Post*, in an article entitled "The Gentleman Who Does Not Yield," cited Washington correspondents who called him "the ablest and most potent advocate in Congress."[48]

In keeping with the Association's drive to educate, at long last a way was found to establish a county law library at the courthouse. Funding, of course, had always been the problem, but a unique remedy was devised in 1931 and approved by the Legislature. For every suit filed at the courthouse a small fee was assessed for the library fund. By late 1932 about $3,000 had been accumulated in this fund to start buying books. The county commissioners agreed to provide space on the top floor of the new Records Building, and by the end of 1935 more than 5,500 law books were on the shelves. During the year 1935 a total of 7,296 persons used the library, with 2,034 of them borrowing books which they could take to the courtroom for reference. Two years later the number of users had climbed to about 10,000 annually. (By 1998 the Dallas County Law Library was in two parts: a civil section in the George L. Allen Sr. Courts Building and a criminal section in the Frank Crowley Courts Building.)[49]

Perhaps the most unique and noteworthy activity was the association's battle with "loan sharks" in Dallas. In late September 1938 the *Dallas Dispatch-Journal* ran a series of articles exposing unethical and usurious actions of these loan companies in which they took advantage of the poor and uneducated. In the concluding article the newspaper challenged the Bar Association to take action to remedy the situation for victims who were unable to afford to hire lawyers. Bar Association President Woodall Rodgers accepted the challenge. He appointed a blue-ribbon forty-member "Anti-Usury Committee" with seven subcommittees to attack the problem on all fronts, including legal assistance to individuals who believed that they had been victimized. A total of 953 complaints were made to appropriate individuals, including city, county and state authorities, and seventy-four suits were filed. The campaign was extended by radio when the committee accepted radio station WRR's offer of thirty minutes free air time, three times a week. During these broadcasts, committee members interviewed the "victims" of loan sharks and presented talks by business, professional, religious, and civic leaders to shed light on the problem. The result of all this activity, as committee chairman Searcy Lee Johnson pointed out, was a "sudden paralysis" in the loan shark racket.[50]

One of the greatest accomplishments of the association during this era was its push to make every Dallas attorney a member. By 1937 membership committee chairman Roy Ledbetter could report that membership stood at 640, up from about 575 at the end of 1933. By the end of the year that figure had grown to 820 out of just about 850 practicing attorneys. It was reported that Dallas, a minor city in size, had the fourth largest Bar Association in the nation![51]

The time was deemed right to hire a full-time executive secretary, and in 1937 Oma Ervin was hired as the first full-time executive secretary of any bar association in the Southwest. But where would she work? The district clerk, George W. Harwood, appeared before the membership in 1938, made a short talk expressing his gratitude for the support given to him by members of the bar since he had assumed office in 1933, and said he had arranged for the organization to have space on the first floor of the courthouse, Room 120, for a permanent headquarters. Room 120 was a fifteen-foot cubicle under the stairway in the Old Red Courthouse, where the new full-time employee installed drapes, pictures of past presidents and other amenities. At the close of 1938 membership had reached 1,015. More than one-fourth of the local members also belonged to the American Bar Association, one of the highest percentages of any bar in the nation. The Dallas Bar itself was the eighth largest in the nation. Of five elected representatives from Texas to the American Bar Association's House of Delegates, three were from Dallas in 1939.[52]

These accomplishments did not go unnoticed. In 1937 the American Bar Association ranked the Bar Association of Dallas as the second best in the nation, just behind that of New York City.[53] When the new president of the Bar Association of Dallas, J. Glenn Turner, delivered his inaugural address in January 1939 at the Dallas Country Club, his opening sentence was: "We have just concluded one of the greatest years in the history of the Bar Association of Dallas." Now, he announced, the Bar Association's goal was to be recognized as the "best bar" in the nation. And having achieved that honor, to maintain and deserve it consistently.[54]

It was not an unrealistic goal. When the American Bar Association met in San Francisco in July 1939, it presented its highest honor, the Award of Merit, to the Bar Association of Dallas. Twenty-one Dallas lawyers were in attendance. The award, presented to Turner, was given, it was said, not just for 1938 but for "a truly remarkable program of achievement covering a long period of years."[55]

DALLAS LAWYERS GO TO WAR

⌘

Chapter Ten

TO MANY KNOWLEDGEABLE persons, the decade of the 1930s, marked so indelibly by the Great Depression and frightening turmoil throughout Europe, was the most perilous time ever for the American nation as well as for the entire world. As 1940 introduced a new decade, the feared apocalypse seemed almost at hand. The very survival of democratic nations was at risk as England, standing courageously alone, withstood Nazi Germany's aerial blitz and braced itself for an impending invasion. In the United States, virtually all discussions on current affairs centered around the question of what should be done.

When in July 1941 the Bar Association of Dallas hosted the annual meeting of the State Bar Association, this issue overshadowed all others. Attendance at the meeting was unusually high. The 2,112 delegates who gathered represented only 326 fewer than those who had attended the American Bar Association's annual meeting earlier in Indianapolis. Two prominent Dallas attorneys welcomed the state's lawyers to Dallas—Woodall Rodgers, mayor of the city, and Roy C. Ledbetter, the Dallas Bar's president.

Hatton W. Sumners, the veteran Congressman and member of the Dallas Bar, declared to the assembled crowd that the only important business before them and before the nation was "preparedness." He challenged his listeners to repair to the cause. "In the great crises of the past when liberty has been imperiled," he said, "it has been the lawyers who have aroused the people and brought them back to a request for the fundamental principles of their government, and you have got to do it again."[1]

His words could hardly have fallen on a more receptive audience. The lawyers of Dallas already had been stepping forward to help their nation prepare for whatever eventuality awaited. Their record of service throughout World War II would be one of extreme patriotism and a willingness to set aside personal gain to work for the defense of their country.

MANY DALLAS lawyers were responding to the international crisis even before the 1941 State Bar meeting. On September 16, 1940, when President Roosevelt signed the Selective Service Act into law providing for the first peace-time conscription in the nation's history, attorneys Robert G. Storey and Shelby S. Cox were appointed to serve as members of the local draft board. Eleven others—all prominent members of the bar—accepted appointment as government appeals agents. Attorney Charles Romick was placed on the advisory board for the Boards of Appeals.[2]

Even as early as September 1939, when Hitler invaded Poland, at least one Dallas attorney, A.J. Beck, responded to the nation's anticipated need for a strong defense. He walked from the office of his firm, Beck & Knox in the Santa Fe Building, to an Army recruiting station, and signed up for the Flying Cadet program. He took his physical at the U.S. Army infirmary at Love Field, passed it, underwent aviation training at Luke Field, Arizona, and became a pilot and second lieutenant. With the advent of war, Beck would serve three years in the Southwest Pacific Theater.[3]

The first day of the draft in Dallas was January 11, 1941, and on that initial day a young lawyer named H. Louis Nichols— destined twenty-two years later to become president of the Dallas Bar Association—was inducted into the Army. He was assigned to the 11th Engineer Combat Regiment at Camp Bowie, Texas, where he still was stationed on the day of the surprise Japanese attack at Pearl Harbor. Five months later, Nichols was commissioned as a second lieutenant in the U.S. Army Corps of Engineers. In 1945 he was sent to Okinawa, and when the war ended he went to Japan as part of the Occupation Forces.[4]

Also an early participant in the war effort was another future president of the Dallas Bar, H. Bascom Thomas Jr., commanding officer of the Dallas Naval Reserve. In May 1941 Thomas and the ninety-four reservists under his command entered into active duty "for the duration." A huge crowd gathered at Union Terminal to see the men depart by train, and a *Dallas Morning News* photographer caught Lt. Commander Thomas with his family at the station. The picture, published on the newspaper's front page, also showed another future president of the Dallas Bar, Thomas' young son, Robert H., who would serve in that capacity in 1978.[5]

Pearl Harbor and the declaration of war prompted an even quicker and more widespread outpouring of volunteerism by bar members. Before the first full year of war had ended, approximately one-fourth of the Bar Association's 1,035 members already were on active duty. They had answered their nation's call without fanfare. Their names were listed at the front of the 1942 volume of *The Dallas Bar Speaks,* and the book was dedicated to them.

The circumstances of those who entered the service varied widely. Harry C. Crump Jr. and Freeman L. Mittenthal, boyhood friends who had graduated from the same high school in 1934 and then started their own partnership in 1939 upon graduation from law school, set aside their ambitions and closed the doors of their firm to join the Army Air Corps. Crump went in as a cadet, and Mittenthal entered the ground forces. Just over a year later Crump, who had become a bombardier on a Liberator, was reported missing in action, later to be confirmed as a casualty.[6] Mittenthal survived the war and returned to Dallas to resume the practice of law.

Assistant District Attorney H.J. Kimball saw his commission as a second lieutenant in the Reserves expire on one day, and then receive in the mail on the following day his draft notice to be inducted as a private at $21 a month.[7] Six months after the United States entered the war, Robert G. Storey, former Bar Association president, president of the Dallas Park Board, and director of Civilian Defense, obtained a commission in the Army Air Corps and reported for duty at Wright Air Field in Dayton, Ohio. Even higher profile activities related to the war effort were ahead for Storey, who also had answered his nation's call to duty in World War I by serving as a lieutenant.[8]

These lawyers—and others who soon followed them—served throughout the world, performing a wide variety of assignments, both as officers and enlisted men. A number of them, but by no means all, were assigned to positions in which their legal skills were of benefit. At least fifteen Dallas lawyers were killed in the service of their country before the war ended.

EVEN IN ITS OFFICIAL activities the Bar Association of Dallas took a keen interest in these critical events. In the spring of 1941 the Bar Association's National Defense Committee sent a strongly worded message to President Roosevelt, Senator Tom Connally, and Congressman Sumners, urging the President to use armed forces to prevent any labor strikes that might hinder the war-preparation effort. The committee warned that some men in positions of power in key industries were neither loyal nor patriotic, some were "agents of foreign governments," and "many of them are communists" seeking to overthrow the government.[9]

In March 1942 the Bar Association declared a complete program of support for the war effort by seeking to involve every one of its more than 1,000 members as part of "a virile, active working unit for aid in the prosecution of the war." The declaration was presented to Mayor Woodall Rodgers and Civilian Defense Director Storey. A number of committees were established to "marshal the forces of the organized bar in order that the full weight of its power may be thrown into the effort to achieve complete military victory." The overall goals included the furnishing of free legal aid to servicemen and their families, supplying trained and informed speakers for the community, and cooperating with every agency contributing to the war program.[10]

James L. Lipscomb headed the war activities committee, under which a number of other committees were formed. J. Glenn Turner did double duty as head of the personnel committee and also the civilian defense committee; Nelson Phillips Jr. chaired a committee on selective service organization; J. Cleo Thompson chaired a committee to make certain that all members were assigned to various duties; William Burrow headed the public relations committee; and Joseph W. Bailey Jr. was named chairman of a committee on legislation.[11]

The uncertain nature of these perilous times was seen in the fate of the chairman of the committee on legislation, Joseph W. Bailey Jr., well known as the son of the former Democratic powerhouse senator from Texas, Joe Weldon Bailey. Not long after his Bar Association committee assignment, young Bailey entered active military service. Within a year he was killed. (As a child, Bailey's father had taken him to see President William McKinley in the White House. Asked by the President to come sit on his knee, young Bailey responded, "Mr. President, I like you, but I can't sit on your knee because you're a Republican.")[12]

When Supreme Court Associate Justice Robert H. Jackson spoke to the Bar Association at a luncheon in July 1942, it marked the first occasion that a Supreme Court justice ever addressed a local bar association in Texas. His comments centered on the war effort, which he termed so vast that a single mind could not comprehend it. Victory was absolutely essential, he stressed, for defeat would exclude the United States from the trade routes of the world and have an impact on the lives of every man and woman. "We must strain every nerve to win, and I mean win completely," he said. "There must be no half victory." After his address in Dallas, Jackson went on to speak at the annual meeting of the State Bar of Texas in San Antonio. In both Dallas and San Antonio he was introduced by Hatton W. Sumners.[13]

When James L. Lipscomb became president of the Bar Association in 1943 he reiterated the importance of war work for the organization above all else. In his inaugural address he said that the principal work of the organization should be directed toward winning the war against the nation's "bestial foes."[14] A noted example of the Bar Association's outward look to other matters lay in the fact that *The Dallas Bar Speaks* ceased publication for the duration of the war. A single edition would be issued afterwards to cover the years 1944, 1945, and 1946.

A LARGE NUMBER of Dallas lawyers, serving on various fronts, performed heroically in combat. Fred (Red) Harris, who later would serve as judge of Dallas County Court at Law No. 3, received the Navy Cross, the Bronze Star, and two Purple Hearts. Charles O. Galvin, later dean of the Southern Methodist University Law School, reported for duty at the Naval Air Station in Dallas in January 1943, and served with the 7th Fleet in the Southwest Pacific in New Guinea, Morotai, East Indies, the Philippines, and other areas.[15]

A.J. Beck, the attorney who in September 1939 had walked from his office in the Santa Fe Building to sign up for the Flying Cadet program, had ultimately found himself in the Southwest Pacific Theater, working on strategy for bombing missions. On one occasion he received permission to go on a bombing mission, but only with the understanding that he would not permit himself to be taken prisoner because of his knowledge of future military plans. He agreed to this condition, and he piloted a P-38 as the last man in the formation. "As we approached the target area," Beck later recalled, "I saw a Japanese fighter at some distance off to our left. I turned to intercept him and then radioed, 'Bandit at 9 o'clock.' I opened fire early, hoping the 20-mm in the nose would reach the target followed by the four 50 calibers. I got a hit, but others in the squadron also scored. I dove after the rapidly descending aircraft, but it was breaking up and I passed it at high speed. Suddenly, I realized I was fast approaching the ocean below. I pulled out of my dive barely feet above the water. Swearing more than a little, I saw another Japanese fighter directly ahead of me, seemingly racing to reach the cover provided by anti-aircraft guns on the shore. He saw me and started taking violent evasive action by making sharp turns to the right and left. I pulled in close, put him in my gun sights and was about to pull the trigger, when he made a very sharp turn to the right, digging his wing into the ocean and going under. . . . Believe it or not, I was credited with the 'kill' although I hadn't wasted a single bullet getting it."[16]

T.D. Wells, a lieutenant (jg), was aboard the aircraft carrier *U.S.S. Wasp* when Japanese torpedoes sank it in September 1942. Wells worked frantically with others in a fruitless effort to save the burning ship by throwing ammunition overboard. Among the last to jump overboard before the ship sank, Wells did so without a life jacket. While paddling in the water he managed to grab a floating 2" x 8" board. He and four other survivors pulled together a handful of other boards and lashed them together by using their shirts as ropes. Three hours later the group, still clinging to their make-shift raft, was rescued by a destroyer. Wells had not been in the Navy long; he had previously served in the Army for a year, then—three days after his discharge—he was sworn into the U.S. Navy as a lieutenant (jg).[17]

George Harvey Penland Jr., who came from a large family of lawyers, was the youngest member of the firm Touchstone, Wight, Gormley and Touchstone before entering the military to serve on a submarine in the Pacific. He died in action on May 4, 1943, and was recommended for the Silver Star for gallantry.[18]

Lt. Albert G. Biggs, formerly of Hughes & Monroe, won the Silver Star for gallantry in action and the Air Medal for participating in twenty-five combat raids. He flew with General Claire Chennault's famous Flying Tigers.[19]

Henry Coke of the firm Coke & Coke was an Army intelligence officer in the Pacific. On a flight in a Liberator bomber, his airplane, seriously damaged by Japanese anti-aircraft fire, had to drop to 500 feet with the crew jettisoning gasoline to lighten the load before it could successfully return to its home base in India.[20]

Lt. Col. Carl L. Phinney, quartermaster for the 36th Infantry Division when it invaded Italy in 1943, won the Silver Star for heroic action when he drove a truck through heavy enemy fire to deliver a radio transmitter that was critical to the success of landing operations.[21]

James G. Blanchette Jr. served at first on the *U.S.S. Lee Fox*, where he was engaged in anti-submarine warfare and escorted convoys across the North Atlantic. His ship next was converted to a high-speed attack transport which carried underwater demolition teams in the Pacific. At war's end, Blanchette was with a group of 2,000 ships in Leyte Gulf preparing for the invasion of Japan. "Since we were scheduled to take in the underwater demolition teams ahead of the first wave, we obviously were delighted over President Truman's decision to drop the 'big bomb,' " he later recalled.[22]

In 1943 Henry P. Kucera, Dallas' city attorney, took a military leave of absence to serve as a major in the U.S. Army. In September that same year Judge Henry King of Criminal District Court No. 2 reported for active duty as a major. (J. Frank Wilson, later to be a district judge himself, was elected by the Bar Association to take his place while King was away.) The future long-time district attorney of Dallas County, Henry M. Wade, lieutenant (jg), had lunch with war correspondent Ernie Pyle a few days before a Japanese sniper killed Pyle at Okinawa.[23]

Robert M. Martin Jr. had a semi-encounter with the famous Major General George S. Patton Jr. which Martin recalled for the Dallas Bar's commemorative *Headnotes* edition observing the fiftieth anniversary of the end of the war. Martin, an enlisted man in the Army, along with other troops from North Africa boarded the headquarters ship, the *Monrovia*, for the landing at Sicily. It was a hot July day. "We were all carrying packs, rifles, canteens and, of course, the inevitable steel helmet, liner and wool cap. All of us had taken off the head gear and had it strapped either to the pack or hanging over an arm. I was the first man at the gangplank, and as I arrived, I saw a full colonel, the highest rank I had ever seen, even at a distance, standing, glaring at me until I got about a foot away. At that point, he exploded with a vituperative discourse on how I was a traitor to my country for not wearing my steel helmet. . . . As he was talking, I looked up on the bridge of the ship and there stood an individual in cavalry breeches, shiny cavalry boots, a short jacket (even before Eisenhower introduced his model), a silver belt buckle about the size of your hand, two pearl-handle revolvers, and, most outstanding, a shiny helmet with two stars on it [as opposed to the standard rough, non-glare helmet]. . . . At that time, I had never heard of George S. Patton Jr., but when I got aboard, I found out that he had quite a reputation in North Africa for being strict about the troops wearing their helmets at all times. . . . The colonel was obviously acting on his orders." Several days later, just prior to the landing, Martin and the other troops on the ship received a letter telling of what lay ahead. The last sentence read: "Go ashore and kill the enemy bastards. Sincerely yours, George S. Patton Jr."[24]

Dallas' women lawyers also saw duty. Margaret W. Scottino, an SMU law school graduate and assistant probation officer for Dallas County, was commissioned as a second lieutenant in the U.S. Marine Corps. Alyne Burton was inducted into the Women's Auxiliary of the Army.[25] Elizabeth Carp, an SMU law school graduate who also joined the WAC, indicated the nature of the entirely new lifestyle she and others were encountering with her report from her basic training course in Iowa. When "the Major" walked back and forth in front of her she nearly "popped" but that her "eyes never wavered."[26]

The war's impact reduced the amount of activity in courtrooms throughout the state, and it also substantially decreased the number of new lawyers entering the profession. In August 1943 then State District Judge Sarah T. Hughes reported that district courts in Dallas were up to date with their case loads. Lawyers could get a trial for their clients in a non-jury or divorce case within thirty days after filing the suit. Jury trials could be obtained within four to six months if both sides were ready. On August 1, 1942, 599 jury cases were pending in the county's district courts. That figure had dropped to 336 on August 1, 1943. So encouraged was Judge Hughes that in the spring of 1945, noting the dockets to be in the best shape in Dallas' history, she advocated having fewer judges in the state but paying them higher salaries.[27]

With so many of the state's lawyers away during the war, there were fewer and fewer law school graduates as well. Their numbers gradually declined to a trickle with each year of the war, from 343 graduates in 1940, to 126 in 1943, to 75 in 1944.[28]

In November 1944 a survey by the American Bar Association showed one out of five Dallas lawyers to be in military service, about the same percentage as at the end of 1942. Of 1,021 full-time lawyers in the county, 214 were in military service.[29]

WHILE THE WAR and the enthusiastic participation of so many Dallas lawyers to work toward its successful completion dominated the first half of the 1940s, other issues occasionally arose to claim the attention of bar members. One that especially captured their interest was an issue that years later would see a dramatic change in attitude. It arose in 1943 after the American Bar Association's board of governors voted for the first time to admit black attorneys to membership in the ABA. The discrimination restricting African-Americans in general from enjoying the full privileges of the American democratic society had seemed especially incongruous to many during a war that was billed as necessary to preserve American freedoms and that saw black citizens losing their lives in uniform for that cause. African-American lawyers in Dallas, still only a handful in number but an increasingly active group, were not permitted to join the Bar Association of Dallas either. Shortly after the ABA's action, the veteran jurist and former mayor William M. Holland presented a resolution at a Bar Association of Dallas meeting on September 11, 1943, calling on the ABA to rescind its vote as a "slap in the face" to all Southern members. "We believe that opening the rolls of membership in the American Bar Association to members of the Negro race," the resolution stated, "will result in grave injury to the association and its influence, if not to its outright destruction, creating, as it will, a source of constant friction, irritation and conflict between the white and Negro races."[30]

A stirring debate ensued. Opponents to Holland's motion were led by Thomas B. Love, George Clifton Edwards, John Davis, Thomas Murnane, Tom L. McCullough, and J. Cleo Thompson (the Bar Association's delegate to the ABA). Finally, a motion to table the resolution succeeded by a vote of 33 to 31.[31]

Still, the matter did not end. At the next Saturday morning legal clinic, D.A. Frank announced that he would move to reconsider the vote at the next meeting, noting that only sixty-four members out of a membership of more than a thousand had voted on Holland's resolution. A large number of members attended the next meeting in the 95th District Courtroom to debate this matter once more. Holland's resolution asking the ABA to rescind its decision eventually was supported by a substantial majority of those present, although an accurate vote count was not taken.[32]

In the next year, 1944, one Bar Association member spoke at a meeting on strategies to circumvent the U.S. Supreme Court decision which required the Democratic Party to open its primaries to Negroes. George Clifton Edwards, angry at sponsorship of a talk on such a subject, submitted a written protest to the Bar Association.[33] The Bar Association responded by inviting Edwards to speak on the subject at one of its Saturday morning legal clinics. In his talk, "Negro Progress and White Justice," Edwards clearly spelled out the insidious nature of discrimination in the law, in economics, in education, and in employment. Lawyers—of all people in society—he said, should recognize the unfairness and unconstitutionality of such discrimination. Applause for his speech was generous, but not unanimous, and a motion by one hostile lawyer to strike Edwards' speech from the minutes was debated and finally tabled.[34]

Several African-American lawyers already were working diligently in Dallas to remedy these inequities, and they were achieving success that helped lay the groundwork for a virtual revolution in American domestic affairs in the next decades. They were responsible for two of the most noteworthy civil rights cases of the era, separate suits which opened up political processes in the South to African-Americans and which signaled an end to segregation in public higher education. The most prominent of these lawyers was William J. Durham (1896-1970), a native of Hopkins County, Texas, who had begun his practice in Sherman after passing the bar examination in 1926. After establishing a successful practice as counsel to an insurance company, Durham began spending much of his time fighting for equal rights through the courts. Already recognized generally as the leading black attorney in the state, in 1943 he moved to Dallas where a group of activists led by A. Maceo Smith and Maynard Jackson were busy organizing African-American voters and building up a political organization in the black community.

Durham, described by John L. Hauer as "unfailingly courteous, patient, and understanding" even when confronted with injustice and prejudice, and the other black attorneys in Dallas such as C.B. Bunkley Jr, Fred Finch Jr., J.L. Turner Jr., D.B. Mason, and

L.A. Bedford Jr. were not eligible to be members of the Bar Association.[35] Their admission to membership and that of other African-American lawyers would not be permitted until two more decades had passed.

One of Durham's early successes was in addressing the issue that schoolteacher George F. Porter had raised nearly three decades earlier—that of inferior pay for black teachers as opposed to their white counterparts. Representing the Dallas Council of Negro Organizations (an umbrella organization for several African-American organizations) in *Page v. Board of Education, City of Dallas*, Durham won a judgment in 1943 which granted pay raises to African-American teachers over a two-year period until their salaries equaled those of white teachers.[36]

It was Durham and the local chapter of the National Association for the Advancement of Colored People, including attorney Crawford B. Bunkley Jr. who challenged the all-white Democratic primaries that had resulted in the important *Smith v. Allwright* decision by the U.S. Supreme Court in 1944. This decision, which required the opening of Democratic Party primaries to African-Americans, was an important first step in dismantling the segregated power structure of the South.

Just after the war, Durham, Bunkley, and the chief counsel for the national NAACP, Thurgood Marshall, who visited Dallas for strategy sessions, turned their attention to discrimination in higher education. The suit they filed, *Sweatt v. Painter*, with Durham as the lead counsel, resulted in a 1950 U.S. Supreme Court decision which declared the University of Texas' all-white law school to be unconstitutional. This case has been viewed as the most important precursor to the 1954 *Brown v. Board of Education* decision which declared "separate but equal" educational facilities throughout the nation to be inherently unconstitutional.

Other gains also occurred during this period. In 1941 the first African-Americans for more than five decades began serving on juries. In October 1942 a grand jury sworn in by Judge Henry King contained for the first time since Reconstruction a black man. He was John King, 62, owner of a farm near Irving. What prompted his selection had been the U.S. Supreme Court's reversal of a death penalty returned against a black man because of the exclusion in Dallas County of African-Americans from grand juries.[37]

Two weeks later, in November 1942, a Dallas *Daily Times Herald* headline reported that there was a "Scheme Afoot Here to Name Negro Judge." African-Americans were said to be organizing to write in the name of J.L. Turner in the November 3 general election to replace Dick Dixon of the 95th District Court. Judge Dixon had left for military service. If indeed there was an organized plan to win write-in votes for an African-American candidate, it went no further. The Dallas Bar Association endorsed William Cramer, and Cramer won the position. J.L. Turner received a single write-in vote. Even that vote had his initials incorrect—"J.T." instead of "J.L." [38]

Another issue pertaining to discrimination of minorities—in this case, women—also remained unresolved during these years. Despite the fact that Sarah T. Hughes sat on the bench in a state district court, and even though women had won the right to vote in 1920, women still were not permitted to serve as jurors in Texas. Judge Hughes critically addressed this question in a Saturday morning legal clinic in April 1943, claiming in her talk that Texas was only "half a democracy." In states where women were permitted to serve as jurors, she said, they performed their duties enthusiastically, unlike men who commonly sought to avoid jury duty. As to the argument that women were subject to being easily swayed by handsome lawyers, this was no more likely than men being influenced by good-looking women, she believed. Women with small children could be exempted from jury service if they asked to be excused, she said. To give equal time to the matter, D.A. Frank spoke the following Saturday in favor of continuing to exclude women as jurors.[39]

Two weeks later, although the Texas Legislature already had spurned a resolution calling for a state-wide vote on the matter, the Bar Association of Dallas continued to debate the issue. While considering a motion opposing women on juries, the constitutional amendment committee, by a vote of 28 to 23, defeated a substitute motion that advocated women on juries. Judge Hughes, seeing that her pet project was doomed, was successful in tabling the original motion against women on juries. The association's minutes thus reflected no official position on the matter.[40] Not until eleven years later in 1954 would women be permitted to serve on juries in Texas.

The issue of women versus men also provided some levity for Bar Association members. In a free-wheeling "quiz show" held in the 14th District Courtroom, three women lawyers competed against three male counterparts before a raucous crowd of lawyers and courthouse workers. Moderator D.A. Frank challenged the panelists with such questions as who wrote the words for the Star-Spangled Banner and what numbered state was Texas when it entered the union. The women, Miss Elizabeth Carp, Mrs. Melody Douthit, and Mrs. Minnie Solomon, defeated the men, J. Frank Wilson, Bart Dummit, and Frank Cain, by a score of 231 to 185.[41]

Yet another matter just after the war's end captured the attention of the Bar Association. This was the push to replace the deteriorating Old Red Courthouse with a new building. All but one of the members present at a meeting in 1945 voted to ask the Dallas County Commissioners Court to submit a bond issue to the voters to build a new courthouse. County Judge Al Templeton described the courthouse as "a crying shame" for a city whose population had doubled in the past twenty-five years. Not long before, a 400-pound ornament had fallen from the courthouse to the street. If it had struck a passer-by, he observed, the county likely would be facing a huge damage suit. Nathaniel Jacks said the county needed a new courthouse far worse than Dallas needed a new city hall, the one at Main and Harwood having been declared inadequate and obsolete only twenty-five years after its construction.[42]

The sole dissenting vote in this resolution to replace the Old Red Courthouse came from U.S. District Judge T. Whitfield Davidson, who pleaded for the county to retain the building in honor of what their grandfathers had done. Other property should be purchased for a new courthouse, he argued. "Let's keep intact the old building that resounded with the voices of the late Charles

Culberson and M.M. Crane, the craggy, white-haired jurist said."[43] Ultimately, of course, Judge Davidson's view prevailed.

A T T H E E N D of the war one of the Bar Association's most active and prominent members, Paul Carrington (1894-1988), told his fellow lawyers—just as Hatton W. Sumners had told them to take the lead in time of war—that they now would be obliged to take the lead in solving the most pressing post-war problems in Dallas and in the nation. These Carrington identified as unemployment and the return of veterans, the relaxation of war-time government controls including those on taxation and housing, international cooperation, and the re-education of Americans on the blessings of and the ideals of democracy.[44]

Carrington was one of the city's most active and visible civic leaders in a busy career that would last for six decades. In 1940 he served both as president of the Bar Association and of the Dallas Chamber of Commerce, then took on a second term as Chamber president. A native of Mexico, Missouri, Carrington graduated from Harvard Law School in 1917. After a stint in the Army as a second lieutenant in World War I, he moved to Dallas to begin his legal career. In Dallas he joined the firm of Etheridge, McCormick & Bromberg (later Carrington, Gowan, Johnson & Walker), where he would remain until 1958 when he withdrew to help found the firm Carrington, Johnson & Stephens. In 1970 he moved on to establish another firm, Carrington, Coleman, Sloman & Blumenthal. From 1960 to 1961 he was president of the State Bar of Texas. Carrington's civic activities, in addition to his Chamber of Commerce work, included leadership roles with the Greater Dallas Planning Council, the North Texas Committee on Economic Development, the Dallas YMCA, and the Circle 10 Council of the Boy Scouts of America.[45]

Especially prominent—in fact, a dominant figure—in Dallas' civic affairs during the war years and immediately after was James Woodall Rodgers (1890-1961), an attorney who specialized in oil and gas matters and whose legal career in Dallas had begun in 1916 after he received a B.A. from Vanderbilt in 1912 and an LL.B. from the University of Texas in 1915. For many years

Rodgers represented Standard Oil Company of Indiana and its Texas subsidiaries. Rodgers, president of the Bar Association in 1938, was elected mayor of Dallas for four consecutive terms, beginning his eight years in the office in 1939. With so much physical energy and resources during these years channeled toward the war effort, Rodgers helped direct the city's attention to the critical planning that he saw as necessary for the post-war period.

Rodgers pushed hard to complete his pet project, the long-time dream of uniting the southern and northern parts of the cities via the "Central Boulevard" link first proposed by George Kessler in his 1911 city plan. Central Expressway, as it would be called, was not finished until after Rodgers' terms as mayor, but recognition of his critical work in starting the project came years later when another expressway tying into Central Expressway was named in his honor—Woodall Rodgers Freeway.

In several other areas Rodgers' civic leadership helped shape Dallas for years to come. One important accomplishment was his role in hiring a nationally recognized city planner, Harland Bartholomew, to develop a new master plan which Rodgers saw as necessary if Dallas were to compete with other cities in the anticipated post-war economic boom. The other was his leading role in 1943 in rejecting an agreement in which Dallas, in partnership with Fort Worth, would build a mid-cities regional airport. Afterwards, Dallas redoubled its efforts to improve the facilities at Love Field with such success that it became one of the nation's busiest airports. Rodgers also led a drive in 1945 for the City of Dallas to annex Highland Park, University Park, and Preston Hollow. Only Preston Hollow residents agreed to the annexation, and afterwards Rodgers advised the Dallas City Council that henceforth only Dallas residents would be permitted to serve on its boards and commissions.

Rodgers was the founder and president of the Greater Dallas Planning Council, and the first president and an organizer of the Dallas Salesmanship Club. In 1942 he was given the Linz Award for outstanding civic service, in 1944 the American Legion Award for citizenship and leadership, in 1955 an award for distinguished city planning from Dallas architects, and in 1961 the "All Time Headliner" award by the Press Club of Dallas.[46]

WITH THE WAR over, one of the great questions for the American nation was whether or not to retain something that had always been anathema to Americans—mandatory military service during peacetime. The debate broke out at a June 1945 meeting of the Bar Association with surprising intensity, lasting two hours before a vote was taken. Following a stirring argument in its favor by Preston A. Weatherred, former commander of the Texas 36th Division, those present at this Saturday morning session voted 27 to 14 to have compulsory military service. The members' sentiment generally reflected national opinion, for when the question arose in Congress, that body approved a continuation of the Selective Service Act.[47]

The aftermath of war saw one of Dallas' lawyers gain international attention through his prominent work in the Nuremberg trials in which leaders of Nazi Germany were charged with war crimes and tried before the International Military. U.S. Supreme Court Justice Robert H. Jackson, the American prosecutor who had spoken to the Dallas Bar in 1942, chose Robert G. Storey (1893-1981)—whose work for combat intelligence service in the Mediterranean theater won for him the Bronze Star and a Legion of Merit—to be his chief assistant in the historic trials. In the prosecution of Herman Goering, Rudolf Hess, and other Nazis, Storey, as deputy prosecutor, helped assemble some 100,000 documents from intelligence files and other sources to produce the guilty verdicts. For his good work this former president of the Bar Association of Dallas was awarded the Medal of Freedom and the French Legion of Honor.[48]

Upon receiving his appointment to help Justice Jackson at Nuremberg, Storey in turn had called upon one of his friends and a former law partner, Edwin Taylor Armstrong, to assist him in the prosecution. Armstrong, who had reported to duty as a lieutenant (j.g.) with the U.S. Navy on April 14, 1942, and since then had seen considerable duty in various non-legal assignments, recently had been assigned to a post in which he did use his legal training in "contract terminations" at Bethlehem, Pennsylvania. Immensely pleased at this rare opportunity in international law, Armstrong contacted his commanding officer, a hard-nosed Naval Academy graduate, and requested permission for the transfer. Armstrong's superior refused. "Although I kept pleading with him as to how much this would mean to my career, he continued to refuse and told me that I was 'his lawyer,' but that he would recommend me for promotion." Armstrong thus missed this unique opportunity.[49] (In 1952 Armstrong would be elected president of the Dallas Bar Association.)

Another Dallas lawyer, however, was able to participate with Storey in the Nuremberg trials. He was George E. Seay, a descendant of pioneer Dallas lawyer Robert B. Seay. Seay, a lieutenant colonel, was in charge of Section VI in compiling evidence against Nazi organizations.[50]

Back in Dallas after his Nuremberg service, Storey, a senior member of Storey, Sanders, Sherrill & Armstrong, accepted in January 1947 an offer to become dean of the Southern Methodist University School of Law. His predecessor, Dean C.S. Potts, who had served as dean since 1927, returned to the classroom as dean emeritus. Almost immediately after his appointment, Storey announced the organization by a group of lawyers, businessmen, and scholars of the Southwestern Legal Foundation, a legal center to be established on the SMU campus. Described at the time as only the third such legal center to be planned in the nation, it would be the first such center to be completed. It became a place where jurists, lawyers, and the lay public could conduct research and study about the needs of a changing world. One of its components would take special advantage of Storey's expertise in international law, but its subjects would also include fields of law of particular interest to the Southwest—oil and gas, insurance, taxation, and labor law. One of the foundation's important functions would be the sponsorship of conferences and seminars in which attorneys, judges, legislators, law school professors, businessmen, and representatives from both management and labor would find solutions to vexing legal problems. Although located on the SMU campus and headed by Storey, the foundation was controlled by a separate board of trustees, many of whom had prominent standing in the Dallas legal community. They included Harold A. Bateman, president of the Bar Association, former mayor Woodall Rodgers, and Congressman Hatton W. Sumners.[51]

Storey's rise to legal prominence had been meteoric. Born in Greenville in 1893, he was admitted to the bar in Texarkana in 1914 after studies at the University of Texas. After service in the First World War as an artillery lieutenant, he became assistant attorney general of Texas in charge of criminal appeals, a position he held from 1921 to 1923. His astuteness and competency won for him appointment to the board of regents of the University of Texas at the youthful age of thirty-one, and he served as a regent from 1924 to 1930. In 1924 Storey became an assistant district attorney in Dallas County; in 1932 he was a delegate to the International Convention of Comparative Law at The Hague; in 1934 he served as president of the Bar Association of Dallas; in 1948 he was elected president of the State Bar of Texas. In 1953 he became the city's second attorney to be elected president of the American Bar Association (Robert E.L. Saner was the first). He was named the outstanding lawyer of the year in January 1955 by the board of directors of the Dallas Bar Association. [52]

Another lawyer from Dallas—this one a native of the city—at whom the national spotlight was directed at the war's end was Tom C. Clark (1899-1977), who in June 1945 was appointed by President Harry Truman to be attorney general of the United States. Clark, the son of the veteran Dallas lawyer William H. Clark (who had become the youngest president of the state bar in 1897 at the age of thirty-six) had moved to Washington, D.C., in 1937 to join the Justice Department. Previously, he had worked with his father and brother in private practice in Dallas from 1922 to 1927. This had followed his graduation from the University of Texas School of Law. Before moving to the nation's capital, he was Dallas County's civil district attorney. His career in the Justice Department had progressed steadily over the years. Prior to his appointment as attorney general he had been assistant attorney general in charge of the criminal division.[53]

Four months after his confirmation by the U.S. Senate, Clark returned to Texas for a round of visits with his lawyer friends in Dallas and other Texas cities. On his first evening in Texas the Dallas Chamber of Commerce and Dallas Citizens Council honored him with a "lavish stag banquet." President Truman sent a message to be read for the occasion: "This should be a proud day for Dallas and for Tom Clark, another home town boy who made good. In honoring him I feel that you are verifying my judgment in appointing him to the exalted post of Attorney General of the United States. We all know that he will do a grand job and will reflect glory on the city and the state that gave him to the nation."[54]

For his part, Clark hastened to tell the crowd that he was "only a small town lawyer." His job as attorney general would be "just a lawyer's job" even though he understood that the office had "a right smart number of lawyers—about 27,000 I understand—working for it."[55]

After a journey into other parts of Texas for brief visits, Clark returned to Dallas to be honored at a luncheon sponsored by the Bar Association of Dallas and the Federal Bar Association. He chose his talk at the luncheon as the occasion to make an important policy statement: federal attorneys must henceforth shut down their private practices and work only for the government. The next morning Clark was honored by a stag breakfast, and then in the afternoon he shook hands with more than 600 persons at the home of his younger brother, Robert L. Clark.[56]

During his term as attorney general Clark would take several positions that were alien to many Texans of the day, including arguing before the U.S. Supreme Court that the off-shore tidelands oil fields were owned not by the individual states but by the federal government. Clark also initiated the Department of Justice's first modern amicus brief on behalf of a civil-rights plaintiff. It resulted in a unanimous high court decision prohibiting discrimination in housing contracts.[57]

Four years later Clark became the first Texan ever to be named to the U.S. Supreme Court. He was sworn in by Chief Justice Fred

M. Vinson on August 24, 1949, in a ceremony in the White House. To observe his ascendancy to the nation's highest court, Clark gave up his practice of wearing gaily colored bow ties in favor of black ones.[58]

Clark would serve on the high court for the next seventeen years, and here too, he often cast votes in opposition to prevailing Southern and Texas opinion. He voted with the majority in *Sweatt v. Painter*, and he also joined in the unanimous opinion of the court in *Brown v. Board of Education* (1954). He ruled in *School District of Abingdon v. Schempp* (1963) that prayers should be kept out of public schools. Despite these positions that generally were described as liberal, Clark often took conservative stances, including his support of McCarthy-era prosecutions. When in 1977 President Lyndon B. Johnson appointed Clark's son, Ramsey, to be the nation's attorney general, Clark resigned from the Supreme Court to avoid any conflict of interest. At Ramsey Clark's suggestion, President Johnson filled Clark's seat by appointing the nation's first African-American to a Supreme Court position, Thurgood Marshall.[59]

THE RETURNING war veterans lost little time in involving themselves in Bar Association activities. In the first election for president after the war, members chose on January 12, 1946, the returned U.S. Navy captain, H. Bascom Thomas Jr., to be president. During the war he had served as commanding officer of a Navy ship in the South Pacific, had seen combat, and was awarded a Bronze Star. A native of Sulphur Springs, Texas, he held an LL.B. from the University of Texas. Thomas' father had been a lawyer; his son, Robert H., became a lawyer (and also a future DBA president), and his grandson Stewart became an attorney.

The veterans, seemingly hungry to participate in the democratic processes which they had helped save, also jumped eagerly into public affairs. One of the earliest and brightest was Will R. Wilson Jr., who as commanding officer of the 465th Field Artillery Battalion in Northern Luzon had accepted the surrender of the forces of General Yamashita. Wilson was an SMU graduate who had grown up in Highland Park and before the war served as president of the Dallas Junior Bar Association. In 1948 Wilson was re-elected district attorney. For many years he would have an outstanding state-wide career as a public official and jurist. In 1949, having gained national attention for strictly enforcing vice laws and chasing gamblers out of town who had been making easy money under lax enforcement, Wilson was elected to the Texas Supreme Court for a six-year term. Afterwards, in 1956, he was elected the state's attorney general, holding that position from Jan. 1, 1957, to January 15, 1963.[60]

In his initial race for district attorney, Wilson had faced several opponents, among them Henry Menasco Wade, a U.S. Navy veteran from Rockwall who had settled in Dallas after the war. So impressed was he with Wade during the campaign that he hired him to be his chief felony prosecutor. When Wilson decided to run for the State Supreme Court, Wade campaigned for and won the right to succeed Wilson as district attorney. Wade became district attorney in 1950, beginning a distinguished career that would set a longevity record for that office in Dallas County—thirty-six years until his retirement on January 1, 1987. During those years Wade achieved national prominence for his work, which included winning a death sentence for Jack Ruby, the slayer of Lee Harvey Oswald [61]

At city hall another Navy veteran and attorney, Wallace Savage, was elected in 1947 to a city council seat. In 1949 he was the upset choice to be mayor of the city, and in 1951 he became state chairman of the Democratic Party's executive committee.

The fact that judges were elected in Texas by popular vote—not appointed—posed a particular dilemma for the public. It was difficult to identify the best candidate for a judge on the basis of a political campaign. Could lawyers make better assessments as to the best candidates? Should their assessments be relayed to the public? Such subjects were debated at a 1946 Bar Association meeting following a judicial committee report that, at least indirectly, criticized two criminal district courts for their large backlog of pending cases.[62] Whether or not this was a fair report and what the public might make of such information were interesting issues. The ensuing discussion prompted the Association to decide that the organization would vote secretly on the qualifications of judicial candidates in the 1946 Democratic primary and publicize the results of the poll as a guide to the public. Regular bar polls on judicial candidates would become a standard part of the Association's activities.[63]

A Time for Streamlining

⌘

Chapter Eleven

AMERICANS IN THE post-war era made a seemingly painless transition from the late 1940s into the 1950s and 1960s. They enjoyed economic prosperity and good times as seldom if ever before experienced, began large-scale residential shifts from cities to new and mushrooming suburbs, and saw college education become a realistic possibility for all economic and social classes. Cold War fears could dampen only slightly an overwhelming feeling that society and all its institutions were advancing inexorably toward a more perfect existence.

In Dallas, too, optimism gave a rosy hue to most affairs. The times were booming and without much domestic conflict or disagreement on goals. Central Expressway, envisioned as early as 1911 by city planner George E. Kessler as an important transportation link between South and North Dallas, was begun and completed. Tightly knit organizations of men who were predominantly business leaders—the Citizens Charter Association and an even more powerful and related group, the Citizens Council—oversaw the city with a paternalistic hand that brought order and efficiency to municipal government and civic affairs. The man known as "Mr. Dallas," banker Robert L. Thornton Sr., served four terms as mayor and managed to "keep the dirt flyin' " as the city grew rapidly in population and its handsome skyline reached ever upward. These days and months and years, it seemed, were ripe for progress, for consolidation, for organization, for planning, for expansion, and for streamlining.

THROUGH THE VERY many years that lawyers had been coming together as a group in Dallas, their forum had always been the "bar association." The precise structure of their bar association had changed at various times over the years as reorganizations occurred amidst frequent efforts to create a more precise and more clearly defined body. In the 1916 reorganization, a charter had been obtained from the State of Texas under the closest designation possible for such an association—that of a "literary society." The occasion had been marked not only by having for the first time an official charter, but also by a name change—from the Dallas Bar Association to the Bar Association of Dallas.

Now, in these heady post-war days, it came to be felt that the Bar Association's charter should be a more proper one. State Senator Fred (Red) Harris and State Representative Dallas Blankenship, both Dallas attorneys, successfully sponsored legislation that made incorporation possible under the organization's actual purpose, that of a "bar association." The lawyers of Dallas became the first in the state to take advantage of this legislation which they had initiated. Their new charter, filed and approved by the secretary of state on November 19, 1947, was signed by ninety-two Dallas lawyers. It brought with it yet another name change, returning to the earlier designation as the Dallas Bar Association.[1] This would be the most lasting reorganization yet for the association. In May 1994 the charter was amended to become perpetual.

The organizational meeting under the new charter was held December 13, 1947, in Judge William M. Cramer's 101st District Court. Only seventeen of the ninety-two who had signed the charter were present, but forty-nine others were represented by proxy. The previous slate of officers, with Harold A. Bateman as president, was continued; all assets and liabilities of the old organization were transferred to the new one; members already in good standing were transferred to the new membership rolls; and the previous by-laws calling for a fifteen-member board of directors and a five-member executive committee were continued. C.K. Bullard was the first chairman of the board of directors. Directors included one female, Hattie L. Henenberg. The purpose of the newly constituted organization was declared in the charter to be "for the protection and advancement of the professional interests of persons licensed to practice law, the advancement of cordial intercourse among lawyers, and the improvement of relations between the Bench and the Bar and the public."[2]

One of the first activities instituted by the Dallas Bar Association under its new name was the creation in 1948 of the Lawyers Reference Service, done in cooperation with and at the suggestion of the Junior Bar Association. The Junior Bar made its recommendation after a survey of similar services in Los Angeles, Chicago, Pittsburgh, Boston, New York, and San Diego. The Service's goal, as summarized by president Robert L. Dillard Jr., was "to make competent legal advice readily available to persons of moderate means, and particularly to make it known publicly that competent legal advice is available at a fixed and very moderate fee."[3]

The referral service also addressed a perennial problem that especially plagued judges, the district attorney, the city attorney, and other officials who were lawyers. Citizens frequently asked them to suggest a lawyer who might represent them. These officials were reluctant to name particular individuals for fear of being accused of favoritism, and the new system provided a convenient solution to this problem. Under the plan the Association's executive secretary, Eula Cates, maintained individual cards bearing the names of more than seventy lawyers who agreed to participate in the program. When an individual requested the name of a lawyer to represent him or her, Ms. Cates simply picked up the first card in the stack and called the attorney listed there to set up an appointment. The card bearing the name of that attorney then would be placed at the back of the stack to be rotated slowly to the front as all cards were referred to in order. The Association's office on the first floor of the Red Courthouse was a convenient location for this public service. After ten months Ms. Cates found that a large number of the calls for legal services came from people seeking lawyers to assist them in obtaining patents for their inventions.[4]

Related to this matter of how a citizen could find a lawyer was another issue—how could an attorney find a salaried position? Beginning in January 1952 the Dallas Bar Association sought to address this problem through the creation of the Lawyer

Placement Bureau, believed to be the first of its kind in the state except for those maintained by law schools. The Placement Bureau was started after Bar Association member Philip I. Palmer conducted a survey of existing placement bureaus in the nation. Any law firm, oil or insurance company, or prospective employer who wished to employ a lawyer on a salaried basis filed its requirements with the Bureau, and conversely, any lawyer seeking work could place his or her credentials with the Bureau. The Bureau operated without cost to those wishing to use its services. The Bar Association's executive director, Miss Evelyn Conway, replaced Eula Cates at the end of 1948 and would serve until 1961, handling all inquiries.[5]

For an attorney—especially one practicing alone—to hang up a shingle and develop a thriving practice strictly on word-of-mouth references was difficult. One vehicle that appeared to be acceptable as a form of advertising was placing one's name, address, and telephone number in a classified legal directory appearing in the city's two newspapers, *The Dallas Morning News* and the *Daily Times Herald*. Even this directory, though, came to be frowned upon by the Bar Association's board of directors which in 1949 declared advertisements in it to be unethical. The board sent letters to both newspapers expressing displeasure at the directory's existence. The committee on legal ethics similarly sent warning letters to all attorneys whose names appeared in the directory.[6]

IN EARLIER DAYS the practice of criminal law was an important aspect of just about every lawyer's practice. As growing numbers in the legal profession became more and more involved with corporate affairs and began to abandon criminal law, they were less and less tied to the courthouse for their routine activities. As these lawyers with predominantly civil practices grew in number and visibility, it began to seem that those who spent so much of their time at the Old Red Courthouse—criminal attorneys—were held in less esteem in the eyes of the public. In the fall of 1949 about seventy-five of these lawyers, concerned about a deterioration in their public image and the growing perception that their work was more tawdry than that of other specialties, decided to form their own organization—the Dallas County Criminal Bar Association. They elected J.E. McLemore Jr. as president and Sam Donosky, a young associate with Hughes & Malone, as vice president. At their first luncheon meeting the group had as their speaker Judge Tom L. Beauchamp of the Court of Criminal Appeals. Beauchamp praised the group "for being frank in your purpose to lead yourselves out of whatever groove others have placed you in."[7]

The Criminal Bar Association declared its objectives to be these: (1) to support proper enforcement and administration of criminal law, (2) to propose criminal laws more just and proper for the betterment of the public, (3) to publicize and stress the necessary place of the criminal lawyer in society, (4) to strive for a high code of ethics among the profession, and (5) to educate the public and themselves on the duties of criminal lawyers and the rights of persons charged with crime.[8]

The Criminal Bar Association quickly assumed a serious intent in living up to its goals. Its regular luncheons included talks from judges, lawyers, and other speakers on interesting and pertinent topics. By 1958 its activities had grown to include mounting a campaign against "bond hustling" and "jail running" (a practice in which lawyers solicited clients among jail prisoners), sponsoring a Little League baseball team, making donations to the Sunshine Home of Dallas (for needy children from broken families), and donating to a fund of the Probation Officers of Dallas County to assist indigent prisoners when placed on probation.[9]

In October 1957 members elected their first woman president, Mrs. Gladys Melton, said to be the only woman in the county to be regularly practicing criminal law. In 1959 members honored her as the Criminal Lawyer of the Year, citing her work as president, her service to indigent defendants, her efforts to achieve better public relations, and her ethical practice of law.[10]

Many of Dallas' criminal lawyers had offices near the courthouse because of its convenience. As this older part of town began to decline and yield in prestige to the uptown area, the offices there tended to be less posh and expansive than those occupied by the city's bigger firms. Even while the criminal lawyers sought to upgrade the image of their specialty, many of them playfully referred to themselves as members of the "skid row bar association."

A typical career pattern for many criminal lawyers after graduation from law school was to work as a prosecutor in the district attorney's office, and then, after several years' experience, to begin their own private practice on the opposite side as criminal practitioners. The best known criminal lawyers in Dallas since the 1920s and into the early 1950s were two partners who had come out of the district attorney's office—Maury Hughes (1894-1955) and Theodore F. (Ted) Monroe (1890-1952). Together they represented defendants in some of the Southwest's most highly publicized criminal trials and gained a national reputation for their skills. Hughes, the former district attorney who in his last year in office had withdrawn his affiliation with the Ku Klux Klan, denounced it, and then fought against it, had become perhaps the most colorful lawyer in town with his sometimes bizarre but always effective courtroom dramatics. Once he fired a pistol before a jury to prove that a certain type of ammunition was compatible with the pistol in question. On another occasion he brought a caged lioness into the courtroom and stuck his hand through the cage bars to prove its gentleness. A native of California who had been reared in Gainesville, Texas, Hughes began practicing law in Dallas in 1913. From 1932 to 1934 he was State Democratic Executive Committee chairman, and in 1934 he lost a race for governor of the state.[11]

Monroe, Hughes' partner from 1923 until 1952, was a native of Kentucky and a University of Michigan Law School graduate. Like Hughes, he began practicing law in Dallas in 1913, and he was assistant district attorney under Hughes. They formed in 1923 a partnership that would last until Monroe's death in 1952. Monroe was said to have a brilliant mind, a deep and impressive voice, and a talent for oratory. During all those years with Hughes, John L. Hauer later recalled, Hughes and Monroe operated as a team at the courthouse, "leaping from their chairs in unison to make an objection, Ted Monroe always the very picture of righteous indignation, visibly shaking and quivering in outrage and speaking in a rich mellifluous voice to the balcony seats, while Hughes spoke quickly and forcefully in what was a comparatively rasping tone."[12]

Sam Donosky, the firm's young associate, described Hughes' irrepressible courtroom wit in an anecdote concerning his defense of an accused bootlegger on a hot summer day before the courthouse was air-conditioned. A dozen bottles of bootleg beer rested on the prosecutor's table as state's evidence. When the prosecutor reached a sweaty and vehement climax in his peroration, he pointed to the bottles of beer and exclaimed, "Look at them! Look at the evidence of shame and of guilt!" From Hughes' parched lips came an anguished and spontaneous cry: "Oh, God, if they were only cold!"[13]

Hughes' son, Robert H. Hughes, also became an attorney. He served as judge of the Domestic Relations Court No. 2 from 1963 to 1968, and also in the Texas Legislature.

ANOTHER ORGANIZATION for lawyers which continued to prosper after its founding in 1929 was the Dallas Junior Bar Association. In September 1951, because of its outstanding work, it won the American Bar Association's annual Award of Merit as the best junior bar in the nation. Edward B. Winn, president, accepted the honor at the ABA's September annual meeting in New York City.[14] The first and largest junior bar association in Texas, by 1962 the Dallas organization had fifteen committees coordinating its varied projects. Its many activities included sponsorship of an auxiliary organization, the Dallas Junior Bar Association Law Wives. Winn followed his presidency of the Dallas Junior Bar with a term as president of the State Junior Bar Association, as did Ben Pickering in 1962. The junior bar associations in the state were affiliated with the State Bar of Texas.[15]

The number of profesional outlets for attorneys with diverse interests kept expanding during these years. By the mid-1950s the Dallas chapter of the Federal Bar Association was holding regular luncheons with speakers such as U.S. District Judge T. Whitfield

Davidson and SMU Law School Dean Robert G. Storey.[16] The Bar Association itself also was recognizing the increasingly complex interests of its own members through the creation of special sections which catered to them. For example, in 1959 the Corporate Counsel Section of the Dallas Bar Association was established for attorneys who were employees of companies, institutions, and associations. By 1961 this special section had about 100 members who met twice a month.[17] It would be only one of a multitude of sections to be created in coming years for those lawyers with special interests.

SMU's law school and the Southwestern Legal Center, both under the leadership of Storey, continued to set high standards for legal education. By 1951 two new buildings had been completed adjacent to one another on the campus, one that later would be named for Storey. The second was Lawyers Inn, a residence hall for students. The work of the law school and the Legal Center, seemingly blended together under Storey's mutual leadership of both, was recognized in 1956 by the Ford Foundation with a $250,000 grant for further development of its Graduate School of American and Foreign Law.[18] In 1958 the Blakley-Braniff Foundation awarded a $375,000 grant for continuation of the program and for research purposes. A part of this program, the Law Institute of the Americas, founded in 1952, regularly brought in attorneys from throughout the Western Hemisphere—especially Latin America—to improve understandings through the study of laws, institutions, and governments of the American nations, and also to train lawyers to handle legal problems arising within the Western Hemisphere. Another element, the Academy of American Law, was designed primarily for lawyers in the Middle East, Far East, and some European nations.[19]

In 1956 the Dallas Bar Association joined the Southwestern Legal Foundation and the State Bar of Texas in hosting an important meeting of the Inter-American Bar Conference at the Legal Center. Some 750 delegates, guests, and observers from throughout the Western Hemisphere attended. One of the main speakers was former President Herbert Hoover, whose talk was broadcast nationally over the National Broadcasting Company.

With so many international delegates in attendance, the U.S. State Department sent a representative to advise the hosts in matters of protocol.[20]

In the spring of 1947 the SMU School of Law, in cooperation with the Legal Center, began issuing a twice-yearly legal journal. At first it was named *Texas Law and Legislation*, but the title was changed after the first year to *Southwestern Law Journal*. The initial issue, 173 pages long, was dedicated to Charles Shirley Potts, dean of the law school from 1927 to 1947. The *Southwestern Law Journal* would grow in prestige and become an important scholarly legal publication over the years.

In 1961 another publication came to be published by the SMU School of Law. This was the *Journal of Air Law and Commerce*, which already was in its twenty-eighth volume when the law school assumed editorial control. This unique journal, published quarterly, was the only scholarly periodical in the English language devoted to the legal and economic problems of aviation.[21]

In 1959 Storey retired as dean of the law school, but retained his leadership of the Southwestern Legal Foundation. He was replaced as dean by Assistant Dean John W. Riehm, who resigned in 1963 to be executive vice president of a law publishing firm in New York. Riehm was succeeded by Charles O. Galvin, a member of the faculty since 1952 who specialized in oil and gas and federal taxation. Galvin, who had grown up in University Park, held degrees from Southern Methodist University, Northwestern University, and Harvard University.[22]

IN 1947 THE State Bar of Texas returned to Dallas for the first time since 1941 to hold its annual meeting. That 1941 Dallas meeting had set an attendance record not yet equaled. While the 1947 convention failed to surpass that mark, falling short of it by some 500, the 1,608 lawyers who came to Dallas made it the second best-attended annual meeting ever for the state. The state's lawyers would return to Dallas in 1951, 1955, and 1963, with 2,396 lawyers registered for the July 1963 convention.[23] The Baker and Adolphus hotels served as central meeting places for sessions.

Hosting these conventions was good practice for the Dallas Bar Association, for in August 1956 a long-awaited event occurred in Dallas, the annual meeting of the American Bar Association. The Dallas Bar Association was the principal host. It was the first time that the ABA had met in the Southwest. Some 8,000 were in attendance for this 79th annual meeting. Among those officially welcoming visitors to the convention were DBA President Dwight L. Simmons, who was joined by Governor Allan Shivers, Mayor R.L. Thornton Sr., and Texas Bar President Newton Gresham. The Dallas attorney who had achieved international fame, Robert G. Storey, a former ABA president, was awarded the organization's most coveted award, the ABA Medal for outstanding service to the legal profession. Storey was cited for his "conspicuous and unselfish service to the cause of American jurisprudence."[24]

Dallas lawyers had always been prominent in professional legal circles, both state and national. When Robert G. Storey served as president of the State Bar in 1948-49 he was the eleventh man from Dallas to hold that position. In 1952-53 another Dallas lawyer, J. Glenn Turner (1905-1975), held the presidency of the State Bar of Texas, thus serving as state bar president at the same time Storey was president of the American Bar Association, a rare double honor for Dallas Bar members. Turner's service was especially important in leading to the construction of a new State Bar headquarters building in Austin.

Several months before assuming the presidency Turner had been named chairman of the finance committee to raise $150,000 in donations to pay for the much-needed new headquarters building. He proceeded with great skill to set up fund-raising activities that ultimately went way over the announced goal and served as an excellent model for such activities. His first step was to get an official ruling from the U.S. Treasury Department that all donations toward the building would be deductible from income taxes. He organized finance committees in all twenty-one Congressional districts of Texas, then announced a memorial plan to honor deceased lawyers with gifts of $1,000 or more. Those contributing $5,000 or more could name the various conference rooms in the facility in memory of deceased attorneys or jurists. As a result of this plan, one conference room in the completed building was named the Clark Family Room for two prominent Dallas lawyers of past years, William Henry Clark and his son, William Henry Clark Jr. The senior Clark had served as president of the State Bar in 1896-97. By the time Turner became president of the State Bar and announced his successor as finance chairman in November 1952, $118,000 already had been raised for the building, and before the drive ended more than $226,000 was raised.[25] When the completed granite and limestone building—debt-free—was dedicated in January 1954, Turner was one of three who presided at the ceremonies.

Since the 1920s the Dallas Bar Association had felt an obligation to provide legal services for those who could not afford to hire an attorney. Over the years this service had been offered in various ways. When Dwight L. Simmons was inaugurated as president of the Bar Association in 1956 he declared that the establishment of an adequate free legal aid clinic in Dallas would be his top priority. He appointed Frank Scurlock as chairman and Ramsey Clark (son of Supreme Court Justice Tom C. Clark) and Judge Julien Hyer to investigate the feasibility of establishing such a clinic. The committee's positive recommendation to the entire membership was overwhelmingly endorsed, and Talbot Rain prepared articles of incorporation for the Dallas Legal Aid Society in 1957. Simmons became president, an office he would hold until his death in 1970. The Commissioners Court authorized the use of office space in the Old Red Courthouse, and the office opened on March 15, 1957, with Paul S. Adams Jr. as the attorney. Funding at first was done through various grants and from members of the Bar Association. Later, it became an agency of the United Way. The first two-year budget was for $30,000. In addition to support from the Dallas Bar Association, support came from the National Legal Aid Association, interested individuals, and beginning in 1961 the United Fund. By 1980 the Dallas Legal Aid Society had five lawyers on its staff.[26]

THE DALLAS BAR Association, just as had been true for

the State Bar, also was in critical need for a new facility, a situation more and more discussed in the late 1940s and remedied at the same time the State Bar moved into its new headquarters. The Bar Association's make-shift office space—a fifteen-foot cubicle in the Old Red Courthouse used since 1936—long since had been outgrown. It had no special meeting rooms, no facilities for meals, and only make-shift office space. As fewer lawyers focused their activities these days on the courthouse, that location was less convenient for most of them. Efforts by the house committee to locate an "uptown" facility that could serve not just as an office but as an accommodations for a "club" began during 1948. When in 1949 it was determined that the expenses for such a place would be too great, the notion was put on hold. While it would be possible to move the office alone "uptown," the housing committee recommended that this not be done unless the new site included club facilities as well.[27]

Finally, in 1954, the house committee, now headed by Robert L. Dillard Jr., successfully negotiated with the Adolphus Hotel to take over the spacious quarters formerly occupied by the City Club. Yearly rental fees were $15,000, a figure that seemed enormous at the time. Monthly dues for members, $3 a year, came under pressure and soon were raised by almost 200 percent. By 1963 dues were $42 a year for those in practice for more than five years and $24 annually for those with less than five years experience. The association's board of directors agreed to launch a program to raise $15,000 in contributions from members for furniture and fixtures.[28] The move into the facilities—so commodious in contrast to the old with offices, dining facilities, and meeting rooms—was completed during 1955 with minimal remodeling and redecorating. In 1957 the first of several major renovations and expansions occurred. After the 1957 renovation members could enjoy a front lounge room with television and hi-fidelity phonograph, paintings rented from the Dallas Museum of Fine Arts, and rugs, chairs, and couches in gold and brown fabrics. The main dining room offered buffet lunches to members and guests, and *Vanity Fair* prints of judges decorated the walls. An auxiliary dining room featured the portraits of all past presidents of the Bar Association, beginning with John J. Good. Executive Secretary Evelyn Conway now was joined on the staff by Mattie Skillern, acting as hostess. The impact of the new space and especially the opportunity to meet and eat together produced a new cohesiveness and solidarity among members. The Adolphus Hotel facilities would serve the Bar Association until 1979, when again it outgrew the space and moved into the Belo Mansion.[29]

Change was in the wind. Just before moving into the new club-like facilities, the Bar Association began publishing in 1960 a weekly four-page miniature bulletin to keep members apprised of the many events occurring. At the same time, annual publication of *The Dallas Bar Speaks* was becoming a burden and running far behind schedule. In 1960, with the 1957-58 issue, publication was discontinued. The legal clinics, which had provided the materials for publication, also underwent a change. From 1959 on, the clinics would be held on Fridays instead of Saturdays, a somewhat delayed response to the nation's adoption of the five-day work week as standard.[30]

One of the more pleasurable social events of the Bar Association that occasionally occurred were luncheons honoring veteran lawyers. Stories of days-gone-by abounded at these affairs. At the April 1949 event, some thirty-three members were honored for having practiced law for fifty years or longer. Judge J.W. Haskell regaled the crowd with recollections of fifty years in North Texas courtrooms.[31] A special luncheon in February 1952 honored the twenty-one living ex-presidents of the DBA. In June 1954 forty-six attorneys who had practiced for more than forty years were guests at a luncheon. They were asked to relate their "most embarrassing moment." The winner, whose tale was not recorded, was J. Hart Willis. At a 1957 luncheon honoring those with forty years' experience, four of the honorees had practiced for more than sixty years. They were W.P. Donaldson, W.H. Shook, H.E. Spafford, and U.S. District Judge William Hawley Atwell.[32]

THE MOST VENERABLE of all at the 1954 luncheon was U.S. District Judge William Hawley Atwell, licensed to practice law in 1880. Atwell, now 84, had been appointed to the federal bench in 1923 by Warren G. Harding. He retired on the last day of 1954, having become eligible for retirement in 1939 but disdaining that option. During his career Atwell heard some 8,000 cases in court, working six days a week and taking few holidays. President Eisenhower expressed his deep appreciation for Atwell's "splendid service."[33] During his many years of public service in Dallas, including years as U.S. Attorney as well as on the federal bench, Atwell had become a recognized leader in civic affairs in the city, and was frequently consulted unofficially on matters pressing to Dallas' welfare. Even after his formal retirement, Atwell continued to preside over non-jury cases and to conduct naturalization hearings. This he did until 1958. Even after that he continued to go into his office. On December 22, 1961, at the age of 92, he died at Baylor Medical Center.

Atwell's retirement in 1954 meant that another veteran jurist became senior judge of the Northern District of Texas. He was U.S. District Judge T. Whitfield Davidson, who had been practicing law since 1903 and had been president of the State Bar in 1927. Replacing Atwell on the bench upon President Eisenhower's nomination was Joe E. Estes, a Dallas attorney who won unanimous backing from the U.S. Senate. Atwell himself swore in his successor in August 1955. Estes' legal training was at the University of Texas, and he had practiced law in Commerce, Tyler, and Fort Worth before coming to Dallas at the end of World War II and heading the firm of Cantwell & Estes. At the time of elevation to the federal bench he was vice president of the Dallas Bar Association.[34]

Another jurist whose long career on the bench ended at about this time was William McLaughlin Taylor (1876-1959), associate justice for the Supreme Court of Texas. Taylor stepped down from his post in February 1951 and returned to Dallas to resume private practice. Except for a three-year term on the Commission of Appeals from 1918 to 1921, Taylor practiced law in Dallas from 1912 to 1935 before beginning service with the Commission of Appeals and then the State Supreme Court. His combined service of nearly nineteen years on the Commission of Appeals and the Supreme Court of Texas was one of the longest in the court's history.[35]

Taylor's son, William M. (Mac) Taylor Jr. (1909-1985), presiding judge of the 134th District Court in Dallas at the time of his father's retirement, would be appointed U.S. District Judge in 1966 by President Lyndon B. Johnson and gain special notice for his supervision of the desegregation of public schools in Dallas as a result of a federal lawsuit. Mac Taylor had grown up in Dallas and earned his law degree from Southern Methodist University in 1932. He had worked as an assistant district attorney for Dallas County and as an assistant city attorney for the City of Dallas before World War II, then served for three and a half years as judge of the 134th District Court before joining the law firm of Strasburger, Price, Kelton, Martin and Unis prior to his appointment by President Johnson.

Taylor's appointment to the federal bench had been preceded by that of Sarah T. Hughes, whose nomination came from President John F. Kennedy. As had been the case in 1935 when she became the state's first female district judge, controversy again surrounded her appointment. This time, though, opposition to Hughes from both the American Bar Association and Attorney General Robert Kennedy was based on her age instead of her sex. Support from her powerful Texas political allies, Vice President Lyndon B. Johnson, U.S. Senator Ralph Yarborough, and especially Speaker of the House Sam Rayburn, prevailed. When she took the oath of office in October 1961 she was sixty-five years old.[36]

THE CITY'S BIGGEST and most prestigious law firms, refraining from involvement in criminal law, usually described themselves as being involved in general civil practice, then listing more specific specialties such as oil and gas, corporate, and insurance. They, along with the growth of population and commerce in Dallas, enlarged their practices and expanded their personnel considerably during this period. Favored locations for their offices were the Republic Bank Building, Mercantile Bank Building (the tallest structure in town since its completion during the war years), and the First National Bank Building. In 1948 Thompson, Knight, Wright, Harris and Weisberg was the largest firm in town with twenty-one lawyers. Next in size was Carrington, Gowan, Johnson & Walker with thirteen attorneys. Two firms had ten lawyers each—Burford, Ryburn, Hincks, & Ford, and Locke, Locke & Purnell. Having eight lawyers each were five firms: Coke & Coke; Leachman, Matthews & Gardere; Robertson, Jackson, Payne & Lancaster; Strasburger, Price, Holland, Kelton & Miller; and Turner, Rodgers, Winn & Scurlock.[37]

By the last year of the 1950s Thompson, Knight, Wright, Harris and Weisberg—now Thompson, Knight, Wright & Simmons—had grown from twenty-one lawyers to thirty-two. The firm that had increased its number the most was the one J. Glenn Turner headed, Turner, White, Atwood, McLane and Francis. In 1959 Turner's firm had twenty-six attorneys compared to just three in 1948. Two law firms listed seventeen attorneys each in the *Martindale-Hubbell Law Directory*—Strasburger, Price, Kelton, Miller & Martin and Locke, Locke, & Purnell. Other large firms included Jackson, Walker, Winstead, Cantwell & Miller with sixteen attorneys, Johnson, Bromberg, Leed & Riggs with thirteen, Burford, Ryburn & Ford with twelve and also Lyne, Blanchette, Smith & Shelton with twelve, and four firms with ten—Carrington, Johnson & Stephens, Coke & Coke, Kilgore & Kilgore, and Leachman, Gardere, Akin & Porter.[38]

These and other firms had, John L. (Jack) Hauer recalled in his book, *Finest Kind!*, a "remarkable abundance of highly skilled, veteran trial lawyers." Most of them were "case-hardened warriors [who] had at one time or another done personal injury work for insurance companies."[39] Rarely did they appear to have openings in the late 1940s, for turnover was minimal. "Someone had to die, or quit practicing for some other reason, such as retirement to create an 'opening' in a law firm," Hauer wrote. Hauer's own experience in the blistering summer heat of 1948 was not too dissimilar from that of Sarah T. Hughes, who in the 1920s had become disheartened at the number of rejections she received because of her sex. But Hauer not only was a man, he was a graduate of the Stanford Law School, co-founder of the *Stanford*

Law Review, and a member of the Order of the Coif. Over a six-week period he visited every law firm in town with no success, interviewing with more than sixty lawyers. Finally, an associate happened to leave Leachman, Matthews, & Gardere, and Hauer was hired. His salary: $200 a month.[40]

The Dallas lawyer who most impressed Hauer in this period with his courtroom ability was Henry W. Strasburger (1898-1972), who began practicing law in Dallas in 1922 after graduating from the University of Texas School of Law. After achieving great success as a litigator in the firm of Touchstone, Wight, Gormley & Frank, in 1940 Strasburger helped form a new firm, Strasburger, Price, Holland, Kelton, & Miller.

Strasburger seemed to have an amazingly intuitive ability to grasp the essential points of the most complicated cases and then to communicate his client's side of the issue in a compelling fashion. Perhaps his ability to touch juries came from his own simple origins. He worked his way through the University of Texas as an undergraduate and law school student, holding at one time four part-time jobs—waiter, railroad baggage man, and carrier for two paper routes. When he first began working for Touchstone, Wight, Gormley & Frank, he was paid an amount representing half the business that he could originate himself. With a family to support he worked during days as a lawyer and at night as a streetcar motorman with Dallas Railway & Terminal Company. Strasburger's ability to memorize was legendary. He frequently recalled the names of entire jury panels during his voir dire examination. "Dallas probably has never seen so subtly ingenious a trial lawyer as Henry Strasburger," Hauer believed, "and certainly he was the greatest crackerbarrel psychologist who ever trod the boards of the Old Red Courthouse."[41] In 1955 Strasburger was elected president of the Dallas Bar Association.

Less and less visible in these post-war days was the genuine, old-time country lawyer who seemed to glory in his rustication. None was more colorful than George Howard "Bud" Crane (1882-1957), who took particular pleasure in contrasting his lack of formal law school training with younger lawyers who boasted of fine degrees from outstanding universities. Crane, who had been a farmer and then a school teacher before being admitted to the bar in 1912, sometimes would show up in court wearing bib overalls, black shoes, and white socks. He had a large practice in divorces. Once in 1948, just after Harry Truman's upset victory over Thomas E. Dewey, Crane arrived for a docket call in State District Judge Sarah T. Hughes' courtroom wearing his bib overalls and atop his head an astonishing new addition—a miner's cap with a light on the front. Crane, as thorough a Democrat as was Hughes, proceeded in the crowded courtroom to crawl back and forth under the counsel tables. When Judge Hughes finally noticed his weird behavior and asked him what he possibly could be doing, Crane replied in his loud and distinctive nasal voice, "I'm looking for a Republican, Judge."[42]

An attorney who began to receive special recognition in 1960 for his long-time service to the City of Dallas as city attorney was Henry Peyton Kucera (1896-1983). Kucera had begun as an assistant city attorney in 1925 under a previous long-time city attorney, James J. Collins, and in 1935 Kucera assumed that position himself. In 1960 the National Institute of Municipal Law Officers presented Kucera its annual Award for Distinguished Public Service, noting his "able work in developing and adapting the principles of municipal law to the solution of the many new and complex problems of modern municipalities."[43] The next year Kucera was elected president of the National Institute of Municipal Law Officers. Born in LaGrange, Texas, Kucera was a graduate of Sam Houston State Teachers College. He later received B.A. and LL.B. degrees from the University of Texas. In World War I he served in the Army as an enlisted man, and in World War II he became a major in the Army with service in Africa, Italy, and Trieste, acting as military governor in Trieste. Kucera had a wide reputation for his unfailing memory. In a courtroom battle an opposing attorney cited a case to make his point, then had to listen as Kucera cited six more cases from memory that successfully refuted the argument.[44]

A FESTERING AND unresolved problem in American society during these seemingly halcyon days was the largely unchallenged discrimination against a major part of the population, particularly African-Americans. The Dallas Bar Association remained segregated, as did other such organizations in the South. By 1952 there were at least twelve black attorneys practicing law in Dallas; none of them were members of the Bar Association.

On May 4, 1952, twelve African-American lawyers met to form their own legal association. They named it the J.L. Turner Legal Association in honor of the lawyer who had practiced in the city from 1896 until his death in 1951. His son, J.L. Turner Jr., presided at the first meeting of the association. Present were Turner, W.J. Durham, Louis A. Bedford Jr., Crawford B. Bunkley Jr., Romeo Williams, Duane B. Mason, L. Clayton Rivers, Jack Terry, U. Simpson Tate, Kenneth F. Holbert, C.W. Ashberry, and Robert Rice. Minutes of that first meeting were recorded on a legal pad as follows:

"Meeting was called to order at 2:30 p.m. by J.L. Turner Jr. who agreed to serve as chairman until a president was elected. Mr. Turner explained the purpose of the meeting was to organize the local attorneys by forming a club and through this club common problems may be solved, the experience of each member may be shared with the group as a whole, and to enjoy the fellowship of other members of the legal profession."[45]

At one of the meetings a few years later the organization decided to challenge the all-white Dallas Bar Association by submitting for membership the names of W.J. Durham and Crawford B. Bunkley Jr. Both of these attorneys had been engaged in civil rights work with growing success. Louis A. Bedford Jr., who would become the unofficial archivist and custodian of the J.L. Turner Legal Association records, recalls that the applications brought no response at all from the Bar Association.[46]

Quite likely, however, the applications caused some soul-searching at the Bar Association. The application of "a colored lawyer" for membership in 1956—perhaps actually a reference to the two applications of Durham and Bunkley—prompted the formation of a committee to study the matter. Minutes of the board of directors meeting, January 12, 1956, reflect that the committee's report was accepted and filed with the executive secretary. Further action was "deferred." The motion was unanimously adopted.[47] Acceptance of African-Americans into the Bar Association would not occur until the next decade.

The 1954 *Brown v. Board of Education* decision by the U.S. Supreme Court was destined to be the springboard for massive changes in the life of the nation, leading indirectly not only to the integration of the Dallas Bar Association but of other associations and institutions. The ruling's significance for Dallas was realized immediately by a few black citizens, who immediately challenged as unconstitutional the Dallas Independent School District's policy of separate schools for blacks and whites. Late in the summer of 1954 the Rev. R.C. McNeil and thirty-two African-American parents, supported by the local chapter of the National Association for the Advancement of Colored People, submitted a petition to Dallas School Superintendent W.T. White, citing the Supreme Court decision as mandating acceptance of students regardless of race or color. White did not agree, arguing that Dallas public schools operated under Texas laws which specifically provided for segregation and that no local school district could alter that situation.[48] In September 1955 the NAACP's chief counsel, Thurgood Marshall, was in town, appearing before U.S. District Judge William Hawley Atwell and beginning what would become an almost eternal legal battle concerning the desegregation of the Dallas schools. It was a struggle that would last far into the 1990s.

In 1961 the federal courts, including especially the 5th Court of Appeals, ordered integration to begin in the Dallas public schools. The Dallas Bar Association's board of directors agreed unanimously to cooperate with the Dallas Citizens Council, a powerful civic group, in promoting the peaceful acceptance of a limited amount of integration into a handful of Dallas schools. The matter was referred to the Bar Association's civic affairs committee to lend any support it could to the peaceful integration of the schools.[49] And, indeed, in the fall of 1961 eighteen African-American first-graders enrolled in eight previously all-white schools without any public disturbance. President John F.

Kennedy and Attorney General Robert Kennedy singled out Dallas for praise in its handling of the sensitive matter. Despite the success of this initial integration of the schools, full-scale desegregation of the school system would not begin until the 1970s.

MOMENTOUS YEARS

⌘

Chapter Twelve

THE ASSASSINATION OF President John F. Kennedy in Dallas on November 22, 1963, marked a great watershed in American history. This shocking deed and the turbulence that followed in the next years stood in sharp contrast from the long and relatively stable years after World War II. Powerful, underlying forces seemed to be unleashed. Images of massive demonstrations, of urban disorders, of alienation, of war in Vietnam, and of other assassinations filled television screens in homes across the nation. Younger generations turned away from the past to embrace and promote the "greening" of America. Neither the legal community nor an institution such as the Dallas Bar Association could escape the impact of this new age.

In those critical and fearful moments from which these changes seemed to spring—mid-day, November 22, 1963—the nation's new president, Lyndon B. Johnson, turned to members of the Dallas Bar Association for advice and assistance.

AT NOON that Friday, Bar Association members gathered for their regular luncheon and legal clinic at their headquarters in the Adolphus Hotel. A few minutes later the presidential motorcade made its way down Main Street amidst cheering crowds en route to the Trade Mart, where the president would speak to a gathering of distinguished Dallasites. A presidential visit was rare for Dallas. The lawyers in the Adolphus crowded around the windows and chatted excitedly as they glimpsed a half block away in the motorcade the president and his wife Jackie, Vice President Lyndon B. Johnson and his wife Lady Bird, and Texas Governor John B. Connally and his wife Nellie.

Just a few minutes later, out of hearing range for the lawyers, rifle shots echoed in Dealey Plaza. The president was fatally wounded; the governor seriously wounded. The shocking event occurred only a few feet from the place where frontier lawyer John Neely Bryan had first camped in 1841 with the intention of founding a city. It took place under the shadow of the Old Red Courthouse, the County Criminal Courts Building, and adjacent courthouse buildings—the places where justice had been administered since the earliest days of Dallas County.

After a race to Parkland Hospital with police escort and a hopeless effort by doctors to save him in the emergency room, President Kennedy was pronounced dead. The nation and the world looked on with shock and grief as television cameras carried live pictures that would continue for the entire weekend. The somber presidential party hurried to Dallas Love Field and boarded *Air Force One*. Before lifting off the ground to return to the nation's capital there were important things to be done. The new president, Lyndon B. Johnson, a Texan with many friends in Dallas, took to the telephone, making calls and decisions especially regarding the oath of office and when it should be taken. After talking to a few key individuals in Washington, D.C., including Attorney General Robert F. Kennedy, he turned his attention to his friends in the Dallas legal community. He wanted their advice and assistance at this critical moment. He first told his secretary, Mary Fehmer, to "get Waddy Bullion." J.W. Bullion, a well-known member of the Dallas bar, for twenty-three years had been counsel to Lady Bird Johnson. Bullion's listing was in the book Ms. Fehmer carried containing telephone numbers for the Vice President's oldest and best friends. But Bullion was out of town in Shreveport.[1]

"Get Sarah Hughes," the president next ordered. Lyndon Johnson had been one of her staunchest champions in persuading President Kennedy to name her to the federal bench despite opposition from the American Bar Association. Judge Hughes' law clerk, John Spinuzzi, said the judge was not there either; she was on her way to the Trade Mart to hear President Kennedy. Johnson took the telephone. "This is Lyndon Johnson. Find her."[2]

Next he called Irving L. Goldberg, another Dallas lawyer who had helped Johnson in his Texas political campaigns and who Johnson later would appoint as an appellate judge for the Fifth Court of Appeals. Goldberg, too, had been en route to see President Kennedy, but by now he had returned home to watch events unfolding on television. "This is Lyndon. Do you think I should be sworn in here or in Washington?" the president asked him. Goldberg thought it should be right away in Dallas. "Who should do it?" Johnson asked. "Sarah Hughes," Goldberg replied. "We're trying to get her here. You try, too," Johnson said.[3]

In his effort to locate the federal judge, Goldberg reached Barefoot Sanders, appointed by President Kennedy to be U.S. Attorney for the Northern District and destined, like Goldberg, to be appointed a federal judge himself. Sanders was in his office, trying to find a federal statute under which the president's assassin could be charged. Agreeing to join in the quest to locate Sarah T. Hughes, he raced upstairs to her office, arriving just as she called to see if there were messages for her. Sanders advised her to go immediately to Love Field. He would obtain clearance with the Secret Service for her to get to *Air Force One*.[4]

Judge Hughes drove to Love Field in her red sports car as quickly as she could. She arrived at approximately 2:30 p.m. and was escorted aboard *Air Force One*. The president thanked her for coming and said he would be ready in a minute or two. The oath of office had been found in the Constitution itself after a worrisome search for it, a Bible was located, and with a dictating machine recording the words—a tape-recorder could not be found—the new president repeated the oath as administered by Judge Sarah T. Hughes before a group of dazed onlookers crowded into the cramped space aboard the airplane: "I do solemnly swear that I will faithfully execute the Office of President of the United States and will, to the best of my ability, preserve, protect, and defend the Constitution of the United States, so help me God."[5] With this done, Judge Hughes got off the plane and *Air Force One* departed for Washington, D.C.

A prime suspect, Lee Harvey Oswald, had been arrested

after allegedly shooting and killing a Dallas police officer in the Oak Cliff section of Dallas. At the downtown Dallas police station, Police Chief Jesse Curry and other law enforcement officials from county, state, and federal agencies joined in questioning Oswald, who denied any involvement. Oswald had no legal representation.

On Saturday afternoon the president of the Dallas Bar Association, H. Louis Nichols, a specialist in municipal zoning cases who had begun practicing law in 1939, received a telephone call from a Dallas lawyer and friend who wondered if Oswald was represented by counsel. Nichols did not know. His friend said that the dean of a law school on the East Coast had told him that the media was reporting that Oswald could not get anyone to represent him in Dallas. Nichols agreed that the matter should be looked into, and he called a friend who was a criminal lawyer to discuss the matter. Since Oswald had not been indicted, there was no legal obligation to appoint an attorney for him at this time, he was told.[6]

Soon Nichols received two more telephone calls from lawyer friends who reported similar concerns about Oswald's lack of representation. Nichols now called District Attorney Henry Wade, who was uncertain himself as to whether Oswald had counsel, but who said he would relay word to Oswald through some of his assistants that he could request legal representation if he did not already have it. Nichols, still concerned, called Police Captain Glen King with the same questions. Captain King suggested that Nichols himself come to the police station for a personal meeting with Oswald to make certain that he knew he could have legal counsel. Just afterwards another telephone call came from a professor at SMU's law school who concurred that Nichols should visit the prisoner himself.[7]

Thus, on Saturday evening, November 23, the president of the Dallas Bar Association visited the city hall jail cell of the accused assassin of President Kennedy. He informed the suspect that he was there to inquire as to whether or not he had a lawyer and, if not, whether he wanted assistance in obtaining a lawyer.

Oswald told Nichols that he would like for a New York

lawyer named John Abt to represent him, that he had already made this request with police officials, and that if Abt were not available he wanted a lawyer who was a member of the American Civil Liberties Union. (Abt earlier had represented the American Communists Gus Hall and John Davis. Oswald also asked Ruth Paine, with whom his wife Marina was living, to call Abt. She did, but he was not home.)[8] Nichols would be welcome to return next week, Oswald said, to see what had developed, and if he had no attorney by then he "might ask" him to find someone to represent him.[9]

Following his interview with Oswald, Nichols briefly visited with Police Chief Curry, then stepped into the third floor of the police station to find himself surrounded immediately by journalists and television cameramen from throughout the world. He reported to them—in words that were relayed around the world—what had transpired in his brief meeting with the Oswald.[10] The huge numbers of reporters who were omnipresent as the investigation continued that weekend would focus the keen attention of the legal community in the months and years ahead toward adopting bar-press guidelines intended to limit pre-trial publicity and to ensure an accused person's right to a fair trial.

On this fateful weekend the eyes of the world centered on Dallas, its law enforcement agencies, and the accused assassin. When nightclub owner Jack Ruby shot Oswald to death on Sunday—the day after Nichols had visited him—the wrath of the nation turned from the alleged assassin to the Dallas Police Department and to the city of Dallas itself. How could they have permitted the prime suspect, while in police custody in the police station, to be shot and killed? It seemed especially painful to have this unexpected event take place before a trial could occur and critical questions be answered. Dallas would face years of opprobrium, not just as the place where the president was shot to death but where his alleged assassin also was permitted to be killed.

Jack Ruby's first attorney was a familiar local criminal lawyer, Tom Howard, who soon was replaced by the famous and egotistical "King of Torts," San Francisco lawyer Melvin Belli, who came to court for Ruby's trial carrying a velvet-covered briefcase. Belli quickly gained a following among members of the press for his affability and story-telling abilities which he demonstrated at some of the popular eateries in the courthouse area. Assisting Belli was Joe Tonahill from Jasper in East Texas and a bright young Dallas lawyer, Phil Burleson (who would become president of the Dallas Bar Association in 1977).

District Attorney Henry Wade, now a veteran having held office since 1950, was joined by his assistants, A.D. (Jim) Bowie, William F. (Bill) Alexander, and Frank Watt, in prosecuting the case in State District Judge Joe B. Brown's courtroom on the second floor of the County Criminal Courts Building. The trial, held in Dallas after Judge Brown denied a request for a change of venue, was certain to bring to the city and to the courtroom another onslaught of journalists from throughout the nation and world.

With enormous pressure for information about the trial, the possibility arose—even in this early period—that it could be televised. Just three weeks after the assassination the Dallas Bar Association's board of directors met to discuss this possibility. Nichols observed that he had received numerous telephone calls and letters from people concerned about the impact on the legal profession if the trial should be televised. He and members of the executive committee, Nichols reported, unanimously believed that it should not be televised. The board forwarded its unanimous resolution to Judge Brown. Broadcasting or televising any of the proceedings would be "detrimental to the due and orderly administration of justice and the maintenance of the dignity and decorum of such proceedings," the board resolved.[11]

Judge Brown agreed. He announced that there would be no televising of the trial itself. The announcement of the jury's verdict, however, could be televised.

The district attorney's office sought the death penalty for Ruby. Belli's defense for Ruby was based on insanity, with a contention that he was a victim of "psychomotor epilepsy," that it had enduced a "fugue state," and that he had suffered a temporary blackout at the time of the shooting.

On March 14, 1964, after a trial of several weeks which once again brought the nation's press to Dallas, the jury returned a verdict of guilty of premeditated murder after deliberating for less than an hour. Ruby was sentenced to death. In the lengthy appeals process that followed, Ruby was represented by a series of attorneys, even briefly by the well-known William Kuntsler and Elmer Gertz, but ultimately by Phil Burleson and Sam Passman.

Financing a lengthy appeal was a problem for Ruby and his family. On October 7, 1964, the Dallas Bar Association's board of directors was briefed on this situation by Burleson and Passman. Ruby was indigent, they were told, and there was concern about preserving all his rights during the appeals process because of the expenses involved. Failure to assure that he exercised all his rights of appeal would not be a good reflection on the community. Burleson and Passman suggested that the Bar Association appoint an ad hoc committee to oversee the appeal. Ruby's family, they said, was prepared to leave his defense in the hands of a Bar Association committee, believing that Ruby did not possess the proper mental condition to make such decisions himself. After considerable discussion as to whether or not such an action would be appropriate for the Association and concluding that it would not be, the directors declined to become involved.[12]

In 1966 Ruby was granted a new trial by the Texas Court of Criminal Appeals on the grounds that a change of venue should have been granted and that his statements to Dallas police immediately after the shooting should not have been allowed into evidence. But no new trial was held. On January 3, 1967, not long after being diagnosed with cancer, Ruby died at Parkland Hospital.[13]

The intense amount of publicity focused on the events surrounding the assassination of President Kennedy prompted a thorough re-examination of the clash of two Constitutional rights—the right of a defendant to a fair trial and the right of freedom of the press. What should be done when these two rights seem to be in conflict? What if Oswald had lived, been convicted, and then had his conviction overturned because of prejudicial publicity?

One of the early thoughtful reactions to this problem came from Paul Carrington, whose past presidency of the Dallas Bar Association, whose status as a member of the House of Delegates of the American Bar Association, and whose many other professional accomplishments lent much authority to his statements. Carrington believed that the situation had presented an almost impossible dilemma in which no adequate standards of conduct existed to guide the press, law enforcement officials, and attorneys. Writing in the *Texas Bar Journal* soon after the incident, he said: "I urge that a State Bar committee . . . explore all the possibilities for avoiding in the future excesses of publicity on the part of attorneys and officers, of our courts, on the part of all law enforcement officials, and on the part of all news media and those connected with them, whenever the publicity relates to a crime or the alleged criminal."[14]

Just as Carrington recommended, the State Bar of Texas appointed a pre-trial publicity study committee. Its chairman was a Dallas attorney, Talbot Rain. Rain and his committee, after lengthy deliberations, recommended voluntary agreements between the bar and press rather than mandatory restrictions.[15] In the next several years Rain's committee held a wide-ranging series of meetings with representatives of the press to accomplish its goals. The result was the adoption of free press-fair trial guidelines by the State Bar of Texas and professional media organizations in the state which sought to minimize or prevent problems stemming from excessive pre-trial news coverage. The recommendations provided much-needed guidelines not only for the press and members of the bar, but also for members of law-enforcement agencies. On a national level, the American Bar Association created the special Reardon Committee to formulate similar guidelines for the press and bar. These, too, were soon adopted.[16]

A decade later in 1973 Carrington would be recognized by the American Bar Foundation as the American Bar Association's outstanding 50-year lawyer. And in 1977 the Texas Bar Foundation recognized him as the "Outstanding 50-Year Lawyer of Texas" for his excellent service to the legal profession and the public.[17]

ONE OF THE CRITICAL issues still confronting the nation was that of bringing equality to the races. The push to gain long-denied civil rights by African-American organizations and by leaders such as Martin Luther King Jr. soon became a national policy under the administration of President Lyndon B. Johnson, who initiated a broad series of federal legislation intended to end discrimination and also to abolish poverty.

By the time of President Kennedy's visit to Dallas, the Dallas Bar Association finally had decided that African-American attorneys should be admitted into membership. The decision to do so, made with some difficulty since it went counter to accepted customs, occurred over a several-month period in 1963 and 1964.

In the summer of 1963, seven years since the last rejection of an African-American attorney's request for membership, Crawford B. Bunkley Jr. (1921-1974) submitted his application for membership. Bunkley was the attorney who, among other civil rights efforts, had helped prepare and argue the important *Sweatt vs. Painter* case in which the segregated law school at the University of Texas was declared unconstitutional. Born in Denison, he had graduated in 1941 with a bachelor of arts degree from Prairie View A&M, then received his LL.B. from the University of Michigan Law School in 1944. Soon after coming to Dallas he had joined W.J. Durham in a partnership.[18]

Prompted by the admission committee's rejection of Bunkley—a rejection which would prevent his name from being brought before the entire membership for approval—President Nichols and John Louis Shook (who attended meetings as an *ex officio* member and director of the State Bar of Texas) reviewed for the directors the bylaws of the Bar Association and its past history concerning applications by African-Americans. At the end of the discussion and upon Shook's motion, the board of directors unanimously voted that Nichols advise the admissions committee that no bylaw or rule of the Bar Association prohibited membership on grounds of race, color, or creed.[19]

Nichols, who earlier had concluded that rejection on the basis of race was wrong, next met with the committee and persuaded it to suspend its action for two weeks on Bunkley's application so that the board of directors could consider the matter. At that meeting, on September 26, Nichols won unanimous approval for the directors to review henceforth any applications denied by the admissions committee.[20]

At the invitation of the directors, the admissions committee attended the directors' meeting on October 8, 1963, to discuss the matter further. Nichols asked committee members to explain their rejection of Bunkley's application, stressing that because of the unusual nature of the matter their reasons should be good and sufficient. Following a lengthy discussion, the report of the admissions committee on the application of Bunkley was approved—that is, his request for membership was denied.[21]

Before the year was over a second African-American attorney submitted his application. He was Fred Finch Jr., a native of Dallas and a *cum laude* graduate of Wiley College. After serving during the war in the Air Force and then working as the assistant personnel officer of Tuskegee Veterans Hospital in Alabama, he had entered Harvard Law School and earned his law degree in 1954. "As a Harvard graduate and with other outstanding credentials, we figured they would have to admit him," Louis A. Bedford Jr., one of the handful of African-American attorneys practicing at the time in Dallas, recalled thirty-five years later.[22]

The admissions committee denied Finch's application just as it had denied Bunkley's. When the board of directors reviewed this action at its December 11, 1963, meeting, Nichols said that he could find no reason to bar Finch from membership. He asked the directors to take the application from the admissions committee, approve it, and submit it to the full membership along with other applications. The directors unanimously agreed to do so. Finch's application then was submitted for approval at a Friday clinic meeting on December 20. After a thorough and painful discussion in which various viewpoints were brought out, his membership was approved.[23]

Five months later Nichols, as immediate past president, moved at a directors' meeting that Bunkley's application now be reconsidered. Discussion revealed that a letter already had been written to him requesting his new application for membership. L.A. Bedford Jr. recalls that the Bar Association's secretary-treasurer, Leonard Hoffman, then visited him, Bunkley, and Durham to solicit their membership applications. Bunkley and Durham declined for the moment, but they urged Bedford, a Dallas native and graduate of the Brooklyn Law School, to take advantage of the offer, which he did. Bedford thus became the second African-American member of the Bar Association.[24]

Among the many accomplishments of what would be a long legal career in the city, Bedford went on ultimately to become a member of the association's board of directors, a trustee of the Dallas Bar Foundation, the first recipient of the DBA's Martin Luther King Jr. Award, and, along with John Estes, the DBA's "Trial Lawyer of the Year" for 1998. He also would be inducted into the National Bar Association's Hall of Fame. As a founding member of the J.L. Turner Legal Association, which would continue to function as an organization for African-American attorneys in Dallas, Bedford became its archivist and historian.[25]

Elsewhere in the city, racial barriers also were slowly being taken down. Joseph Lockridge, one of the city's younger African-American attorneys—and there were beginning to be more and more of them—became in 1966 the first African-American to be elected to the state legislature from Dallas. He was supported by the city's business leadership, by labor, and by both daily newspapers. His exemplary service in his first term in Austin caused his fellow legislators to elect him their "Rookie of the Year." Lockridge, tragically, was killed in an airplane crash in 1968.[26] The Dallas City Council saw its first African-American councilman in 1967 when realtor C.A. Galloway was appointed to complete the term of a councilman who had resigned. Then, in the following year, George L. Allen, a black insurance man, was appointed to a full term of office when two new council seats were created as the result of a charter change. In 1975 Allen and Cleo Steele would become simultaneously the first two African-Americans to become justices of the peace in Dallas County when they were appointed by the commissioners court. (The new courthouse which opened in 1966 later would be named the George L. Allen Sr. Courts Building.) The first black Dallas Independent School District board member, Dr. Emmett J. Conrad, was elected in 1967.

The Hispanic population, another minority group now emerging as a sizable presence in the city, evidently was unrepresented in the Dallas legal profession until 1931. That year Felix H. Garcia (1898-1981), a native of Mexico, earned his law degree from Southern Methodist University and was admitted to the bar. He began his career as a general practitioner in civil and criminal law. During the war Garcia also taught Spanish at SMU. He became a noted speaker on United States-Mexico relations, and in 1951 moved to San Antonio.[27] Robert C. Benavides (1905-1967) began practicing law in Dallas in 1933 after receiving his LL.B. degree from the University of Texas Law School. Benavides represented the Mexican Consul in Dallas, and for fifteen years he was legal advisor to registrants of Selective Service Board No. 27.[28]

An Hispanic attorney who during this period would gain far more visibility for her leadership was a female, Adelfa Botello Callejo. After graduating from high school in Cotulla, Texas, Ms. Callejo moved to Dallas so she could attend the evening law school at SMU. Working at various jobs to support herself, Callejo studied law between 1944 and 1954, moved away from town with her husband, and then returned to Dallas to earn her law degree from SMU in 1961, seventeen years after beginning her studies. Unable to find a position in the district attorney's office—her first choice—or with a firm, she opened her own office and began to develop a specialty in criminal law. Callejo would go on to become president of the Dallas County Criminal Bar Association in 1972, a trustee of the Dallas Public Library, a director of the Dallas Water Advisory Board, a board member of the DFW International Airport, a director of the State Bar of Texas, and a leading spokesperson for the Hispanic community.[29]

Callejo was not alone among lawyers with Hispanic surnames who became visible in the 1960s and 1970s. Frank Hernandez emerged as a recognized leader in the Hispanic community and became active in the Dallas public school desegregation case as a member of a task force appointed by Judge Taylor. In 1976 the county commissioners appointed him to the county court at law, where he served until 1978 as the first Hispanic judge in the county's history. When Hernandez started practicing law in the 1960s he knew of just five other Hispanic attorneys in town— Callejo, Robert Benavides, Filemon Valdez, and Manual Almaguer. The fifth usually was not recognized as being Hispanic—he had anglicized his Hispanic surname because he thought he could attract more clients that way.[30]

Another Hispanic attorney, Florentino Ramirez Jr., in 1973 was president of a new organization composed of some eighty attorneys, the Dallas International Lawyers Association. The organization reflected the increase in foreign business in recent years, an increase that was on the verge of multiplying many times over with the opening in 1974 of the new DFW International Airport.[31]

OF THE 2,443 LAWYERS in the county by the year 1965, 1,428 of them were members of the Dallas Bar Association. Membership was increasing at a good rate; a total of 124 new members had been admitted during the previous year. Members continued to enjoy fellowship at their Adolphus Hotel headquarters, where a new six-year lease was signed effective November 1, 1965, at a monthly rate of $1,600. The thirty weekly clinics during 1964 attracted 2,943 lawyers. A total of 23,303 lunches were served to members at the Adolphus during 1964. Members could buy a hamburger for $1.17 or a buffet meal for $1.78, but inflation was occurring—the price for the buffet meal was raised in 1965 to $2.34, an amount that included service charge and tax.[32]

The 1968 budget provided for total expenditures of $62,815,

with $46,710 of this amount devoted to headquarters expenses (including salaries for the two full-time employees) and the remaining $16,105 allotted to twenty-two committees or activities, the largest amount—$4,450—specified for special services, followed by $3,000 for entertainment and $2,500 for the Lawyer Referral program.[33]

The range of Bar Association activities continued to broaden. Providing portraits of judges in the various courtrooms was a service that had won wide acceptance, and this was an activity that required constant monitoring as new jurists were selected for the growing number of courts or new judges were elected. "Ask Your Lawyer," a weekly radio show presented during 1964 over radio station KRLD, was a continuation of past efforts to reach out to the general public and contribute to the understanding of the legal profession. The program would continue through the 1960s. In the mid-1960s the services of a public relations firm were obtained for special projects such as Law Day functions and also for general public relations efforts. The desire to maintain closer relations with the city's media was highlighted with an annual Press Appreciation Dinner. Pierce Allman later was hired as public relations counsel, a position he held for many years.

In 1970 Bar Association President Frank C. Moore appointed a committee to study and make recommendations for the creation of a non-profit foundation as a vehicle for sponsoring research, forums, scholarships, legal aid for the indigent, and other such activities, as well as being a body for accepting aid, donations, and grants. John N. Jackson, chairman, and his six-man committee reported back in December 1970, and the result the next year was the creation of the Dallas Bar Foundation. A fifteen-member board of trustees elected by the Dallas Bar Association's board of directors directed its activities.[34]

The Association's emphasis on assisting individuals who lacked financial resources was seen in the Pre-Trial Release Program developed in the mid-1970s. Funded by private money and a grant from Governor Preston Smith's Texas Criminal Justice Council, its purpose was to permit certain categories of prisoners to be released on personal recognizance or reduced bond while awaiting trial. Offices were established at the courthouse and the Dallas police station. A staff headed by Robert L. Peacock, who had experience in Travis County as the personal bond office director, investigated individual cases to determine if the accused had sufficient stability and ties to the community to qualify. Charles P. Storey, chairman of the Pretrial Release Committee, said that judges previously had no way of acquiring the necessary information for making these decisions. Barefoot Sanders served as vice chairman of the committee. The Bar Association's objectives for the program included reductions in the number of prisoners in overcrowded jails, reduction in costs in transporting prisoners between jails and court, and the reduction of welfare costs.[35]

Hosting meetings of the State Bar of Texas and the American Bar Association continued to be occasional responsibilities. On August 8-14, 1969, meetings of ABA leaders occurred in Dallas. They had important work to do, and one result was adoption of a new Code of Professional Responsibility which superseded Canons that were sixty years old. [36] Two years later in 1971 the State Bar of Texas held its 89th annual convention in Dallas. Speakers included the former governor of Texas and then secretary of the treasury, John B. Connally. Entertainment activities were highlighted by the appearance of comedian Bob Hope.[37]

A Dallas lawyer who became a national leader in bar activities—the American Bar Association, the State Bar of Texas, and the Dallas Bar Association—was Morris Harrell, a partner in the firm of Rain, Harrell, Emery, Young & Doke. Harrell, a trial lawyer who represented clients in both civil and criminal cases, was noted for his quiet effectiveness rather than for histrionics. His demeanor was demonstrated by an incident occurring at a momentary trial recess when a client felt a need for greater fireworks and asked him to march back into that courtroom and "give the other side hell." Harrell listened patiently, then inquired of his client if it was all right for him simply to return to the courtroom and "just win the suit quietly." The client agreed, and Harrell won the case as promised.[38]

Harrell, a native of Grandview in Johnson County, was the son of Oscar "Slim" Harrell, who had been a major-league baseball pitcher for Connie Mack's Philadelphia Athletics. Harrell earned his degrees, a B.B.A. and LL.B., from Baylor University. Upon completing his law studies in 1942 Harrell served in the U.S. Navy at Guadalcanal, the Philippines, Iwo Jima, and Okinawa before coming to Dallas in 1946 to begin the practice of law under the tutelage of his uncle, W.B. Harrell, who had just completed a term as president of the Dallas Bar Association. In 1947 Harrell became an assistant U.S. attorney in the Northern District, working both in Fort Worth and Dallas.[39] In 1955 he joined Thompson & Knight, and then after five years formed with other attorneys the firm of Rain, Harrell & Emery, later Rain Harrell, Emery, Young, & Doke. In 1962 he became president of the Dallas Bar Association, and then president of the State Bar of Texas in 1970-71.

In 1982 Harrell became the third Dallas lawyer to serve as president of the American Bar Association, following R.E.L. Saner and Robert G. Storey. He was chosen president-elect on the fifth round of a secret ballot by the ABA's House of Delegates early in 1981, and his accession to the presidency the next year was a formality. During his year as ABA president, Harrell traveled throughout the nation and the world, covering an estimated 300,000 miles. (In 1998 the ABA awarded Harrell its most prestigious honor, the ABA Medal for rendering "conspicuous service in the cause of American jurisprudence.")[40]

Other practicing attorneys who gained special attention in these years were those appointed as federal judges by their Texas friend, President Lyndon B. Johnson. William (Mac) Taylor Jr. (see Chapter 11) was sworn in as U.S. district judge for the Northern District on August 18, 1966, by District Judge Sarah T. Hughes. He replaced the veteran Judge T. Whitfield Davidson, who retired November 1, 1965 as the oldest federal judge in the nation. Davidson had been appointed by President Franklin D. Roosevelt in 1936. He had been a delegate to the Democratic conventions that nominated both Woodrow Wilson and Franklin D. Roosevelt.[41]

Irving L. Goldberg (1906-1995), the attorney whom President Johnson had called for advice from *Air Force One* just after the assassination, was named in 1966 appellate judge for the Fifth Circuit Court of Appeals in New Orleans. Goldberg, a native of Port Arthur, Texas, held a bachelor of arts degree from the University of Texas and an LL.B. from Harvard Law School. He moved to Dallas in 1932, and at the time of his appointment he was with the firm of Goldberg, Akin, Gump, Strauss & Hauer. Goldberg took the oath of office in Dallas from Supreme Court Justice Tom C. Clark, formerly of Dallas and the first Texan to become a Supreme Court justice.[42]

Taylor, Goldberg, and Sarah T. Hughes, as the three federal judges in Dallas and frequently working together as a three-judge panel, began in the late 1960s and early 1970s to be the forum for a number of cases challenging the constitutionality of state laws on such subjects as loyalty oaths, sodomy, abortion, obscenity, welfare assistance plans, reapportionment, and primary election fees. Their decisions in these cases often nullified state laws and sent shock waves through the Dallas community and Texas.[43]

Supreme Court Justice Clark, who had sworn in Goldberg, had been the second generation of his family to distinguish himself as a Dallas lawyer, and now his son Ramsey Clark, representing the third generation, was achieving a national reputation. Ramsey Clark was named acting attorney general in 1966 by President Johnson, and in March 1967—just more than three decades after his own father had taken that same position—he became the nation's attorney general.

During his tenure as acting attorney general, Clark swore in yet another Dallas lawyer to a high federal position. In November 1966 Barefoot Sanders became the nation's assistant attorney general in charge of the civil division.[44] In 1979 he would be appointed U.S. district judge for the Northern District by President Jimmy Carter.

AMONG THE new activities of the Bar Association during these energized years was one that resulted from President Lyndon B. Johnson's aggressive "war on poverty" through the

Office of Economic Opportunity. Among the many federal programs spawned through the OEO was one that was innocently conceived but which soon brought to the Dallas Bar Association an unanticipated set of complications. This concerned a new agency, the Dallas Legal Services Project, funded by a federal government grant but contingent upon participation by the legal community. To qualify for the grant, which seemed to be merely an enlargement of the sort of legal assistance the Bar Association had been providing to indigent or low-income persons since the 1920s, the Dallas Bar Association and also the Junior Bar Association and the Dallas County Criminal Bar Association agreed that their members would provide the project with fifty man-hours a week of volunteer time. Its board of directors would be composed of low-income community leaders and members of the bar. Walter W. Steele Jr., counsel to the Project and a law school professor at SMU, explained to the Bar Association's board of directors that the "core" of the new agency's activities would be its "educational aspect."[45]

Little did the Bar Association realize that the Dallas Legal Services Project (DLSP)—which would have its own corps of idealistic, aggressive attorneys—soon would initiate a series of aggressive, high-profile class-action law suits designed not just to improve the economic status of low-income residents but to thoroughly dismantle much of the accepted framework of the city. As DLSP Executive Director Marcus Ranger explained in 1972: "We emphasize law reform cases because the problems of the poor are class problems. Our responsibility under the Office of Economic Opportunity Act is to eradicate poverty. So if the problems of the poor are class problems, the best tool to eliminate them is the class action."[46] The source for many of these suits lay in the person of a young lawyer named Ed Polk, who after working as an attorney with DLSP became its director in 1970. In a three-month period in 1971 under Polk, more than thirty class actions or law reform cases were filed.[47]

A reporter who visited Polk's office in 1969 found posters on his walls bearing the images of Malcolm X and Che Guevara. On Malcolm X's poster were the words, "He Was Ready! Are You?"

Under Guevara's picture were the words, "In Revolution, One Wins or Dies." Polk, thirty years of age, said the two men were his heroes.[48]

One DLSP suit challenged Texas' residency requirements for welfare recipients, another contested rights of the Dallas Housing Authority regarding landlord-client relationships. Polk raised eyebrows when he defended the militant editor of an underground newspaper whose economic status did not seem needy enough to qualify him for DLSP representation. In explaining his own militancy, Polk told a newspaper reporter that the law traditionally had been used to "oppress the people and help the rich get richer." His own goal, he said, was too "improve life for poor people." If such constituted revolution, then he was a "revolutionary."[49]

A particularly volatile, far-reaching case initiated by DLSP during Polk's tenure as director was against the Dallas Independent School District (*Tasby v. Estes*, 1970). In this case, filed in U.S. District Judge William M. Taylor Jr.'s court, it was argued that desegregation in the school district was no more than token and that in fact the district continued to operate a segregated system in which black and Hispanic schools remained markedly inferior to predominantly white schools. The case generated widespread interest and controversy. Public concerns, often expressed with deep emotions, focused on the possibility of large-scale busing of both white and African-American students away from their neighborhoods and into schools across town. As tempers rose, much of the ire was directed toward the federal courts, now perceived to be decidedly liberal or radical in their decisions.

The emerging controversy prompted a special meeting of the Bar Association's board of directors on July 8, 1971, to consider whether or not the Association should take a position regarding the potentially inflammatory situation. Both the Greater Dallas Community Relations Commission, chaired by attorney Sidney Stahl, and the DBA's Urban Affairs Committee wanted the Bar Association to use its influence to calm the situation and to clarify the role of the judicial process. Agreeing to the need, the board of directors prepared a statement that was released the next day by DBA President Timothy E. Kelley. The statement's main point was to emphasize that Judge Taylor could not and would not be influenced by public pressure, that the law would be followed, and that it would prevail. It would be "unreasonable" to assume, Kelley said, that all parties would be pleased with the judge's final decision. "Hysteria or cynicism will not contribute to our stature as a city or our maturity as parents," Kelley continued. "Only sensitive and careful enforcement of the law can assure the best education for all our children and survival of our system of government."[50]

This prolonged and much-publicized case eventually brought about far-reaching changes in the school system. One aspect of it was to introduce busing in which minority and white students were transported across town to integrate previously segregated schools. Judge Taylor's decision also ordered the desegregation of both faculty and staff. The decision was accepted without significant public disruptions at the time, but the phenomenon of "white flight" began to occur. The Dallas public school system ultimately would be made up of predominantly minority students after large numbers of white students either transferred to private schools or moved with their families to suburban school districts. Judge Taylor's jurisdiction eventually was transferred to U.S. District Judge Barefoot Sanders, and into the late 1990s Judge Sanders continued to exercise authority over aspects of the school district as they related to desegregation.[51]

The activist stance of the DLSP caused a great stir among much of the membership of the Dallas Bar Association. Even if it lacked control over the DLSP's actions, the Bar Association was viewed as the DLSP's primary sponsoring organization. The matter began to take up more and more of the directors' time. On February 6, 1970, the directors held a special meeting to discuss the situation and the recent election of Ed Polk as DLSP director. After a thorough discussion, the directors adopted a resolution announcing that it would make no change "at this time" in its support of the Dallas Legal Services Project and expressed a hope that Polk would work with the DLSP's board of directors "in the best interest of the people whom the Project is intended to serve."[52]

Meanwhile, however, the sharing of downtown facilities with the DLSP by the Association's Lawyer Referral Service clearly had become embarrassing. The directors voted on April 16, 1970, to move the Referral Service to a new location in the Main Bank Building.[53]

On July 30, 1970, the directors, responding to further concerns about the Association's ties to DLSP, established a committee to study that relationship and to offer its findings and recommendations to the board. The committee recommended, in effect, to "pack" the board of directors of the DLSP by adding ten additional lawyers to its board, incorporating in the Dallas Bar Association slate the eighteen lawyers presently serving on its board. This effort was successful, although at the same meeting an effort to oust Polk failed. The twenty community members on DLSP's board now were outnumbered by thirty-one lawyers.[54]

Still the issue smoldered as Polk and the DLSP continued to be identified as the lightning rod for social upheaval in Dallas and the abettors of growing unrest in the minority community. On February 15, 1971, the board again discussed the DLSP at length and agreed upon several recommendations and observations: (1) DLSP attorneys should devote a greater proportion of their working time to representing individuals who could not pay for needed legal services, (2) a screening committee should be established to approve all class actions or suits to change existing laws, (3) a committee should be established to determine the eligibility of persons seeking representation by the DLSP staff, (4) DLSP staff attorneys should make greater efforts to settle matters of disputes rather than to institute "media-attracting litigation," and (5) offers to contribute hours of services by members of the Dallas Bar Association were being ignored by the DLSP director. Two other points were added by John Hauer and John Estes. Hauer's point was that Polk "has not demonstrated effectiveness as an administrator nor has he displayed willngness to accept suggestions and guidance from lawyers who are Project Board members." Estes added a seventh point which urged that all thirty-one lawyer members of the board be selected by the DBA board of directors.[55]

These concerns were offered as a public statement on February 23, 1971, by Bar Association President Kelley. "The Dallas Bar Association favors and supports equal justice under law," he said. "We believe that the poor are entitled to the same vigorous and professional legal representation as are all other elements of the community." But, he went on to say, the Dallas Bar Association was "deeply concerned about certain policies and practices of the DLSP," and the recommendations were offered in "a spirit of positive cooperation." An advance copy of the recommendations and comments had been sent to Ron Kessler, president of the Project board of directors.[56]

In June 1971 Polk resigned as director of DLSP. His influence was not over, however, for he soon was named a member of the board. Still concerned, the Dallas Bar Association's board of directors met on November 3, 1971, and in a divided vote authorized Kelley to issue a public statement criticizing the DLSP.[57] Not long afterwards, the question arose as to whether or not the Bar Association still supported DLSP. At a special called meeting of the board, Kelley said he had been requested to contact six Texas Congressmen to advise them of the Bar Association's position. The board authorized him to notify these Congressmen by telephone that the Bar Association continued to support DLSP.[58]

By the end of the year, Polk's tenure in any capacity with the DLSP was over. When he failed in an attempt to prevent the appointment of the more moderate D. Marcus Ranger as executive director, an effort was made to remove Polk from the board. It failed, but it was evident that Polk's influence was diminished. A few days later Polk resigned from the board.[59]

Kelley, who had been drawn into the DLSP controversy during his presidency of the DBA and who had become the subject of intense criticism from County Judge Lew Sterrett, was succeeded as president of the Bar Association by Henry Schlinger. A newspaper story under the headline, "Bar Takes Quieter Key," described Schlinger as a soft-spoken and low-key man whose approach would be in "sharp contrast" to that of his outspoken predecessor. Schlinger said that his "pet projects" would be in the fields of increased public education in the basics of law and an expansion of the pretrial release program instituted in 1970 by the Bar Association.[60] Even though Schlinger would assume a low profile as president, his friends knew him to be second to no one in his dedication to liberal principals.

Meanwhile, Polk had been making headlines of a different nature. After being charged with drunken driving in 1971, he was arrested for missing a trial hearing. He blamed it as "an awkward attempt by a dishonest and unethical district attorney and a perverse judge to assure me an unfair trial." His comments caused the State Bar of Texas to prepare a reprimand against him. After a lengthy legal battle between Polk and the State Bar, a federal district judge ruled that a public reprimand would violate Polk's right to free speech. The reprimand was not issued.[61]

In 1973 Polk left Dallas for San Francisco to take a position at the publicly funded Youth Law Center, an organization aimed at establishing legal rights of juveniles. The DLSP assumed a more moderate stance, focusing its attention on serving individual clients in such matters as divorce, consumer, and landlord-tenant problems. The headlines gradually faded away, and relations between the Dallas Bar Association and DLSP became cordial and coooperative over the next decades.[62]

WHILE POLK and other DLSP attorneys had stretched the limits of acceptability among the legal profession in pushing radical new approaches for old problems, there undeniably was a new spirit emerging in the late 1960s and 1970s that touched all aspects of society, including the Bar Association. Sometimes it was unclear as to what role if any the organization should play. When Dallas police in 1971 arrested scores of individuals in a raid of Lee Park in Oak Lawn, a gathering place for "hippies" suspected to be a prime location for drug deals, widespread violations of constitutional rights were alleged. (Among those caught up in the sweep was a future attorney general of Texas, Jim Mattox, then an assistant district attorney who protested that he was present merely as an observer.) Timothy E. Kelley, Bar Association president, called a special meeting of the board of directors to consider the matter. As a guest he invited the Rev. Bob Jones of the Lee Park Free Church to discuss the police actions as he had observed them. The consensus of the directors, after hearing Jones and discussing the event, was to take no action. The board directed Kelley, who at the time was still DBA president, to make "no comment" if approached by the press.[63]

Vincent W. Perini, who would become president of the Dallas Junior Bar Association and in 1986 president of the Dallas Bar Association, summed up the new attitude among younger lawyers. "We practice people's law," he told the *Dallas Times Herald* in 1970 when he was thirty-one years of age. "Today's new lawyers are finding themselves with an obligation to attack the new problems." Linda Coffee, who had joined in a suit questioning the legality of anti-abortion laws and who was one of a growing number of female attorneys in Dallas, further sought to explain it. "It's safe to call it a movement within our profession and it's related to the changes among college students and their demands."[64]

In keeping with this period's challenges to established society, Coffee initiated the famous *Roe v. Wade*, a case in which the nation's anti-abortion laws were ruled unconstitutional. Arising in 1970 in Dallas County, *Roe v. Wade* would create deep schisms and fierce political debate over the next decades throughout the nation.[65]

Coffee, a University of Texas Law School graduate and former clerk for U.S. District Judge Sarah T. Hughes, had become involved in the women's movement and feminist issues with abortion as a primary concern. She was considering the possibility of having a women's group challenge the state statute prohibiting abortion when an attorney friend contacted her and told her that he had a pregnant client who would be interested in challenging the law. The client was named only as "Jane Roe," although later she would identify herself as Norma McCorvey. Coffee alerted another attorney friend, Sarah Weddington, in Austin, and they filed suit in federal court challenging the state law.[66]

"Wade" in the case citation was none other than long-time Dallas County District Attorney Henry Wade. Actually, he had nothing to do with the case. The case was filed against the state and it named all district attorneys as defendants. Since Wade was the Dallas County district attorney and since the case was filed in Dallas, his name was listed first. The attorney general office for the State of Texas defended the state law.

A three-judge panel, including Sarah T. Hughes, heard the case and declared Texas' statute to be unconstitutional. The U.S. Supreme Court heard the case on October 11, 1972, and on January 22, 1973, it affirmed the right of women throughout the nation to have legal abortions.[67]

In October 1971, the DLSP, representing four inmates in the Dallas County prison, filed a class-action suit (*Taylor v. Sterrett*) alleging that conditions in the jail such as overcrowdedness and lack of recreational facilities violated Texas statutory laws. They claimed that they had been subjected to cruel and unusual punishment, deprived of due process, and denied equal protection. The case was heard in Judge Hughes' federal district court, and on June 5, 1972, having previously visited the jail to inspect conditions herself, she ruled that Dallas County's jail facility failed to meet the minimum requirements of state law and that prisoners were being subjected to cruel and unusual punishment—lack of sufficient bunks, failure to provide recreation facilities, improper censoring of mail, and other things. She ordered the commissioners court to remedy the situation, and she began issuing specific and detailed orders on how it should be done, calling the Dallas County jail a "factory for crime." These directives improved the daily lives of the prisoners, and when Judge Hughes once visited the jail's dining area at lunch, the prisoners recognized her and gave her a standing ovation.[68]

Resistance against Judge Hughes' directives and criticisms against the DLSP attorneys who had instituted the class-action suit were widespread, especially from County Judge W.L. (Lew) Sterrett. The lengthy battle that ensued over a seven-year period culminated on April 27, 1977, when Judge Hughes ordered Sterrett and the four county commissioners to start purchasing land for an entirely new jail facility and to implement plans for building it by July 15. Otherwise, she said, she would permit no additional prisoners to be incarcerated. That November voters approved a bond election with an appropriation of $56.7 million for a new criminal justice center which would include not only a modern jail but a criminal courts building and related office facilities.

A site was chosen at Industrial Boulevard and Commerce Street, and on December 16, 1982, dedication services were held for "the most outstanding new detention facility in the entire nation." Somewhat ironically, the new facility was named the W.L. (Lew) Sterrett Justice Center in memory of the late county judge who had railed so often against the need for jail improvements.[69] It had two buildings, a three-story in-take facility and a nine-story tower containing 918 single bunks for inmates with plans for future expansion up to 4,000 bunks. A recreation area, the lack of which previously had drawn Judge Hughes' ire, was included. Unfortunately, rising costs prevented the construction of the criminal courts building, although a foundation was completed for a projected sixteen-floor structure to be built at a later date. This omission would lead to a protracted debate in the years ahead over the size of the new criminal courts building.

Meanwhile, the Dallas Bar Association observed in 1973 its one-hundredth anniversary, dating its origin to that day when District Judge Hardin Hart had granted the request of attorney John J. Good, the first president, to postpone court activities for two weeks during the month of June so that "jurors, parties, and witnesses" could gather the county's wheat harvest. In honor of its centennial year the Bar Association commissioned a statue by Louis Martin which was placed in front of the Dallas County Government Center facing Commerce Street. The statue, a blindfolded woman of justice bearing sword and scales, was placed atop a six-sided granite pedestal with separate markers commemorating each of the six sovereign nations which Texas had been a part of during its history. A quote from Magna Carta Clause 40 was displayed on the statue: "To No One Will We Sell, To No One Deny or Delay Right of Justice."

One long-standing practice adopted by the Bar Association

that year was the institution of regular evaluations of incumbent judges by members of the bar. This had been recommended in June 1973 by a judiciary committee headed by Waller M. Collie Jr. The board voted in favor of it in September, and the first poll was conducted that fall. There were many objections from state judges, many of whom who viewed the poll as a "popularity contest" that favored Democrats over Republicans. While the DBA had been polling members on judicial candidates since 1946 and releasing the results, the new Judicial Evaluation Poll included all incumbent judges.[70]

The first poll's results were announced by Bar Association President John L. Estes in late December 1973. Ratings were based on responses to thirteen questions such as: Is he a man of good character and integrity? Is he punctual in opening court and keeping appointments? Does he know and apply the rules of procedure? The yes or no responses were calculated by percentages, and in this first poll they ranged in the various categories from a high of 100 percent to a low of 24 percent for one judge in the category of "judicial temperament."[71] Although many judges scored consistently high marks, some did not. "They were more than upset," Estes recalled in 1998. "But the poll has been a real service to the public."[72]

In August 1974, for the second time in its history, the Dallas Bar Association was honored by the American Bar Association for having the outstanding bar organization in the nation. The Award of Merit for Excellence was presented to Estes, who had served as president for 1973, the year it was honored. Estes accepted the award at the ABA annual meeting in Honolulu. The judges who selected the Dallas Bar for the honor cited its overall performance and especially its judicial evaluation poll.[73]

Upon observing its one-hundredth anniversary in 1973 the time seemed right for re-assessment. A "Goals for the Dallas Bar Association" program was established to identify subjects for fuller discussion. It was modeled after the "Goals for Dallas" program which Mayor Erik Jonsson had instituted for Dallas not long after the assassination of President Kennedy. The credo for the DBA's own program was summarized by President-elect

Louis J. Weber, Jr., in these plain-spoken words: "We might get to where we want to go if we could find out where we are and where we want to go and make some plans."[74]

In 1974 members of the Association, joined as well by selected representatives from the Dallas community, spent a three-day retreat at Lake Texoma to discuss and clarify their future goals. Perhaps the most meaningful consensus of all was acceptance of the thesis that the Dallas Bar Association had the right and duty to become active and vocal in the solution of community problems related to the legal system.[75]

BUILDING FOR THE FUTURE

⌘

Chapter Thirteen

FROM ITS EARLIEST DAYS until the 1930s the Dallas Bar Association had no place to call its own. For their meetings, members resorted to finding space in various courtrooms. For their dinners and luncheons, they gathered at hotel dining rooms. In 1937 they were proud to find space for their own office—a fifteen-foot cubicle underneath the stairs in the Old Red Courthouse. In 1955 their move to a club-like setting with dining facilities in the Adolphus Hotel had seemed like a dream come true. But by the 1970s that setting had been outgrown. To accommodate the growing need for space, office and dining facilities had been separated in 1973 when the offices were moved to the adjacent Adolphus Tower. A new and bigger facility was needed to accommodate the Association's ever-expanding activities and its growing number of members. By November 1974 membership reached 2,621 attorneys.

"The Board of Directors and sagacious members realized that the Adolphus had served them well," Jo Anna Moreland, the executive director, recalled later, "but like prospering families who see their rented home falling into disrepair, knew the time had come to make a daring and bold decision."[1]

In 1975 Bar President Charles P. Storey initiated a campaign to raise funds for a new home for the association. A Special New Headquarters Committee, chaired by John L. Hauer, was charged with finding an appropriate location.[2] The search seemed to be successful. Space was located on the third floor of a new and towering mid-town skyscraper, the First International Building at 1201 Elm Street. A brochure announced its selection; and a funding campaign was started in which law firms, individuals, and others pledged approximately $550,000 towards a new headquarters.[3] Complications arose, however, especially concerning unexpected finish-out costs and other variable expenses that seemed certain to escalate. In February 1976 the board of directors declared the First International project to be economically unfeasible, and the idea was dropped.[4]

In fact, a new possibility already had arisen that seemed very exciting, and it began to be pursued at that same board meeting. Jerry Jordan reported that one of Dallas' most historic buildings— the Belo mansion on Ross Avenue between Pearl and Olive streets—might be available. Its purchase would satisfy a need stated in the 1947 charter for the Bar Association to buy its own property and pay rent no longer. The two-story structure with impressive columns that made it look something like a Southern plantation had been built just prior to 1900 by one of the city's most important and influential citizens, Colonel A.H. Belo. Belo was founder in 1885 of *The Dallas Morning News* as a "sister" newspaper to his *Galveston Daily News*, then the state's most important newspaper. Belo himself had moved to Dallas, for the *News* had become an important institution immediately upon its founding, and he chose this location on Ross Avenue, then one of the city's most prestigious residential streets, to build his handsome home. It had been many years, though, since any members of the Belo family had lived there. Two major additions had been made to the structure, and since 1926 it had been occupied as a funeral home. (When the notorious Dallas outlaw Clyde Barrow had been shot to death in an ambush in Louisiana in 1934 his body was returned to the funeral home, where some 30,000 spectators formed long lines to view his remains.)

In February 1976 the board of directors unanimously adopted a resolution that the owner of the property, Mrs. Helen Belo Morrison of Asheville, North Carolina, be approached regarding the possible purchase of the house. On April 28, 1976, President Waller M. Collie, Jr., and Vice-President Robert Thomas and their wives flew to Asheville, North Carolina, to meet with Mrs. Morrison, Belo's granddaughter who had been born in the home in 1902. Over a period of months, Collie and Thomas worked out the details of a purchase option, and on October 15, 1976, Bar President Collie sent a letter to the full membership announcing that he wanted to discuss with them "one of the most important and significant subjects ever to come before the Dallas Bar." The possible purchase of the Belo mansion, he said, would be "the most ambitious project that the Dallas Bar has ever undertaken."[5]

Mrs. Morrison had agreed to sell the property to the Bar Association for $724,000, payable with 29 percent down at the time of closing with the balance in four equal payments over four succeeding years. Preliminary inspections and surveys of the building were made by two architectural firms, both of them reporting that the basic structure remained sound and fully capable of renovation "in such a manner as to reflect its original elegance."

It would have space for a large dining room-meeting place that could accommodate up to 300 people. It would have smaller dining/meeting rooms and a bar overlooking a central atrium-type courtyard, and there would be space for offices and a library. Estimated costs for renovation were approximately $750,000 to $800,000. The location was no more than five to eight minutes walking distance from most downtown buildings, but "downtown" was growing and inevitably would encompass the building's neighborhood.

"I don't think there is any disagreement about the fact that it is a handsome, imposing edifice on beautiful grounds," Collie wrote in his three-page letter to the membership. "Virtually everyone who has seen the premises is absolutely enthusiastic about what this beautiful old home could be as a new headquarters for the Dallas Bar. It is our purpose and intention that, when work on it is completed, it will be the most elegant and beautifully appointed club in Dallas. Certainly no other club, at whatever the initiation and dues cost, can ever hope to match the splendor and grace of its location."[6]

To give members and their spouses an opportunity to examine the property closely for themselves before committing to a project that would cost an estimated $1.9 million, the board of directors held an open house from 4 to 6 p.m. on October 29. Comments were overwhelmingly in favor of the facility; only two negative responses were received. Republic National Bank had indicated a willingness to finance $650,000 of the amount needed on a long-term basis; members who already had made $550,000 in pledges toward the First International Bank location were requested to approve this alternate use of their funds; and approximately $750,000 in additional pledges and funds would be needed.[7]

The appropriate vehicle for handling the transaction was seen as the Dallas Bar Foundation, organized in 1971 but to this point having had little to do. Now was the time for it to serve its basic purpose, although this precise function had not been envisioned. Its charter now was amended to add among its purposes "to preserve historical structures, display historical memorabilia, and conduct historical observances." Thus, it would be the Foundation to whom pledges would be made and it would be the Foundation that would acquire the property and lease it to the Association. The Internal Revenue Service had ruled that the Foundation was tax-exempt, and thus all contributions toward the acquisition of the Belo Mansion would be deductible from income taxes. As usual, all trustees of the Foundation still would be elected by the directors of the Dallas Bar Association.

In February 1977 the Bar Association's board of directors voted to name the prospective new facility the Dallas Legal Education Center, an indication of the organization's increasingly heavy commitment to continuing legal education and to its existence as a professional association dedicated to service to the public and the bar. "Indeed it [continuing legal education] is already the primary activity of the Dallas Bar Association," declared a trio of officers in a 1977 letter to the membership— Collie, now past president; Phil Burleson, president; and Robert Thomas, president-elect.[8] Burleson appointed Thomas as chairman of the New Headquarters Committee, and it would be Thomas who would take the leading role in the acquisition of the property and its renovation.[9] Afterwards, as a salute to his hours of dedication towards the project, Thomas frequently would be referred to as "the father of the Belo mansion." Thomas' dedication to the project was inspired in part, perhaps, by his interest in history and his deep ties to the community. His father, H. Bascom Thomas Jr., had been president of the Bar Association in 1946, and his grandfather, Robert S. Hyer, was the founding president of Southern Methodist University.

Some 500 lawyers, organized into teams, conducted an extensive fund-raising campaign among the membership. By March 31, 1977, the amount of pledges had risen to approximately $750,000. It was estimated now that an additional $600,000 was needed. Jerry Jordan and Jerry Buchmeyer headed a committee to solicit further funds from Bar Association membership. A Special Gifts Division was created to ask families of the city's past great lawyers to memorialize them with donations in their honor. A Community Division contacted corporations, businesses, and foundations for contributions.[10] One special award came from the Texas Historical Commission, which gave a $100,000 grant toward the building's restoration, an amount which Thomas told board members was the largest ever awarded by the Commission in Dallas and possibly in the state.[11]

On September 15, 1977, the transaction for the purchase of the Belo mansion was completed; four days later the purchase of the parking lot property immediately behind the mansion was finalized. The Dallas Bar Foundation now owned an entire block in central Dallas. The work of restoration and remodeling began. The architectural firm of Burson, Hendricks, and Walls was engaged, and Nick LaBranche was selected as general contractor.

In July 1979 the work was completed. The Dallas Bar Association moved into its fine new home on July 23. In addition to meeting rooms, dining area, a bar, and office space, the facility provided space for a law library and for the Dallas Association of Young Lawyers (formerly the Junior Bar Association). Jerry Buchmeyer, president at the time of the move, praised many members for their important work which made it possible, but he especially singled out Robert Thomas, who had served as president during the critical year of 1978 when much of the essential work was done, as "the one person who is more responsible for our new headquarters—and who certainly deserves more credit—than any other." It was Thomas, he said, who "pushed us with his vision, helped raise needed funds, worked constantly with the architects, construction manager and decorator, and was even there to help the movers."[12]

Moving in did not mean that the work was over. A supplementary fund campaign was launched almost immediately which had four parts: (1) the DAYL (Dallas Association of Young Lawyers) campaign to bring in new members, headed by Jerry Lastelick and Tom Craddock with Nina Cortell and Bill Allensworth as co-chairpersons; (2) the Board of Directors Solicitation, headed by chairman Darrell Jordan and vice-chairman Harriet Miers; (3) Community Solicitation, directed by Robert Thomas; and (4) Large Firm Campaign, with Jerry Buchmeyer and past presidents John Estes, Phil Wilson, Waller Collie, and Charles Storey.[13]

The impact of the new headquarters was immediately apparent. Dues income during 1978 had been approximately $165,000; but in 1979 with more than two months still remaining that figure had risen to almost $317,000, an amount anticipated to be $350,000 by year's end. (In addition to an increase in membership, this reflected income from annual dues which had been raised to $120 for lawyers licensed more than five years and $72 for members licensed for fewer than five years.)[14] A total of 334 new members had been admitted to the Dallas Bar Association before the year had ended, and at the first annual membership meeting held at the Belo, fifty-eight new members were accepted, the largest single group ever admitted.[15] Mortgage payments were $6,000 a month as compared to rental payments at the Adolphus of $3,500 per month. Food service at the Adolphus in 1978 had lost the organization $14,000, but during the first two months of operation at the Dallas Legal Education Center (DLEC) a profit of $4,000 already been made through this function. These figures correctly indicated a surge in interest and attendance. During the first full month of operation, August 1979, the DLEC had attracted 1,636 persons; during the same month in 1978 at the Adolphus attendance had been 470.[16]

There had been many uncertainties about the move. Would raising the dues cause resignations of members? Could the minimum monthly guarantee required to support the food service operation be met? Would operating costs be as projected? The answers to all these questions were a resounding yes. "I am pleased to report that the picture looks good," Buchmeyer reported in October in the *Dallas Bar Headnotes*.

As president-elect Robert Edwin Davis reported, in March 1976 the Dallas Bar Foundation had total assets of $388.39. Now, three and a half years later, it owned an entire block in downtown Dallas on which stood a newly renovated and remodeled structure of unique historical significance. The present value of the land and improvements, he wrote, was "well in excess of $2,000,000."[17]

IT WAS CLEAR that the Dallas Bar Association had desperately needed a new facility, although few if any had supposed that it would be so grand. The organization's activities had continued to grow, with one activity frequently spawning another and with the various sections having their own officers and committees.

When Jo Anna Moreland, the executive director, first took her job in 1962, the Bar Association had approximately 1,200 members. Now, upon moving into the new location, that figure had almost tripled to 3,500. The office staff had grown to include not just Ms. Moreland, but her executive assistant who also directed the Lawyer Referral Service, a secretary for the Dallas Bar Foundation, an office assistant, a dining room cashier, and three part-time interviewers for the Lawyer Referral Service.[18] During her seventeen years, Ms. Moreland reported, she had been amazed at the ability of the directors to approach questions from divergent perspectives and come up with a common conclusion. "I have been witness to no politics and no cliques; instead, there is a willingness to share honors as well as responsibility. The people elected and appointed to head the association take their tasks, but never themselves, very seriously indeed."[19] In 1982, upon completing twenty years in her position, Ms. Moreland was honored by the membership with a party and a two-week trip to London, Paris, and Rome.[20]

The Legal Clinics continued as a weekly affair, still meeting at noon on Friday instead of the original Saturday morning sessions. The long, traditional practice of passing flowery memorials to honor deceased members had been modified. In these faster-paced days resolutions were prepared by a sub-committee on memorial resolutions for passage once a year at the annual membership meeting. One constant theme—that of growing specialization—was reflected in the number of sections now existing. By the end of the 1970s these sections generally met once a month, and they had their own officers, committees, and dues assessments. By December 1978 there were eight sections: (1) taxation, with 150 members; (2) probate, trusts, and estates, 150 members; (3) real property, 150 members; (4) family law, 110 members; (5) criminal law, undetermined number of members; (6) sole practitioners, from 40 to 100 members; (7) bankruptcy and commercial law, 90 members; and (8) corporate counsel, 165 members.[21]

The Lawyer Referral Service had come to be a major source of income for the organization as well as a worthwhile service to the community. Those who obtained lawyers from the service paid only a $10 fee, but this amount was expected to bring in approximately $37,500 during 1978. This amount was second as a revenue producer to membership dues, anticipated to be $154,000 for the year. Referral fees were raised to $15 in August 1979. In 1981 the fee was raised again to $20 for a half-hour consultation with a lawyer on the referral list, and during 1981 the Referral Service collected $49,835. During that year 517 lawyers participated on the referral panel, and they served 3,294 clients.[22]

The former Dallas Junior Bar Association, renamed as Dallas Association of Young Lawyers (DAYL) in 1977 (coinciding with a similar name change for the state junior bar group), now had its own office space in the Dallas Legal Education Center. Beginning in 1978 its ties with the Dallas Bar Association had been solidified even further when the board of directors agreed to have the DAYL president attend board meetings as a non-voting member.[23]

The late 70's and early 80's were the years of the "writing presidents," Jerry L. Buchmeyer and John L. Hauer. Buchmeyer, as president during 1979, had begun writing a series of humorous columns for the *Dallas Bar Headnotes* under the title of "et cetera" which continued into the 1980s in the *Texas Bar Journal*. In 1981 the Dallas Bar Foundation published a collection of his columns under the title, *et cetera*. Hauer, who followed Robert Edwin Davis as president in 1981, began writing for *Headnotes* as president-elect a series of reminiscent and humorous columns about lawyers he had known over the years. Generally they appeared under the heading, "Memorable Dallas Lawyers of the Past." Ten years later these columns also would be published by the Dallas Bar Foundation as a book under the title, *Finest Kind!*[24] Frequently, readers of *Headnotes* were treated in the same issue to columns written both by Buchmeyer and Hauer.

In fact, writing a monthly column had become an assignment for all presidents. With the routine publication of the monthly *Dallas Bar Headnotes* in 1977 the president's report became a regular feature of some length rather than the truncated memos which previously had appeared in the weekly newsletters.

BUILDING WAS very much these days on the mind of members of the Bar Association. One concern, and it had always been a concern, was in prodding the county and state to provide sufficient courts and courtrooms. The last new courthouse had been a handsome one, the largest yet built and the seventh courthouse for Dallas County. A white marble structure, it stood twelve stories high and was located adjacent to the Old Red Courthouse at Commerce and Houston streets. On February 4, 1966, Governor John B. Connally and other important public figures participated in a ribbon-cutting ceremony to open the $13 million building. Its official name became the Dallas County Government Center Courthouse (later named for George L. Allen Sr. in honor of the county's first African-American justice of the peace and former Dallas city councilman). Less than ten years after it opened it had been outgrown. The original idea to add upper floors for more space as they were needed was given up by county commissioners as too expensive.

In 1976 the Bar Association asked the Texas Legislature to create fourteen new courts for the county—two criminal district courts, four county criminal courts, four domestic relations courts, two county courts at law, and two juvenile courts. To accommodate them, the construction of another new courthouse facility adequate for years to come would obviously be required. "The obvious truth seems to be that Dallas County has already completely outgrown its courthouse, and that if the administration of justice in our county is to continue to efficiently perform its function, it must have adequate physical quarters in which to do it," Bar President Waller M. Collie Jr. said. The eighth largest city in the nation, he emphasized, ought not to be confronted with the necessity of housing its courts of law in "antiquated, temporary and makeshift space."[25] His comment was an obvious reference to the county commissioners, who had been talking about the possibility of buying an existing building near the courthouse complex to provide space for additional courtrooms. Already, however, the county's courtrooms were scattered in several different locations—the Dallas County Government Center, the old Dallas County Criminal Courts Building, the Records Building, and the Old Red Courthouse. Further separation, it seemed to many, would be short-sighted.

The successful 1977 county bond election—prompted by U.S. District Judge Sarah T. Hughes' finding that Dallas County jails were not in compliance with state statutes—authorized the construction of a new criminal justice complex that would have not just a modern jail to fulfill minimal standards but also a sixteen-story criminal courts building. Creation of a building solely for criminal courts would permit courtrooms in the Dallas County Government Center to be dedicated solely to civil cases. But the $56.7 million approved by voters for the new justice center turned out to be an insufficient amount for both structures, and although a foundation was completed for the criminal courts building, its construction was postponed indefinitely. The 1977 bonds also had included $1.3 million to convert the Old Red Courthouse into a facility for family law courts. But it was discovered that the building had serious structural difficulties, and the cost of remedying the defects would run considerably over $4 million. That idea also was abandoned.[26] Thus, the problem of having a sufficient number of courtrooms and available space for them was escalating.

Opening the Justice Center as a county jail without the adjacent criminal courts posed several problems. One was the logistics involved in transporting prisoners to the courtrooms some six blocks away for trial; another was providing for their meals while away from jail, and yet another was the fact that the district attorney's office, sheriff's department, and other support facilities also would be located several blocks away from the Justice Center. "It's going to cost the Dallas County taxpayers more to open the Criminal Justice facility than not to use it at all," Sheriff Don Byrd told the Dallas Bar Association's Criminal Justice Committee in July 1982, almost a year before the facility actually opened.[27] Completion of the full Justice Center as originally envisioned thus seemed imperative, and in the next few years the Bar Association—stepping into the public limelight— pushed hard for this goal, consistently asking for a bigger facility than County Commissioners were prepared to seek in a bond election.

To address the issue in the most effective and aggressive fashion, at Vincent W. Perini's suggestion, the Bar's officers and directors appointed in 1981 a blue-ribbon Courts and Courts Facilities Planning Department composed of six members who would serve three-year alternating terms.[28] Frank Finn was its first chairman, and he would be succeeded by Judge Craig Enoch of the 101st District Court. In September 1982 Finn and his committee invited incumbents and candidates for the Dallas County Commissioners Court to join them and other members of the Bar Association for an overview of the problem. DBA President Darrell Jordan described the crisis in these terms: "We are fast approaching a time in Dallas County when citizen confidence in our Courts to do their proper jobs will disappear through no fault of the judges, the lawyers or the litigants. When confidence in the courts weakens, respect for the law lessens. If we take away the faith of the citizens in the integrity and effectiveness of the Courts we discourage people that have no other institutions to look to for justice or stability." He emphasized that the Dallas Bar Association's position was that proper and immediate planning for court facilities was absolutely necessary. [29]

Finn presented a video tape which highlighted the problems through interviews with District Attorney Henry Wade, Court of Appeals Chief Justice Clarence Guittard, Sheriff Don Byrd, District Judge Nathan Hecht, and others. Wade pointed out that his staff presently was separated into five different buildings, making it almost impossible to coordinate. He estimated that completion of the Criminal Justice Center would improve the efficiency of his staff by 35 to 40 percent. Sheriff Byrd emphasized the safety hazards in transporting criminal defendants from one facility to another. One segment showed a visiting judge trying a domestic relations case in a ten-foot square jury room adjacent to a normal courtroom in the Old Red Courthouse. The lawyers for both sides were attempting to settle the case, but the judge had no idea where they could go to talk. In conclusion, the video tape showed clearly that the expedient administration of justice in the county depended upon the prompt completion of the Justice Center to include criminal courts and space for the sheriff's and district attorney's offices, all of which originally had been contemplated for the Justice Center. Agreement among those present that the Justice Center should be completed at the earliest date possible was overwhelming. [30]

Not long after the meeting, county commissioners retrieved the early plans for the Justice Center and announced that work would begin to update costs for it in preparation for another bond election. A consultant's report to the commissioners in the summer of 1983 urged that they go ahead with the plans to build a criminal courts building with space for fifty-one courtrooms as well as offices for the sheriff, district attorney, and district and county clerks. [31]

It was understood that an upcoming county bond election would seek to achieve the goal of completing the Justice Center, and now a tug-of-war accompanied by newspaper headlines developed between the county commissioners and the Dallas Bar

Association as to just how big that criminal courthouse should be. The Bar Association hired the former president of the Dallas chapter of the American Institute of Architects as a consultant. Money was raised for a public relations campaign to be directed by Pierce Allman, the Association's public relations counsel. The original 1977 plans had called for a sixteen-story criminal courts building, a size that the Bar Association, its Courts and Court Facilities Department, and DBA spokesman Vincent Perini publicly insisted should be met if future needs were to be accommodated. District Attorney Henry Wade compiled a report which predicted an annual growth in felony cases by 5 percent and misdemeanor cases by 7.5 percent, a growth that concluded that the twenty-four criminal courts in existence in 1984 should become thirty-nine courts in 1990, fifty-four by 1995, and seventy by the year 2000.[32] But County Judge Frank Crowley and County Commissioner Jim Tyson, using population growth projections, insisted that these figures were incorrect, that an eleven-story building was more than adequate. With Commissioner Jim Jackson in agreement, they had a majority on the five-member commissioners court.

Perini, who headed a Bar Association's task force to see that a sixteen-story building was built, termed the eleven-story structure an example of "Central Expressway planning" in which it would be outmoded by the time it could be opened. "If You Liked Central Expressway, You'll Love Crowley's Courthouse" was a slogan being bandied about by lawyers. Tyson, who was in charge of the commissioner's bond election task force, believed that the Bar Association's plan would not be approved by voters because it would contain too much unoccupied space and would be too expensive. "They are looking at a long time in the future and we're looking at what's practical and what will sell," said Tyson.[33]

Dallas Morning News columnist Henry Tatum wrote that both sides were "making the rounds" with drawings and projections that supported their points of view. "A battery of representatives from the judicial courts, district attorney's office and bar association dropped by here recently with pages of statistics that explained why the new building must be 16 stories tall to house all the courts the county will need." A few weeks later, he wrote, Commissioner Tyson visited the newspaper's editorial writers to "explain how off-base" the statistics were. "The two sides are locked into their positions and have no intention of changing. As each week passes, the words become a bit nastier."[34]

With county commissioners holding the upper hand, their point of view ultimately prevailed. They scheduled in 1985 a bond proposition which allowed $50 million toward the construction of a criminal courts building at the W.L. (Lew) Sterrett Justice Center. Because they had maintained that at least $61.5 million was needed, the Bar Association protested and voted to oppose the bond program. In response, the county commissioners agreed to put an additional $11.5 million proposition on the ballot for the voters to consider. This was enough to persuade the Bar Association's board of directors to reverse their position and vote unanimously to support the program. When voters approved a $215 million bond issue on November 8, 1977, $56.4 million of the amount was specified for the new jail. When the building at long last was opened in 1989, it was an eleven-story courthouse adjacent to the new county jail and facing Industrial Boulevard. It contained forty courtrooms and space for the sheriff's department, district attorney, and other county agencies. (A decade later that space continued to be sufficient, for in 1998 it still accommodated all the criminal courts in Dallas County— fifteen district courts, ten county courts, and two county courts of appeal—with unused space remaining.) The slogan used by Dallas' lawyers in striving to get a larger courthouse, "If You Liked Central Expressway, You'll Love Crowley's Courthouse," became, in effect, official. The building was named the Frank Crowley Courts Building in honor of the county judge whose belief that it should be no taller than eleven stories had prevailed.[35]

THE BAR ASSOCIATION's relationship with Southern Methodist University continued to be close. Robert Edwin Davis, the Bar Association's president for 1980, called it a "symbiotic relationship" which provided important benefits for all Dallas lawyers, no matter which law school they had attended. In his

Headnotes column Davis listed nine ways that the law school benefited attorneys in Dallas, and conversely listed six ways in which the city's legal community assisted the law school. Foremost on his first list was the presence of the large law library at SMU, accessible without cost to Dallas lawyers. He also listed among other things its graduate law courses, continuing legal education programs, students and professors, and other services. As to the legal community's contributions to the law school, he described the availability of lecturers and adjunct professors, access to law students for part-time work, fund-raising, general counseling on curriculum, admissions, policies, and others.[36]

Since assuming the position of dean in 1963, Charles Galvin had made many important contributions to the law school. An especially noteworthy one, begun in 1968, was the Hatton W. Sumners Scholarship program endowed by the late and long-time Dallas attorney and Congressman. The program's origin, as related by Galvin, provided an engaging anecdote on Sumners' interesting character. Sumners had decided to retire from Congress at about the time that Robert G. Storey became dean of the law school, founded the Southwestern Legal Foundation and initiated a building program. Dean Storey and Paul Carrington went to see Sumners, a bachelor whose miserliness had become legend, with the idea that he might make a donation towards the new facilities. "It was no secret to anybody that he saved every dollar that he made," Galvin recalled. However, Sumners agreed to give them $25,000 if they would provide an apartment for him in one of the new buildings, Lawyer's Inn, and let him have meals in its dining room for the rest of his life. Galvin and Carrington immediately accepted the offer, thinking that he wouldn't stay for more than a couple of years. As it turned out, he remained there from 1951 until his death in 1962. His grant provided a modest basis for establishing the Hatton W. Sumners Foundation for the study of the "science and art of self government."[37]

Meanwhile, when Galvin joined the law school faculty in 1952 Sumners had asked his help in preparing his will, a process which seemed endless to Galvin because of Sumners' meticulous approach in every detail. When at last finished, the will, deposited in Carrington's law office, specified that the bulk of Sumners' estate would go to his own foundation. Only after Sumners' death and the settlement of his estate was it learned that the various properties he held were worth far more than anyone had realized. Galvin, as dean, soon applied to the foundation, headed by J. Cleo Thompson, for generous scholarships that would permit outstanding students to go through law school absolutely free of charge. The application was approved, and the result, the Hatton W. Sumners Scholarships, became what Galvin described as late as 1995 as "one of the most generous in all legal education."[38] From five to seven outstanding scholars are chosen each year to receive the scholarships which offer full tuition and fees, room and board, and a stipend for textbooks.

Galvin, as dean, also enlisted the support of Dallas real estate developer George M. Underwood Jr. to build a new law library. It was named for Underwood, its principal donor. Upon completion, the Underwood Law Library was described as second in physical size only to the Harvard Law Library.

As enrollment at SMU's day-time law school escalated, enrollment in the evening division declined. Many of Dallas' attorneys had earned their degrees through evening study, first through the old Y.M.C.A. evening school, and then through the continuation of that program by SMU after it assumed control in the mid-1930s. But by the 1960s the program represented a financial drain, and the faculty voted to phase it out by 1969.[39]

Still more changes were forthcoming. Galvin's predecessor as dean, John W. Riehm, had initiated an effort to establish the identity of the School of Law as separate from the Southwestern Legal Foundation. Under Dean Storey the two had often appeared as one. Galvin continued the process to make the two distinctive entities. Tension between the two entities was resolved in 1974 when the Southwestern Legal Foundation, under the direction of Andrew R. Cecil since 1958, moved its offices from SMU to the campus of the University of Texas at Dallas.

In 1970 Galvin resigned as dean to return to the classroom. Professor A.J. Thomas became acting dean, and the search for

Galvin's permanent successor took two years. In 1980, Professor Jeswald W. Salacuse, who had been on the faculty since 1978, was named dean. Salacuse, a Harvard Law School graduate, was a specialist in international business law. He resigned in 1986 to become dean of the Fletcher School of Law and Diplomacy.

SINCE THE CREATION of the Northern District of Texas in 1879 until 1970, there had been only twelve federal district judges to serve in the district. This number began to expand in the 1970s with the creation of new courts. In 1970 Congress authorized one additional judgeship for the Northern District, three more in 1978, and another in 1984. Many of these new positions were filled by Dallas attorneys—Robert Madden Hill, Robert W. Porter, Patrick E. Higginbotham, Barefoot Sanders, Jerry Buchmeyer, A. Joe Fish, Robert B. Maloney, and Sidney A. Fitzwater.[40]

Robert M. Hill (1928-1987), a Dallas native with undergraduate and law degrees from the University of Texas, was appointed to the bench in 1970 by President Richard M. Nixon. During his time on the bench, Judge Hill presided over a number of high profile cases, including the 1979 trial of Billie Sol Estes. In 1984 Hill was appointed by President Reagan to the 5th U.S. Court of Appeals. In 1987 he died after suffering an asthma attack aboard an airliner as he returned with his wife from a vacation in Kenya.[41]

Robert W. Porter (1926-1991) also was named to the bench by President Nixon, his appointment coming in 1974. Porter, a native of Illinois, served in the U.S. Navy from 1944 to 1946. He earned his law degree from the University of Michigan, and in Dallas became a partner in the firm of Thompson, Coe, Cousins, Irons and Porter. During his last years as a judge, Porter presided with an oxygen tank at his side, and when he had trouble breathing he would don an oxygen mask, take a breath, and then return to the business at hand. Judge Porter was ailing from a lung ailment, asbestosis, which he had contracted while working on a Navy ship during World War II. In 1990 he took senior status as a judge because of his illness, and in 1991 he died.[42]

Patrick E. Higginbotham's background was intriguing not just because of his success in the legal profession but because of his youth—he took the oath of office as a federal judge in 1978 at the age of thirty-seven. He was the youngest federal judge in the nation. Higginbotham, upon U.S. Senator John Tower's recommendation, had been nominated by President Gerald Ford to succeed Sarah T. Hughes upon her retirement. A native of Alabama and the son of a dairy farmer, Higginbotham held an undergraduate degree and a law degree from the University of Alabama. He was a former captain in the U.S. Air Force. Until his appointment to the bench he was a member of the Coke & Coke law firm.[43]

Barefoot Sanders was a far more familiar figure to area residents because of his years of public service. Named by President Kennedy in 1961 to be U.S. Attorney for the Northern District, Sanders earlier had served three terms in the Texas Legislature. From 1965 to 1966 he was an assistant U.S. attorney general in Washington, and then he returned to Dallas to practice law in the firm of Clark, West, Keller, Sanders & Butler. Sanders, having been nominated by President Jimmy Carter, took his oath of office from U.S. District Judge William M. (Mac) Taylor Jr. on May 5, 1979.

As an eleven-year-old boy in Dallas, Sanders had achieved his first attention by being named the "Freckle King" at the Texas Centennial in 1936. It was estimated that he had more than 5,000 freckles. After service in in the U.S. Navy during World War II, Sanders attended the University of Texas. He used his middle name, Barefoot (a family surname), rather than his first name, Harold, as a gimmick to win election as head cheerleader. Just afterwards the name proved useful when he campaigned for the student body presidency. White-washed stencils of bare feet on campus sidewalks appeared overnight to promote his candidacy. Once again his campaign was successful; his fellow students elected him to the office. Having become so well known by his middle name, he continued to use it rather than his first name as he began his legal and political career.

In 1979 another familiar figure in Dallas legal circles, former Bar Association president Jerry Buchmeyer, was appointed to the federal bench by President Jimmy Carter. Buchmeyer, the son of an East Texas postal worker, earned his law degree from the University of Texas and was a partner in Thompson & Knight specializing in antitrust law. During his service on the bench Buchmeyer refused to relinquish the humor which had been a part of his personality for so long, and his rulings frequently were marked with passages of wit. In 1983 Buchmeyer was named by *American Lawyer* magazine as the best federal judge in the 5th circuit.[44]

Six years later Buchmeyer made one of the most significant rulings in the history of municipal politics in Dallas. He held that the City of Dallas' method of electing councilmen was unconstitutional because it discriminated against African-Americans and Hispanics. He ordered the city to adopt a new plan for City Council elections in which districts were drawn up with special emphasis on ethnic make-up so that minority candidates would have a better chance at winning a seat. The judge mandated the so-called "14-1" plan (referring to fourteen single-member, geographical districts and a mayor elected at-large) after it had been rejected by the city's voters. His ruling brought a dramatic change to municipal politics in the city with far greater minority participation.[45]

In 1982, upon President Ronald Reagan's nomination, Judge Higginbotham was elevated to the 5th Court of Appeals. He was succeeded in 1983 by A. Joe Fish, a Yale Law School graduate, also upon the appointment of President Reagan. Higginbotham administered the oath of office to his successor. Even though Fish was only 39 years old, he already had served as an associate justice of the state court of appeals and a state district judge.

President Reagan appointed Dallasite Robert B. Maloney to a new federal district judgeship in 1985. Maloney, a Southern Methodist University law school graduate, had been a state representative between 1973 and 1982 and afterwards an associate justice on the Dallas Court of Appeals. At his swearing-in ceremony in January 1986, a special touch of glamour was present in the person of his sister, movie actress Dorothy Malone.

If Patrick Higginboth had astonished many when he became a federal judge at the age of 37, another Dallas appointee in 1986 went a step further. Sidney Allen Fitzwater was only 32 years of age when President Reagan tapped him to be a U.S. district judge upon the recommendation of Senator Phil Gramm. His nomination provoked a storm of criticism from many, including Senator Ted Kennedy of Massachusetts, who led opposition against Fitzwater's appointment. Fitzwater did not fall within American Bar Association guidelines that required prospective candidates to have twelve years of legal experience. But his appointment was confirmed in the U.S. Senate by a 52-42 vote, and Fitzwater became the youngest federal judge in the nation. It was not the first time Fitzwater had gained headlines because of his youth. In 1982, just four years after beginning his law practice with the firm of Rain, Harrell, Emery, Young & Doke, Texas Governor Bill Clements had appointed him to the newly created 298th State District Court at the age of 28.[46]

THE CHANGES that had been occurring in the legal profession in the 1960s—the introduction of what attorney Vincent Perini had labeled "people's law"—continued to escalate over the next years. An especially dramatic change came as a result of the U.S. Supreme Court 1977 decision in *Bates and O'Steen v. State Bar of Arizona* which, along with a 1985 decision (*Zauderer v. Office of Disciplinary Counsel of Supreme Court of Ohio*) opened up for attorneys the right to advertise their services in very direct ways. Attorneys in Dallas and the nation—especially those with sole practices or members of small firms who specialized in fields such as personal injury and divorce—began to make eye-catching appeals through newspaper, magazine, and broadcasting advertisements and commercials. There emerged now vivid images of a new kind of aggressive, energetic lawyer. Through their advertising—often flamboyant in nature—they directly appealed to lower-and middle-income individuals who earlier may have believed it difficult or would have been reluctant to obtain legal representation.

The Bar Association's board of directors in 1977 issued its own recommendations for advertising, noting that *Bates and O'Steen v. Arizona* would have a "profound effect" upon the legal profession. Lawyers should in no way make advertising claims regarding the quality of their own or other's legal services, they stated. Continuing, they specified that "all advertising by a lawyer should be dignified and should convey only relevant and truthful information concerning the availability and terms of legal services."[47]

In order to bring some means of authenticating lawyers' claims of specialties in advertising, a new State Bar of Texas program in the mid-1970s offered certification to those who passed rigorous examinations. Sixty-six Dallas lawyers were among the first group of 298 legal specialists certified in December 1975 in three areas: criminal law, labor law, and family law. The program prohibited lawyers from advertising themselves as specialists unless they were actually certified.[48] Those without certification who did advertise their specialties were required to include a disclaimer stating that they were not "board certified."

The city's larger and more prestigious firms continued to refrain from the new methods of "display" advertising. However, these larger, "main-line" firms also began changing dramatically through a period of meteoric growth in size. Other changes also included the introduction of far higher starting salaries for beginning lawyers, incorporation and designation of firms as "professional corporations," establishment of branch offices in cities such as Washington, D.C., and the development of far more aggressive attitudes in vying for corporate clients.

The remarkable growth spurt of these firms began in the decade of the 1970s and accelerated even more in the boom years of the 1980s. In 1982 the publication *Legal Times* reported that several Dallas firms were among the twenty fastest growing law firms in the nation and that six firms were among the nation's 200 largest. They were Johnson & Swanson; Gardere & Wynne; Strasburger & Price; Akin, Gump, Strauss, Hauer & Feld;

Thompson & Knight; and Jenkens & Gilchrist.[49] In 1985 the firm of Akin, Gump, Strauss, Hauer & Feld in 1985 reported gross revenues of $54.5 million.[50]

An examination of some of the leading Dallas firms demonstrates the unusual growth rate. In 1970, Thompson & Knight (then Thompson, Knight, Simmons & Bullion) continued to be the city's largest law firm, listing in the *Martindale-Hubbell Law Directory* 35 members and associates. A decade later in 1980 Thompson & Knight had doubled in size with 70 members and associates, and just five years later in 1985 it again had virtually doubled its numbers to 130 members and associates.[51]

The law firm that generally was recognized as introducing a far more aggressive and competitive tone in Dallas was a newer one that was organized in 1970 as Hewett, Johnson, Swanson & Barbee but became known in its prime years as Johnson & Swanson. This firm vigorously pursued corporate and public clients, hired outstanding lawyers away from other firms, deeply involved itself in civic affairs, and became the largest law firm in the city with some 375 attorneys in the early 1990s. Its dominant and most visible partner, John Johnson (1942-1993), became the first lawyer ever to serve as chairman of the Greater Dallas Chamber of Commerce and was one of the first lawyers to be a member of the executive committee of the powerful Dallas Citizens Council, an organization whose membership had been limited for most of its existence since 1937 to the city's most powerful businessmen. At its peak, the law firm had offices in Austin, Washington, D.C., and—briefly—Berlin. The death of Johnson from cancer in 1993, internal disagreements among leading partners, and real estate distress beginning in the late 1980s were factors leading to the dissolution of the firm, then known as Johnson & Wortley, in 1995.[52]

Another new firm founded in the 1970s and experiencing rapid growth and prominence was Hughes & Luce (originally Luce, Hennessy, Barnett & Smith). The firm's first demanding assignment was in supervising the liquidation of one of the largest securities brokerage firms in the world, controlled by the interests of Ross Perot. Thereafter, the firm began representing Ross Perot and his Electronic Data Systems Corporation, then moved into other high-profile private-public cooperative ventures in Dallas.[53]

Just as the large Dallas firms expanded rapidly and moved branch offices to other cities, so did other big law firms from other cities open offices in Dallas. The Houston firm of Baker & Botts and the Cleveland-based firm of Jones, Day, Reavis & Pogue were two notable ones.

Notable among those firms that disappeared during these years was Seay, Gwinn, Crawford, Mebus & Blakeney, which dated its origin back to 1871 when Robert Blake Seay arrived in Dallas from Tennessee as a young man determined to make a career on his own rather than stay home and join his brother's successful practice. The firm had grown from 1970 to 1980 from five to twenty-six lawyers. In 1982 the firm merged with Haynes and Boone.[54] For all those years, 1871 to 1982, a Seay had been working in the firm.[55]

Another new development introduced in this period that would continue to grow over the next years was the practice of mediation, an effort to provide alternative methods to the traditional judicial process. The Bar Association's board of directors endorsed the concept on March 26, 1981, after hearing from the director of Dispute Mediation Service, M. Lawrence Hicks. Mediation was a practice intended to relieve the overcrowded courts from minor disputes and also to reduce the costs of litigation.[56]

In February 1962 a speaker before the Dallas Bar Association, Robert A. Wilson, vice president and director for research for the Southwestern Legal Foundation, had told his audience of lawyers that electronic computers soon would be of vital assistance to them. Computers, he advised, had the ability to store large amounts of English language materials, to sort through them quickly in response to a question, and to come up with the exact portion of the stored materials relating to that particular question.[57] It was an early look at the future, for the computer indeed would transform the daily workings of lawyers. By the mid-1970s Dallas attorneys and others had access to a computer program, LEXIS, which permitted faster and more comprehensive research of existing case law. Cases that previously required hours or days to locate now could be found in minutes. Computers began to be used to compare the testimony of one witness against another, to keep track of evidence and court calendars, to draft contracts, wills, and briefs, and to help in tax, estate and pension planning. Computers even permitted lawyers to work at home instead of driving to the office on weekends.[58]

A Dallas attorney who achieved a prominent national reputation during this period was Robert Strauss, a partner in Akin, Gump, Strauss, Hauer & Feld who began to spend more and more time in Washington, D.C. Strauss was an important figure in the Democratic Party, serving as chairman of the Democratic National Committee from 1973 to 1976, chairing President Jimmy Carter's election campaigns in 1976 and 1980, and being ambassador to the Soviet Union and then the Russian Federation from August 1991 to 1992.

AFTER SUCH WOMEN as Hattie Henenberg, Sarah Menezes, Grace Fitzgerald, Helen Viglini, and Sarah T. Hughes had broken through the all-male barriers to begin the practice of law in the second and third decades of the twentieth century, women over the next several decades did not show the steady growth in numbers that might have been anticipated. Difficulties in gaining acceptance within the legal profession continued.

In 1939, fourteen women attorneys were practicing in the city, and by 1956 that number had risen only to twenty-two. By 1969 there were approximately 150 women lawyers in Dallas, by which time barriers still remained.[59]

Evidence of the slowness of female assimilation into the profession could be seen in the number of women lawyers in the U.S. Attorney's office for the Northern District of Texas. After Sarah Menezes had become the first female attorney in the office in the late 1920s, no more than one woman worked in that office until as late as 1975, when the number rose to two. By 1985 there were six women assistant U.S. attorneys in the Northern District office (and thirteen by 1989).[60]

In August 1969 problems for women in the profession were

discussed during a three-day annual meeting of the National Association of Women Lawyers at the Adolphus Hotel. Louise Ballerstedt Raggio, one of Dallas' female attorneys, recalled that when she received her degree in 1952 from Southern Methodist University the law school employment bureau declined accept her application "because there were no placements for women attorneys."[61] Two years later, though, District Attorney Henry Wade hired her as an assistant district attorney after she applied upon the urging of Sarah T. Hughes. As the county's lone female prosecutor, Mrs. Raggio tried a case before an all-woman jury, believed to be a first for the state. She recalled that the women returned a "guilty" verdict, thereby contradicting the common belief that women would be too soft-hearted to convict defendants.[62]

In her work in the district attorney's office, Mrs. Raggio began to concentrate on juvenile problems and domestic relations. In 1956, after two years with the district attorney, she and her husband, Grier, also an attorney, established their own firm, Raggio & Raggio. Mrs. Raggio, as chair of the Texas State Bar's family law section, was instrumental in having rewritten the Texas marital property laws and the Family Law Code to reduce inequities against women. In 1985 she was inducted into the Texas Women's Hall of Fame for her accomplishments. Among the nominees that year were four other female Dallas lawyers: Adelfa Botello Callejo, Harriet Ellan Miers, Margaret Brand Smith, and Hermine Dalkowitz Tobolowsky.[63]

Mrs. Raggio was one of a handful of female attorneys, including Sarah T. Hughes, who in the mid-1960s began meeting once a month at the Adolphus Hotel on an informal basis. They formed a network for advancing women's interests, exchanging information on job opportunities, discussing legislative changes, and seeking to promote more women candidates for the judiciary. Initially, the group preferred not to create a formal organization, but on May 16, 1984, the women incorporated as the Dallas Womens Lawyers Association.[64]

Not until the 1970s did barriers confronting female attorneys begin to fall. This was the result of several factors—the changing nature of the times and the assertion by minorities of their rights, a rapidly rising number of women aspiring to legal careers, and direct legal challenges against law firms that had been reluctant to treat women on an equal basis with men. In 1969 just 6.9 percent of the nation's law students were women; ten years later that figure had risen to 31.4 percent.[65]

Many of these women, including a group from Southern Methodist University law school, were more and more concerned about their lack of opportunities in a male-dominated profession, particularly in the hiring of summer law clerks and associates within firms. A number of SMU law students, joined by four anonymous female practitioners in Dallas whose identities were withheld because they feared reprisals, brought complaints of discrimination before the Equal Employment Opportunity Commission in 1975. The EEOC granted them permission to sue. Several out-of-court settlements were agreed to, and the result was an opening of the profession in Dallas to women to a far greater extent than before.[66]

The end of the earlier and memorable era for women lawyers in Dallas came on April 23, 1985, when the venerable Sarah Tilghman Hughes died of heart failure. U.S. District Judge Robert Hill said of her: "She was the most independent individual—notice I said individual—not woman—that I ever met in my life."[67] Three years before her death her distinguished career already had been celebrated by the Dallas Bar Foundation and the Dallas Bar Association by underwriting a new three-year scholarship at the SMU Law School in her honor.[68]

In that same year death also came to U.S. District Judge William M. Taylor Jr. Surely the case which had been the longest and most complicated for him was the one over Dallas school desegregation. He was remembered as a judge especially for his wisdom, patience, and understanding. Once he had said that he was proudest of the fact that he had never had to hold an attorney in contempt of court.[69]

Not until decades after Judge Hughes' ascendancy to a state district judgeship in 1935 did other women follow in her steps to become judges in Dallas County. Beth Wright in 1957 was appointed judge of the Domestic Relations Court (later the 301st Family District Court), and then was re-elected numerous times to serve through 1974. She was succeeded by Annette Stewart, who served from 1975 through 1983 when she became the first woman appointed to the Court of Appeals for the Fifth Judicial District. In 1978 Joan T. Winn became judge of the 191st District Court and Linda Thomas was elected to preside over the 256th District Court, a position Ms. Thomas held until she resigned at the end of 1986 to become a member of the Dallas Court of Appeals. She is now chief justice. She was succeeded as district judge by Carolyn Wright. Candace Tyson was elected judge of County Court at Law No. 2 in 1980, a position she held until she resigned at the end of 1986 to become a district judge. Frances Harris was elected judge of the 302nd Family District Court in 1982, and that year Nikki DeShazo was elected judge of the County Probate Court. In 1984 Catherine Crier was elected judge for the 162nd District Court, a position she left to become a national figure as a television journalist, originally for the Cable News Network and later for major networks. Frances Maloney in 1984 was elected judge of Criminal District Court No. 4.

When Sandra Day O'Connor became the first women on the U.S. Supreme Court in 1981, the Dallas Bar Association sent a congratulatory message to her. It was duly noted that she was born in El Paso, Texas.[70]

By mid-1985 there were some 150 African-American attorneys in Dallas. Some eighty to ninety of them belonged to the J.L. Turner Legal Association, which continued to be an active force for black attorneys long after they were welcomed into Dallas Bar Association membership.[71] African-Americans also were becoming prominent not just as attorneys but also as judges. After George L. Allen and Cleo Steele both had broken the color barrier in 1975 by becoming justices of the peace, Berlaind Brashear in 1977 was appointed judge of County Criminal Court No. 6. He continued to be re-elected through the 1980s and into the 1990s. Larry W. Baraka was elected judge of Criminal District Court No. 2 in 1984. Other African-Americans would follow.

Hispanics, too, were increasing in numbers. By 1984 the

Mexican American Bar Association was meeting regularly. In 1985 the Dallas Bar Association's Minority Participation Committee, assisted by the SMU Hispanic Law Student Association, conducted a survey of Dallas-based Hispanic attorneys. The survey found that the majority of the Hispanic attorneys had attended law school in Texas, but that 33 percent of them had attended law schools in Massachusetts and California. Seventy-five percent of them were between 30 and 40 years of age.[72]

In 1988 another growing group of minority attorneys, Asian-Americans, founded the Dallas Asian-American Bar Association as a chapter of the National Asian/Pacific-American Bar Association. At the time of the organization's founding, there were approximately fifteen Asian-American attorneys in the Dallas-Fort Worth area; ten years later their numbers had increased to more than 115.

The surge in law school enrollment in the 1960s and 1970s had brought far greater numbers of women and minorities into the legal profession. They began to be elected or appointed as judges, and no longer did it seem odd to see them in courtrooms as prosecutors or in the state legislature or as city council members.

No woman, though, had served as president of the Dallas Bar Association until 1985 when Harriet Miers assumed that office. She had become president-elect in November 1983 after a faithful record of service by having held every office in the Bar Association. Earlier, she had become the first woman elected director. Miers, a 1967 graduate of the Southern Methodist University law school, had clerked for U.S. District Judge Joe E. Estes for two years after finishing her legal education. Afterwards, she became the first woman hired by the firm of Locke, Purnell, Boren, Laney & Neely. Still more recognition awaited her in the 1990s.

CLEARLY, by 1990 the Dallas Bar Association had reached an elevated plateau of success and service. Few if any bar associations in the nation could match its scope of activities or its facility. It was widely recognized as a model of its kind. The schedule of events for a typical month included an unusually wide array of sections and groups that found the Dallas Legal Education Center a comfortable meeting place.

One could obtain just a glimmer of the range of activities by examining the calendar of events at the DLEC for a single month, that of November 1985. Special sections of the Bar Association meeting that month included family law, international law, criminal law, solo and small firm, probate, antitrust, labor, real estate, real property, bankruptcy, construction law, tax, and oil, gas & mineral law. (By 1998 there would be nineteen special sections.) Still other meetings were scheduled there by the Dallas Fellows of the Texas Bar Foundation, the Dallas Bar Foundation board of trustees, the sports law committee, the Federal Bar Association, the State Bar International Law Association, the Dallas Association of Young Lawyers, Women Lawyers Law Librarians, the Mayor's Criminal Justice Task Force, the Grievance Committee, the Dallas Association of Black Women Attorneys, Attorneys for Christ, the Criminal Bar Association, the unauthorized practice committee, the directors of the Dispute Mediation Service, Dallas Trial Lawyers, Lawyers' Wives' Christmas Decorations Committee, ex-FBI agents, and of course the Bar Association's Friday clinic meetings, still in existence after their beginning in 1936.[73]

By the mid-1980s any reasonable observer would have to say that much had been accomplished. The law had changed; attitudes had changed; the profession had changed; the city had changed. And the changes invariably had been for the better. Thus, the lawyers of Dallas could look toward the challenges of the 1990s and the new century ahead with justified confidence.

AFTERWORD

⌘

HOW VERY FAR THE lawyers of Dallas have come since that day in 1849 when seven of them met and drew up a document to request the Texas legislature to adjust the court calendar for Dallas County so they could escape the "severe inclemencies of winter" and the "burning suns of summer." How very many generations of lawyers have passed through Dallas since the 1870s when they began regular meetings to achieve such things as devising a schedule of fees for service and requesting a two-week delay of court so they could help gather the wheat harvest. How long ago it seems to have been when at the turn of the century the town's lawyers reminisced fondly about the older, simpler days when the Bar Association had righted wrongs, turned aside evils, and shared in wholesome camaraderie. And that day in 1936 when the regular Saturday morning clinics began—could it really have been more than sixty years ago? As those in the 1930s laid the foundations for the progressive, expanding organization that the Dallas Bar Association would become, little could they comprehend the frightening perils of the 1940s that lay just ahead of them. After their exhaustive and heroic war-time efforts, how difficult it must have been for them to recognize and to comprehend that unresolved and lingering issues yet remained that had to be faced openly—in particular the assimilation of minorities into the nation's entire social fabric as well as into the legal community itself.

But, indeed, obstacles were faced, resolutions were reached, and mechanisms established to ensure the existence of an association that would enhance both the legal profession and the community at large.

The Dallas Bar Association, still glowing in the pride and comfort of its Belo Mansion headquarters, continued in the 1990s to expand and broaden its reach in a multitude of activities. Members' long-time emphasis on continuing education remained undiminished if not heightened. The traditional weekly luncheon clinic programs still were a major part of the Bar Association's activities. In addition, the separate sections reflecting specialized interest and generally meeting once a month now numbered twenty-four. Evening seminars were meeting four times a year, and still other programs such as the Annual Trial Skills Course were being held.

Further support for DBA members was offered in other ways. The Legal Ethics Committee responded to any written request from a member for advice on subjects of professional responsibility. The Minority Participation Committee encouraged increased minority involvement in Bar Association activities. The Peer Assistance Committee stood ready to help attorneys who had particular health or personal problems. On the important subject of law office economics and management, the Law Practice Committee offered advice and assistance through seminars, symposia, publications and videotapes. Attorneys seeking qualified legal secretaries could turn to the placement service operated in the Dallas Bar Association offices. An annual pictorial roster provided essential information about each member of the Bar Association, and the monthly publication *Headnotes* continued to provide a full range of news concerning the Bar Association.

Recognized more than ever as an essential part of the attorney's career was his or her responsibility to the community. In this regard, the Lawyer Referral Service provided low-cost consultation or referrals for those with a need. A Fee Disputes Committee which included members from the public as well as attorneys sought to settle any disputes that might arise over fees. The Judicial Committee each year conducted judicial polls in an effort to educate the public on the qualifications of judges of all courts of record. The Speakers Committee, the Mock Trial Committee, the Community Involvement Committee, the Legislation/New Laws and Constitutional Amendments Committee, the Criminal Justice Committee, and the *Pro Bono*

Activities Department were just a few of the Bar Association's entities that also were busy addressing issues and subjects believed to be of vital interest to the community. In all, there were forty committees addressing a wide range of law-related and community issues.

The remarkable growth spurt of Dallas law firms that began in the decade of the 1970s and that picked up even more of the pace in the 1980s would be even more pronounced in the 1990s. The editor of the publication, *Of Counsel 700*, declared Dallas in 1998 to be "one of the hottest legal markets in the country."[1] The biggest firm in town by that date had 681 attorneys—considerably more than the entire membership of the Dallas Bar Association in the mid-1930s. A large number of other firms had attorneys numbering in the hundreds.

By 1998 there were twelve U.S. district judges serving the Northern District of Texas, and the two most recent appointees reflected the growing diversity of those who were able to reach the most esteemed ranks of the legal profession. Joe Kendall, who had grown up in the modest Pleasant Grove section of Dallas and had patrolled the streets as a police officer before going on to law school at Baylor University, was appointed to the federal bench by President George Bush in 1992. Sam Lindsay, appointed in 1998 by President Bill Clinton, was an African-American who as the city attorney for the City of Dallas had been the first black man to hold that position. Now he became the first African-American federal judge in the state.

And a member of the Dallas legal community, Ron Kirk, became the first African-American mayor of Dallas upon his election in May 1995. A highly visible and popular public official, Kirk took the lead role in winning public support for two important and controversial bond elections destined to have a huge impact on the city—a long-awaited Trinity River improvement/green-belt plan and a project to build a new basketball arena with surrounding amenities in a barren area immediately northwest of the central business district.

Neither race nor gender appeared to be the significant issue it once had been. After Harriet Miers became the first woman president of the Dallas Bar Association in 1985, she was followed in the 1990s by two other female presidents—Molly Steele in 1997 and Elizabeth A. Lang-Miers in 1998. And Miers herself continued her pathbreaking ways. In 1992 she was elected president of the State Bar of Texas. In 1996 she was elected president of Locke Purnell Rain & Harrell (later Locke Liddell & Sapp), becoming the first woman to lead a major Texas law firm.

Another Dallas attorney who became president of the State Bar of Texas was Darrell Jordan, who held that position during the 1989-90 term. Jordan, a trial lawyer who had been president of the Dallas Bar Association in 1982, became a highly visible Dallas leader in the late 1990s, especially through his leadership of an imaginative plan to place a dome atop the Cotton Bowl. He also continued to be active in the affairs of the American Bar Association.

National awareness of the high standards of the legal profession in Dallas was evident in many ways. The most recent example was recognition of Morris Harrell as the recipient for the American Bar Association's 1998 ABA Medal for having rendered "conspicuous service in the cause of American jurisprudence."[2] Harrell's distinguished record included presidencies of the Dallas Bar Association, the State Bar of Texas, the American Bar Association, and the American College of Trial Lawyers. Harrell's many contributions through the years placed him in the company of such previous award winners as Oliver Wendell Holmes Jr., Thurgood Marshall, Warren Burger, and Sandra Day O'Connor.

ON MAY 2, 1998, in a gala celebration at the Westin Hotel Galleria, the Dallas Bar Association commemorated at its "Law Day Judicial Dinner" its 125th anniversary. Those attending could see on various monitors a new video that related pictorially the 125 years of the organization. Members learned that a sculpture would be commissioned and placed on the grounds of the Belo Mansion to commemmorate the organization's long history. A special guest, U.S. Supreme Court Justice Anthony M. Kennedy, gave an elegant address that, as DBA President Elizabeth Lang-Miers noted in her *Headnotes* column, "demonstrated a breadth of knowledge and depth of thought that made us all proud to be lawyers." [3]

The lawyers of Dallas, indeed, justifiably could feel proud themselves about the sometimes bumpy but always forward-looking journey they had taken over the years. It had been a journey beginning with the arrival in 1841 of the town's founder and first lawyer, John Neely Bryan. It was a journey in time, not over distance, for perhaps more so than for any other profession, lawyers and the community in which they work are bound together in a partnership. No community can grow or prosper in an orderly fashion without the guiding hand of its lawyers, and the lawyers of that community likewise flourish best in a thriving, energetic environment. Happily, for both Dallas and for its lawyers, their partnership reached by 1999 a pinnacle that would represent a challenge for coming generations to match.

PRESIDENTS
DALLAS BAR ASSOCIATION

John J. Good, 1873-75
J.C. McCoy, 1876-77
A.H. Field, 1878-80
W.W. Leake, 1881-85
A.T. Watts, 1886-90
W.B.Gano, 1891-1900
John L. Henry, 1901-08
T.T. Holloway, 1909-15
F.M. Etheridge, 1916-17
Wendel Spence, 1918-19
Joseph E. Cockrell, 1920
Alex Pope, 1921
Hiram F. Lively, 1922
O.O. Touchstone, 1923
Will R. Harris, 1924
Charles D. Turner, 1925
M.N. Chrestman, 1926
Charles F. O'Donnell, 1927
Carl Callaway, 1928
Harry P. Lawther, 1929
Capt. S.M. Leftwich, 1930
W.L. (Jack) Thornton, 1931
C.W. Starling, 1932
Nelson Phillips, 1933
R.G. Storey, 1934
C.C. Renfro, 1935
D.A. Frank, 1936
J. Cleo Thompson, 1937
J. Woodall Rodgers, 1938
J. Glenn Turner, 1939
Paul Carrington, 1940
Roy C. Ledbetter, 1941
J. Frank Wilson, 1942
James L. Lipscomb, 1943
Roy C. Coffee, 1944
W.B. Harrell, 1945
H. Bascom Thomas Jr., 1946
Harold A.Bateman, 1947

Robert L. Dillard Jr., 1948
C.K. Bullard, 1949
Hawkins Golden, 1950
W. Harry Jack, 1951
E. Taylor Armstrong, 1952
Ralph D. Baker, 1953
Franklin E. Spafford, 1954
Henry W. Strasburger, 1955
Dwight L. Simmons, 1956
John Louis Shook, 1957
Conan Cantwell, 1958
John N. Jackson, 1959
Ed Gossett, 1960
Fred T. Porter, 1961
Morris Harrell, 1962
H. Louis Nichols, 1963
Hubert Dee Johnson, 1964
J. Edwin Fleming, 1965
Walter H. Magee, 1966
Mark Martin, 1967
Philip Wilson, 1968
Hugh L. Steger, 1969
Frank C. Moore, 1970
Timothy E. Kelley, 1971
Henry D. Schlinger, 1972
John L. Estes, 1973
Louis J. Weber Jr., 1974
Charles P. Storey, 1975
Waller M. Collie Jr., 1976
Phil Burleson, 1977
Robert H. Thomas, 1978
Jerry L. Buchmeyer, 1979
Robert Edwin Davis, 1980
John L. Hauer, 1981
Darrell E. Jordan, 1982
Jerry Lastelick, 1983
Robert A. Gwinn, 1984
Harriet E. Miers, 1985

Vincent W. Perini, 1986
George C. Chapman, 1987
J. Mike Joplin, 1988
Spencer C. Relyea, 1989
Al Ellis, 1990
Douglas S. Lang, 1991
Orrin L. Harrison III, 1992

Kenneth J. Mighell, 1993
Peter S. Vogel, 1994
Ralph C. "Red Dog" Jones, 1995
Jim Burnham, 1996
Molly Steele, 1997
Elizabeth A. Lang-Miers, 1998
Robert W. Jordan, 1999

CHAIRMEN
DALLAS BAR FOUNDATION

Hugh L. Steger, 1971-75
Spencer C. Relyea, 1976-77
William E. Collins, 1978-82
Robert H. Thomas, 1983-84
Waller M. Collie, 1985-86
John L. Hauer, 1987-90

Robert A. Gwinn, 1991-92
George C. Chapman, 1993-94
Spencer C. Relyea, 1995-96
J. Mike Joplin, 1997-98
Douglas S. Lang, 1999

PRESIDENTS
STATE BAR OF TEXAS

W.L. Crawford, 1887-1888
Seth Shepard, 1891-1892
William H. Clark, 1896-1897
Yancey Lewis, 1908-1909
R.E.L. Saner, 1911-12
E.B. Perkins, 1923-24
A.H. McKnight, 1925-26
T.W. Davidson, 1926-27

Harry P. Lawther, 1932-33
John H. Bickett, Jr., 1945-46
Robert G. Storey, 1948-49
J. Glenn Turner, 1953-53
Paul Carrington, 1960-61
Morris Harrell, 1970-71
Darrell Jordan, 1989-90
Harriet Miers, 1992-93

PRESIDENTS
AMERICAN BAR ASSOCIATION

R.E.L. Saner, 1924
Robert G. Storey, 1953

Morris Harrell, 1982

NOTES

⌘

Chapter One, "The Law in a Frontier Town"

1. At the time of Bryan's arrival the river meandered alongside the foot of today's Dealey Plaza at the Triple Underpass. The river's original bed was diverted to its present artificial channel between levees in a mammoth project in the late 1920s and early 1930s.

2. Lucy C. Trent, *John Neely Bryan: Founder of Dallas* (Dallas: Tardy Publishing Co., 1936), 56.

3. A profile of Holland Coffee (1807-1846) is in Ron Tyler, Editor in Chief, *The New Handbook of Texas*, II (Austin: The Texas State Historical Association, 1996), 188, and Audy J. and Glenna Middlebrooks, "Holland Coffee of Red River," *The Southwestern Historical Quarterly* LXIX (Oct. 1965), 145-162.

4. Z.N. Morrell, *Flowers and Fruits from the Wilderness; or Thirty-Six Years in Texas and Two Winters in Honduras.* (Boston: 1872), 31.

5. Elizabeth York Enstam, ed., *When Dallas Became a City: Letters of John Milton McCoy, 1870-1881* (Dallas: Dallas Historical Society, 1982), 20.

6. Darwin Payne, *Dallas: An Illustrated History* (Woodland Hills, California: Windsor Publications, Inc., 1982), 28.

7. Payne, *Dallas*, 28; John William Rogers, *The Lusty Texans of Dallas* (New York: E.P. Dutton and Co., Inc., 1960), 67.

8. The 16th Judicial District was in existence from 1856 to 1866.

9. *Memorial and Biographical History of Dallas County, Texas* (Chicago: The Lewis Publishing Co., 1892), 557-563; Enstam, ed., *When Dallas Became a City*, 19-21; *New Handbook of Texas*, IV, 382.

10. John H. Cochran, *Dallas County: A Record of Its Pioneers and Progress* (Dallas: Arthur S. Mathis Service Publishing Co., 1928), 193-194; *Memorial and Biographical History of Dallas County*, 181, 192; Walter N. Vernon, *Methodism Moves Across North Texas* (Dallas: The Historical Society, North Texas Conference, The Methodist Church, 1967), 90.

11. The 6th Judicial District was replaced on Feb. 26, 1848, by the 9th Judicial District, which was succeeded in 1856 by the 16th Judicial District.

12. Ochiltree, a native of Fayetteville, North Carolina, began practicing law in Alabama and came to Nacogdoches, Texas, in 1839. Besides serving as a judge, Ochiltree would hold many public offices during the years of the Republic of Texas, including secretary of the treasury and adjutant general. See also *New Handbook of Texas*, IV, 1103.

13. Berry B. Cobb, *A History of Dallas Lawyers, 1840 to 1890* (Dallas: The Bar Association of Dallas, 1934), 1; Rogers, *The Lusty Texans of Dallas*, 67-68; John Plath Green, "Courthouses of Dallas," *Texas Bar Journal*, Nov. 1973, 1045.

14. A.C. Greene, *Dallas: The Deciding Years--A Historical Portrait* (Austin: The Encino Press, 1973), 6, 9-10; Minutes, 6th District Court, 1846-1854, Book A, Texas/Dallas History and Archives Division, Dallas Public Library.

15. Shelby Cox, "Some Early Days and Dallas Judicial History," *The Dallas Bar Speaks, 1949* (Dallas: Wilkinson Printing Co.), 26.

16. Minutes, 6th District Court, 1846-1854, Book A.

17. Wayne Gard, *Frontier Justice*, (Norman: University of Oklahoma Press, 1949), as cited by Rogers, *The Lusty Texans of Dallas*, 67-68.

18. Acheson, *Dallas Yesterday*, 23.

19. *New Handbook of Texas*, II, 410.

20. *Memorial and Biographical History of Dallas County*, 203, 337-38; Enstam, ed., *When Dallas Became a City*, 18; *New Handbook of Texas*, I, 829-30.

21. O.O. Touchstone, "Great Lawyers From Grayson County," *The Dallas Bar Speaks, 1936*, 336-37.

22. Quoted by Berry Cobb, "Texanic Accomplishments in Law," *The Dallas Bar Speaks, 1936*, 456.

23. *New Handbook of Texas*, IV, 103.

24. A reproduction of the original petition, "To the Honl Legislature of the State of Texas," dated Nov. 25, 1849, is at the Dallas Historical Society as document A 39148-H.

25. Maxwell Bloomfield, "The Texas Bar in the Nineteenth Century," *Vanderbilt Law Review*, Jan. 1979, 273.

26. Payne, *Dallas,* 30, 34; Cobb, *A History of Dallas Lawyers*, 29-31.

27. Payne, *Dallas,* 30; Cobb, *A History of Dallas Lawyers*, 12. The bond, according to Cobb, is recorded on Book B, pages 372-73, of the Dallas County deed records, and is repeated in the Minutes of the District Court, Vol. W, Dec. 19, 1888, 223.

28. *Memorial and Biographical History of Dallas County*, 184.

29. Ibid., 199; Green, "The Courthouses of Dallas," *Texas Bar Journal*, Nov. 1973, *1046*.

30. *Dallas County Sheriff's Department Commemorative Edition: 1846-1982* (Dallas: Dallas County Sheriff's Department, 1982) 19.

31. Motion Docket, County Courts, 1849-1853.

32. *New Handbook of Texas*, VI, 206.

33. Entry for Hedgcoxe War, *New Handbook of Texas*, III, 540.

34. Ibid.

35. Cobb, *A History of Dallas Lawyers*, 36; a collection of Good's letters, written during the Civil War, was edited by former Dallas County Judge Lester Newton Fitzhugh under the title *Cannon Smoke: The Letters of Captain John J. Good, Good-Douglas Texas Battery CSA* (Hillsboro: The Hill Junior College Press, 1971).

36. *Memorial and Biographical History of Dallas County*, 199-200; Terrell R. Harper, "Dallas City and County Buildings," *Dallasights: An Anthology of Architecture and Open Spaces* (Dallas: American Institute of Architects, 1978), 84.

37. James D. Lynch, *The Bench and Bar of Texas* (St. Louis: Nixon Jones Printing Co., 1885), 273, 275, as cited in *Memorial and Biographical History of Dallas County*, 38.

38. "Historical Section," *Dallas Morning News*, Oct. 13, 1929, 2.

39. W.D. Wood, "Reminiscences of Texas and Texans Fifty Years Ago," *Texas Historical Association Quarterly*, Oct. 1901, 113-120.

40. Cobb, *A History of Dallas Lawyers*, 38.

41. Ibid., 38-46.

42. Ibid., 46.

43. Cochran, *Dallas County*, 217-219.

44. Payne, *Dallas*, 42-44.

45. Records of the Moore-Cockrell dispute are in Box 24, Case No. 177; Box 26, Cases No. 204 and 205. Stone's suit against Cockrell is in Box 31, Case No. 336. Dallas County District Court Civil Case Papers, 14th District Court, Texas/Dallas Archives and History Division, Dallas Central Public Library.

46. The newspaper account is from Rogers, *The Lusty Texans of Dallas*, 74.

47. Ibid.; Darwin Payne, "A Distressing and Fatal Rencontre," *Sketches of a Growing Town* (Dallas: Master of Liberal Arts Program, Southern Methodist University, 1991) 23-35.

48. *Dallas Herald*, July 31, 1858.

49. Ibid., Jan. 27, 1870.

Chapter Two, "Organizing a Bar Association"

1. Thomas H. Smith, "African Americans in Dallas: From Slavery to Freedom," in Michael V. Hazel, ed., *Dallas Reconsidered: Essays in Local History* (Dallas: Three Forks Press, 1995), 124.

2. The situation is summarized by Payne, *Dallas*, 46, 48.

3. *Houston Telegraph*, July 14, 1860.

4. Cobb, *A History of Dallas Lawyers*, 5; *Houston Weekly Telegraph*, July 26, 1860; *Dallas Herald* "extra," 1860, reprinted in *Dallas Morning News*, Dec. 20, 1890. Judge Burford's description came in a speech he delivered to a pioneer reunion in Garland in July 1892, reprinted in Barrot Stevens Sanders, *Dallas, Her Golden Years* (Dallas: Sanders Press, 1989), 67-68. A lengthy account of the fire appears in the *Memorial and Biographical History of Dallas County*, 291-5.

5. Payne, *Dallas*, 48; *Houston Weekly Telegraph*, July 26, 1860.

6. Hawpe served as sheriff from 1850 to 1854, several years prior to the fire. In his speech in 1892 Judge Burford was quoted as identifying Hawpe as sheriff at the time of the vigilante action. This was either a misquote or Burford had forgotten that Hawpe no longer was sheriff.

7. *Dallas Morning News,* July 10, 1892, as quoted by Sanders, *Dallas, Her Golden Years,* 67-68.

8. Ibid., 48, 57; *Austin State Gazette,* Aug. 4, 1860; *Houston Weekly Telegraph,* July 21, Aug. 7, 1860.

9. See especially William W. White, "The Texas Slave Insurrection of 1860," *Southwestern Historical Quarterly,* Jan. 1949, and a master of arts thesis by Margaret Joan Agnew Telford entitled "Slave Resistance in Texas," Southern Methodist University, 1975.

10. Quoted in the *Houston Telegraph,* Aug. 9, 1860.

11. Payne, *Dallas,* 60.

12. Fitzhugh, ed., *Cannon Smoke,* 196, 132.

13. Cobb, *A History of Dallas Lawyers,* 53-55.

14. Payne, *Dallas,* 60; Randolph B. Campbell, "A Moderate Response: The District Judges of Dallas County During Reconstruction, 1865-1876," *Legacies,* Fall 1993, 4.

15. Letters from Good as quoted in Cobb, *A History of Dallas Lawyers,* 55; see also Fitzhugh, ed., *Cannon Smoke,* 112.

16. John H. Cochran, *Dallas County: A Record of Its Pioneers and Progress* (Dallas: Service Publishing Co., 1928), 87-114 passim; Cobb, *A History of Dallas Lawyers,* 56; Payne, *Dallas,* 60.

17. Cochran, *Dallas County,* 87.

18. Sam Acheson, *Dallas Yesterday* (Dallas: SMU Press, 1977), 22-23.

19. Campbell, "A Moderate Response," 4.

20. Cobb, *A History of Dallas Lawyers,* 15; *Dallas Herald,* Oct. 14, 1865, and Nov. 11, 1865.

21. Ibid., Nov. 4, 11, 1865.

22. Campbell, "A Moderate Response," 5.

23. *Dallas Herald,* Oct. 21, 1865.

24. As quoted by Payne, *Dallas,* pp. 61-62.

25. Cobb, *A History of Dallas Lawyers,* 58-60; Fitzhugh, ed., *Cannon Smoke,* 193.

26. Campbell, "A Moderate Response," 6.

27. Cobb, *A History of Dallas Lawyers,* 60.

28. Dec. 29, 1867.

29. Campbell, "A Moderate Response," 7.

30. Oliver Knight, *Fort Worth: Outpost on the Trinity* (Norman: University of Oklahoma Press, 1953), 48-49.

31. *Dallas Herald,* Dec. 5, 19, 1868; Campbell, "A Moderate Response," 8.

32. Ibid., 8-9.

33. *Dallas Herald,* Oct. 15, 1870, as cited by Campbell, "A Moderate Response," 9, and *Dallas Herald,* Nov. 5, 1870.

34. Campbell, "A Moderate Response," 10.

35. Enstam, ed., *When Dallas Became a City: Letters of John Milton McCoy,* 53-56.

36. Campbell, "A Moderate Response," 15; Payne, *Dallas,* 62; Enstam, ed., *When*

Dallas Became a City, 67; John N. Jackson, "Historical Notes on the Dallas Bar Association from 1873 to the beginning of World War II," *Texas Bar Journal*, Nov. 1973, 1027.

37. Cobb, *A History of Dallas Lawyers*, 15, and *New Handbook of Texas*, V, 480.

38. *Dallas Herald*, March 18, 1876.

39. Cobb, *A History of Dallas Lawyers*, 60.

40. Ibid., 66.

41. Ibid., 67-68.

42. Enstam, ed.,*When Dallas Became a City:*, viii-ix, 8; entry for McCoy in *New Handbook of Texas*, IV, 382-83.

43. Ibid., 15.

44. Ibid., 17.

45. Ibid., 15-17.

46. "Robert Blake Seay Diary Excerpts," A5126, Dallas Historical Society. I have corrected numerous typographical errors in the typewritten manuscript for the sake of readability.

47. The partnership, established sometime in the 1870s with Colonel W.L. Williams, went through a series of name changes over the years. By the 1970s it was Seay, Gwinn, Crawford, Mabus & Blakeney.

48. "Dallas Firm Formed in 1871," *Texas Bar Journal*, June 1976, 496. A brief biography of Seay is found in Lindsley, *A History of Greater Dallas and Vicinity*, II, 375-76.

49. Richard Morgan Jr. to W. Richard Morgan of Savannah, Georgia, Dec. 29, 1871, A506, Dallas Historical Society.

50. Cobb, *A History of Dallas Lawyers*, 73-74.

51. Payne, *Dallas*, 64-65, 70.

52. In addition to his law practice, Record, in partnership with G.W. Guess, had distinguished himself as a member of the Tannehill Lodge and as secretary of the Odd Fellows. He was still a young man (the census of 1870 listed him as thirty-five years of age), yet he had lost through death his wife and four children, evidently of natural causes. Berry Cobb recorded that Record's death "was brought on because of despondency and sorrow" over the loss of his wife and children. Cobb, *A History of Dallas Lawyers*, 13, 14, 71-72; U.S. Census, Dallas County, 1870. The court record is on Page 2, Vol G, 14th District Court.

53. York, *When Dallas Became a City*, 56. The 1870 census for Dallas County listed nineteen citizens in the county who gave their occupations as lawyer or attorney-at-law.

54. Lindsley, *A History of Greater Dallas and Vicinity*, I, 87.

55. The advertisements are on the left-hand column of issues of the *Herald*, rarely changing in content or format. See, for example, the Nov. 9, 1872, issue.

56. F.E. Butterfield and C.M. Rundlett, *Directory of the City of Dallas*, 1875.

57. Lindsley, *A History of Greater Dallas and Vicinity*, I, 478.

58. Ibid.

59. Ibid., 477-78.

60. Cobb, *A History of Dallas Lawyers*, 65.

61. *Norton's Union-Intelligencer*, March 29, 1873, 3.

62. Minutes of the District Court, Book G, p. 312, June 2, 1873, and p. 381, as cited by Cobb, *A History of Dallas Lawyers*, 19.

63. Robert Blake Seay Diary Excerpts, Dec. 4, 1873 entry. A5126, Dallas Historical Society.

64. William B. Carssow, "Organization and Activity of the Texas Bar Association," Committee on History and Tradition of the State Bar of Texas, *Centennial History of The Texas Bar, 1882-1982* (Burnet: Eakin Press, 1981), 2.

65. Lawrence M. Friedman, *A History of American Law* (New York: Simon and Schuster, 1973), 561, 563.

66. A miniaturized version of the poster, "Dallas in 1873: An Invitation to Immigrants," was published in 1980 by Stone-Inge Books, Dallas. A copy of the original poster is in the Texas/Dallas Division of History and Archives, Central Dallas Public Library.

67. Both these advertisements appeared regularly on the front page of *Norton's Union-Intelligencer*, these examples taken from the Jan. 27, 1872, issue.

68. *Norton's Union-Intelligencer*, Feb. 15, 1875, 4.

69. Copy of an undated article appearing in the *Dallas Herald*. Darnell (Addie R.) Collection, 1850-1918, Archives Division, Texas State Library.

70. Cobb, *A History of Dallas Lawyers*, 13; Jackson, "Historical Notes," 1028.

71. Cobb, *A History of Dallas Lawyers*, 19-20. Cobb cites the lists of lawyers in arrears as found in Book L of the Minutes of the District Court, Jan. 24, 1879, July 12, 1879, and Nov. 6, 1879, and in Book N, Jan. 25, 1881.

72. *Dallas Weekly Herald*, March 8, 1873, and April 26,1873.

73. Enstam, ed., *When Dallas Became a City*, 46-47, 59, 61.

74. April 21,1872, cited in ibid., 59.

75. Cobb, *A History of Dallas Lawyers*, 5-6.

76. Lindsley, *A History of Greater Dallas and Vicinity*, I, 95.

Chapter Three, "Attorneys of Ambition"

1. *C.D. Morrison & Co.'s General Directory of the City of Dallas for 1878-79* (Marshall, Texas), 13-14, 15, and 36.

2. "Pioneers Meeting," *Norton's Union Intelligencer*, June 12, 1875; *Dallas Weekly Herald*, Jan. 3, 1877.

3. Ibid., Feb. 3, 1877.

4. Cobb, *A History of Dallas Lawyers*, 15-16.

5. Friedman, *A History of American Law*, 526, 564-65.

6. *Dallas Weekly Herald*, Jan. 27, 1877; *Memorial and Biographical History of Dallas County*, 775.

7. Cobb, *A History of Dallas Lawyers*, 76.

8. Gano's early career is summed up in *Memorial and Biographical History of*

Dallas County, 1004-5. The advertisement is in Morrison's *General Directory*, 1878-79, and also in the *Dallas Weekly Herald*, May 11, 1878.

9.   Donald L. Barlett and James B. Steele, *Empire: The Life, Legend, and Madness of Howard Hughes* (New York: W.W. Norton & Co., 1979), 29-30.

10.   *Dallas Morning News*, Feb. 18, 1920. See also Philip Lindsley, *A History of Greater Dallas and Vicinity*, II, (Chicago: The Lewis Publishing Co., 1909), 268-69, and J.C. Muse, "Col. W.L. Crawford—A Colorful Character," *The Dallas Bar Speaks, 1936*, 233-246.

11.   *The Dallas Bar Speaks*, 153-54.

12.   "Postmaster A.B. Norton," *Dallas Weekly Herald*, Nov. 18, 1876.

13.   Ibid.

14.   Ibid.

15.   *Dallas Daily Herald*, March 24, 30, 1881. Scott seems to have been born in 1840, but the date of his death is unknown. *Dallas City and County Directory for 1881-82*. Payne, *Dallas: An Illustrated History*, 76.

16.   *Dallas Weekly Herald*, Oct. 6, 1881.

17.   *Biographical and Historical Memoirs of Pulaski, Jefferson, Lonoke, Faulkner, Grant, Saline, Perry, Garland and Hot Springs Counties, Arkansas* (Chicago: Goodspeed Publishing Co., 1889) 132, 133, 146.

18.   U.S. Census for 1880, Memphis, Tennessee, Supervisor's District No. 5, Enumeration District No. 139, page 13.

19.   *Dallas Daily Herald*, Dec. 13, 14, 1882.

20.   "Divorce Suits," *Dallas Morning News*, Oct. 6, 1885.

21.   Wiley's career as an entrepreneur is discussed fully in Thomas H. Smith, " 'Cast Down Your Buckets: A Black Experiment in Dallas,' " *Dallas Reconsidered: Essays in Local History*, Michael V. Hazel, editor (Dallas: Three Forks Press, 1995), 144-157.

22.   *Dallas Morning News*, Feb. 10, 1992, 1A, 6A.

23.   Darwin Payne, *Big D: Triumphs and Troubles of an American Supercity in the 20th Century* (Dallas: Three Forks Press,) 180.

24.   *Dallas Weekly Herald*, Jan. 27, Feb. 3, 1877. The quote from the *Caldwell Eagle* is repeated in the *Herald*, Feb. 3, 1877.

25.   Ibid., Feb. 9, 1878, 2.

26.   Cobb, *A History of Dallas Lawyers*, 7.

27.   *Dallas Weekly Herald*, Nov. 17, 1877, 2..

28.   Ibid., March 23, 1878, 4.

29.   Charles D. (Chuck) Cabaniss, editor, *United States Attorney for the Northern District of Texas . . . From Saddlebag to Briefcase: Published for the Bicentennial Observance of the Establishment of the Office of United States Attorney, 1789 - 1989* (n.p., 1989), passim.

30.   *Dallas Morning News*, Oct. 1, 1935, VI, 15.

31.   *Dallas Weekly Herald*, Jan. 27, 1881, 5.

32.   Ibid., Feb. 17, 1881.

33. "The Bar Meeting," *Dallas Morning News*, Oct. 14, 1885, 8.
34. *Dallas Weekly Herald*, March 23, 1878, 3.
35. Ibid., June 1; 1878, 3.
36. "Response to Dedication of 'The Dallas Bar Speaks,'—1937," *The Dallas Bar Speaks, 1938*, 155.
37. *Dallas Weekly Herald*, July 7, 1877.
38. Ibid., April 14, 1881, 14.
39. Ibid., Dec. 22, 1877, Jan. 12, 1878.
40. Ibid., Jan. 27, 1881, and July 7, 1881.
41. Maxwell Bloomfield, "The Texas Bar in the Nineteenth Century," *Vanderbilt Law Review*, Vol. 32, No. 1, Jan. 1979, 268-69.
42. Ibid., July 20, 1882, and Traylor Russell, chairman, *Centennial History Of The Texas Bar* (Burnet, Texas: Eakin Press, 1981), 1, 8-9.

Chapter Four, "A New Red Courthouse"

1. William D. Elliott, "Practicing Law in 1888," *Daily Commercial Record*, Oct. 25, 1988, 4, 23-24, and William E. Collins, "Thompson & Knight: The First Hundred Years," an unpublished history.
2. "The Dallas Bar and the Dallas Bar Association," *Daily Commercial Record*, Oct. 25,1988.
3. Elliott, "Practicing Law in 1888."
4. Lindsley, *A History of Greater Dallas and Vicinity*, I, 477.
5. Ibid., 479.
6. *New Handbook of Texas*, V, 619.
7. *Dallas Morning News*, Oct. 14, 1885, 8.
8. Ibid.
9. Lindsley, *A History of Greater Dallas and Vicinity*, I, 21-25.
10. Harold F. Thompson, "William Thompson: A Texas Portrait," *Texas Bar Journal*, Jan. 1966, 26.
11. Ibid. and Collins, "Thompson & Knight," 16.
12. Collins, "Thompson & Knight," 16-17.
13. Ibid., 27.
14. Ibid., 31.
15. Lindsley, *A History of Greater Dallas and Vicinity*, II, 86-87.
16. *Hubbell's Legal Directory*, 1929 (New York: The Hubbell Publishing Co., 1928), 606.
17. A biographical portrait of Locke is given by his grandson, Maurice E. Purnell, in "Maurice E. Locke: A Texas Portrait," *Texas Bar Journal*, May 1966, 359-60, 403-404.
18. *Dallas Morning News*, July 14, 1886, 4.
19. Cobb, *A History of Dallas Lawyers*, 18; *Proceedings of the Fifth Annual Session of the Texas Bar Association* (Austin, 1886), 23.
20. *Dallas Morning News*, July 13,1886, p. 1.

21. Ibid., p. 8.

22. *Centennial History of the Texas Bar*, 48.

23. Cobb, *A History of Dallas Lawyers*, 64-65.

24. Lindsley, *A History of Greater Dallas and Vicinity*, II, 279-80; *Memorial and Biographical History of Dallas County*, 925.

25. "The Centennial of the Court of Appeals for the Fifth District of Texas, 1993," 2, a historical document prepared to commemorate the Fifth District's centennial anniversary on Oct. 1, 1993.

26. Ibid., 4.

27. *Dallas Morning News*, Feb. 8, 1890.

28. Cobb, *A History of Dallas Lawyers*, 7.

29. John Plath Green, "The Courthouses of Dallas," *Texas Bar Journal*, Nov. 1973, 1044-46.

30. *Dallas Morning News*, Nov. 14, 1890, 8.

31. Acheson, *Dallas Yesterday*, 149-151.

32. James William Madden, *Charles Allen Culberson: His Life, Character and Public Service* (Austin: Gammel's Book Store, 1929), 13-14.

33. *New Handbook of Texas*, II, 435-36.

34. Acheson, *Dallas Yesterday*, 234.

35. *Dallas Morning News*, Sept. 19, 1895.

36. Madden, *Charles Allen Culberson*, 221; Payne, *Dallas*, 113-14.

37. Madden, *Charles Allen Culberson*, 35-38.

38. Ibid., 221. For a general description of the prize-fight controversy, see Anthony Fazio and Daniel Clark, "Gentleman Jim and Fighting Bob," *Sketches of a Growing Town: Episodes and People of Dallas from Early Days to Recent Times*, edited by Darwin Payne (Dallas: SMU Master of Liberal Arts Program, 1991), 66-75.

39. *The Independent*, Dec. 19, 1907, 1499-1500.

Chapter Five, "New Times, New Century"

1. Philip Lindsley, *A History of Greater Dallas and Vicinity*, I, 473-74, 480.

2. Ibid., 474.

3. *Daily Times Herald*, Oct. 3, 1905; Oct. 1, 1909.

4. Ralph W. Yarborough, "A History of Law Licensing in Texas," *Centennial History of the Texas Bar*, 184-87.

5. George Edwards, *Pioneer-at-Law*, (New York: W.W. Norton & Co., Inc., 1953), 73; Dallas City Directory, 1902.

6. *Daily Times Herald*, Jan. 5, 1911; Lindsley, *A History of Greater Dallas and Vicinity*, II, 52-53, 80, 82-83, 85.

7. Ibid., 84, 161-62, 285-86, 153-54.

8. *New Handbook of Texas*, IV, 306; Patricia E. Hill, *Dallas: The Making of a Modern City* (Austin: University of Texas Press, 1996), 104.

9. Lindsley, *A History of Greater Dallas and Vicinity*, II, 124.

10.   Hill, *Dallas: The Making of a Modern City*, 40.

11.   Lawrence Goodwyn, *Democratic Promise: The Populist Movement in America* (New York: Oxford University Press, 1979), 509, cited by Hill, *Dallas*, 41.

12.   *New Handbook of Texas*, III, 1042.

13.   Hill, *Dallas*, 46-48; Payne, *Big D*, 38-40.

14.   *New Handbook of Texas*, II, 797-98; Edwards, *Pioneer-at-Law* , 26-27, 43. Edwards provided basic details about his education and admission to the bar in a sworn statement given to the Dallas Bar Association in 1929. His statement and others are contained in a huge unnamed binder at the Bar Association headquarters. References to this collection of sworn statements hereinafter will be referred to as "1929 Sworn Statements."

15.   Lindsley, *A History of Greater Dallas and Vicinity*, II, 64-65.

16.   Collins, "Thompson & Knight."

17.   Ibid.

18.   *Daily Times Herald*, Dec. 9, 15, 1906.

19.   *Ibid.*, Jan. 9, 1907.

20.   *Ibid.*, Dec. 28, 1908.

21.   *Ibid.*, Jan. 7, 1911.

22.   *The WPA Dallas Guide and History*, (Dallas Public Library Texas Center for the Book and University of North Texas Press, 1992), 82-83.

23.   Lindsley, *A History of Greater Dallas and Vicinity*, II, 412-13; *New Handbook of Texas*, VI, 149-150.

24.   *New Handbook of Texas*, VI, 875.

25.   Ibid., I, 833.

26.   Ibid., VI, 1074.

27.   Ibid., I, 283. See especially John L. (Jack) Hauer's vivid account of Atwell in *Finest Kind: A Memorable Half Century of Dallas Lawyers* (Dallas: The Dallas Bar Foundation, 1992),175-204.

28.   William Hawley Atwell, *Autobiography* (Dallas: Warlick Law Printing Co., 1935),14-15.

29.   Acheson, *Dallas Yesterday*, 163-64.

30.   Payne, *Big D*, 10-19.

31.   Bill Minutaglio and Holly Williams, *The Hidden City: Oak Cliff, Texas* (Dallas: Elmwood Press and The Old Oak Cliff Conservation League, 1990), 77.

32.   A tribute to Judge Martin in the Minutes of the Dallas Bar Association, July 18, 1927, on the occasion of his death.

33.   William Neil Black, "Empire of Consensus: City Planning, Zoning, and Annexation in Dallas, 1900-1960," (Ph.D. dissertation, Columbia University, 1982), 247.

34.   City of Oak Cliff, et al. v. State of Texas, Texas Supreme Court, 79 SW Reporter 1.

35.   Black, "Empire of Consensus," 248.

Chapter Six, "The Rule of Law Under Challenge"

1. *Daily Times Herald*, Feb. 24, 1910.
2. Ibid., Feb. 25, 1910.
3. Ibid.
4. Ibid.
5. Ibid.
6. Ibid., Feb. 28, 1910.
7. Ibid. and March 2, 1910.
8. Ibid., March 1, 1910.
9. Ibid., March 3, 1910.
10. Ibid., March 4, 1910.
11. Ibid.
12. Ibid., March 5, 1910.
13. Ibid, March 7, 1910.
14. Ibid., March 10, 1910.
15. Ibid., March 8, 1910.
16. Ibid., March 9, 1910.
17. Ibid. March 16, 1910.
18. Ibid., March 28, April 1, 1907.
19. Payne, *Big D*, 41-48.
20. Ibid.
21. Ibid.
22. Deborah Reynolds, "Executions—Dallas Style: 1853 to 1925," a paper prepared in 1996 for Southern Methodist University's Master of Liberal Arts program.
23. Ibid.
24. This subject is treated in detail in Payne, *Big D*, "Embracing the Ku Klux Klan," and also in Payne, *"Dallas Morning News* and the Ku Klux Klan," *Legacies*, Spring 1997, 16-27.
25. John Hauer, *Finest Kind: A Memorable Half Century of Dallas Lawyers* (Dallas: The Dallas Bar Foundation, [n.d.], 91-92.
26. They are identified along with committee members on an oversized paper, "Names of Members of Ku Klux Klan," a copy of which is in the collections of the Dallas Historical Society, A42166. The document is undated but internal evidence rather clearly indicates mid-1922.
27. Payne, *Big D*, 80-83.
28. *Dallas Morning News*, April 2, 1922.
29. Ibid., April 4, 1922.
30. Ibid.
31. Ibid., April 5, 1922.
32. Ibid.
33. *New Handbook of Texas*, II, 389-90.
34. Payne, *Big D*, 82-93.

35. Ibid., 95-96.

36. The divorce is Cause No. 15166, Vol. 8-14, 513, District Court Minutes, as cited by Jim Monaghan, *Divorces, Dallas Co., Texas, 1846-1905* (Dallas Genealogical Society, 1998), 119.

37. Harold B. Pressley, "Locke Purnell Rain Harrell: History of the Firm," typescript, Nov. 1991; Rogers, *The Lusty Texans of Dallas*, 249.

38. Pressley, "Locke Purnell Rain Harrell," 30.

39. Ibid., 30-31; and *Daily Times Herald*, Sept. 11, 1924.

40. Pressley, "Locke Purnell Rain Harrell," 31.

Chapter Seven, "Breaking the Gender Barrier"

1. *Dallas Morning News*, May 17, 1916.

2. Harold A. Bateman, "Foreword," *Dallas Bar Speaks, 1947*, 10th volume (Dallas: Wilkinson Printing Co.). In 1947 the association would take on a new corporate charter after the Texas Legislature passed a statute making this possible, and it would become once again the Dallas Bar Association.

3. *Memorial and Biographical History of Dallas County*, 83-4.

4. A brief biography of the firm in typescript was prepared by the firm under the title, "Johnson, Bromberg & Leeds."

5. *Dallas Morning News*, May 17, 1916.

6. *The Daily Times Herald*, May 19, 1916.

7. *Dallas Morning News*, May 21, 1916.

8. John N. Jackson, "Historical Notes on the Dallas Bar Association from 1873 to the beginning of World War II," *Texas Bar Journal*, Nov. 1973, 1029-30.

9. Ibid. and *Daily Times Herald*, June 14, 1916.

10. Ibid.

11. Extracts from the code were reprinted in *Dallas Morning News*, June 14, 1916.

12. *Dallas Morning News*, Jan. 10, 1917.

13. *Bradwell v. The State* , 83 U.S. Reports 130.

14. June Sochen, *Herstory: A Woman's View of American History* (New York: Alfred Publishing Co., Inc., 1974), 103, 202.

15. Mrs. Ward's career is summarized briefly in an obituary, "Hortense Ward," *Texas Bar Journal*, Dec. 1945, 585, and also in *New Handbook of Texas*, VI, 818-19.

16. *Daily Times Herald*, Dec. 27, 1914.

17. The Dallas City Directory for the year 1914 lists Mrs. Aveilhe as a law firm clerk; the 1915 directory lists her as an attorney in Atwell's office; and she is not listed anywhere in the 1916 directory.

18. Sworn statement by Henenberg, June 8, 1929, in Bar Association of Dallas survey of all Dallas lawyers, 1929.

19. Dallas City Directory, 1916.

20. "Memorials," *Texas Bar Journal*, Feb. 22, 1975, 186; *Daily Times Herald*, Feb. 1, 1925.

21. "In 1925 an All-Woman Supreme Court Was Appointed," *Daily Commercial Record*, Oct. 25,1988.

22. Vivian Anderson Castleberry, *Daughters of Dallas: History of Greater Dallas Through the Voices and Deeds of its Women* (Dallas: Odenwald Press, 1994) 256.

23. Cabaniss, *United States Attorney for the Northern District of Texas. . . From Saddlebag to Brief Case* , 80.

24. *Daily Times Herald*, Feb. 1, 1925; Phyllis K. Glickman, "Women Attorneys of Dallas From 1914 to 1954," a research paper prepared for the SMU Master of Liberal Arts program, Nov. 29, 1997, and in the possession of the author.

25. *Daily Times Herald*, Feb. 1, 1925; Minutes, Dallas Bar Association, Jan. 13, 1926; sworn statement by Ms. Fitzgerald in Bar Association of Dallas survey of lawyers, 1929.

26. *Daily Times Herald*, Feb. 1, 1925; Minutes, Dallas Bar Association, April 11, 1925.

27. Glickman, "Women Attorneys of Dallas From 1914 to 1954."

28. Ibid.; Minutes, Dallas Bar Association, Dec. 8, 1920.

29. *New Handbook of Texas*, VI, 1003.

30. Minutes, Dallas Bar Association, June 28, 1919.

31. Glickman, "Women Attorneys of Dallas From 1914 to 1954"; *Daily Times Herald*, Feb. 1, 1925; *New Handbook of Texas*, VI, 1003-1004; and Castleberry, *Daughters of Dallas*, 255.

32. Sarah T. Hughes to Haughton Tilghman, March 10, 1922, as cited in Opal Howard Allread, "Sarah T. Hughes: A Case Study in Judicial Decision-Making," Ph.D. dissertation, The University of Oklahoma, 1987, p. 31.

33. Minutes, Dallas Bar Association, Jan. 12, 1927.

34. Ibid., and *New Handbook of Texas*, III, 774-75.

35. *Daily Times Herald*, Feb. 1, 1925.

36. Minutes, Dallas Bar Association, May 15,1926.

37. Ibid., Nov. 22, 1930. The Lawyers' Wives' Club has its own set of minutes, maintained since that first meeting in the Chrestman home. The first entry states the founding date as March 17, but later material, including the "History of the Dallas Lawyers' Wives Club," printed in the organization's yearbooks, gives the date of March 18.

38. Quoted in Payne, *Big D*, 8.

39. Ibid., 30.

40. Black, "Empire of Consensus," 122.

41. Spann v. the City of Dallas, Texas Supreme Court, 235 SW 513; Black, "Empire of Consensus," 148.

42. Payne, *Big D*, 70-71.

43. *New Handbook of Texas*, II, 1005.

44. Payne, *Big D*, 49-53; Ernest Sharpe, *G.B. Dealey of the Dallas News* (New

York: Henry Holt and Co., 1955), 172-74.

Chapter Eight, "A Surge of Maturity"

1. Harold B. Pressley, "Locke Purnell Rain Harrell: History of the Firm," 9-11, a typescript.
2. Ibid., passim.
3. Maxine Holmes and Gerald Saxon, eds., *The WPA Dallas Guide and History* (Dallas Public Library, Texas Center for the Book, University of North Texas Press, 1992), 167-69.
4. "What Oil Industry Means to Dallas," *Dallas*, Feb. 1922.
5. *Daily Times Herald*, May 7, 1915.
6. Ibid.
7. *Dallas Morning News*, June 6, 1915.
8. "The Dallas Bar and the Dallas Bar Association," *Daily Commercial Record*, Oct. 25, 1988.
9. Pressley, "Locke Purnell Rain Harrell," 29.
10. Lindsley, *A History of Greater Dallas and Vicinity*, II, 84; *New Handbook of Texas*, VI, 1086-87.
11. Payne, *Big D*, 61-63.
12. *Daily Times Herald*, Sept. 19, 1919.
13. Ibid; *New Handbook of Texas*, VI, 1087.
14. Evan A. Young, *Lone Star Justice: A Biography of Justice Tom C. Clark* (Dallas: Hendrick-Long Publishing Co., 1998), 5-8.
15. Minutes, Dallas Bar Association, April 3,1920, and Jan. 8, 1927.
16. Ibid., Jan. 8, 1927.
17. "Robert E. Lee Saner," *Texas Bar Journal*, March 1962, 207-208, 251-54, 257.
18. Ibid., 253-54.
19. A copy of *The Jeffersonian*, 1932 edition, in the collections of the Texas/Dallas History and Archives Division, Dallas Public Library, provides much of the information given here. An undated clipping in the CTX Bio Clips, Box 20, Texas/Dallas History Division, provides a brief biographical sketch of Priest.
20. Mary Martha Hosford Thomas, *Southern Methodist University: Founding and Early Years* (Dallas: SMU Press, 1974), 118.
21. Typescript by A.F. Henning, "The Story of Southern Methodist University, 1910-1930," II, 355. This two-volume history of the university's early days is in SMU's Fondren Library.
22. John J. Kimpisty, "The SMU School of Law: Reflecting on the First Two Decades," a research paper, Nov. 30, 1997, prepared for the Master of Liberal Arts program at SMU and in the author's possession.
23. *Daily Times Herald*, May 10, 1925. The Bar Association did not pay for the salaries out of its own budget; presumably direct donations were made to

Southern Methodist University.

24. "W.A. Rhea," *Texas Bar Journal*, Aug. 1941, 411-12, and Nov. 1955, 665. Harvey Wingo, "A Modification & Updating of a Brief History of S.M.U. Law School, Originally Written By Professor Joseph W. McKnight for Publication in *The Brief*, Summer 1978," a manuscript in the possession of the author.

25. Kempisty, "The SMU School of Law," 5.

26. *Dallas Morning News*, March 6, 1947. Minutes, Dallas Bar Association, Nov. 10, 1928. Other members of the first graduating class were John Harold Goode, James Franklin Gray, Dewitt Harry, Ellis P. House Jr., Autry Norton, Harry Samuel Pollard, John Wales Randall, Ely Straus, Paul Leslie Williams, and Hubert Delaney Wills. They are listed in the 1928 edition of the *Rotunda* yearbook.

27. Minutes, Dallas Bar Association, May 3, 1924.

28. Ibid., Jan. 3, 1925, Jan. 8, 1927.

29. "Introduction," *The Dallas Bar Speaks, 1936*, xiv.

30. C.A. Matthaei, "The Junior Bar Association of Dallas," *The Dallas Law Journal*, Feb. 1929, 5.

31. Minutes, Dallas Bar Association, June 4, 1929.

32. Ibid., Aug. 28, 1929.

33. "State Junior Bar of Texas," *Texas Bar Journal*, May 1962, 361.

34. "Junior Bar Association," *The Dallas Law Journal*, Aug. 1929, 14. Membership Roster, ibid., Dec. 1932, 18.

35. "Presentation of Pictures of Judges by Bar Association of Dallas," ibid., Aug. 1929, 5-6.

36. Minutes, Bar Association of Dallas, April 21, 1926.

37. Ibid., Nov. 17, 1928.

38. Ibid., March 2, 1929.

39. Ibid., March 9, 1929.

Chapter Nine, "Acclaimed for Good Works"

1. Collins, "Thompson & Knight: The First Hundred Years," 98.

2. *Hubbell's Legal Directory* (New York: The Hubbell Publishing Co., 1928), 610, and *Martindale-Hubbell Law Directory* (New York: Martindale-Hubbell, Inc., 1939), 1551.

3. Collins, "Thompson & Knight," 95-96; and Martindale-Hubbell Law Directory (New York: Martindale-Hubbell, Inc., 1935), 1551.

4. Minutes, Bar Association of Dallas, Jan. 8, 1932, 4-5.

5. Ibid., Jan. 21, 1933, 114.

6. *New Handbook of Texas*, V, 183.

7. *Spann v. the City of Dallas*, Texas Supreme Court, 235 SW 513.

8. Black, "Empire of Consensus," 148-156.

9. Lombardo v. City of Dallas, Texas Supreme Court, 73 SW 2nd 475.

10. The others were Hugh S. Grady, H.P. Kucera, A.A. Long, and W. Hughes Knight.

11. Minutes, Bar Association of Dallas, Dec. 30, 1933, 213-216.

12. Ibid., Dec. 16, 1933, 189-191.

13. These incidents are covered fully in the *Daily Times Herald*, March 6-13, 1931, and they also are described by George Clifton Edwards' son, George Edwards, in *Pioneer-at-Law* (New York: W.W. Norton & Sons, 1974), 107-121. The quotation is from the *Daily Times Herald*, March 7, 1931.

14. *Daily Times Herald*, March 8, 1931.

15. Minutes, Bar Association of Dallas, March 6, 1931, 473-74.

16. *Daily Times Herald*, March 8, 1931.

17. Ibid., March 9, 10, 17, 1931.

18. Ibid., March 12, 1931.

19. Edwards, *Pioneer-at-Law*, 161; Patricia Evridge Hill, *Dallas: The Making of a Modern City* (Austin: The University of Texas Press, 1996), 148-150.

20. The letter is quoted by Edwards, *Pioneer-at-Law*, 171-72.

21. *Roster, The Bar Association of Dallas*, 1934.

22. *Daily Times Herald*, April 30, 1930.

23. Ibid., July 24, 1930, and Aug. 24, 1930.

24. Hughes' legislative career is discussed by Opal Howard Allread in "Sarah T. Hughes: A Case Study in Judicial Decision-Making," Ph.D. dissertation, University of Oklahoma, 1987. The quotation is on page 48.

25. Ibid., 59.

26. *Daily Times Herald*, Feb. 5, 1935.

27. Minutes, Bar Association of Dallas, Jan. 16, 1932, 7-8.

28. Ibid., April 15, 1932, 39-40.

29. Ibid., March 12, 1934, 248-49.

30. "Legal Education and Admissions to the Bar," *The Dallas Bar Speaks, 1936*, 32.

31. Minutes, Bar Association of Dallas, April 15, 1932, 35.

32. Letter from Committee on Legal Education to Members of the Supreme Court of Texas, March 25, 1932, recorded in Minutes, Bar Association of Dallas, April 18, 1932, 47-50.

33. Associate Justice William Pierson to M.N. Chrestman, April 12, 1932, recorded in Minutes, Bar Association of Dallas, April 18, 1932, 51.

34. " 'The Dallas Bar Speaks'—and What a Story!" *Journal of the American Judicature Society*, Vol. 22 No. 4 (Dec. 1938), 157; Storey, "Legal Education and Admissions to the Bar," 136; "109 Pass Bar Exam," *Texas Bar Journal*, Aug. 1941, 279.

35. Ibid., 139.

36. Minutes, Bar Association of Dallas, Dec. 20, 1934, 285.

37. *Texas Bar Journal*, Nov. 1955, 664.

38. "Introduction," *The Dallas Bar Speaks, 1936*, xiii.

39. "Harry P. Lawther," *Texas Bar Journal*, April 1961, 319-20, 364.

40. *Dallas Morning News*, Jan. 10, 1937.

41. Minutes, Bar Association of Dallas, June 5, 1937, 158-59.

42. Proceedings of the Fifty-Eighth Session of the Texas Bar Association, *Texas Law Review*, Oct. 1939, 157-163.

43. *Texas Bar Journal*, Jan. 1954, 60-62.

44. Minutes, Bar Association of Dallas, March 21, 1936, 4-5, and March 28, 1936, 9-12.

45. Ibid., Feb. 6, 1937, 123, and Feb. 13, 1937, 125-26.

46. William E. Leuchtenburg, *Franklin D. Roosevelt and the New Deal, 1932-1940* (New York: Harper & Row, 1965), 234.

47. Minutes, Bar Association of Dallas, Sept. 11, 1937, 163.

48. May 10, 1941.

49. Minutes, Bar Association of Dallas, Dec. 12, 1932, 88, and Jan. 11, 1936, 398-99; " 'The Dallas Bar Speaks'—and What a Story!" 157; the Hon. John A. Rawlins, "History of the Dallas County Law Library," *The Dallas Bar Speaks, 1940*, 281-87; and *Dallas Morning News*, April 12, 1998.

50. "Bar Association of Dallas vs. Loan Sharks," *The Dallas Bar Speaks, 1938*, 227.

51. "The Bar Association in 1937," *The Dallas Bar Speaks, 1937*, 1-2.

52. "The Dallas Bar and the Dallas Bar Association," *Daily Commercial Record*, Oct. 25, 1988; "Executive Offices Aid Local Bar Work," *Texas Bar Journal*, Jan. 1940, 5; E. Taylor Armstrong, "The Bar Association of Dallas in 1939," *The Dallas Bar Speaks, 1939*, 1-2, 4-5.

53. "Inaugural Address," *The Dallas Bar Speaks, 1939*, 15.

54. Ibid.

55. The citation is reprinted in the Bar Association's 1940 application for a second Award of Merit, a copy of which is included in the Bar Association minutes, volume 3, 447.

Chapter Ten, "Dallas Lawyers Go to War"

1. "Our Business Is Preparedness," *Texas Bar Journal*, Aug. 1941, 421.

2. "Lawyers Aid in Draft," ibid., Nov. 1940, 491.

3. A special issue of the Dallas Bar Association's *Headnotes*, Oct. 20, 1995, paid tribute to the World War II veterans with recollections of their military service. Beck's account is on page 7.

4. Ibid., 8.

5. *Dallas Morning News*, May 14, 1941.

6. "Men o'War," *Texas Bar Journal*, March, 1942, 49, and ibid., Nov. 1943, 499.

7. "In Chambers We Learn," ibid., May 1941, 243.

8. "Men o' War," *Texas Bar Journal*, June 1942, 155.

9. Minutes, Bar Association of Dallas, Jan. 4, 1941, 430-31.

10. *Dallas Morning News*, March 25, 1942.
11. Ibid.
12. *New Handbook of Texas*, I, 336.
13. *Dallas Morning News*, July 2, 1942.
14. "Inaugural Address," *The Dallas Bar Speaks*, 1943, 1.
15. *Headnotes*, Oct. 20, 1995, 7, 9.
16. Ibid.
17. "Men o'War," *Texas Bar Journal*, Dec. 1942, 455-56.
18. Ibid., Sept. 1943, 305.
19. Ibid., Nov. 1943, 498.
20. Ibid., 499-500.
21. Ibid., Oct. 1944, 320.
22. *Headnotes*, Oct. 20, 1995, 10.
23. *Texas Bar Journal*, Aug. 1943, 278, Nov. 1943, 500, and June 1945, 307.
24. *Headnotes*, Oct. 20, 1995, 4,6.
25. *Texas Bar Journal*, Nov. 1943, 499, and Jan. 1943, 7.
26. Ibid., Sept. 1943, 308.
27. "In Chambers We Learn," *Texas Bar Journal*, Sept. 1943, 310; "Sarah T. Hughes Advocates Fewer Judges With Better Pay," ibid., May 1945, 228.
28. "The Lawyers Returning From the War," ibid., Nov. 1944, 352-53, 373-74.
29. Ibid., 358.
30. "Dallas Bar Asks A.B.A. to Reconsider Election of Negroes," *Texas Bar Journal*, Dec. 1943, 543.
31. *Dallas Morning News*, Sept. 12, 1943.
32. Ibid., Oct. 3, 1943.
33. "Association Activities," ibid., Sept. 1944, 284.
34. The speech is described at length in George Edwards, *Pioneer-at-Law* (New York: W.W. Norton & Co., Inc., 1974), 208-214.
35. John L. (Jack) Hauer, *Finest Kind!* (Dallas: The Dallas Bar Foundation, [n.d.]), 148.
36. Ibid., 73-74.
37. *Dallas Times Herald*, Oct. 5, 1942.
38. Ibid., Oct. 29, 1942; *Dallas Morning News*, Nov. 4, 1942.
39. *Dallas Morning News*, April 4, 1943.
40. Ibid., April 18, 1943.
41. Ibid., July 11, [194?]. The precise year of this debate is not visible on the clipping in the files of Texas/Dallas History and Archives, Dallas Public Library.
42. Ibid., Nov. 4, 1945.
43. Ibid.
44. "Association Activities," *Texas Bar Journal*, Feb. 1946, 63-64.
45. *Dallas Morning News*, May 29, 1988.
46. Payne, *Big D*, 194, 197-200, 207-218; *New Handbook of Texas*, V, 650.

47. *Dallas Morning News,* June 24, 1945.
48. Ibid., Oct. 6, 1957; *Texas Bar Journal,* March 1947, 95.
49. *Headnotes,* Oct. 20, 1995, 7.
50. George E. Seay Jr. to William D. Elliott, Nov. 10, 1997.
51. "Legal Center Established at S.M.U.," *Texas Bar Journal,* June 1947, 225-26.
52. "Storey New Dean SMU Law School; Potts Becomes Dean Emeritus," ibid., March 1947, 95; *Dallas Morning News,* Oct. 6, 1957; *Texas Bar Journal,* March 1955, 121; Minutes, Dallas Bar Association, Jan. 28, 1955.
53. "Tom C. Clark," *Texas Bar Journal,* June 1945, 253.
54. "Texas Lawyers Honor Tom Clark," ibid., Nov. 1945, 503.
55. Ibid., 519.
56. Ibid., 520.
57. *New Handbook of Texas,* I, 137.
58. "Tom Clark Is First Texan to Serve on U.S. Supreme Court," *Texas Bar Journal,* Nov. 1949, 498.
59. *New Handbook of Texas,* I, 138.
60. *Texas Bar Journal,* Jan. 1951, 6.
61. Payne, *Big D,* 227-28.
62. *Dallas Morning News,* Jan. 22, 1946.
63. *Texas Bar Journal,* Feb. 1946, 64.

Chapter Eleven, "A Time for Streamlining"
1. Minutes, Dallas Bar Association, Dec. 13, 1947; *The Dallas Bar Speaks, 1947,* ix.
2. Minutes, Dallas Bar Association, Dec. 13, 1947.
3. Inaugural speech by Robert Dillard in *The Dallas Bar Speaks, 1948,* xiv.
4. *Daily Times Herald,* Feb. 1, 1948; Minutes, Dallas Bar Association, Feb. 23, 1949; *Dallas Morning News,* Oct. 10, 1948.
5. *Texas Bar Journal,* March 1952, 131; Minutes, Dallas Bar Association, Dec. 22, 1948, Feb. 23, 1949.
6. Minutes, Dallas Bar Association, Nov. 17, 1949.
7. "Dallas Criminal Lawyers Fight Unjust Criticism," *Texas Bar Journal,* Nov. 1949, 498, and Dec. 1949, 565.
8. Ibid., Nov. 1949, 498.
9. Ibid., Oct. 1958, 646.
10. Ibid., Oct. 1959, 577.
11. Hauer, *Finest Kind!* 92, and ibid., Sept. 1955, 542.
12. Ibid.; *Texas Bar Journal,* Oct. 1952, 537.
13. Hauer, *Finest Kind!,* 97.
14. *Texas Bar Journal,* Oct. 1951, 581.

15.   "State Junior Bar of Texas," ibid., May 1962, 361-62, 368.

16.   Ibid., Dec. 1955, 703, and June 1956, 416.

17.   Ibid., Nov. 1961, 1076.

18.   Ibid., April 1956, 192.

19.   Ibid., Nov. 1958, 672; Wingo, "A Modification & Updating of a Brief History of S.M.U. Law School, Originally Written by Professor Joseph W. McKnight for Publication in *The Brief*, Summer 1978."

20.   *Texas Bar Journal*, May 1956, 255-56.

21.   Wingo, "A Modification & Updating," 4.

22.   "Galvin Named Dean," *Texas Bar Journal*, Dec. 1963, 1006.

23.   Ibid., Aug. 1947, 294, and Aug. 1963, 574.

24.   Ibid., Sept. 1956, 574, 576.

25.   Ibid., Jan. 1954, 12, and Dec. 1952, 599.

26.   *Dallas Bar Headnotes*, May 19, 1980, 8-9.

27.   Dallas Bar Association Minutes, Dec. 3, 1948, Feb. 23, 1949, and June 23, 1949.

28.   Ibid., Nov. 1, 1954.

29.   Ibid., Jan. 7, 1955; Jo Anna Moreland, "Just Lookin' for a Home," *Dallas Bar Headnotes*, Aug. 7, 1979, 4; Charles J. Winikates, "Our Bar in Dallas," *Texas Bar Journal*, May 1963, 386.

30.   Minutes, Dallas Bar Association, March 27, 1959.

31.   *Texas Bar Journal*, June 1949, 304.

32.   Ibid., Sept., 1954, 546; *Dallas Morning News*, June 5, 1954.

33.   "William Hawley Atwell," *Texas Bar Journal*, Feb. 1955, 54.

34.   "Joe E. Estes," Oct. 1955, ibid., 557; *Dallas Morning News*, Aug. 9, 1955.

35.   "William M. Taylor," *Texas Bar Journal*, Dec. 1959, 679, and Sept. 1959, 546.

36.   Rowland Evans and Robert Novak, *Lyndon B. Johnson: The Exercise of Power* (New York: The New American Library, 1966), 314-15.

37.   Figures are from the *Martindale-Hubbell Law Directory, 1948*, vol. 3 (Summit, N.J.: Martindale-Hubbell, Inc., 1948).

38.   Ibid., 1959.

39.   Published by the Dallas Bar Foundation, undated, 25.

40.   Ibid., 21-22.

41.   Ibid., 31.

42.   Ibid., 4.

43.   "Henry P. Kucera," *Texas Bar Journal*, Nov. 1960, 729.

44.   "Kucera Elected National Municipal Officer," ibid., Nov. 1961, 1063.

45.   The minutes were reprinted in *Dallas Morning News* on Feb. 10, 1992, 6A.

46.   Telephone interview with Bedford, Aug. 19, 1998.

47.   Dallas Bar Association Minutes, Jan. 12, 1956.

48.   Glenn M. Linden, *Desegregating Schools in Dallas: Four Decades in the*

Federal Courts (Dallas: Three Forks Press, 1995), 16-17.

49. Dallas Bar Association Minutes, April 14, 1961.

Texas Bar Journal, May 1957, 210; June 1957, 283; and May 1963, 386.

Chapter Twelve, "Momentous Years"

1. William Manchester, *The Death of a President: Nov. 1963* (New York: Harper & Row, 1967), 272.

2. Ibid.

3. Ibid., 272-73.

4. Ibid., 274.

5. Lyndon Baines Johnson, *The Vantage Point: Perspectives of the Presidency, 1963-1969* (New York: Holt, Rinehart and Winston, 1971), 15.

6. *Hearings Before the President's Commission on the Assassination of President Kennedy*, VII (Washington, D.C.: U.S. Government Printing Office, 1964), 326; telephone interview with H. Louis Nichols, Sept. 2, 1998. In the intervening years Nichols did not remember the names of the attorneys who had called him.

7. Ibid., 327-28.

8. Gerald Posner, *Case Closed: Lee Harvey Oswald and the Assassination of JFK* (New York: Random House, 1993), 347.

9. Ibid., 329.

10. Ibid., 330.

11. Minutes, Dallas Bar Association, Dec. 11, 1963.

12. Ibid., Oct. 7, 1964, and Nov. 30, 1964.

13. Posner, *Case Closed*, 400-403.

14. Paul Carrington, "Too Much Publicity," *Texas Bar Journal*, Feb. 1964, 128.

15. *Dallas Morning News*, Feb. 25, 1968.

16. Ultimately viewed themselves as restrictions upon attorneys' freedom of speech, restrictions under Reardon which severely limited lawyers' abilities to discuss pending cases were relaxed in the years to come.

17. *Texas Bar Journal*, Sept. 1977, 689.

18. Ibid., Oct. 1974, 991.

19. Minutes, Dallas Bar Association, Aug. 22, 1963.

20. Ibid., Sept. 26, 1963.

21. Ibid., Oct. 8, 1963.

22. *Texas Bar Journal*, Nov. 1986, 1125; interview with Louis A. Bedford Jr., Aug. 25, 1998.

23. Minutes, Dallas Bar Association, Dec. 11, 1963; *Dallas Bar Association Weekly Bulletin*, Dec. 16, 1963; telephone interview, H. Louis Nichols, Sept. 1, 1998, and Mrs. Jo Anna Moreland, Sept. 4, 1998. On March 16, 1986, Finch and his wife, Mildred, were found stabbed to death in their Dallas home. The case remained unsolved through 1998.

24. Interview with Louis A. Bedford Jr., Sept. 22, 1998.

25. "Lawyers with Commitment," *Dallas Bar Headnotes*, Sept. 1, 1998.

26. Payne, *Big D*, 336.

27.   *Texas Bar Journal*, Dec. 1981.
28.   Ibid., Oct. 1967, 825.
29.   *Dallas Times Herald*, Nov. 26, 1972, *Dallas Morning News*, May 23, 1982, and biographical sheet in clippings file, Texas/Dallas History and Archives Division, Dallas Public Library.
30.   Telephone interview with Frank Hernandez, Sept. 23, 1998.
31.   *Dallas Morning News*, Sept. 13, 1973.
32.   Minutes, Dallas Bar Association, Nov. 16, 1965.
33.   Ibid., Feb. 22, 1968.
34.   Minutes, Dallas Bar Association, Dec. 10, 1970, March 4, 1971, and April 21, 1971.
35.   Ibid., June 25, 1970.
36.   *Texas Bar Journal*, Sept. 1969, 610.
37.   Ibid., June 1971, 466.
38.   Ibid., Aug. 30, 1987.
39.   *Dallas Morning News*, Oct. 17, 1983.
40.   Ibid.; "Elite Company," *Dallas Bar Headnotes*, June 1998.
41.   *Texas Bar Journal*, Nov. 1966, 887-88, and Nov. 1965, 931, 934.
42.   Ibid., Nov. 1966, 886.
43.   Opal Howard Allread, "Sarah T. Hughes: A Case Study in Judicial Decision-Making," PhD dissertation, University of Oklahoma, 131.
44.   *Texas Bar Journal*, Dec. 1966, 1039.
45.   Minutes, Dallas Bar Association, Oct. 19, 1966.
46.   *Dallas Morning News*, July 23, 1972.
47.   Ibid.
48.   *Dallas Times Herald*, June 3, 1969.
49.   Ibid.
50.   The statement is included in the minutes of the Dallas Bar Association, July 8, 1971.
51.   For an overview of this entire prolonged court case, see Glenn M. Linden, *Desegregating Schools in Dallas: Four Decades in the Federal Courts* (Dallas: Three Forks Press, 1995).
52.   Minutes, Dallas Bar Association, Feb. 6, 1970.
53.   Ibid., April 16, 1970, and May 28, 1970.
54.   Ibid., Oct. 8, 1970; Oct. 14, 1970; *Dallas Times Herald*, Oct. 16, 1970.
55.   Minutes, Dallas Bar Association, Feb. 15, 1971.
56.   Ibid., Feb. 23, 1971.
57.   Ibid., Nov. 3, 1971.
58.   Ibid., Dec. 1, 1971.
59.   *Dallas Morning News*, July 23, 1972.
60.   *Dallas Times Herald*, Jan. 26, 1972.
61.   Ibid., April 4, 1974.
62.   *Dallas Morning News*, June 5, 1973, and Aug. 21, 1986.
63.   Minutes, Dallas Bar Association, Dec. 9, 1971.

64. *Dallas Times Herald*, June 24, 1970.
65. *Roe, et al v. Wade*, 410 U.S. 113.
66. Castleberry, *Daughters of Dallas*, 354.
67. *Roe v. Wade*, 314 F. Supp. 1217, and *Roe v. Wade*, 410 U.S. 113.
68. *Taylor v. Sterrett*, 344 F. Supp. 411; *Dallas Morning News*, April 16, 1983, and Hauer, *Finest Kind!*, 164.
69. Dedication Program, Dec. 16, 1982, Dallas County jail clippings file, Texas/Dallas History and Archives Division, Dallas Public Library.
70. Minutes, Dallas Bar Association, June 22, 1973, Sept. 6, 1973.
71. The results appeared in a chart in *Dallas Morning News* on Dec. 30, 1973.
72. "Lawyers with Commitment," *Dallas Bar Headnotes*, Sept. 1, 1998, 14.
73. *Dallas Times Herald*, July 25, 1974; *Dallas Morning News*, July 29, 1974.
74. "Goals for the Dallas Bar Association Program," attachment to ibid., May 9, 1973.
75. "Setting Goals for the Bar," *Dallas Times Herald*, Oct. 8, 1974.

Chapter Thirteen, "Building for the Future"
1. Jo Anna Moreland, "Just Lookin' for a Home!" *Dallas Bar Headnotes*, Aug. 7, 1979.
2. Minutes, Dallas Bar Association, Jan. 7, 1975.
3. Waller M. Collie, Jr., to members of the Dallas Bar Association, Oct. 15, 1976.
4. Minutes, Dallas Bar Association, Feb. 25, 1976.
5. Collie to members of the Dallas Bar Association, Oct. 15, 1976.
6. Ibid.
7. "Chronology—Dallas Legal Education Center," *Dallas Bar Headnotes*, Aug. 7, 1979; Waller M. Collie, Jr., to members of the Dallas Bar Association, Oct. 15, 1976.
8. Collie, Burleson, Thomas to Dallas Bar Association, "An Exciting New Concept for the Use of the Belo Mansion," March 31, 1977.
9. Minutes, Dallas Bar Association, Feb. 2, 1977.
10. Ibid.
11. Ibid., Jan. 26, 1978.
12. "President's Report," *Dallas Bar Headnotes*, Aug. 7, 1979.
13. Ibid., Sept. 17, 1979.
14. Minutes, Dallas Bar Association, Nov. 3, 1978.
15. Ibid., Nov. 2, 1979.
16. *Dallas Bar Headnotes*, Oct. 22, 1979.
17. Ibid., Sept. 17, 1979.
18. Ibid., June 4, 1979.
19. Ibid.
20. Ibid., Aug. 16, 1982.
21. Minutes, Dallas Bar Association, Dec. 19, 1978, attachment #2.
22. Ibid., Aug. 30, 1979, and Jan. 18, 1982.

23. Ibid., May 25, 1978.
24. Sub-titled, *A Memorable Half Century of Dallas Lawyers (plus a few from out-of-town)*.
25. *Dallas Times Herald*, Dec. 2, 1976.
26. "President's Report," *Dallas Bar Headnotes*, Nov. 27, 1978.
27. "Byrd, Bar Meet on Jail," ibid., July 19, 1982.
28. Minutes, Dallas Bar Association, June 25, 1981.
29. "Bar Takes Tough Stance on Center," ibid., Sept. 20, 1982.
30. Ibid.
31. *Dallas Times Herald*, Aug. 28, 1983.
32. *Dallas Morning News*, July 30, 1984.
33. Ibid., July 30, 1984.
34. Ibid., Aug. 3, 1984.
35. The Dallas Bar Association, relying on three separate studies and figures from District Attorney Henry Wade, had projected a need for thirty-one criminal district courts by the year 1990, more than twice as many as had actually existed. "In a Nutshell," *Dallas Bar Headnotes*, July 16, 1984.
36. "President's Report," ibid., Nov. 17, 1980.
37. Charles O. Galvin, "Comments on the History of the Sumners Fellowship Program," a typescript prepared by Galvin and sent to Dean C. Paul Rogers, SMU Law School, Jan. 11, 1995. See also Southern Methodist University's brochure, "Hatton W. Sumners Scholarship Program."
38. Ibid.
39. Wingo, "A Modification & Updating of a Brief History of S.M.U. Law School, Originally Written By Professor Joseph W. McKnight for Publication in *The Brief*, Summer 1978."
40. Phyllis Macon, secretary to Senior U.S. District Judge Barefoot Sanders, compiled information on the Northern District judges in a document, "History of the Northern District of Texas Judges," Oct. 14, 1998.
41. *Dallas Morning News*, May 17, 1984, and Oct. 20, 1987.
42. Ibid., Nov. 7 and 8, 1991.
43. *Dallas Times Herald*, Feb. 7, 1978.
44. Cited in "High Profile," *Dallas Morning News*, April 26, 1987.
45. Ibid., March 29, 1990; *Dallas Morning News*, Dec. 17, 1990.
46. *Dallas Morning News*, March 19, 1986, April 22, 1986.
47. Minutes, Dallas Bar Association, June 27, 1977.
48. *Dallas Morning News*, Dec. 24, 1975.
49. Cited in *Dallas Bar Headnotes*, Oct. 18, 1982, 5.
50. "Weathervane," *Dallas Morning News*, July 7, 1985.
51. Figures cited and in the paragraph following, with the exception of 1998, are from the *Martindale-Hubbell Legal Directories*. The 1998 figures are from *Texas Lawyer*, cited by Dallas Morning News, Aug. 30, 1998.
52. *Dallas Morning News*, Nov. 24, 1985, March 23, 1985, and Dec. 31, 1994.

53. "Origin and Growth of Hughes & Luce," undated typescript prepared by Hughes & Luce.

54. Typescript history of the firm, "1970-1980. . . . A Decisive Decade," provided by Durwood D. Crawford, a former partner in the firm.

55. George E. Seay Jr. to William D. Elliott, Nov. 10, 1997.

56. Minutes, Dallas Bar Association, March 26, 1981.

57. "Dallas Lawyers Hear Speakers on Space, Briefing Computers," *Texas Bar Journal*, March 1962, 230.

58. "Lawyers Find Computers Transforming Traditions, *Dallas Morning News*, Oct. 28, 1985.

59. The 1939 and 1956 figures were obtained from the Dallas telephone directories; the 1969 estimate comes from the *Dallas Times Herald*, Aug. 3, 1969.

60. Charles D. (Chuck) Cabaniss, editor, *United States Attorney for the Northern District of Texas . . . From Saddlebag to Brief Case*, a booklet published in 1989 by the U.S. Attorney's office.

61. *Dallas Times Herald*, Aug. 3, 1969.

62. Louise B. Raggio, letter to the editor, *Texas Bar Journal*, Feb. 1998, 110.

63. Castleberry, *Daughters of Dallas*, 375-77.

64. Louise Raggio to Nina Cortell, Feb. 16, 1999.

65. "Women Have Their Day in Court—as Lawyers," *U.S. News & World Report*, Nov. 17, 1980, 86-87.

66. Southern Methodist University Association of Women Law Students, et al., v. Wynne & Jaffee and Thompson, Knight, Simmons, & Bullion, Nos. 77-2346 and 77-2347, U.S. Court of Appeal, Fifth Circuit, July 30, 1979.

67. "In Memoriam," *Dallas Bar Headnotes*, May 20, 1985.

68. "SMU Scholarship Named for Judge Sarah T. Hughes," ibid., May 17, 1982.

69. "Taylor Recalled for Patience, Wisdom as Judge," *Dallas Morning News*, June 19, 1985.

70. Minutes, Dallas Bar Association, Sept. 24, 1981.

71. "Bar Group Aims to Open Doors for Black Attorneys," *Dallas Morning News*, Sept. 26, 1985.

72. "Survey of Hispanic Bar Creates Profile of Second Generation," *Dallas Bar Headnotes*, July 15, 1985.

73. "DLEC Calendar," ibid., Oct. 21, 1985.

Afterword

1. The editor of the publication, Larry Smith, was quoted in *Dallas Morning News*, Aug. 30, 1998.

2. "Elite Company," *Headnotes*, June 1998.

3. "A Stellar Month," ibid.

INDEX

At Law, No. 2, 90
Court of Appeals, 5th District, 76, 153, 174, 277
"court-packing" plan, 175-76
courthouses (see also Old Red Courthouse) 9, 14-15, 17, 48, 60, 77-79, 193-94, 260, 261-65
Courts and Courts Facilities Planning Department, 262-63
Cowart, Bob, 43-44, 83, 97
Cox, Shelby S., 116, 181
Craddock, Tom, 257
Cramer, William, 192, 204
Crane, Edward, 120
Crane, George Howard, 219-220
Crane, Martin M., 113, 114-115, 121, 176, 194
Crane, M.M. Jr., 113
Cravens, John E., 11, 15
Crawford, Katherine, 117-18
Crawford, M.L., 83, 91, 117, 142
Crawford, Col. William L., 54, 66, 75, 79, 81, 83, 113, 117-18, 121, 142, 146, 173
Crawford, William L. Jr., 142
Crawford, William L., 117-18
Crier, Catherine, 278
Criminal Bar Association, 207
Criminal District Court (1873-76), 49
Criminal District Court (1893-present), 76, 91, 102-104
Criminal District Court No. 2, 91, 161
criminal law, 206-209
Crockett, John M., 10-11, 13-15, 19-20, 27-29, 30, 35, 41, 51
Crowley, Frank, 264
Crowley, Frank Courts Building, 177, 265
Crozier, N.R. Jr., 148
Crump, Harry C. Jr., 182
Crutchfield Hotel, 18
Culberson, Charles Allen, 79-82, 88, 94, 97, 115, 143, 151, 194
Culberson, Dave, 54, 79
Curry, Jesse, 227, 228

DFW Airport, 236
Dabney, L.M., 120
Dallas Association of Black Women Attorneys, 280
Dallas Association of Young Lawyers, 256, 257, 259, 279
Dallas Bar Association, vii, ix-x, petition of 1849, 13; 1849-1853 "roll of attorneys," 15; early meetings, 42-43; founding of, 45-46; first president, 47; charter of 1878, 62-63; memorials, 63-64; and court dockets, 90-91; charter of 1916, 119-123; and admission to the bar, 123-25; and first women members, 129-130; growth in 1920s, 145-46; and founding of SMU law school,149-151; and free legal assistance, 151-52; involvement with civic organizations, 153-55; progress during 1930s, 158; and women members in 1930s, 166; growing complexity, 169-170; and standards for practicing law, 170-71; beginnings of Saturday morning clinics, 172-73; *The Dallas Bar Speaks*, 173; accomplishments of late 1930s, 177-79; and World War II, 183-84; and Old Red Courthouse, 193-94; charter of 1947, 203-205; establishment of referral service, 205-206; legal aid clinic, 213; Adolphus Hotel as headquarters, 213-15; and Nov. 22, 1963, 224; DBA president visits Oswald, 227-28; admission of African-Americans, 232-34; growth in 1960s, 236-37; Dallas Bar Foundation, 237; involvement with DLSP, 240-46; centennial observance, 249; judicial poll, 250; goals program, 250-51; and Belo mansion, 252-57; impact of move to Belo, 257-58; legal clinics moved to Friday, 259; referral

service, 259; and drive for new justice center, 260-65; and SMU law school, 265-66; advertising guidelines, 271-72; and minority membership, 278-79; first woman president, 279; activities in 1980s, 279-280; and 1990s, 281-83; 125th anniversary, 284-85.
Dallas Bar Foundation, vii, ix-x, 237, 255, 256, 258, 279
Dallas Bar Headnotes, 187, 260
Dallas Bar Speaks, 173, 182, 184, 215
Dallas Chamber of Commerce, 135, 154, 273
Dallas City Council, 14-1 plan, 270
Dallas Citizens Council, 222, 273
Dallas City Plan Commission, 160-61
Dallas, general descriptions of, 3, 9, 14, 31, 46-50, 64, 67, 84, 95-96, 100, 132-34, 137-38, 145, 156-57, 203
Dallas County Citizens League, 114-116, 117
Dallas County Criminal Courts Building, 139-140, 225, 261
Dallas County Government Center (see George L. Allen Sr. Courts Building)
Dallas County "Motion Docket" of 1849-1853, 15
Dallas during Civil War, 23-29
Dallas Independent School District, 242-43
Dallas International Lawyers Association, 236
Dallas Junior Bar Association (see also Young Lawyers Club and Dallas Association of Young Lawyers), 152-53, 209
Dallas Junior Bar Association Law Wives, 209
Dallas Law and Debating Club, 107
Dallas Law Journal, 146
Dallas Lawyers Auxiliary, 131-32

Dallas Legal Aid Society, 213
Dallas Legal Education Center (also Belo mansion), 255, 259
Dallas Legal Services Project, 241-46, 248
Dallas Morning News, 8, 67, 112, 134-35, 206, 253
Dallas School of Law (see YMCA law school)
Dallas Trust & Savings, 135-36
Daniels, Sarah, 166
Darnell, Nicholas H., 27
David, Edmund J., 34, 35
Davidson, T. Whitfield, 174, 193-94, 209-210, 216, 239
Davis, John, 176, 189
Davis, Robert E., 258, 265-66
DeBogory, Eugene, 176
DeGolyer, Everette Lee, 157-58
DeShazo, Nikki, 278
Dickson, J.M., 70
Dickson, R.J., 152
Dillard, Robert L. Jr., 205, 214
diploma privilege, 170-71
Dixon, Richard J., 148, 192
Domestic Relations Court, 130, 277
Donaldson, W.P., 215
Donosky, Sam, 207, 209
Douglass, Mildred M., 166
Douthit, Melody, 193
Downs, J.T., 46
Duls, William H., 173
Dumas, J.P., 5
Dummit, Bart, 193
Dunigan, Florence, 166
Durham, W. J., 190-91, 221, 232
Dyer, William J., 15

Eakins, Felix, 14
Easton, John C., 13, 15
Eblen, Jim, 68-69, 83
Eckford, J.J., 70, 120
Edmunds, George F., 75
Edwards, George Clifton, 88-89, 103, 151, 162-66, 189, 190
Edwards, W.M., 46, 83
Eisenhower, President, 216

Hall, William H., 70, 85
Hamilton, Peter J., 151
Hare, Silas, 4
Harper, Hallie, 128
Harrell, Morris, 238-39, 284
Harris, John C., 120
Harris, Frances, 278
Harris, Fred (Red), 184-85, 204
Harris, William R., 90, 151, 176
Harston, Dan, 116
Hart, Hardin, 34, 35, 42, 45, 249
Harwood, Alexander, 15
Harwood, George W., 178
Haskell, J.W., 215
Hatcher, W. Gregory, 176
Hauer, John L., 190, 208, 218-19,
    244, 252, 259, 260
Hawpe, Trezevant C., 15, 24, 28
Hay, Phillip, 24
Hay, Stephen, 104-105
Head, Louis, 155
Hecht, Judge Nathan, 263
"Hedgecoxe war," 16-17
Henenberg, Hattie Leah, 126-127,
    152, 166, 168, 204, 275
Henry, John L., 55, 83, 119, 122,
    142
Henry, William T., 98, 142
Hensley, Captain Charles, 6
Hernandez, Frank, 236
Hexamer, Frances, 127
Hicks, M. Lawrence, 274
Higginbotham, Patrick E., 268, 269,
    270, 271
Hill, Robert Madden, 268, 277
Hispanic attorneys, 235-36, 278
History of Dallas Lawyers, 170
Hoffman, Leonard, 234
Hogg, Governor James S., 69, 76,
    79, 80, 94, 115
Holbert, Kenneth F., 221
Holland, Frank P., 81, 95
Holland, M.A., 113
Holland, W.C., 46, 142
Holland, Robert B., 150
Holland, William M., 90, 120, 123,
    142, 174, 189

Holloway, T.T., 119, 121, 122
Hord, William H., 11, 25, 96
Hord's Ridge, 7, 8, 11, 13, 14, 96-
    97
Horton, D.O., 32
Houston, Andrew Jackson, 61
Howard, Tom, 229
Huff, Charles C., 120
Hughes, George Ernest, 130
Hughes, Howard Jr., 54
Hughes, Maury, 111-112, 116, 129,
    163, 208-209
Hughes, Robert H., 209
Hughes, Judge Sarah T., 59, 127,
    130-31, 166-69, 188, 192-93, 217,
    218, 220, 225, 226, 239, 240, 247,
    248-49, 261, 269, 275, 276, 277
Huitt, John, 8
Hunt, G. Drummond, 120
Hurt, J.M., 69, 81
Hyer, Julien, 213

insurance as a legal specialty, 72,
    74, 86-87, 138-39
integrating the Bar Association,
    189, 232-34
integrating Dallas Independent
    School District, 222-23
Inter-American Bar Conference,
    210-11
Irish, Gilbert Haven, 89

Jack, William Harry, 152
Jacks, Nathaniel, 193
Jackson, Jim, 264
Jackson, John N., 237
Jackson, Maynard, 190
Jackson, Robert H., 184, 196
jail, Dallas County, 248-49, 261-62
Jefferson Law School, 128, 131,
    147-49
Jennings, Pat, 25
Johnson, John, 273
Johnson, Lyndon Baines, 71, 131,
    200, 217, 224-26
Johnson, Searcy Lee, 178
Joiner, C.M. "Dad," 139, 156

Jones, the Rev. Bob, 247
Jones, Erin Bain, 151
Jonsson, Erik, 250
Jordan, Darrell, 257, 262-63, 284
Jordan, Jerry, 256
Journal of Air Law and Commerce, 211
judicial evaluations, 201-202, 250
Juergens, Henry F., 167
Justice Center (see Sterrett, W.L. [Lew], Justice Center)

Karcher, J.C., 157
Kearny, Jerome, 83, 87-88
Kelly, J.T., 160
Kelley, Timothy E., 243, 245, 247
Kendall, Joe, 283
Kennedy, Anthony M., 284-85
Kennedy, President John F., 169, 217, 222, 224-26
Kennedy, Robert, 223, 225
Kennedy, Ted, 271
Kerfoot, John D., 41
Kessler, George S., 89, 133, 195, 203
Kimball, H.J., 182
King, Glen, 227
King, J. Henry, 148, 187, 191
King, John, 191-92
Kirk, Ron, 283
Knight, C. Tom, 113
Knight, Robert E. Lee, 72-73, 90
Kucera, Henry P., 187, 220
Ku Klux Klan, 82, 87, 110-117, 118, 162, 165
Kuitunen, Denise, viii
Kuntsler, William, 230
LaBranche, Nick, 256
Lamar, Lucius Q.C., 117
Lane, John W., 27, 4
Lang, Otto, 133
Lang-Miers, Elizabeth A., 284
Lanham, S. W.T., 98
Lastelick, Jerry, 257
Latimer, James, 12-13, 14
Law Day Judicial Dinner, 284
law firms: Akin, Gump, Strauss,

Hauer & Feld, 272-73, 275; Ault & Wellborne, 46; Baker & Botts, 274; Barksdale & Eblen, 46; Beck & Knox, 181; Bookout & Edwards, 43; Burford, Ryburn, Hincks & Ford, 218; Burson, Hendricks, and Walls, 256; Burford & Morgan, 46; Cantwell & Estes, 216; Carrington, Gowan, Johnson & Walker, 194, 218; Clark, West, Keller, Butler & Ellis, 70; Clark, West, Keller, Sanders & Butler, 269; Carrington, Coleman, Sloman & Blumenthal, 194; Carrington, Johnson & Stephens, 218; Coke & Coke, 186, 218, 269; Crawford, Muse, and Allen, 102; Etheridge, McCormick, and Bromberg, 120, 194; Gardere & Wynne, 272; Goldberg, Akin, Gump, Strauss & Hauer, 240; Good & Bower, 46; Haynes and Boone, 274; Hewett, Johnson, Swanson & Barbee, 273; Hughes & Luce, 273-74; Hughes & Monroe, 186; Hughes & Tucker, 43; Jackson, Walker, Winstead, Cantwell & Miller, 218; Jenkens & Gilchrist, 273; Johnson and Swanson, 272, 273; Johnson & Wortley, 273; Johnson, Bromberg, Leed & Riggs, 218; Jones, Day, Reavis & Pogue, 274; Kilgore & Kilgore, 218; Leachman, Gardere, Akin & Porter, 218; Leachman, Matthews & Gardere, 218, 219; Locke Liddell & Sapp, 284; Locke & Locke, 117-118, 138, 141; Locke, Locke & Purnell, 218; Locke, Purnell, Boren, Laney & Neely, 279; Locke Purnell Rain & Harrell, 284; Lowrance and Bates, 133-34; Lyne, Blanchette, Smith & Shelton, 218; McClure & Goldthwaite, 43; Morgan & Gibbs, 43; Priest, Herndon, and Ledbetter, 131; Rain, Harrell &

Mays, L.M., 120
McNicholl, Jimmie, 152
McCormick, A.P., 61
McCormick, Ernest, 175
McCormick, J.M., 120
McCorvey, Norma, 247
McCoy & McCoy, 46
McCoy, John Clavin, 6, 7-8, 14, 15, 20, 24, 27, 29, 34-35, 37-38, 42, 48, 51, 83
McCoy, John Milton, 34, 37-38, 43, 47, 48-49, 83, 146
McCraw, William S., 145, 164
McCullough, Tom L., 189
McCutcheon, Currie, 108
McDermett, Cora, 7
McDermott, Eugene, 157
McDonald, W.L., 70
McKinley, William, 184
McKnight, A.H., 174
McLaughrin, Lauch, 92
McLemore, J.E. Jr., 207
McNeil, the Rev. R.C., 222
McPherson, J.B., 14
Mead, E.K., 164
mediation, 274
Melton, Brian, viii
Melton, Christina, viii
memorials by Bar Association, 47, 63-64
Melton, Gladys, 207
Menezes, Sarah C., 127-128, 131, 164, 166, 168, 275
Mexican-American attorneys (see Hispanic attorneys)
Mexican American Bar Association, 278
Miers, Harriet, 257, 276, 279, 283-84
Miller, Barry, 91, 161
Miller, T.S., 83, 86
Millermore, 162
Miner, Fred, 61
Mittenthal, Freeman L., 182
Monroe, Theodore F., 208-209
Moore, Andrew M., 20-22
Moore, Frank C., 237

Moreland, Jo Anna, 252, 258
Morgan, Richard, Jr., 36, 40-41, 45, 66, 98
Moroney, W.J., 164
Morris, Martin L., 97-99
Morrison, Helen Belo, 253-54
municipal government, 154-55
Murnane, Thomas, 189
Muse, Cavin, 142, 162
Muse, E.B., 104, 113, 125-126, 142
Muse, J.C., 102, 113, 120, 142
Muse, J.C. Jr., 142
Muse, John B., 113, 142

NAACP, 191
Nash, Thomas F., 83
Nation, Carrie, 92
National Association of Women Lawyers, 276
National Exchange Bldg., 85
Naylor, Isaac, 20
Neff, Governor Pat, 127, 130
Nelms, W.W., 107-108
New Deal, criticisms of, 158-59
Newton, Samuel G., 14
Nichols, H. Louis, 181, 227-28, 229, 232-34
Nicholson, E.P., 15, 20, 24
Ninth Judicial District, 11, 13
North Texas Building, 85
Northern District of Texas (U.S.), 60-61, 134, 268, 275, 283
Norton, Andrew Banning, 32-33, 44-45, 47, 55-56, 58, 61, 76, 134
Norton's Union Intelligencer, 47, 78

Oak Cliff, 96-99, 134
Oates, Burrell, 105, 108-110, 140
Ochiltree, William Beck, 9
O'Connor, Sandra Day, 278
O'Daniel, W. Lee, 174-75
O'Day, Paul, 117-118
oil and gas as legal specialty, 139, 156-58
O'Keefe, Pat, 152
Old Red Courthouse, 3, 5, 77-79, 110, 140-41, 175, 193-94, 225,

Rodgers, Woodall, 177, 180, 183, 194-96, 198
Roe v. Wade, 247-48
Romick, Charles, 181
Ross, Lawrence Sullivan, 76
Ross, Mary, 173
Rothblum, Phillip J., 112
Ruby, Jack, 228-230
Ryan, John W., 103, 108
Ryburn, F.M., 172

SMU Hispanic Law Student Association, 278
Sadler, S.P., 150
Salacuse, Jeswald W., 268
Sanders, Barefoot, 226, 238, 240, 243, 268, 269
Saner, Robert E. Lee, 146-47, 198, 239
Savage, Wallace, 201
Schlinger, Henry, 245-46
Scott, R.W., 29-30, 32
Scott, Sam H., 56-58
Scottino, Margaret W., 188
Scurlock, Frank, 213
Seay, George E., 197
Seay, Harry L., 96
Seay, Robert B., 38-40, 41, 45, 47, 65, 83, 96, 102, 106, 197, 274
segregation, residential, 134
Selecman, C.C., 149-150
Seventh Judicial District, 34
Shepard, Seth, 75
Shivers, Governor Allan, 212
Shook, John Louis, 232
Shook, W.H., 215
Simmons, Ann, vii
Simmons, Dwight L., 212, 213
Simpson, Cecil Lane, 86
Simpson, James P., 66, 113
Sixth Judicial District, 9, 11
Sixteenth Judicial District, 11, 17, 29, 30
Sixty-eighth District Court, 91, 160
"skid row bar association," 208
Skillern, Mattie, 215
Smith, Ashbel, 5

Smith, Rev. James, 11
Smith, Maceo, 190
Smith, Margaret Brand, 276
Smith, Sam, 25
Smith, W.J.J., 85-86, 121
Smith v. Allwright, 191
Smithdeal, C.M., 113, 120
Sneed, H.H., 46, 47
Solomon, M.B., 148
Solomon, Minnie, 193
Southern Methodist University Law School, 149-151, 171, 172, 197-98, 210-11, 265-68, 277
Southland Life Ins. Co., 86
Southwestern Law Journal, 211
Southwestern Legal Foundation, 197-98, 210-11
Southwestern Life Insurance Co., 86, 138-39
Spafford, H.E., 215
Spann, John R., 133
Spell, W.E., 174
Spellman, John M., 86
Spence, Alex, 164
Spence, Wendel, 120
Spinuzzi, John, 225
Starling, C.W., 150, 153, 158
State Bar of Texas, 175, 180, 181, 210, 211, 212-13, 231, 238
Steele, Cleo, 235, 278
Steele, Molly, 284
Stemmons, John M., 46, 53
Sterett, William G., 83
Sterrett, W.L. (Lew), 245, 248-49,
Sterrett, W.L. (Lew) Justice Center, 249, 261-65
Sterling, Ross, 164
Stewart, Alton E., 167
Stone, Barton Warren, 15, 20, 21, 24, 28
Storey, Charles C., 238, 257, 266
Storey, Robert G., 169, 171-72, 176, 181, 182, 183, 196-98, 210, 211, 212, 239, 266, 267
Strasburger, Henry W., 219
Strauss, Robert, 275
Stroud, Martha Joe, 128

Stuart, Dan, 80-81
Sumners, Hatton William, 91-92, 143, 176-77, 183, 184, 194, 198, 266-67
Sweatt v. Painter, 191

tax, state occupation, 47
Tannehill Masonic Lodge, 7
Tarrant, E.H., 15-16
Tasby v. Estes, 242
Tate, J. Waddy, 164
Tate, U. Simpson, 221
Tatum, Henry, 264-65
Taylor, William M. Sr., 167, 216-17
Taylor, William M. Jr., 217, 236, 238, 240, 243, 277
Templeton, Al, 193
Templeton, M.B., 121
Terry, Jack, 221
Texas Bar Association, 173, 174, 175 (see also State Bar of Texas)
Texas Election Bureau, 134
Texas Emigration and Land Co., 5
Texas Historical Commission, 256
Texas Supreme Court, 127, 130, 132, 160-61, 171, 173
Thomas, A.J., 267
Thomas, Bascom Jr., ix, 164, 181-82, 200
Thomas, Cullen F., 120
Thomas, J.E., 102
Thomas, James Dickinson, 97
Thomas, John, 8
Thomas, Linda, 277-78
Thomas, Robert, vii, ix, 182, 200, 253-54, 255-57,
Thompson, Adam, 65-66
Thompson, J. Cleo, 174, 175, 183, 189, 267
Thompson, J.W., 83
Thompson, William, 71-72, 73, 89-90, 120
Thornton, R. L., 154, 203, 212
Thornton, W.L. (Jack) 154
Thurman, J.M., 46
Tobolowsky, Hermine, 276
Tonahill, Joe, 229

Tower, John, 269
Trammell, Claude, 163
Truman, Harry S., 198-99, 220
Tucker, Charles Frederick, 76, 84, 97
Turner, Charles D., 150
Turner, J. Glenn, 178-79, 183, 212-13
Turner, J. L. 58-59, 190, 192, 221
Turner, J. L. Jr., 221
Turner, J.L. Legal Association, 59, 234, 278
Turney, James, 15
Tyson, Candace, 278
Tyson, Jim, 264, 265

Ulrickson Plan, 154
Underwood, George M. Jr., 267
Union Terminal, 141, 143
Urban Affairs Committee, DBA, 242
Urbish, Regina, 166

Valdez, Filemon, 236
Vann, Holly, 109
Viglini, Helen, 127, 128-29, 166, 167, 275
Vinson, Chief Justice Fred, 199-200
Vinson, Dr. R.E., 122

Wade, Henry M., 187, 201, 227, 229, 248, 263, 264
Wade, Melvin, 33
Walker, Albert, 120, 126
Ward, Hortense S., 125, 126
Watt, Frank, 229
Watts, A.T., 43-44, 66, 69, 70, 75
Weatherred, Preston A., 196
Weber, Louis J. Jr., 251
Weddington, Sarah, 247
Weisberg, Alex F., 124, 160
Wellborn, Olin, 44, 47, 69, 92-93
Wells, Ammon Scott, 59
Wells, T.D., 185-86
Westerfeld, Claud C., 167-68
White, Alexander, 61
White, John, 175
Wight, Allen, 176